American Public Discourse

A Multicultural Perspective

Edited by
Ronald K. Burke

UNIVERSITY PRESS OF AMERICA

Lanham • New York • London

Copyright © 1992 by
University Press of America®, Inc.
4720 Boston Way
Lanham, Maryland 20706

3 Henrietta Street
London WC2E 8LU England

Library of Congress Cataloging-in-Publication Data

American public discourse : a multicultural perspective / edited by
Ronald K. Burke.
p.   cm.
Includes bibliographical references.
1. Minorities—United States.   2. Pluralism (Social sciences)—
United States.   3. United States—Ethnic relations.   4. United
States—Race relations.   5. Speeches, addresses, etc., America.
I. Burke, Ronald K.
E184.A1A6365   1992   305.8'00973—dc20   92–14800 CIP

ISBN 0–8191–8752–6 (cloth : alk. paper)
ISBN 0–8191–8753–4 (pbk. : alk. paper)

 The paper used in this publication meets the minimum requirements of
American National Standard for Information Sciences—Permanence
of Paper for Printed Library Materials, ANSI Z39.48–1984.

Acknowledgements

I am grateful to several individuals for helping this anthology become a reality. I am especially indebted to Professor Richard Jensen of the University of New Mexico for his invaluable assistance in helping me obtain texts of Chicano oratory. I am indebted to Owanah Anderson, Executive Director of the National Commission on Indian Work of the Episcopal Church, for directing me to resources containing American Indian female speeches. Special thanks goes out to Mozelle Cherry, Custodian of the Ohoyo Resource Center; Ann Allen Shockley, Associate Librarian for Special Collections and Fisk University Archivist; and Christine Marin, Curator/Archivist of the Chicano Research Collection, Hayden Library, Arizona State University

I wish to thank the following individuals and institutions for their kind assistance in helping me gain permission to reprint the discourses in this volume: Suzanne Harrell, Rights and Permissions of the University of Oklahoma Press; F.E. Abernethy, Secretary-Editor of the Texas Folklore Society; Frederick T. Courtright, of Macmillan Publishing Company; Florence B. Eichin of Penguin, USA; Ralph J. Burant, Director of Publications of Family Service America; Editors and staff at Spelman College Archives; Iris Eaton, Journals Editor at Howard University Press; James E. O'Brien, Editor of *Together* magazine; Richard Reynolds, Communications Director of *Mother Jones*; Betty Smith, President International Publishing Company, Inc.; Marian Reiner, Agent for the Proprietor, Joan Daves Agency; Administrative Personnel, The John Marshall Law School; Ralph Oman, Register of Copyrights, Library of Congress; Carol Schreiber, copyright & permissions, Harper & Row, Publishers, Inc.; Thomas F. Daly, Editor, *Vital Speeches of the Day* and the staff at Martin Luther King, Jr. Center for Nonviolent Social Change, Inc., Atlanta, Georgia.

Others who must not be overlooked are: Interlibrary Loan Personnel, Bird Library, Syracuse University; Arents Room Staff, Bird Library, Syracuse University; J. Tyler, Cornell University Libraries; D.F. Peterson, Manuscript Cataloger, The Quaker Collection, Haverford College Library; The Schlesinger Library staff, Radcliffe College; Dina Schoonmaker, Head, Special Collection, Oberlin College Library; Professor Sabine R. Ulibarri of The University of New Mexico; Professor Matt Meier of Santa Clara University; Lydia R. Aguirre, C.S.W., Texas Department of Health; Julie R. Kidd of Frewsburg, New York; Sedelta Verble of The Department of Agriculture, Austin Texas; Geraldine Ferraro and her staff; Henry Cisnero's office and staff; and the staff of The Associated Publishers, Inc, Washington, D.C. Finally, I wish to thank Rita Schlegel, Denise Breault, and Wendy Dameron for their administrative assistance.

n.b. Every reasonable effort has been made to trace the owners of copyright materials in this book, but in some instances this has proven impossible. The publisher will be glad to receive information leading to more complete acknowledgments in subsequent printings of the book and in the meantime extends its apologies for any omissions.

Contents

Native American Males (continued)

CHAPTER THREE.

African American Females

CHAPTER FOUR.

African American Males

African American Males (continued)

CHAPTER FIVE.

Mexican American Males

CHAPTER SIX.

Mexican American Females

Mexican American Females (continued)

CHAPTER SEVEN.

White American Females

Preface

American Public Discourse: A Multicultural Perspective is an anthology of speeches by African Americans, Mexican Americans, Native Americans, and White American Females. In the context of this volume the term *multicultural* will be understood as "a racial, ethnic, or gender group smaller than the larger controlling group of America's social system." With all due respect to the White American male it should be noted that he has contributed powerful and oft-times moving oratory to the growth and development of this country, but because he represents the larger controlling group it is not appropriate for him to be placed in with these groups. Also, White American men have had easier access to the public platform, their works have been anthologized repeatedly, and they have not encountered the prejudice and bias that have kept minority voices from being heard.

The purpose of this anthology is to provide the reader with examples from the abundant amount of distinctive American minority rhetoric available that has yet to be anthologized. Some of those minority orations scattered in various locales throughout the nation are brought together here for the first time. The present editor has collected speeches of minorities who have been able to utilize America's public platform effectively while simultaneously battling against discrimination and racial prejudice. The groups included in this book may attribute a significant part of their success to their creative rhetorical strategies. Those strategies are important, moreover, because they have helped to establish the group's unique identity in American society. Clearly, minority rhetoric is unusual because of the many cultural variables and the special ways its speakers manage ideas.

It is important that these minority American speeches: 1) Inform students (speech communication or others) of the large amount of untapped primary sources that are available for further study. 2) Provide a more comprehensive source of discourses which will affect the interpretation of the history of American public address. 3) Ensure that the story is told about each and every group that has contributed to the shaping of this nation.

An attempt has been made—in most cases—to have the speeches of each minority cover the period from the mid-nineteenth century to the present. But the available orations within certain minority groups did not allow for particular time frames. That is because many of the speakers mentioned in the anthology relied more

Preface

on oral than written history. With the appearance of this book perhaps there will be a more conscious effort by historians to retain or record speeches that are important to certain cultural groups.

Inasmuch as this is the first book to compile a collection of American minority speeches crucial questions emerged that had to be resolved by the editor: 1) What groups will be represented? 2) What speakers will be included in the book? 3) What will be the book's format?

As to what groups would be represented it was decided that the volume would include orations of groups who have been successful at gaining access to American public speaking platforms. While it is recognized that several other groups may also fit into this category arbitrary decisions had to be rendered. Groups with available speeches and the groups with the greatest visibility were chosen. As to what speakers would be included it was decided that orators with a widely-publicized reputation would not be the sole consideration. Regardless of their notability, the speaker, had to address an intellectual, a moral, or a spiritual matter associated with the particular ethnic, racial, or gender group they represented. As to the books format it was decided that each chapter would be a collection of speeches by certain identifiable minority groups rather than by dividing each chapter into topical patterns. The reason being that when the speeches of a particular minority group are read in the aggregate their thematic focus may have a greater impact on the reader. Additionally, the reader will have the opportunity to identify the particular groups' approach to their audience as they move through these selected addresses.

The student may wish to study a particular group's oratory for many various reasons. This could be done by considering any of the following questions:

How much of a role does religion play in the particular group?

How much of a role does politics play in the particular group?

How has the group communicated with the White American male? How much of a role did a quest for human rights play in the group's struggle?

What rhetorical strategies did the group use to gain visibility? Does each group employ significantly different rhetorical strategies?

These questions will lead to other stimulating thoughts. In addition to the speeches a selected bibliography is included as a tool to enlarge upon many of the

Preface

issues with which the speakers are concerned. Preceding each speech are explanatory headnotes providing— when possible—biographical sketches and background information pertinent to the speaker and the speech. An index of themes appropriate to the speeches is included also. This book should be useful to students of public address, written composition, history and criticism of American oratory, and to students of the social sciences and American history. At the very least, this volume will aim at attempting to avoid a narrow interpretation of the history of American Public Address. It is hoped that this collection will stimulate scholars to publish other volumes of this kind.

I

Introduction

Chapter One is comprised of six speeches by successful Native American women professionals who address a wide variety of issues. They express their dissatisfaction with the lack of educational, political, and economic opportunities available for Indian women. Clearly, the expressed purpose of the speakers is to articulate their common desire for improvement in the Native American life style. According to one spokesperson they "speak for themselves, about themselves and to each other in past, present and future perspectives."

The first speech is by the keynote speaker Owanah Anderson who sets the tone for the Indian Woman's Educational Equity Awareness Conference held at Tahlequah, Oklahoma on April 3-5, 1981. Anderson recommends persuasive strategies the audience members should employ to achieve their goals. She charges her conferees to take three "pathways" to help them through the difficult times ahead. First, she suggests that they look at "the roads other minority groups have traveled." Second, her advice is to work arduously to attain political power. Third, she believes it especially important that Native American women study thoroughly the "total scope of the White women's movement." To Anderson the imperative is: "Time has come when we must recognize that we cannot cope as islands, for we each are part of the main—the main body moving in a rapid and changing course."

The second speech by Dr. Shirley Hill Witt "Past Positives/Present Problems," deals with the crucial issue of Indian women moving between two worlds. That is, the Native American world of the "reservation, the tribes, and the community" and the Anglo sphere of the "White man's world, the American way." Aware of the inadequate preparation an Indian woman receives to enter into the Anglo world Witt conducted her own study to find out how successful Native American women achieved their own level of success. One of her interviewees remarked that success for an Indian woman today is to learn how to take the best of both worlds—the Indian and non-Indian worlds. The "good indication" of success however, was summed up by another interviewee who said that "verification and validation" from the Indian people was the "ultimate sense of success." Witt concludes her speech with an indication of what the future could promise: "I fully and firmly believe that to the extent that the world of the Great White Father is willing to open itself to Native Americans, Indian women have a unique vision and contribution to bring to this nation."

The third speech by Nancy Butterfield "Squaw Image Stereotyping," asserts that the image of Indians portrayed in the media has been damaging. The Indian woman has been depicted as a "sullen drudge" who follows obediently "three paces behind her man." That portrayal was supposed to acknowledge the Indian male's strength and superiority. The Indian maiden, moreover, has been portrayed to us, says Butterfield as a "mysterious, wild, untamed creature" who possesses an unearthly quality. These images were a result, says the speaker, of the nineteenth century poets and writers like Henry Wadsworth Longfellow who authored *The Song of Hiawatha*. But contrary to that widespread stereotype Indian women in colonial times had a greater economic, social, and political status than their white counterparts, said Butterfield. Even though the Native American woman has changed her ways to meet the needs of our modern high-tech society Butterfield affirms that: "she will always exist at the center of her family, the strength of her tribe, and a life-bringer and sustainer of her people."

The fourth speech by Dr. Rayna Green entitled "Contemporary Indian Humor" is a clever satire of the Anglo's insensitivity toward the American Indian. In addition to sharing humorous anecdotes with her listeners Green relates how she and her colleagues plan to develop a "unique cultural institution"—THE MUSEUM OF THE PLAINS WHITE PERSON. As Green describes the museum it is obvious she is rendering an attack on the Anglo anthropologists who have exploited Indian culture in the past. Her use of humor upholds the judgment that a comic spirit teaches us to be responsive and to question our actions.

The fifth speech of Dr. Ethel Krepps is concerned with Indian women as change agents. She informs her audience that she has been in a position to observe Native American women as change agents. As a result of seeing how women made a difference in many various contexts Krepps suggests specific areas where Indian women can succeed. She states that there is a need for unity among women to provide for improvement. Every effort must be made says Krepps to "maximize" the available resources, skills, and talents of all Indian women. Another point important to Krepps is: "During the next 100 years, progress for American Indian women will depend upon how willing Indian women are to work for and with each other as change agents."

The sixth speech closes the chapter with Helen Maynor Scheirbeck's remarks, "Retrospect and Prospect: The Past, Present, and Future For Indian Women." Scheirbeck offers a comprehensive listing of the principles and policies to be followed for the successful improvement of Indian women. Also, Scheirbeck says all Indians must acknowledge their differences and "seek out the truth about each other." The imperatives are: educate the children, unite to stop cultural genocide, and talk to young women and girls to encourage them to seek their full potential.

In the past unfortunately, American Indian oratory has "been so buried in archives as to be almost lost."[1] It is hoped that these selections will stimulate the reader to seek out more information to gain a better understanding of Native American women.

---

1 W.C. Vanderwerth, ed., *Indian Oratory,* New York: Ballantine Books, 1971., p. vi.

Owanah Anderson (Choctaw)

"Keynote: Charting New Directions."

Owanah Anderson is founder and director of the Ohoyo Resource Center in Wichita Falls, Texas. She is a Texas resident who has studied at the Harvard University Graduate School of Education. At this time she is Executive Director of the National Committee on Indian Work of the Episcopal Church. This speech was delivered at the "American Indian Women's Educational Equity Awareness Conference" on April 3, 1981 at Northeastern State University, Tahlequah, Oklahoma. In this keynote address Anderson sets the tone for the theme of the conference: "Indian Women at the Crossroads: Identifying Guideposts."

This speech is reprinted from Sedelta Verble, ed, *Words of Today's American Indian Women: Ohoyo Makachi*, (Wichita Falls, Texas: Ohoyo Resource Center, 1981), pp. 5-10.

Many years ago, when I was a child, my grandmother used to say to me, "If anyone asks you if you are Indian. . .You tell them no. You tell them you're Choctaw."

Almost 300 of us Indian women are together today, and each of us is keenly aware of our right to be identified as a member of a sovereign nation. We each subscribe to that right. But, haven't we now traveled beyond that narrow and constraining requirement to identify ourselves solely as a Choctaw. . .solely as a Pawnee, Menominee, Chippewa, Seneca or Alabama- Coushatta?

As we consider charting new directions—directions to survive against a new national course—must we not first consider the necessity to think of ourselves as one people? We all share a certain commonality—our commonality as the continent's original people. We all share a similar heritage—a proud heritage and a sad one. Time has come when we must recognize that we cannot cope as islands, for we each are part of the main—the main body moving in a rapid and changing course.

A distinct new national course was charted in November, 1980, and as people economically deprived, by all existing criteria, we Indian people must once again figure out how we are going to survive.

We now have Reagan Administration budget recommendations, and we find Indians bear a disproportionate share of cut-backs. Indian housing recommendations: zero. Yet, we are the most poorly housed of any of the nation's people. CETA programs in dire jeopardy. Yet, Indians have the highest unemployment of any of the nation's people. Education funds: drastic cuts recommended. Yet, we have the dubious distinction of poorest educational attainment of all this nation's people.

How do we cope against these odds?

I suggest that we first take stock of the fact that we are at the crossroads. We *must* chart new courses. We *must* explore alternatives. We *must* cope with the reality that after half a century the nation has pivoted sharply away from politics to "affect social change. This is reality, and naught can come from lamentations. Too long we have wrung our hands and lamented—lamented loss of our lands, lamented encroachment on our heritage, lamented our physical defeat. And, we women have borne the brutal brunt.

I submit to you three pathways—pathways which can lead us once again through hardships ahead. First, let us examine the roads other minority groups have traveled. Second, let us impact political power. Third, let us re-examine the scope, the total scope, of the women's movement.

In my state, as in the states of many of you, there is an ever-growing Hispanic population. Our Hispanic sisters also come from diverse backgrounds as we do. The Mexican-American most frequently differs in priorities, goals and thrust from the Puerto Rican; the Chicana differs from the Cuban; the California Hispanic differs from the Texas Hispanic. Yet, from community level to the national level, I have observed that our Hispanic neighbors can generally coalesce and come out eventually in the political arena with a position to positively impact the general Hispanic community. Take, for instance, bilingual education. Two months ago, an Administration policy was announced which would have dismantled bilingual ed. Reaction rippled clear across the Hispanic community, forces went into immediate action; lobbying was leveled from every angle. The most recent word is: bilingual ed. will survive.

Let us learn from the Hispanics. Let us learn how to maintain our tribal distinctiveness but keep it internal, and how to present an external coalition to the common good of us all. How hard this is for us. How deep are our divisions. How long has the U.S. government pitted us one against the other. How conditioned we are to turf-protection. To turn this around we have to begin within our own selves, our own attitudes. How guilty we are of knocking each other.

I stole this story from a California friend. It illustrates my point so well — and so painfully. An Indian and a White man went fishing together. They were using live crab for bait. The lid on the White man's bait bucket kept coming off

— the crabs kept climbing up and pushing the lid off. Finally, the White man had to get a rock and put it on the lid of the bait bucket. Off the lid came again, and the White man had to get a bigger rock to hold down the lid. Finally, he had three or four big rocks stacked on top of his lid. The White man said to the Indian man, "How come you're having no trouble keeping your bait in the bucket?" The Indian man said, "I've got Indian crabs." "What do you mean Indian crabs?" The Indian man replied, "Every time one of my crabs starts climbing up the side of my bucket, the rest of them pull him back down again."

We do this to each other. Let one Indian surface in any sort of visibility — and the rest of us start pot-shotting...detracting...diminishing...criticizing, and before it's all said and done, somebody pops up with the unkindest cut of all: "She (or he) *really* isn't Indian."

Where this all leads is to an awesome fact: we don't have a voice in the political arena, the arena where policy is made, policy that determines our life-style. Policy that determines whether a hospital will be completed, whether a sanitation system will be finished, a school kept open, a scholarship funded. We are politically powerless—yet no people's lives are as inextricably entwined under the federal thumb as we are. We must learn how to participate in shaping policies...not merely wail and lament equities after the fact. We must learn how to act, not merely re-act.

We will remain powerless until we quit cutting each other down... until we recognize that what happens to the Crow in Montana does, in fact, impact the Choctaw of Oklahoma...until we come to grips with the fact fishing rights in western Washington is an issue about which the land-locked Cherokee of Oklahoma must needfully be concerned.

We will remain powerless until leadership of our national Indian organizations enter into real dialogue with each other. It isn't that we don't have national organizations but its too infrequently we hear of them coming up with common priorities...with a unified voice...with a solid position. Let us hope that the coming convocation of our leadership, next month in Washington, may bring a new beginning. This meeting of vast numbers of our leadership is set for early May. I think it significant to point out that the effort is being orchestrated by a woman, our Menominee colleague, Ada Deer.

We will remain powerless until we learn to seize power. Seizing power begins at your own ballot box. Far too many Indians don't vote. Too many of us don't participate—participate in the process of choosing our Congressman or our tribal council. Much emphasis of the conference will be on leadership development and on impacting the political process, and how to impact it from the grassroots up. So, let us now turn to the much maligned topic of the women's movement. I ask that we re-assess its scope. Let us look at it to determine what is—and what is not—applicable to Indian women. Much has been written about how and why Indian women haven't flocked in droves to join the women's movement. Some say that Indian women are—or were—equal within our own cultures. Some say the women's movement is simply a whim of upper middle class White women. Some say Indian women have been too busy simply surviving to take part in movements, generally. Some have been side-tracked on certain controversial bits and pieces.

I say to you the heart and soul of women's movement is sheer economics. It will continue to be an economic issue for so long as there remain those awful inequities in the pay check. For as long as a woman draws 59c for every dollar a man draws. For so long as a woman is the last hired and the first fired. For so long as this nation is willing to accept as a matter of course that a woman is automatically worth less at the payroll office simply because she was born female. And, what happens at the payroll office *is* an Indian woman's issue. More than one-third of our women are in the work force and ours remains the lowest median annual income of all the nation's ethnic women. For those working outside the home: $1695 is a yearly average, according to the latest available statistics. Employer of the greatest number of Indian women is Uncle Sam himself—but our grade levels are way below the national average. Our Indian women who work at BIA are at an average of GS 4; at IHS at an average of 5.19. The overall average at BIA is 7; and at IHS 6.

There's an ever-increasing number of Indian women who work because we have to. We're the head of the family. Our children must be fed and child support can't be counted on. Last summer we heard from Reuben Snake, chairman of Nebraska Winnebagoes, that 67 percent of the households on his reservation were headed by women. The same pattern is emerging in urban areas. It's merely another myth—that the Indian woman sticks to the house and minds the kids. Such is a luxury that fewer and fewer can afford. And, in the spirit of sisterly concern, we must respond to the needs of the Indian woman who is required to play the dual role of wage earner and full- time mother, and is often ill-prepared for the wage earner role.

During the past three years I served on President Carter's Advisory Committee for Women, and in that capacity I sat in public hearings across the United States. I listened carefully as women in North Carolina, in Florida, and in Denver related their problems. I heard the recommendations—recommendations for federal initiatives to alleviate the problems. I observed there wasn't a great deal of difference between the problems of Indian women and the problems of the rest of the women. Ours were just more so.

The President's Advisory Committee for Women developed a final report and presented it to the President in the Cabinet Room of the White House on December 17 (1980). The report spoke to housing—and Indian people are the poorest housed. The report spoke to child care—and we heard Indian women's testimony across the country on this problem. The report spoke to domestic violence—and this, too, is surfacing as a painful problem for Indian women. The report spoke to women's education needs and opposition to sex discrimination and sex bias and stereotyping in our children's school books. This, truly, is an Indian woman's problem. We're all weary of being depicted solely as squaws, and we're galled that the textbooks of our children, by and large, reveal that no more than two American Indian women have ever graced this continent: Pocahontas and Sacajawea.

I challenge you to look again at the women's movement. To review the blueprint for change. I challenge you to pick out those issues with which you can relate: like employment, like affirmative action, like vocational choices for Indian girls. Give your support to those you can relate to, that you agree with. Bypass the rest. I did. Link with organizations which have already done the groundwork; you need not reinvent the wheel.

And, remember, too: The Census Bureau has just released figures which inform there's now 1,418,195 of us counted. We grew 71 percent—more than any other ethnic group in the land. I like to say that there's more of us now than any time since the Buffalo went: my anthropologist friends like to point out that there's more of us now than there's probably ever been. We survived manifest destiny; we survived White men's diseases; we survived the Trail of Tears which was trod by the foremothers of many of us here today. We survived corrupt Indian agents and insensitive White school teachers. We've survived poverty and pestilence and federal bureaucracy.

We not only survived but we no longer think of ourselves as a defeated people. Instead, a rejuvenated spirit prevails across the length and breadth of Indian country; a contagious resurgence that combines the best of the old and the best of the new. We women shall prevail. We shall prevail as Indian women. We'll move together to new horizons. Through coalition building, through participating in the political process, through expending our energies within the political parties of our choice, through getting behind our elected leaders (or, if we can't get behind them...get them out). Through linkage with in-place organizations focused on our priorities we will be a force to be reckoned with.

Shirley Hill Witt (Akwesasne Mohawk)

"Past Positives/Present Problems."

At the time of this speech Shirley Hill Witt was the Director of the Rocky Mountain Regional Office, United States Commission on Civil Rights. She has served as consultant for numerous government and international agencies including UNESCO. A widely published author she has lectured throughout the world for the U.S. State Department. She took her Ph.D. degree in Anthropology from the University of New Mexico in 1969. She is a Colorado resident. This speech was presented at the American Indian Women's Educational Equity Awareness Conference in Tahlequah, Oklahoma on April 3, 1981.

This speech is reprinted from Sedelta Verble, ed., *Words of Today's American Indian Women: Ohoyo Makachi,* (Wichita Falls, Texas: Ohoyo Resource Center, 1981), pp. 11-19.

LIVING IN TWO WORLDS

There is no Native person in North America who is untouched by the Anglo world, the White man's world, the American way. Nor are any of us immune to its infectiousness. Yet few self-identifying American Indians live exclusively in the non-Indian world. To be "Indian" carries for many a sense of homeland (reservation, tribe, community) and duty to one's people, no matter where one currently resides...or whether one ever returns...or whether those duties are ever discharged. Thus Native peoples are aware of and practice to varying degrees two, often widely contrasting, life-styles. To move between these two worlds can be a feast of appreciation for human ingenuity, or it can be the bitterest trap.

Whether they live in an apartment in Minneapolis or attend the Bureau of Indian Affairs School on the San Juan Pueblo in New Mexico, Indian children typically learn two sets of ways—neither of them perfectly. No human knows his or her own culture perfectly, but what one culture has created is certainly learnable by members of another and is limited only by our intelligence and our opportunity to learn. And so, most Native people nowadays grow up with a two-track cultural background and find themselves participating to greater or lesser extent both in the Indian world as defined by their tribal affiliation, and in the White man's world. This term, "The White man's world," by the way, is not to be taken as a quaint archaic phrase: the world of the White *woman* is, for the most part, invisible to Indians. Even if it weren't invisible, it is irrelevant, since the White *man's* world is the one making an impact upon Indian life and Indian individuals. It is still the Great White Father (sic), who determines the quality of life for Native people as well as all other Americans, male and female.

FROM STRENGTH BEFORE COLUMBUS

As many as 280 distinct aboriginal societies existed in North America prior to Columbus. *Not* surprisingly, some tribes practiced the oppression of women by men. But, in several, the roles of Native women stand in stark contrast to those of Europeans. These societies were matriarchal, matrilineal, and matrilocal—which is to say that women largely controlled family matters, inheritance passed through the female lines and upon marriage the bride usually brought her groom into her mother's household.

In a matrilocal household, all the women were blood relatives and all the males were outsiders. This sort of residence pattern was frequently seen among agricultural societies in which women bore the responsibility for farming while the men went off to do the hunting. It guaranteed a close-knit working force of women who had grown up with each other and with the land.

Although the lives of Native American women differed greatly from tribe to tribe, oftentimes their life- styles exhibited a great deal more independence and security than those of the European women who came to these shores. Indian women, in many cases, had individual freedom within tribal life that women in so-called "advanced" societies were not to experience for generations. Furthermore— and in contrast—Native women *increased* in value in the estimation of their society as they grew older. Their cumulative wisdom was considered one of society's most valuable resources.

NEW NATIVE WOMEN SPEAK: PAST POSITIVES/PRESENT PROBLEMS

In recent years I have sought out successful native women to find out how they have achieved their current levels of success in the Indian world, or the Anglo world, or both. I have asked them about how things were for women in their grandmother's lives and in their own. And, finally, I have asked them to tell me about themselves today, about the problems and the victories they have experienced.

What I will be sharing with you for the remainder of my talk will be the words and thought of these women, as best as I could capture their ideas on paper.

TRADITIONAL VS. MODERN ROLES

What were the joys and the conflicts between traditional vs. modern roles? Options for women in the past have been limited for *all* cultures, given the reality of women's biology and the limited control women have had over determining pregnancy. Thelma Stiffarm (Gros Ventre/Cree) observed that, "In my mother's generation it was expected that the women would stay home and raise the children. My generation has conflict when remembering how nice it was growing up with my mother always there. I don't know if it was *Indian* culture or *white* culture since *all* women stayed home then." Rain Parrish (Navajo) said, "Traditionally, every woman should have a child. Females were to give birth, to give life." But Bella McCabe, also a Navajo, feels that whereas not all sheep and goats are good mothers, not all *women* are made to be mothers. There are other important roles for them to play instead. The traditional roles of Native women often extended far beyond the hogan or tipi door. "In my tribe," says Stiffarm, "Indian women were always given the opportunity to do whatever they wanted and were always encouraged to do so. We've always had Indian tribal council women. We had women warriors." McCabe reports that in Navajo life, "It's a woman's land and everything is centered around the woman. If anyone is oppressed, it's the Navajo men." Parrish describes a major transition for Navajo women from owners and controllers of their homesteads and flocks to a modern, less secure way of life. She says, "Traditionally, women's work was in the home. After losing her sheep in the sheep reduction program (in the 30's), she had to go *outside* the home for work. There had to be a whole re-establishment of roles." Speaking about today she observes that, "Often these days the men aren't working and *they* are in the homes. Now the BIA is starting a new sheep reduction program. I think there will *continue* to be a breakdown in the family, a real fragmentation. I don't know who'll come through it." McCabe says, "Indian men recognize the necessity for some wives to work: it's no problem, and anyone who knows how to should handle the money. My grandmother always had her purse with the family money on a string under her skirt."

While the traditional cultures viewed women's roles as primarily being involved in family and household needs, many tribal groups expected women to play key roles in the political and religious areas of Native life. As Stiffarm indicated, some even had women warriors such as those known as the "brave-hearted women" among the Dakota, one reincarnate today being an organization called W.A.R.N. (Women of All Red Nations) to serve the needs of their people. Movement into the Anglo world of work and education is seen as necessary, or an opportunity. It is not *necessarily* seen as a major threat to traditional concepts of women's behavior.

PERCEPTIONS OF ANGLO MEN AND WOMEN

But what are their perceptions of Anglo men and women? The White world into which Indian women foray for training and work is often hostile, always confusing universe. Connie Uri (Choctaw/Cherokee) is frank about her perception of that world. She says that:

"Racism has stood in my way in my career. To be female and Indian gives you a double bind. In medical school, the first day of anatomy the teacher told me I wasn't worth teaching and he wouldn't do it. The medical school was segregated, two blacks, two Jews, two women, and we were all put at one end of the laboratory to work on cadavers. The lab assistants had to help us since the teacher refused to."

Rayna Green (Cherokee) sees the *stereotype* as standing in the way. "What needs to be changes in non-Indian culture," she feels, "is the image of Indian women seen as dupes and drudges and dumb squaws. As they really are, as superstars, is how they *should* be seen." McCabe also recognizes that the dumb-Indian-squaw-drudge stereotype exists:

"I've served on committees with Anglo groups and it always surprises me that I've always been introduced as an Indian or a Navajo, and then I think people give each other the nod which means, "There's a dumb person.""

Green observes that, "In the White world, being *poor* and *female* more than being an *Indian* has been the burden to attaining success." Uri has found the generalized Indian noncompetitiveness as a handicap. Yet, she says, "I've learned to be more aggressive through the years—but I've got a long way to go to catch up with these punks I'm going to law school with." Bernice Moffett (Nez Perce) remarked that, "It is in the Anglo world that I am walking two paces behind men." Stiffarm, when asked what *White males* need to learn about Indian women to make this a better world, responded, "I'd educate them to learn that women, Indian and non-Indian, are *not* a threat: that there are plenty of opportunities around and that there are *enough* to go around."

Ramona Bennett (Puyallup) feels that, "White men are paranoid. The White man has built his strength on an imaginary supremacy and knows it. He drinks and pushes and competes and destroys a lot of lives keeping up this supremacy pretense. I should pray." she said, "that someday they would rest better and feel better. It would be wonderful if they built a higher regard for women of their race and other races. They have a strong anger, fearing someone will get in front of them."

Anne Marr Medicine (Seneca/Mohawk) essentially agrees. She said, "I've had the good fortune of knowing a number of fine White males, but arrogance is the big problem. They're afraid. If we could erase the fear they have of women and other races I think we could go a long way toward solving problems."

Uri expressed sadness over the lack of communication between Indian and White women. She said:

"I had a lot of hope a few years ago about White women: they were asserting themselves against male dominance and I *thought*   they'd look upon Indian women as their sisters. But after Wounded Knee II, talking with White women, I came away with a bad feeling that they couldn't comprehend the needs of the Indian people. Their total ignorance of the problem was bad: they judged Indian people by their own standards. I told some NOW women that it took 200 years for them to get rid of bras which *we* weren't wearing when *they* arrived here."

Mary White Eagle Natani (Winnebago) feels that, "They try to relate to Indian women, but because of their own upbringing it's hard for them." She said that, "Their concern with outward things, clothes, etc., needs to be changed."

Bennett expressed this opinion more forcefully:

"White women, I would hope, would reinstitute the values that they traditionally had. The women of all races have that strong family and community sense, but White women are too competitive. They compare their children to others' children, their heritage to others, their values are based on how jealous others are of them instead of having things to share.   Their children are put in little boxes and are raised in isolation. They grow up so alone, so lost, and their boys become very aggressive and girls become gossipy and cloistered and they never get away from that. It affects how they treat us."

Fern Eastman Mathias (Dakota) also sees this insularity. "They aren't thinking about other kinds of women," she observes, "the wide range of women. They're only thinking about their own selves and their own culture. They have life too easy. Put them on the reservations for a while and see how they do."

Anne Marr Medicine is more optimistic, however. "I'm feeling a little bit better about White women. I'm meeting some very good people. I'm getting an affinity for some and I hope it grows. Even shopping in a supermarket, though, there is so much hostility in South Dakota I just want to shake some of those White women."

Stiffarm, while sympathetic to the women's movement in this country, nonetheless agreed with Uri and feels her priorities lie elsewhere:

"White women have a mistaken idea that all minorities have the same problems. If I have to choose between an Indian problem or a woman's problem, I'll always choose the Indian problem to work on. Indians have priority for me. There are plenty more *women* attorneys than *Indian* attorneys, *male* or *female*."

OBSTACLES TO SUCCESS

Adequate preparation for life in the Anglo world is a necessity that severely strains the ability of many Indian families. Those who are on the reservations must rely on the most part on the BIA to teach the children skills they will need to know if they leave the economic desert of reservations for greater opportunities elsewhere. But the task is too rarely accomplished in a full and adequate way. When reservation families move to Phoenix in hopes of finding employment," said Phyllis Bigpond, an Oklahoma Yuchi who is assistant director of Phoenix Indian Center, "It is usually the wife-mother who becomes the wage earner and head of the household. She works for sheer necessity because her husband can't get a job. Some who come to the city go right to work—no problems, no help needed," she said. "But many are completely devoid of city survival skills. They lack job training, transportation, telephones, housing, reading and language skills, child care, food. Talk about frustrated people."

Grace McCullah (Navajo) feels that:

"Indian women, in general, are more aggressive than Indian men—certainly more aggressive at finding and holding jobs. When the family comes to the city, *somebody* has to do something. So the mother goes to work. She flat *can't* be intimidated by discrimination. She's got to put the bread on the family table for survival. Tribal roles used to be clearly defined, but with the erosion of tribalism and with sheepherding, for instance, diminished as a way of life, the man has nothing in the contemporary sense to replace those strong structural roles. For him, the role is *gone;* for the woman, the role is not so eroded. She can get *some* kind of job, usually, and the job and her children become her discipline and her reinforcement. In the city it's the *women* who deal with the money, the government, the salesman. Yet, in the Anglo-dominated city, the White society says the father should be the primary wage earner and head of the household."

Natani placed blame for her past career difficulties on the shoulders of the educators:

"What stood in *my* way was a lack of direction early on, people at various schools who tracked me into home economics could have helped me find what I really wanted to do. I went to the mission boarding schools and BIA schools. It took me 15 years of working to find out what I really wanted to do: what to take in school, how to go about it. I was a file clerk for the BIA. I wanted to work with *people* but I didn't know how or who."

Self-consciousness haunts Native women when they penetrate new zones or new heights in the Anglo world. McCabe expresses a common exasperation:

"I'm always seen as being the 'Indian.' Always the *representative*.. Especially with ultra-liberals. But I'm not a representative: I only represent *myself* but I guess we're always a representative whether we like it or not. I'm conscious of being *watched* a lot. I guess I am being an ambassador because I'm educating the non - Navajo people about my people."

Green confesses that, "I don't find myself being schizophrenic except when I'm being pressed to act more 'Indian' by others, usually Anglo. It's also discomforting to be asked to plan for whole Indian groups." Yet she sees one clear advantage. "Being an educated Indian women who interfaces with the non- Indian world, I am so unique that I *can* have an impact on aiding Indian people to become what they *want* to become." Mathias finds that, *"Male dominance* in organizations has stood in my way. They just don't look at females as leaders. I'm talking about both White men and Indian men."

SUCCESS IN TWO WORLDS

When the discussion turns to the lives of the Native women   and   their opportunities, what can be the *assessment* and *measure* of one's "success" when it must span two worlds which do not often mesh well with one another? Stiffarm counsels us that:

"You learn to take the best from both cultures, living an   Indian life is a very different way of life. You have to *share* things, you must learn to give away everything you have, to learn not to be materialistic, to be kind, to show   deference, to take care of old people, and to treat children with respect as individuals. You have to be very strong to do all those things. Taking the best of the White w o r l d is a lot easier than Indian ways."

She then told a story.

"I had a white shawl that I loved very much. My mother recognized that I was getting too attached to it and made me give it away—to someone I didn't even know. Whites feel that if you *work* for something you *keep* it. In the Indian world you have to give it away. So when I hear young Indian people say, 'I want to go back to the old way, I say it's hard to be nice to people all the time.!'"

She feels that, "Success for an Indian woman today is to learn how to take the best of both worlds. Each culture has good things to learn. For example, the White world has good schools. The Indian world has sharing and caring. A successful Indian woman can put together a good life taking the best from the White world and the Indian world." Bennett sees a successful woman as "a person taking part in the traditional culture but also being involved in the national movement for Indian survival, and being able to function realistically in both cultures."

Natani also recognizes this need for a "two-world" competency for successful functioning. She feels that the successful Indian woman is the one who is able to live in both worlds. It's not degrees or money that make a person a success.

The present-day Indian woman who pursues an education and a career outside the home and "off-res" sometimes has much to contend with. Green observes that, "My having gotten a Ph.D. is not well thought of at all. It is seen as dangerous, threatening, and non-Indian. My status in the non-Indian world, although good, is inherently threatening. It threatens my credibility as an *Indian* person." Stiffarm notes that, "My being an attorney *does not* impress my people. They never ask how my job is going—they judge me on how I treat my mother and how I participate in the Sun Dance."

Medicine says, "I've had to make some trade-offs. You can't have an Iroquois longhouse in the middle of the urban area. But in order to do my thing I have to move away from home. I'm caught adrift because I have to move physically farther and farther away."

"I'm sure my reservation sisters think I have achieved success simply because I directed an agency with a $2 million budget—but I am uncomfortable in the role of primary breadwinner for my children and myself. Is its success to struggle— maybe until I die--for our basic comforts? Like the divorced White women around me who are heads of households, I'd like to marry a man who would help support the family, help share the struggle. That, now, would be 'success.'"

But another Navajo, Carol Kirk, has a different view: "For me success will be the day I can return home. I don't think of myself as an urban Indian woman. I regard Phoenix as a necessary stopover, strictly temporary. I get through each day by dreaming of the beautiful tomorrow when I can go home again."

Bennett believes that while, "success must be defined as competency in both the Anglo and Indian worlds, the *ultimate* success is to be found at home. As a chairwoman of the Puyallup Nation, there is no greater honor possible. There is nothing better for me later...being a governor, or a judge or a senator. No other honor or glory could be greater than being honored by my people."

An assessment by Green perhaps best sums up the issues explored here today.

"A good indicator of success for an Indian woman is when a woman has reached the place where she can work for and with her own people, where she has influence enough to be effective. For some it's educational attainment in the non-Indian world which is very useful, or it can be traditional wisdom in the Indian world. A Ph.D. is not very useful on the reservation. It would be best to get the credentials in *whatever sphere* you operate, to have attained credentials in *both* worlds would be ideal, but the *ultimate* sense of success for me would be *verification* and validation in the Indian world."

I fully and firmly believe that to the extent that the world of the Great White Father is willing to open itself to Native Americans, Indian women have a unique vision and contribution to bring to this nation, now as in the past. As Rain Parrish hopes, it may be that for Native women:

It is time to ascend to the mountain tops
To begin to chant the music of our visions.

Nancy Butterfield (Red Lake Chippewa)

"Squaw Image Stereotyping."

Nancy Butterfield in a former Assistant Editor of *The Indian Voice,* a publication of Small Tribes of Western Washington. She is an accomplished author whose articles are concerned with Indian civil rights complaints, Indian women's stereotypes, battered women and women leadership. This address was delivered at the American Indian Women's Educational Equity Awareness Conference at Tahlequah, Oklahoma on April 3, 1981. In this speech she destroys the myth that Native American women are without individuality.

This speech is reprinted from Sedelta Verble, ed., *Words of Today's American Indian Women: Ohoyo Makachi,* (Wichita Falls, Texas: Ohoyo Resource Center, 1981), pp.20-24.

The subject that I'm going to be speaking on today, "Squaw Image Stereotyping," is something that was kind of mulling around in my mind for about the last five years and finally, after going through some processes and talking to a lot of other people, I started to put these things down on paper.

In 1976 and 1977 I lived here in Oklahoma, in Shawnee, and was working for Central Tribes of the Shawnee area. At that time I had an opportunity to get acquainted with a lot of really great Indian women around the Shawnee area who were also interested in women's issues. One of the things that we were able to do was pull together a group of Indian women and form the Shawnee Women's Political Caucus. Kaye Warren of the Sac and Fox tribe, who's here today, and also Wanda Peltier, who was wife of the late Potawatomi chairman, Gerald Peltier, were very active in forming the organization. We held a lot of discussions about the status of Indian women today and how that's changed over the years. We started questioning things like the policies of the Bureau of Indian Affairs (which are unwritten policies but they still exist) of putting women at the bottom of the career ladder in clerk-typist positions. While there is an Indian preference policy, there is no policy which enables women to ascend the career ladder the same way men do. Another thing we looked at was the practice of Indian Health Service of enabling the non-Indian spouse of a male tribal member to have all and full health care benefits of tribal members, but the non-Indian spouse of a female tribal member gets nothing. So, in other words, a woman who marries outside the tribe is, in the eyes of Indian Health Service, waiving her rights as a tribal member for her family.

In talking about these things i decided to find out more about how we go to where we are now. I talked to a lot of people, I read a lot of articles. The paper that I'm presenting I feel like I really can't take credit for myself. Most of the information

I have taken from other sources—from talking to other women, from my own upbringing and just from a number of different places. So, I feel that I have taken all these ideas, these concepts, and set them in writing.

At the time I first wrote the article Wanda Peltier was involved with a newspaper published in Norman called *The Sister Advocate*.. If it weren't for Wanda, I probably never would have written this because she kept bugging me and bugging me, saying, "You know, nothing's really ever been written by Indian women about the situation and we really would like to have something." So she gave me a deadline: we're going to press next Wednesday, we need to have something from you to put in there. So, I got everything together that I had gathered from all these sources and put it down on paper. The article was later picked up by OHOYO and reprinted in their newsletter. the response that I had was really surprising. It alerted me to the fact that there is such a hunger among Indian women to read and see and experience more information about ourselves— more positive things about ourselves. Because those images just don't exist in the media.

You all know how Indian women have been portrayed in the media. It has not been a positive image so I hope that in sharing with you today the things that I have gathered from you—from Indian women as a whole-that we can start within our own minds to turn the tide of being a part of that negative self-image. I want to start out with a quote that is an anonymous quote. It's something that has been kicking around for a long time and I'm sure that even if you haven't heard the quote before that it's ring will be familiar. You will have heard the theme before.:

"Pity the poor squaw. Beast of burden, slave;
Chained under female law from puberty to grave."

Is that really the way it's been? The anonymous author of these lines displayed a misconception about the lives of Indian women which is not only prevalent in non-Indian society today, but which has also had a destructive influence on the contemporary roles and aspirations of Indian women themselves.

The familiar image of the Indian women as a sullen drudge who lives out her days in powerless and subordinate existence, is one which was first fostered by White male historians and missionaries, who interpreted what they saw in Indian society from their own framework of male superiority. This image was perpetuated by careless observers and uninformed persons and has made its way intact into the twentieth century. It has had a profound personal effect on the lives of Indian women in the way we are seen by the rest of the world and in the way we see ourselves. Many Indian women of my generation have grown up believing the Hollywood version of the male-female relationships among Indian people: that the woman walked three paces behind her man to show deference to him and to acknowledge his superiority. When in actuality, the reason the Indian male preceded the female was to protect her from unexpected danger in the wilderness. It was, as the elders put it. "to make the way safe for her."

The other less common, but every bit as persistent, myth surrounding the American Indian woman is the view of her as a mysterious, wild, untamed, intriguing creature who possessed a kind of unearthly quality. This fairy tale is usually applied only to Indian women who lived in the past, of course, none of us who exist today, and is largely the result of the nineteenth century romanticism of poets and writers. People like Henry Wadsworth Longfellow and the Poem of "Hiawatha," you know, all of those kinds of images. While this vision of Indian women is more appealing, it still prevents us from being acknowledged and taken seriously as full and complete human beings. If there is any doubt that the myth or the desire to identify with it still exists, we need only to consider the numbers of times we have all heard a Caucasian person assert that his or her bloodline is graced by the presence of a Cherokee great-grandmother (who was often also a princess). In reality, most Indian women led neither inferior nor privileged existence, but were an important and integral part of the life and direction of the tribe. Many of the largest and most highly developed Indian tribes were matrilineal societies, women of these tribes were the Iroquois and Delaware in the east, the Creek, Choctaw, Chickasaw and Seminole in the south, the Pawnee, Otoe, Missouri and Crow in the Great Plains and the Navajo and the numerous Pueblo tribes in the southwest.

In matrilineal societies, membership in the tribe or clan, ownership and inheritance of property, or hereditary right to public office, developed through the female line.

With regard to the tribe's property, weapons and ceremonial articles usually belonged to men, but instruments for cultivating the soil, preparing foods, cleaning skins, making clothes and tipis and other household articles belonged to women. A woman could build and own a house and in most tribes the dwelling in which a family lived belonged to the mother.

In most tribes the woman could under no conditions be deprived of her belongings by her husband, even if their marriage was dissolved. Divorce was a simple matter which could be initiated either by the wife or the husband. In tribes where women owned the home and its contents the woman could divorce her husband by placing the belongings outside the door and he had no choice but to comply. Following such a divorce, the man or woman was free to remarry.

In her book, *Founding Mothers*, written about colonial women, Linda Grant DePaw states that Indian women at that time had a greater economic, social and political status than their White counterparts in colonial society. The mothers of the tribe often had the final say when the warrior's council disagreed and they could stop the tribe from going to war by refusing to provide trail rations and moccasins. They also had the final say in the fate of captives taken during the war in many tribes. Native American women were also less economically dependent on their husbands. The economic security of the tribe, important male relatives to help the woman if something happened to her husband, and the freedom to divorce, helped the Indian woman to maintain a strong and independent status.

Going back into history to the different tribal stories of creation, women played key roles. Joan LaFrance, who is a Chippewa tribal member, and is with the Seattle American Friends Service Committee office, has written that "the female person is usually the primary force in the creation of the living world. Earth Mother brings forth life. She often works along with the male forces, but according to the creation myths, she is never inferior to the male forces and often she appears as the strongest force." This is a sharp contrast to the Christian story of creation, where the creating force is given a male identity and creates woman from man. Indian woman need not struggle with the question whether God is male or female. Indian women and the female image have always been a part of the creation.

Within traditional religious ceremonies and healing rituals, Indian woman still have major roles. However, so much of the operation of tribes today has been drastically altered and influenced by the domination of European and political and social systems, that in areas relating to employment and education, even within her own tribe, an Indian woman faces the same obstacles and difficulties confronted by non-Indian women. The structure of Indian economic and social service programs, most of which are federally funded and often developed by non-Indian planners, is based on the usual vertical hierarchy or responsibility, which exists in all other American corporations and institutions, with executives at the top who are always male and secretaries and clerk/typists at the bottom who are always female. This is in direct contrast to the way in which tribes historically functioned, with authority and responsibility shared cooperatively and with individual roles and positions of authority often determined by age rather than by sex. The composition of the Bureau of Indian Affairs demonstrates clearly that Indian women have in some areas been deprived of their traditional equal status. Even with its recently professed commitment to Indian self-determination and preference given to Indian people for employment, BIA executive and supervisory personnel are overwhelmingly male with most female employees at the bottom of the ladder in clerical jobs.

Indian Affairs Commissioner, William Hallett, has recently issued a directive to superintendents of Bureau of Indian Affairs Area offices directing that affirmative action programs intent on bringing more Indian women into executive level jobs be implemented. This is too new to see any results yet but we're all watching.

Though the life of a Native American woman has changed with the necessity to survive in today's technological society, and though some of her important roles have been misplaced in this transition, she will always exist as the center of her family, the strength of her tribe, and a life-bringer and sustainer of her people. These qualities, along with her unwaivering spirit of determination, equip her to face the contemporary challenges of health care, employment and educational needs of her people and to insure for her an important part in their solution.

Rayna Green (Cherokee)

"Contemporary Indian Humor."

Rayna Green took her Ph.D. in Folklore and American Studies at Indiana University in 1973. She has served as Distinguished Visiting Professor at Dartmouth College, Hanover, New Hampshire, and, she is Project Director the National Native American Science Resource Center. She is Special Consultant in the National Endowment for the Humanities on Indian Affairs and American Association for the Advancement of Science. Her latest publication is *Native American Women: A Bibliography*. This after-dinner speech was presented on April 3, 1981 at the Ohoyo Resource Center Conference on Educational Equity Awareness in Tahlequah, Oklahoma.

This speech is reprinted from Sedelta Verble, ed., *Words of Today's American Indian Women: Ohoyo Makachi,* (Wichita Falls, Texas: Ohoyo Resource Center, 1981), pp. 48-54.

I am humbled before the stature that people like Mary Natani have reached—people who have been my role models and my teachers and after whom I can only hope that I could aspire to some real stature of that kind. There are lots of people out here and I want to say "thank you" my dear friends: Ruth Arrington, Wathene Young, Carol Young, Nellie Buffalomeat, Wilma Mankiller, Kay Frank, Betty Lombardi, and dear, dear, friends and my dear relatives, my dear people. I am truly grateful to be here. One, I am always grateful to come here and get decent food. As you can see, I've been praying to God for years not to take me while I'm in a Taco Bell but at least to let me go eating grape dumplings. A couple of times a year I can go home and do that. I'm really grateful for that.

But I'm always grateful to come home for a number of other reasons. To see friends. I'm glad the business that I'm in gives me a pretense and an excuse to do this. I'm just delighted to be here before you tonight.

Before I start speaking, though, there is one award that has been omitted. I've had several discussions with people this afternoon. We really felt that some award was necessary for this distinguished person of great merit. It's an unusual, unusual kind of merit. I want to speak about this person just briefly. She has done something that by and large we just don't hear of much in Indian Country. At least, not in the last few years. I believe it is a model we can all aspire to. Many of you heard of Ada Deer's recent triumph where she mugged a mugger on the streets of Washington, D.C. and came out smiling. The poor man was taken down to the jail because he made the unfortunate mistake of mugging a Menominee. All I can say is, I'm staying out of

Wisconsin from now on. The poor man was taken back to the jail bleeding and his clothes torn. The poor fellow is certainly going to give up a life of crime after this.

But we decided, really, that Ada deserved something so that she could mug him more in Indian style. Leslie Wolfe thought of that very thing. If Ada would come forward we want to present her with something so that she can carry on her new found career. Ada, where are you? We felt this deserved a really special weapon so that Ada will not ruin her hands. They've been insured now by Lloyd's of London for millions of dollars and we want to present this to Ada. This is one hatchet we're not going to bury. (Leslie and Rayna present Ada with an enormous stone tomahawk.) We felt it was something to be proud of and it beats Mace. It only weighs eight pounds.

Well, as I said, I'm really grateful to be here. I'm particularly—I always enjoy the food. I know you can tell that. I'm grateful to be away from Hanover, N.H., and the Ivy League where basically, dinner almost always consists of one chicken breast and a broccoli spear and a glass of sherry. I've really grown tired of it, in addition to freezing to death. So, I'm always glad to get back to Oklahoma.

Owanah Anderson asked me to address something that was relevant to the concerns of the women gathered here and the concerns of the Indian people gathered here. I tried to think what special talent I might have that I could talk to you about that would give you something to carry away with you—that would inspire you and would inspire Indian children. I just searched and searched my mind and I finally hit upon it...well, I'm a scholar and that's what I do in this world. I write and I do research. Most often most Indian people don't have much use for scholars, especially the kind I am...an anthropologist. I worried and worried. I thought, "Gee, here I am getting up before Indian people again and here I am an anthropologist and those are the kinds of people that have just ripped us off."

I'm always a little embarrassed about it. I tried to think of some things I can tell you. My family, as you might guess, both my Cherokee and my non-Indian family, are really dubious about my scholarship. When I first started to go off and get a Ph.D., I got a fellowship to go to the Smithsonian and I was going to do a book, or my dissertation, actually I called my mother, I was so excited and so proud. I called my mother and said—this is my way of saying how your family keeps you humble—"Oh, Mother, I've gotten a fellowship and I'm going off to Smithsonian and I'm going to write a book." I knew she wouldn't know what a dissertation was so I didn't want to go and explain it. She said, "Oh, that's wonderful, I'm so proud of you. Everyone in the family will be so proud of you. It's just marvelous you're doing it. Now what will you have to do to write this book? Won't you have to teach or something?" I'd been teaching for years, of course, and working hard and she knew that I'd have to do something-it just didn't come free. Nothing in our life ever did. So she said, "What do you have to do?" And I said, "I don't have to do anything, Mama, they're just going to give me this money and I'm going to go to the Smithsonian and write this book." There was a long silence and finally she said, "You mean to tell me that someone will pay you just to lay up and write?"

I realized then it was going to be a hard time in the next few years. People were not necessarily going to reward me for having done that. So I tried to think about what use Indian scholars like myself can be to Indian people. And I thought of all kinds of things. You know, we write all the time and do research and I'm grateful that Owanah and Ohoyo gave me the chance to do something that would actually get out to Indian people: the bibliography on Native women. Most of the things I write get published in places that no one will ever read them and so I'm always grateful for the chance to do something that will be useful to Indian people. I want to tell you about a few of those things that scholars, young Indian scholars, like myself, and one much better than I am, are involved in and there's some very exciting things. I want to share those with you.

One of those things, for example, we are involved in, a number of us are now consulting for some new TV series, Norman Lear, who has produced the soap, *Maude*—all these TV situation comedies—now we are producing Indian TV situation comedies. I really am so excited about this. Just think, Indian people will be on television. They won't be saying, "Um, my people call it Mazola." We have been changing this to actually produce real Indian commercials. Toni Eagleshield is going to come out and she is going to say, "You people call them mushrooms, my people call them magic." She's going to have a little white powder in one spoon and she's going to say, "My people call it...(Smiling and deeply sniffing.) We've been thinking of giving her a glue tube, but we decided that would be tacky. We know you will share in the excitement of these new commercials. We really believe we can sell the products. We're marketing a commercial fry bread mix very soon. Owanah doesn't know it yet but she's going to pose for it. She's going to be the Indian Aunt Jemima. We knew you'd be happy about that.

But the two things that excite us most are two serials we're working on. Charlie Hill and some of us are working on a Navajo soap opera. It's about a modest little Navajo family, a bunch of sheepherders, and it's called *Yazzie and Harriet*. The most exciting one is an Indian science fiction serial. It's call *SkinTrek*.. We're very excited 'about that too. The computer is an old Indian man that calls everyone "my son" and leads them all astray, regularly. "Yes, my son, go two million miles, turn right..." Well, that's one of the things we're involved in doing.

We have an Indian professional series where professional Indians appear and talk about their careers and it's called *Doctors, Lawyers,* and you guessed it, *Indian Chiefs*. That's a nice one. We're doing a very exciting study now— a group of anthropologists and social scientists are doing a study on the Indian extended family. Basically the theme of it has to do with the alternatives to the nuclear family. One of the scholars that's working with us said that he thinks the Western nuclear family is just like nuclear power—difficult and dangerous. One of the reasons I came here is because I have been commissioned to do an article on the Indian women's movement. Particularly, on the Marxist/Socialist/Leninist/Indian Feminist movement. So I'm here interviewing all the Marxist/Socialist/Leninist Indian feminists in Tahlequah. But the town phone booth wasn't big enough so we're doing the interviewing over here in the Community Center tomorrow and I hope I'll see all of you there. Don't mind the photographs and microphones. They're for the permanent record of Uncle Sugar who, of course, wants to know about all these people.

I am presently working on another project, too. Many people want to know why the Indian women's movement didn't really join the majority women's movement in this country. I've come up with a new theory of why they have not joined the women's movement. You've all heard that one of the first things in the movement did was to burn their bras. I've really decided why Indian women didn't do that. Being the shape most of us are in, we were afraid they'd have to bring the fire trucks in from ten miles around. So you can understand why we were reluctant to join that movement. We figured we stopped air pollution in eastern Oklahoma from not doing that kind of burning.

But the thing I'm most excited about recently is the grand project. This is a multi-million dollar project, it's been funded by all the major foundations in the country. It's very exciting. As you know, all over the country, the Cherokee Nation and many of the Indian nations all over the country have established their own museums. I've done a great deal of museum consulting for the National Endowment and for the tribal museums, for the Indian Museum Association. But I had found a real lack of a particular kind of museum that I really feel we need. And this is going to be a major cultural institution. I want to tell you about it because I am so thrilled to be part of this. This idea, I have to give credit, was originally hatched up by the ex-chairman of the Winnebago tribe, Lois LaRose, and myself, late one night in a serious scholarly discussion in Albuquerque. Basically what we want to develop is a unique, cultural institution. I know you will be thrilled. This is an institution that is meant for Indian people. It is something we've been needing for a long time. It's something that is particularly needed to meet a very special, critical need. The museum is called *Museum of the Plains White Person*. It meets this critical need that I spoke of. It's very serious. You see, we began to be very worried. As you know their (White people's) culture is dying out. Very soon, very soon there will be very few White persons. We worry about this. What will the last surviving White persons do when they have no one to ask what their language was like, what their customs and clothes were like. So, we began to worry about this and we came up with the idea of the *Museum of the Plains White Person*. As I said, it's been met with great reception all over the country. Foundations have rushed to pour money in. Indian people have given money for it. I can't tell you how many shawl and blanket raffles have gone on to pay for this museum. And I want to tell you something about the museum and perhaps this will inspire some of you to go to those few White people that you know are living out there and quickly acquire artifacts from them before they disappear. Because, you know, they don't know how to take care of them. We worry about this. It's quite serious.

The first big collection that we are working on, and this is really inspiring, is the bone collection. As you know, all museums have to have a bone collection. We have begun a national campaign to acquire the bones of famous White people. We want little Indian children to be able to come in and study these and Indian scholars want to pore over them, the different skull shapes and so forth. And, of course, when we do acquire them we will acquire them permanently. As you know, they cannot be given back once they have been handled. We do need to study them for years. And so we are acquiring these. We have just acquired, I think, what is a quite moving find. One of the most important ones. We have just acquired the bones of John Wayne. As you realize what great significance this can have for the scholars, what a study of his bones will tell us about these people and what their lives were like. Well, so that's very important.

There are a number of other famous bones that we want to acquire and I am sure you can begin to guess whose we have our sights on. It's going to be thrilling. The collection will be quite large, of course. We have planned to make the collection as large as it needs to be with as many samples. So, we are going to begin a massive grave excavation all over the country. We have, through our legal offices, which have become very sophisticated, as you know, acquired clear title to at least 80 percent of all the graves in White cemeteries all over the country. We plan to move in with steam shovels right away. We've acquired Mr. Peabody's big coal shovel which did strip mining up at Northern Cheyenne in order to begin and it's going to be an amazing project.

I'll tell you a few things about some of the other collections that I think are quite exciting. We are going to have collections of their food, for example—their food ways. We are going to reconstruct a McDonald's in its entirety. In that we're going to have true-to-life plastic exhibits of white bread, mayonnaise, iceberg lettuce and peanut butter which will be everywhere—smeared all over everything. Primarily stuck to the roof of everyone's mouth. We are going to have several exhibits about their customs. We want to have some performing arts there and we have found the last of a number of White people who know their dances and songs and who have preserved these intact and we are going to have everyday, living exhibits of the two-step, the fox-trot, the disco and other dances. This is going to be very exciting when children come to visit, particularly.

We have acquired exhibits of their costumes. In fact, in the condominium that we are going to reconstruct in its entirety, inside the museum, there will be a typical little family with the gentleman in the three-piece suit and a briefcase and the other artifacts of their civilization.

We have found one very unusual thing that I do want to tell you about. It's an archaeological remain that we have found somewhat in the vicinity of what used to be called "Los Angeles." It's very interesting. It proves that their culture was very flighty. They seemed to change rulers quite regularly. It's kind of interesting. In fact, we found an archaeological artifact that indicates that they changed rulers regularly. It's a big thing they used to call a neon sign—and it says "Queen for a Day." We are going to do some more excavation to determine just how they did depose their rulers and how they transferred power.

Well, I think you'll agree that this is one of the most exciting things that Indian people have done—one of the most exciting contributions that we could make. As young Indian scholars we are deeply pleased to be able to make this. I should tell you something about the Board of Trustees. It will be composed entirely of distinguished Indian people and one little old White lady from Nebraska who speaks no Indian languages. However, she is going to be the representative for the total culture as we feel that anyone of her age and status would be able to speak for all of them. We know they'll be pleased to have a representative. We did find her the other day and we plan to spray and fix her permanently so she will remain on the board.

Well, I think you'll agree that this is a very exciting contribution for young scholars to make and I hope you've begun to see the wonderful things that scholars like myself, humble, well-trained in Western ways, can perform for tribes. I was just talking to Chief Swimmer this morning and telling him some of these things. He agreed that this was just marvelous—a great potential—and that we could, in fact, count on the tribe's hiring at least 20 young scholars to help the tribe to do some of these projects for economic development and for the betterment of the nation in the future. One of the things we did help the tribal council understand recently is about this CERT which the tribe has just joined, and that it actually is the Council of Energy Resource Tribes. the council had thought that it was a breath mint and that they were buying stock in it when they joined. But we've straightened that out for them. We were happy and pleased to do that kind of linguistic translation for the tribe.

Well, I don't want to burden your patience with all this scholarly dry dissertation anymore except to thank you and hope that some of you will look forward to hiring some of us someday. We feel we have skills that Indian people can use and, particularly, that Indian women can use as they march forward to take over—and that's what this is all about. And so, we're planning on the takeover right away. But we'll be gentle. I'm pleased that young scholars will be involved in this and I want to thank you for hearing me and hope that we'll be seeing you soon with some more of these exciting projects.

Ethel Krepps (Kiowa/Miami)

"Indian Women As Change Agents For Indian Policy."

Ethel Krepps is an Oklahoma resident who is a licensed registered nurse and holds a Bachelor of Science degree. She has a Doctor of Jurisprudence from the University of Tulsa College of Law and is author of Western Publications' *A Strong Medicine Wind*. A practicing attorney for Native American Coalition Krepps has also served as Kiowa Tribal Secretary. In addition, she is National vice-president of the American-Indian Alaska Native Nurses Association. This address was delivered at the Ohoyo Educational Conference, Tahlequah, Oklahoma, April, 1981.

This speech is reprinted from Sedelta Verble, ed., *Words of Today's American Indian Women: Ohoyo Makachi*, (Wichita Falls, Texas: Ohoyo Resource Center, 1981), pp. 35-39.

AREAS IN WHICH INDIAN WOMEN ARE ACTIVE

I am in a position to see Indian women as change agents in many vital areas. First, as a practicing attorney, I am aware of Indian women and their involvement in advancing legal arguments in which Indian people are the beneficiaries.

Second, as a licensed registered nurse and the national vice-president of the American Indian-Alaska Native Nurses Association, I am aware of health issues in which Indian women are formulating policy to Indian health problems.

Third, as a member of the governing body of my tribe, I have had the opportunity to travel on behalf of the tribe to present testimony on issues and also attend national conferences and conventions and observe personally what Indian women are doing on a national scale to advance Indian rights, causes and Indian self-determination.

Fourth, as an Indian student currently participating in the Masters in Business Administration in Tribal Management (MBA/TM), at Northeastern State University in Oklahoma, and having previously obtained the degrees of R.N,, B.S. and J.D. through formal education, I am aware of the concern of Indian women as both students and educators as they lobby educational upgrading benefits and opportunities that will benefit all Indian people.

In all these critical areas I have seen women acting as change agents for Indian policy as they are involved in all areas in various Indian issues and are advancing Indian rights, interests and self-determination. As an Indian women involved within the national Indian community, I see how Indian women of today respond to Indian issues either as individuals or within Indian women's organizations.

INDIAN ORGANIZATIONS IN WHICH INDIAN WOMEN ARE ACTING AS CHANGE AGENTS

I observe women as change agents operating within organizations and changing or implementing Indian policy as that policy affects Indian people. Today's Indian woman is visible in many organizations. Some of the organizations are: North American Indian Women's Association, Inter-Agency Task Force on American Indian Women, National Congress of American Indians, Native American Rights Fund, Bureau of Indian Affairs, Indian Health Service, American Indian-Alaska Native Nurses Association, Native American Coalition, and National Indian Education Association.

Indian women are also involved in tribal governments, either as tribal chairpersons or judges and are serving on tribal councils or tribal committees. Indian women are acting as change agents in the formation and implementation of Indian policy in many organizations and on many issues.

FACTORS THAT MAKE INDIAN WOMEN CHANGE AGENTS

Indian women are a unique blend of tradition and contemporary make-up. They must have a wide command of abilities, skills and also have broad knowledge of Indian issues to be an effective Indian women leader. They must not only be aware of Indian issues, they must be aware of and understand the unique relationship which Indian people have with the United States government. Indian women must also be aware of their individual tribal culture and tradition, and they must be knowledgeable of current non- Indian issues such as equal opportunity, affirmative action, and civil rights.

HOW INDIAN WOMEN ARE ACTING AS EFFECTIVE CHANGE AGENTS

As women of all colors struggle to establish themselves as equals in today's world, Indian women face a truly difficult challenge. They not only face the same challenges for equality as other women, but they face many additional differences which must be overcome if they are to be effective change agents.

First, Indian women must determine for themselves where their interest is regarding Indian issues. All areas of Indian issues are critical for Indian people, so in whatever area an Indian woman decides her interest or talent lies, she could be an effective change agent.

Second, after she has determined her particular area of interest and concern, she should continue to be aware of what other benefits Indian organizations are striving to obtain for Indian people and be supportive of their efforts as well.

*The area of education seems to be very critical as Indian women are in the process of catching up after years of being denied the opportunity for an education due to various factors, whether it was an early marriage, or living in a remote area far from a serious academic setting, or even tribal custom which might have prevented the Indian woman from obtaining an adequate education. Whatever the factors involved, Indian women have been denied too long the opportunity for an equal education.

*In the health area, Indian women as nurses and administrators are struggling against truly outrageous problems regarding the health of Indian people. Serious problems regarding rampant diabetes, cirrhosis of the liver, and simple problems regarding proper health care and prevention of disease. In the legal field, knowledge and insight are being gained in legal rights. Heretofore, Indian people have been denied these rights because they had no advocate to advance their legal arguments. The "Maine Land Case," in which the Penobscot and Passamoquoddy tribes were awarded millions of dollars and thousands of acres after their legal arguments were raised in state court proceedings, is a case in point.

*Indian tribes, under P.L. 93-638, are being allowed the opportunity to become self-governing and sovereign in their own right.

These are only a few of the critical areas facing Indian women today as they strive to become effective change agents. All of these responsibilities weigh upon the shoulders of Indian women as they strive to uphold themselves, their Indian sisters, their respective tribes and all other individuals and families. They must also balance their responsibility to their families.

INSIGHT REGARDING THE CRITICAL INDIAN ISSUES

Indian women as change agents have to be equally skilled at raising the issues, making the arguments and presenting the solutions which are most acceptable to the Indian community; all the while saying just enough to make change, but not saying too much to cause an anti-Indian backlash.

AREAS WHERE INDIAN WOMEN CAN BE EFFECTIVE CHANGE AGENTS

The following areas seem to be the most crucial issues in need of effective change:

*Equal opportunity needs to become a reality.

*The economic status of Indian women needs to be drastically improved.

*Indian women need to be moved into positions where they can have input into policy affecting Indians.

*Formal education must be made readily available to a   certain percentage of the total number of Indian women per population.

*Alternative opportunities to formal education need to be made available to Indian women.

*Indian women need to be made aware of health issues specifically involving the future of the Indian people which involve obtaining their consent, i.e., sterilization and other surgical procedures, and family planning instructions.

*There should be more Indian women represented in the tribal governments and managing tribal resources. After   all, at least half of a given tribe are women. The practice of oppressing Indian women in tribal government should cease.

*Indian women need to be consulted on other issues effecting the future of Indian people such as the definition of an Indian.

All women have the challenge to become change agents. We need to collect ourselves as a group resource to provide for the betterment of all Indian women, whatever skills or talents we have to offer, so as to maximize the skills and talents of all Indian women. A chain of Indian women is only as strong as its weakest link. When the average overall GS grade level for Indian women employed by IHS is 4.88, it is a reflection on all Indian women and their ability to be a productive wage earner or head of household.

THE FUTURE OF INDIAN WOMEN

If we are to become effective change agents, a look backward is good, for we have come some distance from yesterday. The look at where we are today is still not that bright. However, the most important time frame for Indian women to be striving for is the future if we are to be truly effective change agents. Something constructive must take place. Action is necessary. What future changes will we plan for our young Indian children? What will their future be like 100 years from now? Will Indian women still be the lowest paid worker; will her voice still be silent around the tribal council or conference table; will her economic stratification be more pronounced even than it is today? The society of Indian women of the future won't be much different than today's unless we make the earnings of Indian women equal to those of others, nor will the situation improve unless we raise her opportunities to obtain an equal education so she can compete with advanced job skills.

Some Indian women of the future may still choose the traditional way of life and continue to live on Indian reservations. However, she must be afforded the opportunity of choice. She must not be prevented from achieving full economic of social equality if she so desires. Indian women are born and live for the same reasons that any other human being is born and lives. They work for the same reasons that other people who work must work, for economic security, and their basic necessities of life are the same as other employees. Her self- actualization and desires for a fulfilling life are the same.

During the next 100 years, progress for American Indian women will depend upon how willing Indian women are to work for and with each other as change agents. Unity for progress is essential. Change is inevitable. The question becomes: what kind of change agent today will be effective and sufficient enough to change this situation 100 years from now?

There are important questions of policy still ahead and Indian women need to be a part of that policy making as effective change agents.

Helen Maynor Scheirbeck (Lumbee)

"Retrospect And Prospect: The Past,
Present, And Future For Indian Women."

Helen Scheirbeck is an Education Consultant and resident of Virginia who holds a Ph.D. from Virginia Polytech Institute and State University. She is former Director of the National Indian Information Project in Washington, D.C. Also, she was Project Coordinator of the National Commission on International Year of the Child. She is past Director Office of Indian Affairs, U.S. Office of Education. This speech was presented at the Ohoyo Conference, Albuquerque, New Mexico, September, 1979.

Sedelta Verble, ed., *Words of Today's American Indian Women: Ohoyo Makachi*, (Wichita Falls, Texas: Ohoyo Resource Center, 1981), pp. 171-177.

I have not been attending Indian conferences over the past several years because I have been finishing a doctorate. Yet, when I received this invitation I knew I would be coming to this meeting because of its very nature, the involvement of Indian women.

I want to talk briefly about Indian women in America's past and then speak of our challenge today and in the future because the future is tomorrow and tomorrow and that time is always upon us.

THE PAST

Our past as Indian women is as checkered as the geography of the nation. We are many people, many tribes, speaking many languages, and representing a diversity of cultures. It was that way when we were discovered by Amerigo Vespucci or Christopher Columbus, and named Indians, later changed to American Indians, and now called by some Native Americans.

In the early days, legends, folk tales, skinpaintings, and whispers, tell of peace, prosperity, other Indians, battles with strange new groups and horses, spirits and "new gods," wars, famine, and new homelands. In those days, Indian people and their life-styles quickly responded to new circumstances and events—and obviously were ready to adapt materials, things, and concepts which improved their lives. We must always remember that the outside pressures on Indian people came at various times. The Pueblo Indians and Indians along the Eastern seaboard, the Passamaquoddy and the Penobscot in Maine, the Iroquois in New York, the Powhatan Confederacy in Virginia, the Croatan and Cherokee in North Carolina, and the Creeks in Florida— all felt the impacts of European cultural imperialism 200 years before the rest of

Indian America. After the 1830s, the European migration to America increased and from then until 1900, Indian people throughout the land felt the impact of the American settlers, the U.S. Cavalry, the Buffalo Soldiers, and the wrath against Indian tribes and communities.

During this period, several things occurred in the American consciousness and was reflected in the nation's history and literature. The myths of the American Indian man and woman evolved and after taking their place in the literature have stayed to portray us to this day.

WHAT ARE THESE MYTHS?

Indian men are either the noble savage (tall, dark, breech-clothed, Mohawk-plaited hair) from the literary pictorial of Rousseau or the blood-thirsty savage (tall, wild-looking Bowie knife-swinging, pinto-riding man) from the era of Daniel Boone, Davy Crockett, and George Custer. Indian women are either a fair-skinned, beautiful storybook princess, who always saves a White adventurer from the cruel ax of her tribesmen as Pocahontas did and then is carried away to be the toast of English society; or a fat, dumpy squaw—who is the jackie of all trades—the childbearer, the food gatherer and preparer, the seamstress, the house and village-keeper in times of war and peace. In short, the drudge.

Both images of Indian women and men are grossly exaggerated at both ends of the scale but are still prevalent throughout this nation today. There were some truths in our past which need to be maintained and built upon:

*The concept of sharing and caring for our clans/tribes/young/ old.

*Functional education for everyday living.

*Awareness and keen acknowledgment of the spiritual world.

*The will to survive.

TODAY'S POSITIVE ISSUES

Let me discuss with you some of the positive and negative issues at work in Indian affairs today.

American Indian tribes and communities have seen tremendous strides since 1964. Much of this is a result of the civil rights movement in this nation, a movement which:

*Created an awareness of cultural diversity and the needs of minority children in the country.

*Created the Indian advocacy desks in the federal government outside the Bureau of Indian Affairs. These desks became the advocates and orienters about Indians to the new policy-makers. They became the cutting edge for new Indian resources throughout the Federal government.

*Passed education programs for disadvantaged children which gave financial assistance to tribal and community groups of cultural enrichment programs. Developed by Indian people, these programs also brought the role models into the classroom, Indian people who came through Teacher Corps and Title I ESEA, etc.

*Expanded educational opportunities for Indians in the last decade. Encouraged movement of Indians into higher education and the professional schools. We now have a limited number of doctors, lawyers, teachers, businessmen, as a re sult of this. Title IV, the Indian Education Act, has helped expand the dialogue between Indian parents and the public   schools. It has brought more cultural enrichment into the classroom and created a greater awareness among Indians about each other and their needs.

This era has also seen a movement to make political governments on the reservation—the tribal councils, into more viable local governments with more direct power and Indian involvement in tribal issues. Phenomenal growth in the Federal budgets and services to reservation Indians has occurred.

TODAY'S NEGATIVES

Let's review for a moment some of the negative things which have happened in this era. Although there has been phenomenal expansion in the Federal budgets to bring social services to Indian people wherever they live, very little growth has occurred in trained Indian man and woman power. Thus, there is no assurance that these social services are of top quality and that Indian people are receiving full benefits. There have been intensive political wars between Indians living on reservations and in urban areas, and those who have never lived on reservations but lived historically in Indian communities. These divisions were encouraged by White politicians and have been intensified by particular national Indian political leadership. These groups are lobbying full-time to cut whole segments of Indian people out of Federal programs and grossly distorting the truth about who is and is not an Indian. When one realizes that over 52 percent of the Indians do not live on reservations the severity of this problem becomes evident.

In spite of increased expenditure on Indian programs at Federal levels, no clear or uniform data base on Indians- women/children/reservation/urban, etc., is available.

With increased educational opportunities has come a large number of educated Indians. Two things have happened:

*These educated Indians have come out of the educational system which has turned them on to the opportunities in the American economy, and turned them off to assisting and serving Indian communities. They have lost sight of their traditions and commitment to Indian people.

*Up until this time I've talked about the Indian man and woman in the context of the Indian community or tribe. That is because in our struggle to maintain our Indianness we have always been concerned about our family, our relatives, our tribe, our community, our future as a race of people.

INDIAN WOMEN

American history recorded few things about Indian women. What were they? One I've already mentioned—Pocahontas saving Captain John Smith. The other, Sacajawea guiding the Lewis and Clark expedition westward to Oregon.

I've spent the last four years of my life pouring through the archives, nationally and in the state of North Carolina, concerning Indian education. I found recorded only a few things about Indian women. The first Indian woman finished Philadelphia Medical School for Women in 1848. No name or tribe was given in the Commissioner of Indian Affairs' reports.

Those same reports record that the Indian girls at Albuquerque Indian School sewed 400 sets of pantaloons for the Indian girls at a number of the large off-reservation boarding schools in the 1880s.

In my own community of Lumbee Indians in North Carolina, our first teacher to have a four-year degree, from Carson Newman College, Tennessee, was a Ms. Ruthie Sampson who came back to teach in the Indian schools of Robeson County.

I am merely illustrating the consistent quiet, effective, but invisible role of Indian women in their communities and the circumstances in which they found themselves.

Now what of this future of Indian women? We are the backbone, heart, and brains of our people. You and I, and our daughters, are the mothers of this and future generations of Indian children. We are the cultural carriers of our generation today and tomorrow.

It is from our hearts, and minds that the future will be built. There can be either scattered, caged, remnant bands of Indians tucked away on reservations, in urban ghettos, isolated rural communities, or assimilated and acculturated Indians living in Los Angeles, Chicago, Washington, D.C. and New York; or there can be strong, happy, assertive (yes, assertive) coalitions of Indian tribes, communities, and people in the United States.

I hope each Indian woman here in this room will pledge herself to this last alternative. For if we do not, the Indian world and its people are doomed to extinction. Oh, there will be a few traditional Sioux, Hopi, Navajo and other groups tucked away, but the majority of the Indian people will be scattered to the winds.

How do we (you and I) build this strong coalition of Indian tribes, communities, and people?

We begin by acknowledging the diversity among all Indians- -in cultures, in physical appearance, and legal definition.

We stop pretending that the only Indians who are real Indians are traditional reservation Indians.

We acknowledge that the great majority of Indians are people in transition who need an opportunity to relearn and restore values that they cherish from their cultures.

We stop living in a White woman's stereotype of Indian women. That is 20 pounds of turquoise, dyed black hair and painted olive complexion. This is a sensitive area and I do not mean to offend anyone. I'm just stressing that if a White photographer wants you to wear feathers and beads and you don't feel that is you, you are still an Indian woman, and don't do it! Americans must learn to deal with us as we really are!

Begin seeking the truth about all Indians. If someone is preaching hate and division about and against other Indians, find out the truth yourself and set the record straight.

Consciously raise your children with a broad knowledge and understanding of tribal legend, folk-ways and histories. This will take creativity and work on your part.

Access the true plight of Indian women where you live and band together to change the cultural genocide taking place in your community against women, children, and men.

Personally talk and encourage women and young girls to seek their full potential in skills and career development. Reinforce the concept of career development and the relaying of skills, opportunities, and service back to Indian people, both in your own tribe and in other tribes.

Out of this meeting let's begin to reinforce and support each other in whatever we are pursuing. Let's begin to monitor laws, legislation pending in Congress, Federal programs and see where Indian women are in each instance. Let's take positions and ensure a fair share for Indian women and girls in jobs, services and programs.

Let's move together against medical experiments using Indian women for sterilization and other purposes. Move against medical directors and Federal officials who do this—expose them in the press and ask for their resignations. Let's make sure medical information and services are open to Indian women, where and when they need them.

In employment we (you and I) must use Title IX to look at Federally funded programs at the tribal, state, and Federal levels to assure that Indian women who wish to do so may work in those jobs, competently and with an opportunity for growth. In this area, we need to call upon our sisters in the women's movement to assist us with their skills in breaking down these barriers.

I must say a special word about my work in education—for it has been the main instrument used in breaking up the Indian way of life. Education is a critical instrument in the ultimate development and growth of Indian people.

For generations our people on and off the reservation and in non-reservations communities, have been subjected to totally non-Indian formal education. This meant traditions had to be reinforced in the homes by parents, who themselves had been "mainstreamed" in their normal education. Today, the Redwoman must encourage her child and children in the community to seek and obtain an education.

Some cultural aspects of Indian life are being brought into the classroom as a result of the compensatory education programs and the Indian Education Act. Indian women as cultural transmitters and teachers must begin coming together to assess and assist in forming these activities. It is this effort which can correct stereotypes which America has about Indian women and Indians, generally. It is also this effort which can build a base for unity among all Indian people, which reconizes our differences and similarities as Indian people.

All of us in this room are people of color. That simply means we are non-White. Indian women must lead the way in their tribes and communities to wipe out distrust and hate against other minorities. These people are human, too, and have been subjected to the same cultural oppression as Indians. The great majority of other minorities do not wish to be digested up in the great "American Melting Pot." They want to marry their own kind, live comfortably, and have freedom of opportunity open to them.

As Indian women, we must build a strong, caring concern for each other and all Indian people. We must structure a coalition out of this meeting to assist each other on common and particular concerns.

We must also join our sisters in the women's movement, majority and minority, to fight for women's equal rights. We must educate them about us, seek their assistance, learn about them, share their concerns and fight together. I have talked of Indian people, tribes and communities because as Indian women we strive to protect and strengthen our people. This is not inconsistent with our fight to develop, achieve, and be strong Indian women who can interpret and work for themselves and Indian people in any career in or outside of the Indian world.

Please take a minute and list your vision for Indian people. I have a dream for Indian women and *it is not one which says:* "My people are tired, poor, hungry, I shall fight no more." Let me say in reverence to Chief Joseph, how sad my heart always is when I read or hear that statement.

II

Introduction

Chapter two contains six speeches—three by nineteenth century American Indian warriors and three by twentieth century American Indian activists. It should be no surprise to the student of Native American history that the subject matter of the orations spoken by these Indian males has not changed much over many decades. In fact, the issues have remained the same. The Native American's greatest concern is how Indian land is managed and controlled by the U.S. government. Moreover, Indians have been disappointed that their freedom of movement over the countryside has been restricted. And, that restriction came by way of the reservation. The poor relations between the Indian and the Anglo have created three main issues: 1) An ongoing program by the Indian to sensitize the non-Indian about the danger of the eroding natural resources. 2) An attempt to inform the white man that the Indian's deep-seated need for freedom of movement must not be curtailed. 3) The wish that the federal, state, and local governments do not disregard Indian rights as sovereign nations. For too long now governments have been ignoring treaties that granted tribes land, hunting rights, and sovereign jurisdiction.

Oratory has, and, is a high priority in the Native American's life. Most students of American oratory are aware of Red Jacket the Seneca Chief's reply when asked how he had distinguished himself as a warrior. He answered: "A warrior? I am an orator! I was born an orator!" Other great Indians have claimed a place in history for their eloquence but they are too numerous to include here. The speeches selected for this chapter however, represent a balance between the warrior-diplomat and the modern day Indian pragmatist.

The first speech "I Will Fight No More Forever," by Chief Joseph (which received mention from Helen Maynor Scheirbeck in Chapter One (page 40) as evolved into a classic oration. Chief Joseph delivered the short speech on the occasion of his surrender to Generals Howard and Miles on October 5, 1877. For eleven weeks the Nez Perce fought the United States Calvary as they traveled over the northwest for some sixteen hundred miles. Chief Joseph and his tribe engaged ten separate military commands and fought thirteen battles and skirmishes. In nearly every case they defeated the Cavalry or fought them to a standstill. Finally living conditions among the tribe's people became so wretched and miserable that Chief Joseph submitted to surrender. His little speech has been a source of frustration for the very proud Native Americans for many years. The overpowering force of the American Army eventually brought Chief Joseph and other tribes to a situation where they were forced to capitulate. Chief Joseph's statement is a metaphor for the greater struggle for power between the two nations.

The next speech by the Apache Cochise is "You Must Speak Straight So That Your Words May Go As Sunlight To Our Hearts" In this eloquent discourse Cochise reiterates the familar American Indian position: "Resist the White man by preventing him from taking land that rightfully belongs to the Native American." Cochise presented this speech at a council at the agency at Canada Alamosa in September of 1866. United States Army General Gordon Granger conducted the council.

The speech "The White Man Thinks We Don't Know About The Mines But We Do." is spoken by Blackfoot Chief of the Crow tribe. He presented this discourse at a council held with the United States Board of Indian Commissioners at the Crow Agency in Montana on August 15, 1873. In the address Chief Blackfoot discussed three issues: 1) He outlined the territory his people claimed and dominated. 2) He challenged the treaty commissioners to give guarantees of what the government would do if the Crows sold their land. 3) He informed his listeners that the Indians were aware of the mineral wealth of the area.

The speech by Hank Adams "Manifesto Addressed to the President of the United States from the Youth of America," is from a series of discourses compiled "on the occasion of the 1970-71 White House Conference on Children and Youth." Adams began his speech by tracing the historical relationship between the Indian and the United States government. In his speech Adams asked the United States government to affirm its good faith with the Native American and respect and provide legal support to the tribal communities. Moreover, Adams suggested that the Indian be encouraged to unify their institutions that govern their lives through a "system of good local government drawn in the context of our tribal-reservation existence." Clearly, Adams wanted to see the Bureau of Indian Affairs dismantled and subsequently replaced by a decentralized system.

Following Adams' speech is an oration by Russell Means in which he expresses his fear of cultural assimilation. In no way does he wish for his people to become completely westernized. He claimed that the Western influence on the American Indian was a form of "cultural genocide." His concern was to inform his brothers and sisters on how to "resist this genocide."

The reader is directed to compare and contrast the rhetorical choices of Means and Peter MacDonald the orator who ends this chapter of speeches. MacDonald presented an inaugural address when he assumed the office of Chairman of the Navajo Nation. MacDonald seeks social cohesion, unity, and promises a vigorous leadership. It is apparent that both Means and MacDonald hold vastly different world views.

Chief Joseph (Nez Perces) (1840-1904)

"I Will Fight No More Forever."

Chief Joseph of the Nez Perces was born in 1840 and died in 1904. Not a large tribe the Nez Perces lived in the northwest mountainous country. More often than not the tribe was reported to be at peace with the white people and their Indian neighbors. Chief Joseph assumed the position of chief from his father at about thirty-one years of age. His record of leadership quickly attracted many writers and historians. His fame as a leader came when he and his tribe attempted to escape white rule and move from the United States to Canada in 1877. This little speech was spoken on the occasion of the Nez Perces surrender to Generals Howard and Miles on October 5, 1877.

From *Indian Oratory: Famous Speeches by Noted Indian Chieftains*, by W.C. Vanderwerth. Copyright (c) 1971 by the University of Oklahoma Press.

Tell General Howard I know his heart. What he told me before, I have in my heart. I am tired of fighting. Our chiefs are killed. Looking Glass is dead. Toohoolhoolzote is dead. The old men are all dead. It is the young men who say yes and no. He who led on the young men is dead. It is cold and we have no blankets. The little children are freezing to death. My people, some of them, have run away to the hills and have no blankets, no food; no one knows where they are—perhaps freezing to death. I want to have time to look for my children and see how many I can find. Maybe I shall find them among the dead. Hear me, my chiefs. I am tired; my heart is sick and sad. From where the sun now stands I will fight no more forever.

Cochise (Apache) (-1874)

"You Must Speak Straight So That Your Words May Go As Sunlight to Our Hearts."

Cochise the remarkable leader of the Apaches was for years a constant source of perturbation to the United States Army. Highly skilled in guerilla warfare tactics and aware of the location of every crevice and corner and stream and river in the countryside the Apaches ambushed white travelers or settlers, wagon trains, and "whatever else offered itself as a target." For ten years Cochise and his small group of Indians fought a bloody war with the U.S. Army in southern Arizona. In 1872 Cochise finally surrendered to General Oliver O. Howard. Cochise's date of birth is unknown but we know he died in June of 1874. This speech was given at a council held at the agency at Canada Alamosa in September of 1866. General Gordon Granger conducted the affairs at the council.

From Indian Oratory: Famous Speeches by Noted Indian Chieftains, by W.C. Vanderwerth. Copyright (c) 1971 by the University of Oklahoma Press.

The sun has been very hot on my head and made me as in a fire; my blood was on fire, but now I have come into this valley and drunk of these waters and washed myself in them and they have cooled me. Now that I am cool I have come with my hands open to you to live in peace with you. I speak straight and do not wish to deceive or be deceived. I want a good strong and lasting peace.

When God made the world he gave one part to the white man and another to the Apache. Why was it? Why did they come together? Now that I am to speak, the sun, the moon, the earth, the air, the waters, the birds and beasts, even the children unborn shall rejoice at my words. The white people have looked for me long. I am here! What do they want? They have looked for me long; why am I worth so much? If I am worth so much why not mark when I set my foot and look when I spit?

The coyotes go about at night to rob and kill; I can not see them; I am not God. I am no longer chief of all the Apaches. I am no longer rich; I am but a poor man. The world was not always this way. I can not command the animals; if I would they would not obey me. God made us not as you; we were born like the animals, in the dry grass, not on beds like you. This is why we do as the animals, go about of a night and rob and steal. If I had such things as you have, I would not do as I do, for then I would not need to do so. There are Indians who go about killing and robbing. I do not command them. If I did, they would not do so. My warriors have been killed in Sonora. I came here because God told me to do so. He said it was good to be at peace—so I came! I was going around the world with the clouds, and air, when God spoke to my thought and told me to come in here and be at peace with all. He said the world was for us all; how was it? When I was young I walked all over this country, east and west, and saw no other people than the Apaches. After many summers I walked again and found another race of people had come to take it. How is it? Why is it that the Apaches wait to die—that they carry their lives on their finger nails? They roam over the hills and plains and want the heavens to fall on them. The Apaches were once a great nation; they are now but few, and because of this they want to die and so carry the lives on the finger nails. Many have been killed in battle. You must speak straight so that your words may go as sunlight to our hearts. Tell me, if the Virgin Mary has walked throughout all the land, why has she never entered the wigwam of the Apache? Why have we never seen or heard her?

I have no father or mother; I am alone in the world. No one cares for Cochise; that is why I do not care to live, and wish the rocks to fall on me and cover me up. If I had a father and a mother like you, I would be with them and they with me. When I was going around the world, all were asking for Cochise. Now he is here—you see him and hear him—are you glad? If so, say so. Speak, Americans and Mexicans, I do not wish to hide anything from you nor have you hide anything from me; I will not lie to you; do not lie to me. I want to live in these mountains; I do not want to go to Tularosa. That is a long way off. The flies on those mountains eat out the eyes of horses. The bad spirits live there. I have drunk of these waters and they have cooled me; I do not want to leave here.

Blackfoot (Crow) (-1877)

"The White Man Thinks We Don't Know about the Mines, But We Do."

A member of the Mountain Crow Tribe in the Yellowstone Territory little is known of Chief Blackfoot's childhood. And, his date of birth is not recorded anywhere. He became Chief of the Crow Tribe in the 1850's and in the 1860's he advanced to head Chief of the Mountain Crows. Active in tribal affairs he represented his people at treaties and participated in many council meetings. He became famous for his long harangues and eloquence at council meetings. In 1877—in his late eighties—Chief Blackfoot died of pneumonia. This speech was presented at the council held at the Crow Agency in Montana on August 15, 1873.

From Indian Oratory: Famous Speeches by Noted Indian Chieftains, by W.C. Vanderwerth. Copyright (c) 1971 by the University of Oklahoma Press.

On this side of the river and on the other side is our country. If you do no know anything about it, I will tell you about it, for I was raised here. You mark all our country, the streams and mountains, and I would like to tell you about it; and what I say I want you to take to your heart. You make us think a great deal today. I am a man, and am talking to you. All the Indian tribes have not strong arms and brave hearts like we have; they are not so brave. We love you and shake hands with you (at this point he shook hands with Commissioner Brunot). We have gone to Judith Basin a great deal, and you wish us to take it for a reservation. All kinds of men go there; trappers and hunters go there poisoning game. The Sioux Indians, Crees, Santees, Mandans, Assineboines, Gros Ventres, Piegans, Pen d'Oreilles, Flatheads, the Mountain Crows, the River Crows, Bannacks, Snakes, and Nez Perce Indians and white people, all go there. You wish us to take the Judith Basin for a reservation. All these Indians will come, and we will likely quarrel; that is what we think about it.

Judith Basin is a small basin; a great many people go there; we all go there to eat buffalo. I have told you about the Sioux when they come to fight us. We go a long way from our camp. All Indians are not as strong as we are; they give up and run off. If you have two dogs, if they go to fight, and you catch them and pull them apart, when you let them go they fight again. So it is with the Sioux and Crows.

You tell me the railroad is coming up the Yellowstone. If you move this place away from here, the Sioux will be like a whirlwind; they will come and fight the whites; that is true as I tell you. Along Prior Mountain is the Crow Trail. We listen to you, and what I tell you is true. The young men do not care what they do. We want some of them to go to Washington with Major Pease (agent for the Crows), and what they say there will be all right. I will tell you what we will do; neither of us will live forever; in time both of us will die. We will sell the part of our reservation containing the mountains from Clark's Fork below the mountains, and the valleys we will not sell. The Crow young men will go to Washington and fix it up, and come back and tell us about it. We will sell the range of mountains to Heart's Mountain and Clark's Fork. The young men will sell it at Washington, and they will say to the Great Father at Washington, that the Crows have a strong heart and are willing to sell their land. When you buy this and give us plenty for it, we will talk about the rest, if you want to buy it.

Those mountains are full of mines. The whites think we don't know about the mines, but we do. We will sell you a big country, all the mountains. Now tell us what you are going to give for our mountains. We want plenty for them. Am I talking right? The young men think I am talking right. Every one here is trying to get plenty. The railroad is coming. It is not here yet. You talk about Judith Basin. I have heard about it. I want to see what you will give for the mountains; then we will talk about the rest of our land. You think you have peace with the Sioux; I do not think you have. You want to shake hands with them. We want to know, whether you are going to fight the Sioux or not; we want to know. We will see what the young men will do at Washington; if they hear what is good, we will do it. The railroad will not be here for some time, and before that we will be part of the time on this side and part of the time on the other side of the river. In the Gallatin Valley, if you sell a house and a little piece of ground, you get paid for it. I know that is the white man's way of doing. The white men are all around us. On the other side of the river all those streams belong to the Crows. When the Sioux come there, we can run them off into the river. We are friends; when our friends get horses stolen, we give them some. Many of our horses are stolen here; four of my horses are gone now; last night some horses were stolen. The Sioux took them along the mountains. On the other side of the gap, there are plenty of houses full of everything. In Gallatin Valley are plenty of cartridges; the Crows have none. If the Sioux come, I do not know what we shall fight them with.

See all these old women! They have no clothing; the young men have no good blankets. We would like the Nez Perces, when they raise camp, to come here; they die with the Crows; they help to fight the Sioux. The last commission told us we could eat buffalo a long time. While we are here, the Flathead Indians take our horses. I would like you to take our part and stop them.

Hank Adams (Assiniboine-Sioux)

"Manifesto Addressed to the President of the United States from the Youth of America."

When this discourse was addressed to the President of the United States in 1970 Hank Adams was twenty-seven years old. An Assinoboine-Sioux from Poverty Flats, Fort Peck Reservation, Montana, Adams was reared in Indian communities in western Washington State. In the 1970's he led the Survival of American Indians Association as they struggled to protect salmon fishing rights guaranteed by U.S. treaties. He edited the newsletter *The Renegade* and worked as a researcher and writer. He was a lobbyist in Washington D.C. for the National Congress of American Indians and the National Indian Youth Council. Moreover, he participated in the formation of a national Indian Culture Center on Alcatraz Island.

Reprinted with permission of Macmillan Publishing Company from *Manifesto Addressed to the President of the United States from the Youth of America*, edited by Alan Rinzler. Copyright (c) 1970 by Macmillan Publishing Company.

The American Indian has not been a beneficiary of this nation's strengths, but rather a continuing victim of its weaknesses—and our own. Dispossessed of a continent and confined to the unnatural existence of the reservations, the Indians' lives, remaining lands and other resources were entrusted unto the care and control of the United States government to be administered in our "own best interests," without Indian interference.

Indians did not become citizens under the Fourteenth Amendment in 1868 because of the sovereign character of our tribes and our owing allegiance to them. The granting of citizenship to all Indians in 1924, however, brought no material change to Indian lives. Subsequent years have brought forth still greater misery, despair and sterile conditioning.

The national mood has periodically been such as to demand a commitment in public policy toward alleviating and dispelling chronic problems that, in the public mind, have been endemic to the Indian personality and ecological condition. The national maturity necessary for devising effective programming and rendering productive assistance, nevertheless, has already been lacking.

Today the Indian people approach the future with the most negative economic, education and employment rates in the nation. As reformist Ralph Nader wrote in 1956 and appropriately repeated in 1969 Congressional testimony, Indians remain "a people without a future."

Indians retaining tribal affiliations—which federal agencies generally count as their self-ascribe service populations—number substantially fewer than 500,000 people. Significantly, Indians have owned and still possess many resources that have not been available to millions of other impoverished people in urban slums, ghettos and rural areas. Among these: the tribes collectively own 2 percent of United States territory, or 55 million acres of land containing valuable mineral, timber, water and fishery resources; they have more than $250 million in the United States Treasury; and they are serviced by a federal Indian program currently budgeted at $525 million annually (this does not includes state and private programs).

The resources and services, however, are not distributed uniformly among the native American Indian populations. Poverty is. Present federal programming may offer little more to the Indian future than poverty in perpetuity—and bureaucratic positions for white men. With properties estimated as valuing nearly $10 billion, apart from further improvements and economic exploitation, Indians have been consigned to a role of being wealthy landholders, while remaining functional paupers.

The reasons, oddly, are move obvious than inexplicable.

Public policy and federal programming throughout the national history have always manifested ambivalent, contradictory social and political attitudes toward Indians.

One continuing hope for Indians has been the judicial standard arrived at early in the life of the nation by the United States Supreme Court. Justice John Marshall's declaration that Indians occupy a legal dimension as political sovereigns——being, in the first instance, independent nationals possessing the right of nations and original title to the soil—was difficult to reconcile with public attitudes, which ranged from holding that Indians were social inferiors to doubting if they were even possessed of sufficient "human traits" to argue against a policy of outright extermination and disposal. The objectives common to subsequent national Indian policy thus became those of reducing or extinguishing the force of Indians' natural and distinct political rights, and of "elevating" their "social and human character" from that of "Indians."

The features common to the several hundred treaties between the federal government and the tribes were the cession of Indian land title to the United States and the tribes' declaration of dependence upon the United States in exchange for its protection. These documents established the doctrine for the federal government to assume complete political control over the lives and properties of Indian tribes and individuals, control to be exercised, in the first instance, by the Congress.

Functional control over Indian lives, however, has been exercised most fully by the Bureau of Indian Affairs, established in 1849 in the Department of Interior after being originally in the War Office. The primary function of the BIA was to undertake the final civilizing measures upon the Indian population through the dispensation of goods and welfare services provided gratuitously by the Congress or under the provisions of the various treaties.

The Indian Bureau's major responsibility shifted to the management of Indian properties and funds when the Congress decided in the 1880's that tribal lands should be divided up and allotted in trust to individual Indians. It was agreed that breaking up tribal communities to commit all Indians to agrarian life would have an "overwhelming civilizing effect"—caring nothing for the respective tribal experiences and ignoring all the implications of the industrial revolution.

Ensuing exploitation of Indian vulnerability resulted in the loss of two thirds of reserved lands from Indian ownership before Congress decided, in 1934, to take the corrective action necessary. Further land allotments were then prohibited. Consequently, most Indian property owners today are over thirty-five years in age. Since then, 13.5 million acres of land have passed into divided ownership through lines of inheritance—with federal restrictions upon approved use so extreme as to totally remove this acreage from productive utilization and benefit either by the multiple owners, individual interests or tribes.

The lease of Indian lands to non-Indians has been the most common form of BIA property management. In 1967 this was reflected by non-Indians securing only 56.6 percent of the total $105,200,000 gross income drawn from Indians' nonirrigated agricultural-range lands. Non-Indians grossed $52,400,000 in lease of just 2.13 million acres of select Indian agricultural lands out of the total 44.2 million acres in use. Irrigated lands present similarly distressing figures.

Simply stated, Indians are now making their major investments in their least productive lands at a much lower rate of return than that which accrues to non-Indians who lease the Indians' most productive agricultural lands.

The unemployment rate among Indians is reportedly 40 percent; yet 79,000 Indians, or 60 percent of the Indian labor force, are presently unemployed or underemployed, according to confidential figures provided last year to the Bureau of the Budget. The BIA anticipates the reservation labor force will, at a 1 percent rate of annual increase, number 140,000 by 1973—but realistically assumes "no improvement in employment rates" in its program projections for the next five years.

The BIA's Industrial Development Program is cited as its major program for creating reservation employment. The IDP accounted for less than two hundred new jobs annually in its first decade of operation, and its total payrolls amounted to a per capita income increase to reservation Indians of slightly more than $10—during a period in which national per capita income has increased over $700. In 1966 the BIA declared it had attracted twenty-six new industrial plants to Indian areas to create 1,700 new jobs. In 1968 it was disclosed that these plants had produced only 319 jobs, generating an average annual wage of only $2,912.

Programs in employment assistance, relocation and vocational training are centrally designed to remove more than thirty thousand Indians from the reservation each year; there is no comparable assistance in training or job development if the same persons desire to stay on the reservation. Programs that tend to serve large family units generally provide considerably less income than the $3,120 average income that institutional vocational trainees were found to be earning three years after completion of training, according to a BIA justification for funding requests last year.

The results of BIA job development programs do not compare favorably with the bureau's own internal growth. Last year the BIA and the Public Health Service-Indian Division asked Congress to approve 923 new permanent positions for their combined employee structures; the bureau alone estimated it will need 6,252 additional employees by 1973-having advanced to 16,177 by mid-1967. PHS-ID entered the fiscal year of 1968 with 6,694 authorized permanent positions.

Significantly, in the same period Indian family income, drawn primarily from nonfederal sources, increased 18 percent to $1,600 per year; federal expenditures for Indians increased by 400 percent. If paid directly to 400,000 Indians, current expenditures would provide more than $6,500 per five-member family unit.

Present programming is actually not keeping pace with growing problems. The existence and demands of one program only attest to the failures of others. Under current dropout rates, 95,000 of the present 162,000 Indian elementary and secondary school students can be expected not to complete high school. Though only 16,000 out of 57,000 housing units now designated as substandard are considered renovatable, only a mere 2,400 new housing starts annually are programmed. Health and disease problems are becoming more visible in their severity rather than becoming radically improved.

What needs to be done? The present Congress and Administration are fully committed to errors of the past and are primarily engaged in carrying forward the burdensome foundations for continuing failures. The Indians leadership is so enveloped by fear and insecurity that they protectively embrace and defend these foundations, while damning their manifest errors.

There must be qualitative reform of the federal-Indian relationship now with consequent commitment to effect the dramatic changes such reform requires.

The Bureau of Indian Affairs should be abolished prior to 1976, in order that a third "century of dishonor" may not begin. We may assume that all its employees are qualified to secure honest jobs in other pursuits.

A new agency, headed by a Cabinet-level director, to sustain the federal-Indian relationship should be established in the Executive offices of the President. This unit should have at least one representative selected by each tribal unit in the nation, including an ordinate number of Aleuts and Eskimos, and a professional staff not exceeding the number of native American staff (apart from clerical support). Its principal function would be to provide and administer community development grants to the local-tribal governments and to contract with various Indian communities and urban organizations for the conduct of essential services programs. It could redirect funds to priority needs and programs of local communities through absorbing the present funding levels while effecting elimination of the related programs. The full dimensions of its role would be established by collective Indian determination.

Revision of the trust relationship is required to eliminate restrictive aspects while continuing its beneficial elements. Congress should enact legislation to continue tax exemptions for Indian properties and income derived therefrom until the year 2000, and prohibiting alienation of any and all properties from Indian ownership for the same period of time. With these provisions in force, the status of trust and its management responsibilities could be dispensed with.

Trust funds now held in the United States Treasury could conceivably be consolidated under some form of corporate trust to provide a continuous investment and limited- development fund for enabling collective utilization and circulation of Indian monetary resources. Such a nationally consolidated fund could enable their conversion for collateral use of working capital under reasonable interest and return rates, as opposed to their present nonuse.

Essentially, this nation must now affirm its good faith with the Indian people and its own spirit of government by respecting and providing legal support to the tribal communities in their distinct political and cultural dimensions. In a sense, we need a chance to unify the institutions that govern our lives through a system of good local government drawn in the context of our tribal- reservation existence—and granted positive standing within the systems of both federal and state governments.

Given command of our own resources and afforded appropriate assistance, we will have the means and mechanics to bring economic solutions to our economic problems. We can develop processes of education—drawing upon the strengths of cultural diversity and free from the design of cultural devastation—that will allow us to remain at home in our communities while providing us with the academic advancement and social mobility necessary to take up residence within any element of American life. We could bring security to our families through adequate employment and income for heads of families, enabling them to meet the personal needs and social concerns of all family members.

The real question is whether this post-Columbian nation can summon the integrity and courage to abort the maladapted mission of the Bureau of Indian Affairs and abolish it. If not, there is small chance of advancing solutions to problems in any major sphere of concern. If not, this post-Apollo nation will have lost the benefit of its most creative human experiences and will continue to give but misguided direction to the destiny of its pre- Columbian people.

Russell Means (1930-)

"For the World to Live 'Europe' Must Die."

Co-founder of the activist American Indian Movement (AIM) and a member of the Ogala Lakota Tribe Russell Means addressed several thousand people during the Black Hills International Survival Gathering in the Summer of 1980. Held on the Pine Ridge Reservation in South Dakota the meeting protested the damage done to the environment of American Indian land throughout the Western United States. Means has organized several AIM groups in cities and on reservations. He participated actively in the takeover of Wounded Knee, South Dakota in the Spring of 1973.

In addition to complaining about the destruction of the natural environment Means addressed the assumed superiority of the European mind set. He stated: "A lopsided emphasis on human by humans—the Europeans' arrogance of acting as though they were beyond the nature of all related things— can only result in a total disharmony and a readjustment which cuts arrogant human beings down to size, gives them a taste of that reality beyond their group or control and restores the harmony."

Reprinted with permission from *Mother Jones* magazine, (c) 1980, the Foundation for National Progress.

The only possible opening for a statement of this kind is that I detest writing. The process itself epitomizes the European concept of "legitimate" thinking; what is written has an importance that is denied the spoken. My culture, the Lakota culture, has an oral tradition, so I ordinarily reject writing. It is one of the white world's ways of destroying the culture of non-European peoples, the imposing of an abstraction over the spoken relationship of a people.

So what you read here is not what I've written. It's what I've said and someone else has written down. I will allow this because it seems that the only way to communicate with the white world is through the dead dry leaves of a book. I don't really care whether my words reach whites or not. They have already demonstrated through their history that they cannot hear, cannot see; they can only read (of course, there are exceptions, but the exceptions only prove the rule). I'm more concerned with American Indian people, students and others, who have begun to be absorbed into the white world through universities and other institutions. But even then its a marginal sort of concern. It's very possible to grow into a red face with a white mind; and if that's a person's individual choice, so be it, but I have no use for them. This is part of the process of cultural genocide being waged by Europeans against American Indian peoples today. My concern is with those American Indians who choose to resist this genocide, but who may be confused as to how to proceed.

(You notice I use the term *American Indian* rather than *Native American* or *Native indigenous people* or *Amerindian* when referring to my people. There has been some controversy about such terms, and frankly, at this point, I find it absurd. Primarily it seems that American Indian is being rejected as being European in origin—which is true. But all of the above terms are European in origin; the only non-European way is to speak of Lakota—or, more precisely, of Oglala, Brule, etc.--and of the Dine, the Miccosukee and all the rest of the several hundred correct tribal names.)

(There is also some confusion about the word *Indian*, a mistaken belief that it refers somehow to the country, India. When Columbus washed up on the beach in the Caribbean, he was not looking for a country called India. Europeans were calling that country Hindustan in 1492. Look it up on the old maps. Columbus called the tribal people he met "Indio," from the Italian *in dio*, meaning "in God.")

It takes a strong effort on the part of each American Indian not to become Europeanized. The strength for this effort can only come from the traditional ways, the traditional values that our elders retain. It must come from the hoop, the four directions, the relations; it cannot come from the pages of a book or a thousand books. No European can ever teach a Lakota to be Lakota, a Hopi to be a Hopi. A master's degree in "Indian Studies" or in "education" or in anything else cannot make a person into a human being or provide knowledge into the traditional ways. It can only make you into a mental European, an outsider.

I should be clear about something here, because there seems to be some confusion about it. When I speak of Europeans or mental Europeans. I'm not allowing for false distinctions. I'm not saying that on the one hand there are the by-products of a few thousand years of genocidal, reactionary, European intellectual development which is good. I'm referring here to the so-called theories of Marxism and anarchism and "leftism" in general, I don't believe these theories can be separated from the rest of the European intellectual tradition. It's really just the same old song.

The process began much earlier. Newton, for example, "revolutionized" physics and the so-called natural sciences by reducing the physical universe to a linear mathematical equation. Descartes did the same thing with culture. John Locke did it with politics, and Adam Smith did it with economics. Each one of these "thinkers" took a piece of the spirituality of human existence and converted it into a code, an abstraction. They picked up where Christianity ended; they "secularized" Christian religion, as the "scholars" like to say—and in doing so they made Europe more able and ready to act as an expansionist culture. Each of these intellectual revolutions served to abstract the European mentality even further, to remove the wonderful complexity and spirituality from the universe and replace it with a logical sequence: one, two, three, Answer!

This is what has come to be termed "efficiency" in the European mind. Whatever is mechanical is perfect; whatever seems to work at the moment—that is, proves the mechanical model to be the right one—is considered correct, even when it is clearly untrue. This is why "truth" changes so fast in the European mind; the answers which result from such a process are only stop-gaps, only temporary, and must be continuously discarded in favor of new stop-gaps which support the mechanical models and keep them (the models) alive.

Hegel and Marx were heirs to the thinking of Newton, Descartes, Locke and Smith. Hegel finished the process of secularizing theology—and that is put in his own terms—he secularized the religious thinking through which Europe understood the universe. Then Marx put Hegel's philosophy in terms of "materialism," which is to say that Marx despiritualized Hegel's work altogether. Again, this is in Marx' own terms. And this is now seen as the future revolutionary potential of Europe. Europeans may see this as revolutionary, but American Indians see it simply as still more of that same old European conflict between *being* and *gaining*. The intellectual roots of a new Marxist form of European imperialism lie in Marx'—and his followers' links to the tradition of Newton, Hegel and the others.

Being is a spiritual proposition. *Gaining* is a material act. Traditionally, American Indians have always attempted to *be* the best people they could. Part of that spiritual process was and is to give away wealth, to discard wealth in order *not* to gain. Material gain is an indicator of false status among traditional people, while it is "proof that the system works" to Europeans. Clearly, there are two completely opposing views at issue here, and Marxism is very far over to the other side from the American Indian view. But let's look at a major implication of this; it is not merely an intellectual debate.

The European materialist tradition of despiritualizing the universe is very similar to the mental process which goes into dehumanizing another person. And who seems more expert at dehumanizing other people? And why? Soldiers who have seen a lot of combat learn to do this to the enemy before going back into combat. Murderers do it before going out to commit murder. Nazi SS guards did it to concentration camp inmates. Cops do it. Corporation leaders do it to the workers they send into uranium mines and steel mills. Politicians do it to everyone in sight. And what the process has in common for each group doing the dehumanizing is that it makes it all right to kill and otherwise destroy other people. One of the Christian commandments says, "Thou shalt not kill," at least not humans so the trick is to mentally convert the victims into nonhumans. Then you can proclaim violation of your own commandment as a virtue.

In terms of the despiritualization of the universe, the mental process works so that it becomes virtuous to destroy the planet. Terms like *progress* and *development* are used as cover words here, the way *victory*   and *freedom*   are used to justify butchery in the dehumanization process. For example, a real-estate speculator may refer to "developing" a parcel of ground by opening a gravel quarry; *development* here means total, permanent destruction, with the earth itself removed. But European logic has *gained* a few tons of gravel with which more land can be "developed" through the construction of road beds. Ultimately, the whole universe is open—in the European view—to this sort of insanity.

Most important here, perhaps, is the fact that Europeans feel no sense of loss in all this. After all, their philosophers have despiritualized reality, so there is no satisfaction (for them) to be gained in simply observing the wonder of a mountain or a lake or a people in *being*. No, satisfaction is measured in terms of gaining material. So the mountain becomes gravel, and the lake becomes coolant for a factory, and the people are rounded up for processing through the indoctrination mills Europeans like to call schools.

But each new piece of that "progress" ups the ante out in the real world. Take fuel for the industrial machine as an example. Little more than two centuries ago, nearly everyone used wood—a replenishable, natural item—as fuel for the very human needs of cooking and staying warm. Along came the Industrial Revolution and coal became the dominant fuel, as production became the social imperative for Europe. Pollution began to become a problem in the cities, and the earth was ripped open to provide coal whereas wood had always simply been gathered or harvested at no great expense to the environment. Later, oil became the major fuel, as the technology of production was perfected through a series of scientific "revolutions." Pollution increased dramatically, and nobody yet knows what the environmental costs of pumping all that oil out of the ground will really be in the long run. Now there's an "energy crisis," and uranium is becoming the dominant fuel.

Capitalists, at least, can be relied upon to develop uranium as fuel only at the rate at which they can show a good profit. That's *their* ethic, and maybe that will buy some time. Marxists, on the other hand, can be relied upon to develop uranium fuel as rapidly as possible simply because it's the most "efficient" production fuel available. That's their ethic, and I fail to see where it's preferable. Like I said, Marxism is right smack in the middle of the European tradition. It's the same old song.

There's a rule of thumb which can be applied here. You cannot judge the real nature of a European revolutionary doctrine on the basis of the changes it proposes to make within the European power structure and society. You can only judge it by the effects it will have on non-European peoples. This is because every revolution in European history has served to reinforce Europe's tendencies and abilities to export destruction to other people's, other cultures and the environment itself. I defy anyone to point out an example where this is not true.

So now we, as American Indian people, are asked to believe that a "new" European revolutionary doctrine such as Marxism will reverse the negative effects of European history on us. European power relations are to be adjusted once again, and that's supposed to make things better for all of us. But what does this really mean?

Right now, today, we who live on the Pine Ridge Reservation are living in what white society has designated a "National Sacrifice Area." What this means is that we have a lot of uranium deposit here, and white culture (not us) needs this uranium as energy production material. The cheapest, most efficient way for industry to extract and deal with the processing of this uranium is to dump the waste by-products right here at the digging sites. Right here where we live. This waste is radioactive and will make the entire region uninhabitable forever. This is considered by industry, and by the white society that created this industry, to be an "acceptable" price to pay for energy resource development. Along the way they also plan to drain the water table under this part of South Dakota as part of the industrial process, so the region becomes doubly uninhabitable. The same sort of thing is happening down in the land of the Navajo and Hopi, up in the land of the Northern Cheyenne and Crow, and elsewhere. Thirty percent of the coal in the West and half of the uranium deposits in the U.S. have been found to lie under   reservation land, so there is no way this can be called a minor issue.

We are resisting being turned into a National Sacrifice Area. We are resisting being turned into a national sacrifice people. The costs of this industrial process are not acceptable to us. It is genocide to dig uranium here and drain the water table— no more, no less.

Now let's suppose that in our resistance to extermination we begin to seek allies (we have). Let's suppose further that we were to take revolutionary Marxism at its word: that it intends nothing less than the complete overthrow of the European capitalist order which has presented this threat to our very existence. This would seem to be a natural alliance for American Indian people to enter into. After all, as the Marxists say, it is the capitalists who set us up to be a national sacrifice. This is true as far as it goes. But, as I've tried to point out, this "truth" is very deceptive. Revolutionary Marxism is committed to even further perpetuation and perfection of the very industrial process which is destroying us all. It offers only to "redistribute" the results—the money, maybe—of this industrialization to a wider section of the population. It offers to take wealth from the capitalists and pass it around; but in order to do so, Marxism must maintain the industrial system. Once again the power relations within European society will have to be altered, but once again the effects upon American Indian peoples here and non-Europeans elsewhere will remain the same. This is much the same as when power was redistributed from the church to private business during the so-called bourgeois revolution. European society changed a bit, at least superficially, but its conduct toward non-Europeans continued as before. You can see what the American Revolution of 1776 did for American Indians. It's the same old song.

Revolutionary Marxism, like industrial society in other forms, seeks to "rationalize" all people in relation to industry—maximum industry, maximum production. It is a materialist doctrine that despises the American Indian spiritual tradition, our cultures, our lifeways. Marx himself called us "precapitalists" and "primitive." *Precapitalist* simply means that, in his view, we would eventually discover capitalism and become capitalists; we have always been retarded in Marxist terms. The only manner in which American Indian people could participate in a Marxist revolution would be to join the industrial system, to become factory workers, or "proletarians" as Marx called them. The man was very clear about the fact that his revolution could only occur through the struggle of the proletariat, that the existence of a massive industrial system is a precondition of a successful Marxist society.

I think there's a problem with language here. Christians, capitalists, Marxists. All of them have been revolutionary in their own minds, but none of them really mean revolution. What they really mean is a continuation. They do what they do in order that European culture can continue to exist and develop according to its needs.

So, in order for us to *really* join forces with Marxism, we American Indians would have to accept the national sacrifice of our homeland; we would have to commit cultural suicide and become industrialized and Europeanized.

At this point, I've got to stop and ask myself whether I'm being too harsh. Marxism has something of a history. Does this history bear out my observation? I look to the process of industrialization in the Soviet Union since 1920 and I see that these Marxists have done what it took the English Industrial Revolution 300 years to do; and the Marxists did it in 60 years. I see that the territory of the USSR used to contain a number of tribal peoples and that they have been crushed to make way for the factories. The Soviets refer to this as "The National Question," the question of whether the tribal peoples had the right to exist as peoples; and they decided the tribal peoples were an acceptable sacrifice to industrial needs. I look to China and I see the same thing. I look to Vietnam and I see Marxists imposing and industrial order and rooting out the indigenous tribal mountain people.

I hear a leading Soviet scientist saying that when uranium is exhausted, *then* alternatives will be found. I see the Vietnamese taking over a nuclear power plant abandoned by the U.S. military. Have they dismantled and destroyed it? No, they are using it. I see China exploding nuclear bombs, developing uranium reactors and preparing a space program in order to colonize and exploit the planets the same as the Europeans colonized and exploited this hemisphere. It's the same old song, but maybe with a faster tempo this time.

The statement of the Soviet scientist is interesting. Does he know what this alternative energy source will be? No, he simply has faith. Science will find a way. I hear revolutionary Marxists saying that the destruction of the environment, pollution and radiation will all be controlled. And I see them act upon their words. Do they know *how* these things will be controlled? No, they simply have faith. Science will find a way. Industrialization is fine and necessary. How do they know this? Faith. Science will find a way. Faith of this sort has always been known in Europe as religion. Science has become the new European religion for both capitalists and Marxists; they are truly inseparable, they are part and parcel of the same culture. So, in both theory and practice, Marxism demands that non-European peoples give up their values, their traditions, their cultural experience altogether. We will all be industrialized science addicts in a Marxist society.

I do not believe that capitalism itself is really responsible for the situation in which American Indians have been declared a national sacrifice. No, it is the European tradition; European culture itself is responsible. Marxism is just the latest continuation of this tradition, not a solution to it. To ally with Marxism is to ally with the very same forces that declare us an acceptable cost.

There is another way. There is the traditional Lakota way and the ways of the other American Indian peoples. It is the way that knows that humans do not have the right to degrade Mother Earth, that there are forces beyond anything the European mind has conceived that humans must be in harmony with *all* relations or the relations will eventually eliminate the disharmony. A lopsided emphasis on humans by humans—the Europeans' arrogance of acting as though they were beyond the nature of all related things—can only result in a total disharmony and a readjustment which cuts arrogant humans down to size, gives them a taste of that reality beyond their grasp or control and restores the harmony. There is no need for a revolutionary theory to bring this about; it's beyond human control. The nature people of this planet know this and so they do not theorize about it. Theory is an abstract; our knowledge is real. Distilled to its basic terms, European faith—including the new faith in science—equals a belief that man is God, Europe has always sought a Messiah, whether that be the man Jesus Christ or the man Karl Marx or the man Albert Einstein. American Indians know this to be totally absurd. Humans are the weakest of all creatures, so weak that other creatures are willing to give up their flesh that we may live. Humans are able to survive only through the exercise of rationality since they lack the abilities of other creatures to gain food through the use of fang and claw.

But rationality is a curse since it can cause humans to forget the natural order of things in ways other creatures do not. A wolf never forgets his or her place in the natural order. American Indians can. Europeans almost always do. We pray our thanks to the deer, our relations, for allowing us their flesh to eat; Europeans simply take the flesh for granted and consider the deer inferior. After all, Europeans consider themselves godlike in their rationalism and science. God is the Supreme Being; all else must be inferior.

All European tradition, Marxism included, has conspired to defy the natural order of all things. No theory can alter that simple fact. Mother Earth will retaliate, the whole environment will retaliate, and the abusers will be eliminated. Things come full circle, back to where they started. *That's* revolution. And that's a prophecy of my people, of the Hopi people and of other correct peoples.

American Indians have been trying to explain this to Europeans for centuries. But, as I said earlier, Europeans have proven themselves unable to hear. The natural order will win out, and the offenders will die out, the way deer die when they offend the harmony by overpopulating a given region. It's only a matter of time until what Europeans call "a major catastrophe of major proportions" will occur. It is the role of American Indian peoples, the role of all natural beings, to survive. A part of our survival is to resist. We resist not to overthrow a government or to take political power, but because it is natural to resist extermination, to survive. We don't want power over white institutions; we want white institutions to disappear. *That's* revolution.

American Indians are still in touch with those realities— the prophecies, the traditions or our ancestors. We learn from the elders, from nature, from the powers. And when the catastrophe is over, we American Indian peoples will still be here to inhabit the hemisphere. I don't care if it's only a handful living high in the Andes. American Indian people will survive; harmony will be reestablished. *That's* revolution.

At this point, perhaps I should be very clear about another matter, one which should already be clear as a result of what I've said. But confusion breeds easily these days, so I want to hammer home this point. When I use the term *European*, I'm not referring to a skin color or a particular genetic structure. What I'm referring to is a mind-set, a world view that is a product of the development of European culture. People are not genetically encoded to hold this outlook; they are *acculturated* to hold it. The same is true for American Indians or for the members of any other culture.

It is possible for an American Indian to share European values, a European world view. We have a term for these people; we call them "apples"—red on the outside (genetics) and white on the inside (their values). Other groups have similar terms. Blacks have their "oreos"; Hispanics have "coconuts" and so on. And, as I said before, there are exceptions to the white norm: people who are white on the outside, but not white inside. I'm not sure what term should be applied to them other than "human beings."

What I'm putting out here is not a racial proposition but a cultural proposition. Those who ultimately advocate and defend the realities of European culture and its industrialism are my enemies. Those who resist it, who struggle against it are my allies, the allies of American Indian people. And I don't give a damn what their skin color happens to be. Caucasian is the white term for the white race; *European* is an outlook I oppose.

The Vietnamese Communists are not exactly what you might consider genetic Communists, but they are now functioning as mental Europeans. The same holds true for Chinese Communists, for Japanese capitalists or Bantu Catholics or Peter "MacDollar" down at the Navajo Reservation or Dickie Wilson up here at Pine Ridge. There is no racism involved in this, just an acknowledgment of the mind and spirit that make up culture.

In Marxist terms I suppose I'm a "cultural nationalist." I work first with my people, the traditional Lakota people, because we hold a common world view and share an immediate struggle. Beyond this, I work with other traditional American Indian peoples, again because of a certain commonality in world view and form of struggle. Beyond that, I work with anyone who has experienced the colonial oppression of Europe and who resists its cultural and industrial totality. Obviously, this includes genetic caucasians who struggle to resist the dominant norms of European culture. The Irish and the Basques come immediately to mind, but there are many others.

I work primarily with my own people, with my own community. Other people who hold non-European perspectives should do the same. I believe in the slogan, "Trust your brother's vision," although I'd like to add sisters into the bargain. I trust the community and the culturally based vision of all the races that naturally resist industrialization and human extinction. Clearly, individual whites can share in this, given only that they have reached the awareness this continuation of the industrial imperatives of Europe is not a vision, but species suicide. White is one of the sacred colors of the Lakota people—red, yellow, white, and black. The four directions. The four seasons. The four periods of life and aging. The four races of humanity. Mix red, yellow, white and black together and you get brown, the color of the fifth race. This is a natural ordering of things. It therefore seems natural to me to work with all races, each with its own special meaning, identity and message.

But there is a peculiar behavior among most Caucasians. As soon as I become critical of Europe and its impact on other cultures, they become defensive. They begin to defend themselves. But I'm not attacking them personally; I'm attacking Europe. In personalizing my observations on Europe they are personalizing European culture, identifying themselves with it. By defending themselves in this context, they are ultimately defending the death culture. This is a confusion which must be overcome, and it must be overcome in a hurry. None of us have energy to waste in such false struggles.

Caucasians have a more positive vision to offer than European culture. I believe this. But in order to attain this vision it is necessary for Caucasians to step outside European culture—alongside the rest of humanity—to see Europe for what it is and what it does.

To cling to capitalism and Marxism and all the other "isms" is simply to remain within European culture. There is no avoiding this basic fact. As a fact, this constitutes a choice. Understand that the choice is based on culture, not race. Understand that to choose European culture and industrialism is to choose to be my enemy. And understand that the choice is yours, not mine.

This leads me back to address those American Indians who are drifting through the universities, the city slums and other European institutions. If you are there to learn to resist the oppressor in accordance with your traditional ways, so be it. I don't know how you manage to combine the two, but perhaps you will succeed. But retain your sense of reality. Beware of coming to believe the white world now offers solutions to the problems it confronts us with. Beware, too of allowing the words of native people to be twisted to the advantage of our enemies. Europe invented the practice of turning words around on themselves. You need only look to the treaties between American Indian peoples and various European governments to know that this is true. Draw your strength from who you are. A culture which regularly confuses revolution with continuation, which confuses science and religion, which confuses revolt and resistance, has nothing helpful to teach you and nothing to offer you as a way of life. Europeans have long since lost all touch with reality, if ever they were in touch with it. Feel sorry for them if you need to, but be comfortable with what you are as American Indians.

So, I suppose to conclude this, I should state clearly that leading anyone toward Marxism is the last thing on my mind. Marxism is as alien to my culture as Capitalism and Christianity are. In fact, I can say I don't think I'm trying to lead anyone toward anything to some extent I tried to be a "leader," in the sense that the white media like to use that term, when the American Indian Movement was a young organization. This was a result of a confusion I no longer have. You cannot be everything to everyone. I do not propose to be used in such a fashion by my enemies; I am not a leader. I am an Oglala Lakota patriot. That is all I want and all I need to be. And I am very comfortable with who I am.

Peter MacDonald

"Inaugural Address to the Navajo Nation."

Peter MacDonald had already served several four-year terms as Chairman of the Navajo Nation when he delivered the following address. Here he once again assumed that office. MacDonald delivered this inaugural speech on January 13, 1987 in Window Rock, Arizona. In this discourse MacDonald outlined his program for the future and pledged a proactive leadership. Unlike his contemporary Russell Means who gave a critical analysis of western culture MacDonald presented his vision for the future for his people, stressed the need for unity, and asked for cooperation among the tribes.

This speech is reprinted with the kind permission of the editor of *Vital Speeches of the Day*, March 15, 1987, pp. 342-344.

Fellow Navajo Tribal Members; distinguished guests, ladies and gentlemen: One hundred and twenty years ago, we, the Navajo People returned from the Long Walk to reclaim this land as our home. Today I feel, I, too, have completed a long and difficult journey, and have returned home to serve my People. Honored Navajo elders, Navajo youth, Navajo Brothers and Sisters. . .with a humble heart and a soaring spirit, once again I accept your call to the Chairmanship of the Navajo Nation.

For the next four years, I will lead you with great determination—and as I look around this exciting country of ours, I see a wealth of opportunity for all of us.

Our great Navajo Nation is a small, but vital part of the greatest nation on earth. We must take every advantage of the prosperity around us.

The Navajo Nation is one of America's last economic frontiers. We have precious resources waiting to be tapped intelligently. Resources like our land, water, minerals, natural beauty and most of all, ourselves. We need to direct these resources to meet and conquer the challenges of the future. Today, we must come out of our long hibernation, and enter into spring. Let us forge ahead along the path toward economic self-sufficiency. Let us, once and for all, share in the beauty of America! Our challenge is unmistakable.

Since I first became your Chairman in 1971, the Navajo population has doubled. By the year 2,000, it could double again. If we are to prosper as a nation, we must create jobs, for ourselves today, and for our children tomorrow.

This puts an enormous responsibility on our shoulders. Today on the Reservation, one of every two Navajos cannot find work. There are simply not enough jobs to go around. Day by day, the situation grows worse.

It is not acceptable that our children suffer the humiliation of not being able to find work. It is no less a tragedy when our children must leave family and friends in order to seek jobs in a strange city. All *around* us, hundreds of millions of dollars are invested every day.

These are private investments, not public grants. These dollars build power plants. They fund banks, and construct office parks, and open stores, and create *jobs*. We see the fruits of these private investments every time we *leave* the Reservation. I say to you that it is now time to see them here on the Reservation!

Our goal must be to go out, and find these jobs, and bring them home.

And here is how we will do it:

First, by streamlining our own bureaucracy. I learned recently that a company which came here wanting a business- site lease, had to obtain *thirty-seven* different approvals and wait countless months. That's appalling. Bureaucracy has been the death of our good intentions. It is time we used our power as a Government to attract business to Navajo, not frighten them off with unnecessary delay and red tape.

Second, we will start paying attention to the needs of the business world. We will offer each serious investor a package of incentives which will help insure the profitability and security of their investments. We will turn to the Federal Government to aid us in this effort to make Navajo a magnet for free enterprise which complements our resource base and human skills. *Navajo* skills! *Navajo talents*!

And third, we will work *hard*. We will not rest until we have identified every potentioal business partner. We will not rest until we have studied their needs, made them proposals and *sold them on us*. We will not get those jobs by sitting here in Window Rock and shuffling paper. We will get them by going after them. We will get them by letting the world know that Navajo means *business*! And business means *jobs*!

Our drive to attain economic self-sufficiency must also focus on education. Every year, more than 2,000 Navajo youth graduate from high school. Only three out of ten can afford to go on to college. *This* is *a national disgrace*, and it must be stopped. Money is keeping the classroom doors shut to our Navajo children. We must open those doors, and open them *wide*!

Our goal for the next four years is clear. We shall see to it that no Navajo children be denied a college education because of inability to pay. We must double or triple our scholarship funds. We must provide a full package of educational assistance to those who need it. We must not deny our sons and daughters the chance to develop our most precious natural resource: their minds.

It may be 1987 across America, in Gallup and Flagstaff and Farmington. But on this Reservation we still live with housing and health care standards from the last century. Let me be very clear; the traditional Navajo values do not include poverty! We produce more power than any other American community—and still, thousands of homes are without electricity! Our reservation contains great bodies of clear blue water—and still, thousands of Navajos must drive ten miles or more to get water for basic cooking and washing needs. This is wrong, wrong, *wrong*!

We know it's 1987. And *we* know that each and every Navajo have what every American in 1987 is entitled to as a matter of right!

We are, after all, not only American Indians but Indian *Americans*. Sixteen-thousand Navajos are veterans of our wars. When America needed a secret code to shorten the Second World War, we offered our language. On the sands of Iwo Jima, and in the forests of Germany and the jungles of Viet Nam, we gave our lives. Fifty percent of our Navajo families are families of veterans. But we have no veteran benefits—*no* health care, *no* housing loans, *no* educational assistance.

Why?

Our sacrifices to this country were no less great because we are Navajos. Our needs as veterans are no less worthy because we live on our Reservation. This Administration will see to it that veterans benefits no longer stop at the Reservation line!

Together, we will fight for our fundamental human rights as Navajos. We will insist upon a solution to the Navajo- Hopi land issue which respects human dignity. We have suffered as we watched 6,000 of our own people uprooted from the land of their forefathers. Today, they are *refugees* in their own country. Their human rights have been abused in a manner that our leaders in Washington would never allow if it had occurred in Afghanistan, or in South Africa.

Believe ME when I say that I will not rest, until I know that these Navajos have adequate housing and health care. I will not rest until I know they have adequate land for their crops and sheep. And I will not tolerate *others* being removed from their homelands against their will.

These are our goals, our vision as a People. In my heart I know we will succeed in our quest if we move forward together. In times past our common bond as the Navajo People has kept us from despair. We survived the Long Walk. . .we survive Kit Carson and Fort Sumner. . we survived the days of livestock reduction and termination. And we shall survive these days of Gramm-Rudman budget cuts and forced dislocations—if we face them as One. *Together* we are strong. Together, we are invincible.

Here we are—assembled, a Tribe united, with the 1986 Navajo election behind us. Today I assume office with a mandate from you not to undo all the important achievements of past administrations, but to build upon them. Now leaders must always build upon the accomplishments of their predecessors. For instance, during the late 1970's we seized the initiative and established taxation on our Reservation to improve our tribal income. Today, many court battles and two Administrations later, our right to tax is a recognized reality.

We will move forward as a Nation. And everyone of us here today has a special role to play.

To the private sector, I say simply: Do business with us. Explore us, challenge us; we won't let you down. We understand your past frustrations. You must understand that those days are behind us now. You have seen what our people can do with their hands. Now come discover what we can do with our minds!

To state governments, I say: Let's not waste our energies quarreling over jurisdiction. We have common enemies to worry about, like the pollution which threatens our air and water. Or the economic stagnation which wastes our talents. We must trust and respect each other.

To the Federal Government, I say: you are our Trustee. We hold our Treaty relationship with you sacred. It is written that you will help us. We need your help, but in a way that will make us less in need of it in the future. Give us a hand so that we may walk with both feet. Cooperate with us to manage and protect our God-given resources. Give us the legislative tools we will need to realize our true economic potential.

To my fellow Navajo Tribal Council members, I say: bring us ideas from across the Reservation. Tell us what our constituents are saying and what they need. We will have a working council. Be prepared to work long and hard as leaders. All of us will need to go where the opportunities lie for our People. You won't have to wait outside my door, or ask any staff attorney's approval to go out there and do what the voters elected you to do.

Finally, let me speak to you, my Navajo constituents.

During the past months I spoke some very simple truths in chapter after chapter—that was my strength. I simply said things we all know to be true.

—our people lack jobs
—our children are poorly educated
—our young adults cannot continue on to college
—our houses do not keep out the cold
—6,000 of our people have been made refugees in their own land
—our veterans have been forgotten and abandoned

I am here because you *believed me*, when I said WE could do something about those problems. Not me, but WE; me and you.

—not just the Chairman's Office
—not just the tribal government, but all of us—you and me together, every man, woman and child.

In the past, we have united against common enemies. We have fought paternalism and colonialism and racism. Now, we must unite around the common purpose:

—to house the homeless,
—to repatriate our refugees,
—to honor our obligations to our veterans,
—to educate our young,
—to provide higher education to our young adults,
—to create jobs for the unemployed

In the past our greatest progress has come from our unity as a people. Our sovereignty is based on that unity. That unity gave us the strength to create a new program that brought tax money to our Reservation. Now with new authority given to tribal governments by Congress and with new tools that states and municipalities have tested, we can forge new strategies that will bring additional capital to the Reservation, new jobs, new businesses.

We can create a whole new arsenal of economic tools. But it will take more than new businesses, new capital and new tax revenues.

We have people and we have problems. We must put the two together. We must use our people to solve our problems. We must mobilize our human resources to meet our needs— these are the ways. It can be done, but only if we work together.

The wealth of our people *is* our people. I am not just talking about the individual Navajos. I am talking about how we can help each other: that is the Navajo way.

The most efficient economic system ever created *is* the family. And the Navajo family, the extended Navajo family, the clans, has strength greater than the nuclear family.

The Navajo Nation itself is the greatest family of *all*. We are bound together by blood and by history, by geography and by culture, by sovereignty and by tradition.

—are we not all one people?
—are we not all one family?
—are we not all one nation?

That unity gives us strength; we must find ways to tap that strength. We can do it if we build on the family and if we mobilize our own resources to address our own problems.

No individual can do it alone. No Chairman can do it alone, it will take all of us. But it can be done, you have my word. You have my oath.

So today, I pledge myself to a new partnership; between the Chairman's office and the Tribal Council, between the government here in Window Rock and the chapters spread out across the Reservation, between those of us on the Reservation and those many Navajos residing off the Reservation.

But above all between the Navajo people of today and the Navajo people of the 21st century, our children and their children and their children's children. Let this day be known not simply as an inauguration of a new Chairman, but as the beginning of a new partnership—*of* and *by* and *for* the Navajo people.

A partnership that mobilizes our most precious resources, *our people*, to meet our most critical needs.

A partnership that builds family and clan and community and chapters.

A partnership that builds homes and creates jobs and businesses, that rights wrongs and creates opportunities, that educates our children and provides scholarships for our young adults.

Together we can.
Together we will. I need you.
We need each other.

Our journey the next four years will not be easy. The Navajo path has always been full of obstacles as well as opportunities. But we have always walked together with dignity, toward the summit of our destiny.

Our hibernation is over. A new spring is just beginning to dawn across this wonderful land of ours. Together we have, together we can, and together we will surely triumph. Thank you, and God Bless You.

III

Introduction

Chapter three consists of three discourses by nineteenth century social activists Charlotte Forten, Maria W. Stewart, and Ida Wells-Barnett. Also, included are three discourses by renowned twentieth century women: Patricia Roberts Harris, Sadie T.M. Alexander, and Edith S. Sampson. These twentieth century speakers condemn the ever- present evil of prejudice and are adamant in their support of the attainment of education for African Americans. In these orations, moreover, the diverse backgrounds that each individual woman speaker brings to the public platform is quite apparent.

The first speech is by the deeply religious Maria Stewart (America's first black woman political writer) who developed her own evangelical speaking style in which she proclaimed religion as being "held in low repute among some of us." She believed that followers in Christ would be saved and "shine forth in the kingdom of their father." Saddened that the "rising generation" would not improve Stewart asked mothers to extend their influence over their husbands and children to nourish a spirit of "Christian love and unity." In addition, she asked that they be charitable with one another.

The second speech is by Charlotte Forten, a writer, poet, and abolitionist who published many of her writings in antislavery tracts. This poem expresses the concerns of the socially conscious reformer of the nineteenth century. It reflects the sincerity, humility, charity, and reverence embodied in the archetypical antislavery activist.

The third speech is by newspaper correspondent and editor Ida Wells-Barnett. Wells-Barnett spent the greater part of her adult life speaking out against the horrible crime of lynching. In this piece she alludes to the "New Cry." A Southern Bishop and some influential white citizens advised the public to have compassion for the genteel southern women who had been allegedly "victimized" (raped) by African American men. Wells-Barnett asserted that this strategy had its effect on the press and the pulpit to the point that even "the better class of "Afro-Americans" did not give lynching "the investigation nor condemnation it deserved." Her speech warned that the vigilantes or lynch mobs had left the out-of-the-way places and were becoming more and more active in the broad daylight in large cities.

The fourth speech is Patricia Harris's seminal oration on the need to differentiate between issues of law and issues of morality when they are intertwined within a particular point in question. Harris defines clearly the term law and the term morality.

Then she continued to say that we should not have to wait for cases to come before the court to decide on an issue. We should be conducting public discussions and forums on issues of deep concern to all of us, she declared. In this way "national dialogue" would help us appreciate the good lawyers who serve us and guard against the "would-be custodians of morality." The fifth speech of Sadie T. M. Alexander is an inspirational message to the graduates of Spelman College. She suggested to the people who will someday attain the tops jobs not to forget their friends at the bottom. Also, she forewarned the listeners that they should prepare themselves "to live in the highly competitive world in which we will find ourselves as the walls of segregation come tumbling down." The sixth speech is Edith Sampson's "Choose One Of Five" in which she discussed five life styles a college graduate could adopt with ease. Four of the life styles are insensitive and lack an interest in the affairs of men and women. But the examples are interesting because four of the five are life-styles in which one could find comfort. The fifth is a choice that asks the listener to be true to his or her integrity.   Choice five she claims is where the thoughtful person has to live continuously with the knowledge that there are no simple answers to life's perplexities.

Charlotte L. Forten (1838-1914)

"Poem"

Charlotte L. Forten was born in Philadelphia in 1838. Her valuable contribution to the continuous struggle against prejudice is the classic Journal she kept which describes a young African American woman's reactions to the white world around her. Forten's perceptions of the activities of the abolitionists are informative and helpful to the student of abolitionism. She taught in Massachusetts and then she participated in a social experiment with freed African Americans of the Sea Islands. She died on July 23, 1914. She read this poem at her own graduation exercises from Salem Normal School in 1856. Subsequently she submitted the poem to the Boston antislavery newspaper, *The Liberator* Edited by William Lloyd Garrison.

The poem appeared in the March 16, 1856 issue of *The Liberator*.

> In the earnest path of duty,
>> With the high hopes and hearts sincere,
> We, to useful lives aspiring,
>> Daily meet to labor here.
>
> No vain dreams of earthly glory
>> Urge us onward to explore
> Far-extending realms of knowledge,
>> With their rich and varied store;
>
> But, with hope of aiding others,
>> Gladly we perform our part;
> Nor forget, the mind, while storing,
>> We must educate the heart,—
>
> Teach it hatred of oppression,
>> Truest love of God and man;
> Thus our high and holy calling
>> May accomplish his great plan.
>
> Not the great and gifted only
>> He appoints to do his will,
> But each one, however lowly,
>> Has a mission to fulfill.
>
> Knowing this, toil we unwearied,
>> With true heart and purpose high;—
> We would win a wreath immortal
>> Whose bright flowers ne'er fade and die.

Maria W. Stewart (1803-1879)

"An Address Delivered at the African Masonic Hall in Boston, February 27, 1833."

Born a free black in Hartford, Connecticut in 1803, Maria W. Stewart worked as a servant in the household of a minister where she remained until the age of fifteen. Although she did not receive a formal education it is apparent in this speech that she had some religious- oriented training. Held in contempt by her contemporaries for controversial public speaking appearances Stewart eventually ceased her personal campaign of being a representative speaker for black women. The writer of a biographical sketch of Mrs. Stewart stated: "[T]hat she was then, as now, a very devout Christian lady, a leader in all good movements and reforms, and had no equal as a lecturer or authoress in her day." This speech is a plea to the free men of color to raise their voices and protest on behalf of black oppression.

The speech appeared in William Lloyd Garrison's antislavery tract *The Liberator* in two installments, on April 27, and May 4 of 1833.

African rights and liberty is a subject that ought to fire the breast of every free man on color in these United States, and excite in his bosom a lively, deep, decided and heart-felt interest. When I cast my eyes on the long list of illustrious names that are enrolled on the bright annals of fame among the whites, I turn my eyes within, and ask my thoughts. "Where are the names of our illustrious ones?" It must certainly have been for the want of energy on the part of the free people of color that they have been long willing to bear the yoke of oppression. It must have been the want of ambition and force that has given the whites occasion to say, that our natural abilities are not as good, and our capacities by nature inferior to theirs. They boldly assert that, did we possess a natural independence of soul, and feel a love for liberty within our breasts, some one of our sable race, long before this, would have testified it, notwithstanding the disadvantages under which we labor. We have made ourselves appear altogether unqualified to speak in our own defense, and are therefore looked upon as objects of pity and commiseration. We have been imposed upon, insulted and derided on every side; and now, if we complain, it is considered as the height of impertinence. We have suffered ourselves to be considered as dastards, cowards, mean, faint-hearted wretches, and on this account, (not because of our complexion,) many despise us and would gladly spurn us from their presence.

These things have fired my soul with a holy indignation, and compelled me thus to come forward, and endeavor to turn their attention to knowledge and improvement; for knowledge is power, I would ask, is it blindness of mind, or stupidity of soul, or the want of education, that has caused our men who are 60 or 70 years of age, never to let their voices be heard nor their hands be raised in behalf of the color? Or has it been for fear of offending the whites? If it has, O ye fearful ones, throw off your fearfulness, and come forth in the name of your Lord, and in the strength of the God of Justice, and make yourselves useful and active members in society; for they admire a noble and patriotic spirit in others—and should they not admire it in us? If you are men, convince them that you possess the spirit of men; and as your day, so shall your strength be. Have the sons of Africa no souls? Feel they no ambitious desires? Shall the chains of ignorance forever confine them? Shall the insipid appellation of "clever Negroes," "good creatures," any longer content them? Where can we find amongst ourselves the man of science, or a philosopher, or an able statesman, or a counsellor at law? Show me our fearless and brave, our noble and gallant ones. Where are our lecturers on natural history, and our critics in useful knowledge? There may be a few such men amongst us, but they are rare. It is true, our fathers died and bled in the revolutionary war, and others fought bravely under the command of Jackson, in defense of liberty. But where is the man that has distinguished himself in these modern days by acting wholly in the defense of African rights and liberty? There was one—although he sleeps, his memory lives.

I am sensible that there are many highly intelligent gentlemen of color in these United States, in the force of whose arguments, doubtless, I should discover my inferiority; but if they are blest with wit and talent, friends and fortune, why have they not made themselves men of eminence, by striving to take all the reproach that is cast upon the people of color, and in endeavoring to alleviate the woes of their brethren in bondage? Talk, without effort, is nothing; you are abundantly capable, gentlemen, of making yourselves men of distinction; and this gross neglect, on your part, causes my blood to boil within me. Here is the grand cause which hinders the rise and progress of the people of color. It is their want of laudable ambition and requisite courage.

Individuals have been distinguished according to their genius and talents, ever since the first formation of man, and will continue to be whilst the world stands. The different grades rise to honor and respectability as their merits may deserve. History informs us that we sprung from one of the most learned nations of the whole earth— from the seat, if not the parent of science; yes, poor, despised Africa was once the resort of sages and legislators of other nations, was esteemed the school for learning, and the most illustrious men in Greece flocked thither for instruction. But it was our gross sins and abominations that provoked the Almighty to frown thus heavily upon us, and give our glory unto others. Sin and prodigality have caused the downfall of nations, kings and emperors; and were it not that God in wrath remembers mercy, we might indeed despair; but a promise is left us; "Ethiopia shall again stretch forth her hands unto God."

But it is of no use to us to boast that we sprung from this learned and enlightened nation, for this day a thick mist of moral gloom hangs over millions of our race. Our condition as a people has been low for hundreds or years, and it will continue to be so, unless, by the true piety and virtue we strive, to regain that which we have lost. White Americans, by their prudence, economy and exertions, have sprung up and become one of the most flourishing nations in the world, distinguished for their knowledge of the arts and sciences, for their polite literature. Whilst our minds are vacant and starving for want of knowledge, theirs are filled to overflowing. Most of our color have been taught to stand in fear of the white man from their earliest infancy, to work as soon as they could walk, and call "master" before they scarce could lisp the name of mother. Continual fear and laborious servitude have in some degree lessened in us that natural force and energy which belongs to man; or else, in defiance of opposition, our men, before this would have nobly and boldly contended for their rights. But give the man of color an equal opportunity with the white, from the cradle to manhood, and from manhood to the grave, and you would discover the dignified statesman, the man of science, and the philosopher. But there is no such opportunity for the sons of Africa, and I fear that our powerful ones are fully determined that there never shall be. Forbid, ye Powers on High, that it should any longer be said that our men possess no force. O ye sons of Africa, when will your voices be heard in our legislative halls, in defiance of your enemies, contending for equal rights and liberty? How can you, when you reflect from what you have fallen, refrain from crying mightily unto God, to turn away from the fierceness of his anger, and remember our transgressions against us no more forever. But a God of infinite purity will not regard the prayers of those who hold religion in one hand, and prejudice, sin and pollution in the other; he will not regard the prayers of self- righteousness and hypocrisy. It is possible, I exclaim, that for the want of knowledge, we have labored the hundreds of years to support others, and been content to receive what they chose to give us in return? Cast your eyes about—look as far as you can see—all, all is owned by the lordly white, except here and there a lowly dwelling which the man of color, midst deprivations, fraud and opposition, has been scarce able to procure. Like king Solomon, who put neither nail nor hammer to the temple, yet received the praise; so also have the white Americans gained themselves a name, like the names of the great men that are in the earth, whilst in reality we have been their principal foundation and their support. We have pursued the shadow, they have obtained the substance; we have performed the labor, they have received the profits; we have planted the vines, they have eaten the fruits of them.

I would implore our men, and especially our rising youth, to flee from the gambling board and the dance hall; for we are poor, and have not money to throw away. I do not consider dancing as criminal in itself, but it is astonishing to me that our young men are so blind to their own interest and the future welfare of their children, as to spend their hard earnings for this frivolous amusement; for it has been carried on among us to such an unbecoming extent that it has become absolutely disgusting. "Faithful are the wounds of a friend, but the kisses of an enemy are deceitful." Had those men amongst us, who have had an opportunity, turned their attention as assiduously to mental and moral improvement as they have to gambling and dancing, I might have remained quietly at home, and they stood contending in my place. These polite accomplishments will never enroll your names on the bright annals of fame, who admire the belle void of intellectual knowledge, or applaud the dandy who talks largely on politics, without striving to assist his fellow in the revolution, when the nerves and muscles of every other man forced him into the field of action. You have a right to rejoice, and to let your hearts cheer you in the days of your youth; yet remember that for all these things God will bring you into judgment. Then, O ye sons of Africa, turn your mind from these perishable objects, and contend for the cause of God and the rights of man. Form yourselves into temperance societies. There are temperate men amongst you; then why will you any longer neglect to strive, by your example, to suppress vice in all its abhorrent forms? You have been told repeatedly of the glorious results arising from temperance, and can you bear to see the whites arising in honor and respectability, without endeavoring to grasp after that honor and respectability also?

But I forbear. Let our money, instead of being thrown away as heretofore, be appropriated for schools and seminaries of learning for our children and youth. We ought to follow the example of the whites in this respect. Nothing would raise our respectability, add to our peace and happiness and reflect so much honor upon us, as to be ourselves the promoters of temperance, and the supporters, as far as we are able, of useful and scientific knowledge. The rays of light and knowledge have been hid from our view; we have been taught to consider ourselves as scarce superior to the brute creation; and have performed the most laborious part of American drudgery. Had we as people received one half the early advantages the whites have received, I would defy the government of these United States to deprive us any longer of our rights.

I am informed that the agent of the Colonization Society has recently formed an association of young men, for the purpose of influencing those of us to go to Liberia who may feel disposed. The colonizationists are blind to their own interest, for should the nations of the earth make war with America, they would find their forces much weakened by our absence; or should we remain here, can our "brave soldiers" and "fellow citizens," as they were termed in time of calamity, condescend to defend the rights of the whites, and be again deprived of their own, or sent to Liberia in return? O, if the colonizationists are real friends to Africa, let them expend the money which they collect in erecting a college to educate her injured sons in this land of gospel light and liberty; for it would be most thankfully received on our part, and convince us of the truth of their professions, and save time, expense and anxiety. Let them place before us noble objects, worthy of pursuit, and see if we prove ourselves to be those unambitious Negroes they term us. But ah! methinks their hearts are so frozen towards us, they had rather their money should be sunk in the ocean than to administer it to our relief; and I fear, if they dared, like Pharaoh king of Egypt, they would order every male child amongst us to be drowned. But the most high God is still able to subdue the lofty pride of these white Americans, as He was the heart of that ancient rebel. They say though we are looked upon as things, yet we sprang from a scientific people. Had our men the requisite force and energy, they would soon convince them, by their efforts both in public and private, that they were men, or things in the shape of men. Well may the colonizationsists laugh us to scorn for our negligence; well may they cry, "Shame to the sons of Africa." As the burden of the Israelites was too great for Moses to bear, so also is our burden too great for our noble advocate to bear. You must feel interested my brethren, in what he undertakes, and hold up his hands by your good words, or in spite of himself his soul will become discouraged, and his heart will die within him; for he has, as it were, the strong bulls of Bashan to contend with.

It is of no use for us to want any longer for a generation of well educated men to arise. We have slumbered and slept too long already; the day is far spent, the night of death approaches, and you have sound sense and good judgment sufficient to begin with, if you feel disposed to make a right use of it. Let every man of color throughout the United States, who possesses the spirit and principles of a man, sign a petition to Congress to abolish slavery in the District of Columbia, and grant you the rights and privileges long before this the mountains of prejudice might have been removed. We are all sensible that the Anti-Slavery Society has taken hold of the arm of our whole population, in order to raise them out of the mire. Now all we have to do is, by a spirit of virtuous ambition to strive to raise ourselves; and I am happy to have it in my power thus publicly to say that the colored inhabitants of this city, in some respects are beginning to improve. Had the free people of color in these United States nobly and boldly contended for their rights, and showed a natural genius and talent, although not so brilliant as some; had they held up, encouraged and patronized each other, nothing could have hindered us from being a thriving and flourishing people. There has been a fault amongst us. The reason why our distinguished men have not made themselves more influential is, because they fear that the strong current of opposition through which they must pass, would cause their downfall and prove their overthrow. And what gives rise to this opposition? Envy. And what has it amounted to? Nothing. And who are the cause of it? Our white sepulchres, who want to be great, and don't know how; who love to be called of men "Rabbi, Rabbi," who put on false sanctity, and humble themselves to their brethren, for the sake of acquiring the highest place in the synagogue, and the uppermost seats at the feast. You, dearly beloved, who are the genuine followers of our Lord Jesus Christ, the salt of the earth and the light of the world, are not so culpable. As I told you, in the very first of my writing, I tell you again, I am but as one drop in the bucket—as one particle of the small dust of the earth. God will surely raise up those amongst us who will plead the cause of virtue, and the pure principles of morality, more eloquently than I am able to do.

It appears to me that America has become like the great city of Babylon, for she has boasted in her heart,—"I sit a queen, and am no widow, and shall see no sorrow." She is indeed a seller of slaves and the souls of men; she made the Africans drunk with the wine of her fornications; she has put them completely beneath her feet, and she means to keep them there; her right hand supports the reins of government, and her left hand the wheel of power. And she is determined not to let go her grasp. But many powerful sons and daughters of Africa will shortly arise, who will put down vice and immorality amongst us, and declare by Him that sitteth upon the throne, that they will have their rights; and if refused, I am afraid they will spread horror and devastation around. I believe that the oppression of injured Africa has come up before the majesty of Heaven; and when our cries shall have reached the ears of the Most High, it will be a tremendous day for the people of this land; for strong is the arm of the Lord God Almighty.

Life has almost lost its charms for me; death has lost its sting and the grave its terrors; and at times I have a strong desire to depart and dwell with Christ, which is far better. Let me entreat my white brethren to awake and save our sons from dissipation, and our daughters from ruin. Lend the hand of assistance to feeble merit, and plead the cause of virtue amongst our sable race; so shall our curses upon you be turned into blessings; and though you shall endeavor to drive us from these shores, still we cling to you the more firmly; nor will we attempt to rise above you; we will presume to be called equals only.

The unfriendly white first drove the native American from his much loved home. Then they stole our fathers from their peaceful and quiet dwellings, and brought them hither and made bond men and bond women of them in utter ignorance, nourished them in vice and raised them in degradation; and now that we have enriched their soil, and filled their coffers, they say that we are not capable of becoming like white men, and that we never can rise to respectability in this country. They would drive us to a strange land. But before I go, the bayonet shall pierce me through. African rights and liberty is a subject that ought to fire the breast of every man of color in the United States, and excite in his bosom a lively, deep, decided and heartfelt interest.

Ida Wells-Barnett (1869-1931)

"The New Cry"

Born in Holly Springs, Mississippi in 1869, Ida Wells- Barnett later attended the Methodist Freedmen's Aid Society's Rust College in that village. Upon graduation she moved to Memphis and undertook a teaching career. After six years she left teaching and became editor and half-owner of a newspaper *Free Speech* which took an uncompromising stand against lynching. Forced to leave Memphis by whites who attacked and destroyed her office and print shop, she traveled to New York City in 1892 where she published her first pamphlet *Southern Horrors*. Subsequently she settled in Chicago and continued her crusade by lecturing and publishing pamphlets until her death in 1931. Wells said: "The very frequent inquiry made after my lectures by interested friends is, 'What can I do to help the cause?' The answer is, 'Tell the world the facts,'" In the speech that follows Ida Wells-Barnett reported "the facts" to the world.

Ida Wells-Barnett, *On Lynchings*, (New York: Arno Press and the New York Times, 1969), pp. 21-25. *(See acknowledgement page iv)*

The appeal of Southern whites to Northern sympathy and sanction, the adroit, insidious pleas made by Bishop Fitzgerald for suspension of judgment because those "who condemn lynching express no sympathy for the *white* woman in the case" falls to the ground in the light of the foregoing.

From this exposition of the race issue in lynch law, the whole matter is explained by the well-known opposition growing out of slavery to the progress of the race. This is crystallized in the oft-repeated slogan: "This is a white man's country and the white man must rule." The South resented giving the Afro-American his freedom, the ballot box and the Civil Rights law. The raids of the Klu Klux and White Liners to subvert reconstruction government, the Hamburg and Ellerton, S.C., the Copiah County Miss., and the Lafayette Parish, La., massacres were excused as the natural resentment of intelligence against government by ignorance.

Honest white men practically conceded the necessity of intelligence murdering ignorance to correct the mistake of the general government, and the race was left to the tender mercies of the solid South. Thoughtful Afro-Americans with the strong arm of the government withdrawn and with the hope to stop such wholesale massacres urged the race to sacrifice its political rights for sake of peace. They honestly believed the race should fit itself for government, and when that should be done, the objection of race participation in politics would be removed.

But the sacrifice did not remove the trouble, nor move the South to justice. One by one the Southern States have legally(?) disfranchised the Afro-American, and since the repeal of the Civil Right Bill nearly every Southern State has passed separate car laws with a penalty against their infringement. The race regardless of advancement is penned into filthy, stifling partitions cut off from smoking cars. All this while, although the political cause has been removed, the butcheries of black men at Barnwell, S.C., Carrolton, Miss., Waycross, Ga., and Memphis, Tenn., have gone on; also the flaying alive of a man in Kentucky, the burning of one in Arkansas, the hanging of a fifteen year old girl in Louisiana, a woman in Jackson, Tenn., and one in Hollandale, Miss., until the dark and bloody record of the South shows 728 Afro-Americans lynched during the past 8 years. Not 50 of those were political causes; the rest were for all manner of accusations from that of rape for white women, to the case of the boy Will Lewis who was hanged at Tullahoma. Tenn., last year for being drunk and "sassy" to white folks.

Those statistics compiled by the Chicago "Tribune" were given the first of this year (1892). Since then, not less than one hundred and fifty have been known to have met violent death at the hands of cruel bloodthirsty mobs during the past nine months.

To palliate this record (which grows worse as the Afro- American becomes intelligent) and excuse some of the most heinous crimes that ever stained the history of a country, the South is shielding itself behind the plausible scream of defending the honor of its women. This, too, in the face of the fact that only *one-third* of the 728 victims to mobs have been *charged* with rape, to say nothing of those of that one-third who were innocent of the charge. A white correspondent of the Baltimore Sun declares that the Afro- American who was lynched in Chestertown, Md., in May for assault on a white girl was innocent; that the deed was done by a white man who had since disappeared. The girl herself maintained that her assailant was a white man. Then that poor African was murdered, the whites excused their refusal of a trial on the ground that they wished to spare the white girl the mortification of having to testify in court.

This cry has had its effect. It has closed the heart, stifled the conscience, warped the judgment and hushed the voice of press and pulpit on the subject of lynch law throughout this "land of liberty." Men who stand high in the esteem of the public for Christian character, for moral and physical courage, for devotion to the principles of equal and exact justice to all, and for great sagacity, stand as cowards who fear to open their mouths before this great outrage. They do not see that by their tacit encouragement, their silent acquiescence, the black shadow of lawlessness in the form of lynch law is spreading its wings over the whole country. Men who, like Governor Tillman, start the ball of lynch law rolling for a certain crime, are powerless to stop it when drunken or criminal white toughs feel like hanging an Afro-American on any pretext.

Even to the better class of Afro-Americans the crime of rape is so revolting they have too often taken the white man's word and given lynch law neither the investigation nor condemnation it deserved.

They forget that a concession of the right to lynch a man for a certain crime, not only concedes the right to lynch any person for any crime, but (so frequently is the cry of rape now raised) it is in a fair way to stamp us a race of rapists and desperadoes. They have gone on hoping and believing that general education and financial strength would solve the difficulty, and are devoting their energies to the accumulation of both.

The mob spirit has grown with the increasing intelligence of the Afro-American. It has left the out-of-the-way places where ignorance prevails, has thrown off the mask and with this new cry stalks in broad daylight in large cities, the centres of civilization, and is encouraged by the "leading citizens" and the press.

Patricia Roberts Harris (1924-   )

"The Law And Moral Issues."

Lawyer, educator, and U.S. Ambassador to Luxembourg, Patricia Roberts Harris was born in Mattoon, Illinois on May 21, 1924. She took her A.B. degree—*summa cum laude*—from Howard University in 1945. Subsequently she undertook graduate study at the University of Chicago and then removed to George Washington University earning a law degree and editing the university's *Law Review*. She has held several government positions and among them were Assistant Director of the American Council on Human Rights, a lawyer in the Criminal Division of the Department of Justice, Co-chair of the National Women's Committee for Civil Rights, a member of the Commission on the Status of Puerto Rico, and Alternate Representative to the 22d general assembly of the United Nations. She has been on the Law faculty at Howard University.

This discourse appeared originally in *Journal of Religious Thought*, vol. xxi, 1964-65, Number 1, 65-72; it is reprinted with the kind permission of the editor.

Law and morality frequently meet as the powers of government are sought to enforce and reinforce private notions of morality.

As a matter of fact, the early history of this country is a history of a surprisingly successful effort to mold the law to conform to the notions of morality of the majority community. The Puritans, in rejecting the theory of the law as the reflection of the will of the sovereign, sought instead to make it a manifestation of the Puritan ethic (an ethic which figured only recently in a debate, with the Puritan ethic affirmed as a great American principle which could not successfully be opposed). Frequently, however, these most excellent men, the Puritans, confused the ethics of individuals, the leaders of the community, such as Governor Winthrop, with the preferences of the majority, with a result not unlike the Gilbert and Sullivan quotation from *Iolanthe*:

> The Law is the true embodiment
>   Of everything that's excellent.
> It has no kind of fault or flaw,
>   And I, my Lords, embody the Law.

The wish carried by these lines that the law be "the true embodiment/Of everything that's excellent" subsists today and results in attempts either to retain or to secure an enunciation of law which conforms to individual or group conviction with respect to what is excellent in the sense of what is morally sound.

And if it is the purpose of law to so order society that it may achieve the goals it has set for itself, the adoption of that part of the moral code deemed to constitute the imperative for the living of the good life would seem essential.

Any discussion of law and morality may be brought to naught if, it is not admitted that neither the term law nor the term morality has clear and inherent meaning on which even reasonable lawyers, philosophers, or theologians will agree. I use the word *will*, rather than *can*, because the inherently disputatious nature of the three disciplines suggested, law, philosophy, and theology, accord high value to the identification and maintenance of differences and distinctions; and even though the objective experience of students of the disciplines might well lead to a substantial agreement with respect to the meaning of the terms (and surprisingly often has), in order to avoid catering to our mutual disposition to disputation and argumentation, I shall define, admittedly roughly, the meaning assigned to the words in this discussion.

By law, I mean that body of rules and regulations established by official governmental units to control public and private behavior, the observance of which is secured by the threat of the imposition of penalties in the nature of fine, imprisonment, or withdrawal of a government granted benefit.

By morality, I mean that body of concepts of right behavior accepted by substantial segments of our society as standards for the evaluation of the conduct of individuals. I am not concerned with whether or not the law is enforced; it is, for present purposes, denominated law if there exists, wither under statute or subsisting precedent, the power to give effect to the law. With respect to morality, for purpose of discussion it is deemed to subsist if the concept of right behavior is applied in making judgments about the character of individuals or is the position asserted to be moral is articulated consistently as a value to be adopted by society in general and individuals in particular.

Thus, so far as my definition is concerned, the law is that men may not commit adultery. This is the law, according to S22-301 of the District of Columbia Code, despite the fact that prosecution for adultery is rare.

Also, adultery is considered immoral—is contrary to the Ten Commandments—and even among my somewhat radical friends, there is no disposition to consider such behavior desirable, even though records of divorces, and our general knowledge of modern behavior, suggest that significantly large numbers of persons engage in adulterous activity.

In illustrating that which is for present purposes denoted as law and that which is denoted as morality. I have also suggested the most apparent relationship between the two.

But as suggested in the citation of the criminal code of the District of Columbia, both laws and the articulation of moral codes live beyond the period when either can be deemed to be imperative for the appropriate ordering of society. For while I would join all who would condemn adultery, our sophisticated society now admits that its existence does not necessarily end, or even imperil, the marital or family relationship; and when it does, requirements of our domestic relations law for support of the injured spouse and children make it wiser to apply funds which might be used for a fine to that support and to permit freedom, rather than incarceration, in order to encourage the earning of sufficient money.

Nevertheless, the Damoclean Sword of possible criminal penalty hangs over the head of the wrongdoer, never really to fall, and seldom even to deter, but present to reassure us that law is the "true embodiment/Of everything that is excellent," for it supports our morality!

But if honesty is a value—if we, as I believe we do, purport to judge behavior on the basis of its honesty—we must find immorality in the continued existence of laws that derive from notions of morality which are in process of reevaluation. It is here, it seems to me, that each person concerned with the effectuation of both law and morality must come to grips with the questions of the appropriate merging of special and general moral concepts with legal pronouncement.

Lawyers and clergymen play special roles as the interpreters and enforcers of law and morality and, through such roles, occupy positions of trust in evaluating law and morality in the context of the community's responsibility in the enforcement of each. The identification of moral imperative has been the special responsibility of the philosopher and his kinsman, the theologian. But the interpretation of these insights has been a role that communities have expected the clergy to identify for the laity and to lead the laity in discussion of the nature of morality and its practical consequences for the religious communicant.

I question if today this is the role played by significant numbers of the clergy. But a short time ago a great (great in the sense of large) religious body in a nearby southern state congratulated its clergy for remaining in communication with the laity on the moral issue of racial adjustment—for not getting too far ahead on the membership on the moral issue. The custodians and articulators of moral values were complemented for not having articulated these values so clearly they could be understood, and possibly rejected, by their parishioners.

Again, in a southern city, where a Negro church was desecrated and lives lost, four days after the tragedy the report was that not a single white minister and not a single white church had been in communication with the desecrated house of worship.

But in that city, on the day of the desecration, one voice spoke to the city and to the world of the immorality of the event, and that voice was not the voice of a minister. It was the voice of a lawyer.

This fact serves to highlight a surprising phenomenon in our present-day society. That phenomenon is that the debate about the ethical content of the law, and the moral and societal imperatives it represents, is today most likely to start with the legal profession.

With due regard to the magnificent contribution made by the clergy and others in the civil rights movement, the impetus for the present activity was the adoption of concepts riven from the rigors of legal combat, the 1954 school desegregation cases.

The debate about the appropriate role of religious observances in the publicly supported institutions of this nation had no real force until the enunciation of lawyers as advocates and of lawyers as judges required an examination of the moral imperatives of our pluralistic society. Only recently, three members of the Supreme Court opened what I hope will be a national debate about the morality of the death penalty for rape where the life of the victim was not placed in jeopardy, asking if life should be taken to preserve any value other than another life.

Thus, lawyers, rather than seeing law as "the true embodiment/Of everything that's excellent," subject it to a continuing critical scrutiny, seeking to ascertain if the law does in truth support the highest ethical and moral values of the society as it is expected to do, or if, instead, it perverts them. It is true that, in our legal system, this scrutiny is often possible for the lawyer only as he contends for the interest of his clients or as he sits in judgment of the competing contentions of disputants. Herein, of course, lies a significant limitation upon the effectiveness of the lawyer as lawyer in this area. (Of course, the lawyer as citizen or as legislator can and does make a contribution, but the chief contribution made by the lawyer to the confrontation of law and moral assertion has been in his formal activities as advocate.)

But no such limitation exists in fact or in practice upon the rest of society, and there is no reason why the aforementioned issues or any other should await the fortuitous appearance of the client whose interests permit the articulation of a demand for a reexamination of the moral base of the law.

For example, it is appalling that there has not been general national debate, of sustained duration and significant strength, on the imposition of the death penalty for rape. But the social fear of dealing with a sex crime in our eminently respectable churches and elsewhere, is, no doubt, the explanation for lack of concern about this serious issue.

But then how do we explain the failure of our community's moral leadership to examine critically and honestly the implications of the imposition of the death penalty for any crime? Why must we await a Chessman case to consider the moral issue involved in capital punishment?

The quick answer is, of course, that there are legal questions which only the expertise of the lawyer can deal with. But clearly they are not. Whether or not we are permitted to pray in public schools is a legal issue, but whether or not we ought to pray in school is a question with which we are all competent to deal. Whether rape of murder carries with it a death penalty or not is a legal question, but if either should, morally, or ideally, carry the death penalty is a question requiring the reconciliation of competing social values—a moral issue, which must be decided by the community. Whether or not the Fourteenth Amendment prohibits distinctions based on race is a legal question, but whether or not a democratic society can be democratic in the presence of public or private racial distinction is an issue involving judgments about the worth of the human spirit and the dignity of men—a moral question.

Thus, the decision with respect to the morality that ought to be reflected in our law is a decision to be made as a result of the enlightening activity of public debate focused upon the identification of moral values and the societal imperatives which flow from these values in the form of law. But such debate must have leadership which is sustained and itself enlightened. The strictures of present debate in these suggested areas and others is due largely to the fact that those to whom the society has delegated the task of providing moral leadership have all too frequently interpreted morality in its most narrow and parochial terms.

There is a fear of identifying broad value areas and of testing specific acts against competing broad value assertions. Today, de Tocqueville could not say of 110 Americans, as he did in 1835:

> They have all a lively faith in the
> perfectability of men...they all consider
> society as a body in a state of improvement,
> humanity as a changing scene, in which nothing
> is or ought to be permanent, and they admit that
> what appears to them today to be good may be
> superseded by something better tomorrow.

Instead, there is a general wish not to rock the boat; not to change the imperfections of today's world, because the world of tomorrow, if we change things, may be worse. But another observation of de Tocqueville's, "a republic could not exist...if the influence of lawyers in public business did not increase in proportion the power of the people," has meaning today.

For, as has been suggested, the most frequent initiators of significant national dialogue are these custodians of the law and not the would-be custodians of morality....

Sadie T.M. Alexander (1898-   )

"Founders Day Address."

Sadie T.M. Alexander has four degrees from the University of Pennsylvania: the B.S., *cum laude* 1918; the M.A. 1919; the Ph.D. 1921; and the L.L.B. 1927. She is the first black women in the United States to earn the Ph.D. degree, the first black women to receive a law degree from the University of Pennsylvania, and the first black woman to be admitted to the Pennsylvania bar. She holds membership in many organizations concerned with human rights. She chairs the Philadelphia Commission on Human Rights, is a member of the Lawyers' Committee on Civil Rights and an active member of the National Committee of the American Civil Liberties Union. In this address delivered on April 11, 1963 at Spelman College she claims that social activism works not only to free the individual, but works to make America free as well.

This speech which originally appeared in the *Spelman Messenger*, vol. 79, May 1963, Number 3, 13-25, is reprinted with the kind permission of the *Spelman College Archives*.

Dr. Manley, Members of the Board of Trustees, Members of the Faculty, Students, and Friends of Spelman College.

I consider it a privilege and honor to have been invited to deliver the Founders Day Address at your renowned institution. The high academic standing of Spelman is recognized not only by your membership in the Southern Association of Colleges and Schools, and the appearance of your College on the approved list of the Association of American Universities, as well as the American Association of University Women, but more important, by the distinction attained in the life of our country by too many of your graduates for time to permit me to enumerate.

When Spelman College was established on April 11, 1881, only sixteen years after the Civil War, both Negroes and concerned whites, such as your founders, Sophia B. Packard and Harriet E. Giles, realized that the Negro had only been freed from physical shackles, and that if the mind of the Negro was to be freed so that he could develop the ability and will to secure for himself and posterity the rights guaranteed under the Constitution or the Bill of Rights, emphasis must be placed upon education. At the beginning, as evidenced by the training provided the eleven students of the first class of your college, who were "eager to learn to read the Bible and write well enough to send letters to their children," the courses of study involved only the most rudimentary elements, such as learning to read, write, and count. From this meager start developed classes in sewing, cooking, millinery, and more training, but as public education began to fulfill these needs, Spelman along with similar Negro institutions, began to train for leadership.

From your college and other Negro colleges and universities came most of the professional men and women who have assumed leadership at the local and national level. There is indeed little racial strategy today which was not to some degree developed by them, including the pickets and sit-ins. In 1913, my uncle, Doctor Nathan F. Mossell (a graduate of Lincoln University, class of 1879, and of the University of Pennsylvania Medical School, class of 1882, from which latter institution he was the first Negro to receive a degree from any department), having protested in vain to the Mayor of Philadelphia against the showing of *The Birth of a Nation*, led more than one thousand Negroes in a march from the heart of the Negro population to the center of the city, where the theater was located. This tumultuous demonstration broke up the show. Moreover, the relatively small number of men and women who were trained at the eastern and western colleges and universities made notable contributions among these were Doctor W.E.B. Du Bois, the first historian to study sympathetically and scientifically Negro communities and institutions; Carter G. Woodson, who dedicated his life to recording and preserving Negro history; Abram Harris in economics; E. Franklin Frazier in sociology; Ralph Bunche in political science; and Charles Houston, who brought the first successful civil rights action, taught and gave the inspiration which produced Thurgood Marshall and his volunteer staff of consultants.

It is my confirmed opinion that had it not been for the continuous, never-ending efforts and demands of the American Negro to "secure these rights" guaranteed by the fundamental laws of the nation, the United States might have forgotten and lost its claim to being a democracy. Not until the Hitler holocaust did the Jews in America join our fight for equality. Not until the Japanese- Americans were placed in concentration camps did they even form an organization of their own people. The Negro ministers, whose church doors have always been open to us; the pioneer political and social workers of the stature of Walter White and Eugene Kinckle Jones, educators, such as Mary McLeod Bethune and John Hope, and Negro lawyers, such as Charles Houston, Austin Walden, Raymond Pace Alexander have carried on a relentless battle to keep alive and give meaning to the rights guaranteed American citizens.

In the Far East, Asia, Western Europe, Central and South America, college students have over the years taken the lead in effecting social change. Two years ago in Japan, I witnessed the demonstrations of students against rearmament. I also saw students in Chile marching in protest against an increase in bus fares. I have seen unnumbered hordes of students in India stopping all traffic as they filled the streets of New Delhi protesting the delay of the United States in shipping wheat. Where there has been hunger, imperialism, dictatorship, exploitation, college students have in many countries often demonstrated against what they believe to be unjust. In the United States and England, the usual protest has been, until recently, by debate rather than by positive action. In this country, it was the southern Negro student who first undertook sustained direct action. First he started the sit- ins and later was joined by freedom riders. These activities reflect a growing sense of security of an increasing middle class and the effect of world pressure on the United States to root out and destroy discrimination. The rise of twenty-one independent African states has had tremendous influence on Negroes in the United States and has caused them to be determined to secure freedom for the oppressed peoples of their native country.

You students of Spelman College, and your counterparts in other colleges and universities of the United States, will live after graduation in communities of a nation where there is constant agitation and action for the eradication of the situations which cause us to be called Negroes rather than Americans. Your problem will be one of strategy and techniques. You must realize the calculated risk inherent in any leadership efforts, and be prepared to face criticism if your approach proves not to be generally acceptable to the community or if you refuse to join a movement which, after careful consideration, you do not believe is sound morally and technically. What is the best approach?

I am by no means wise enough, nor foolish enough, to offer you the answer. . . .However, based upon long years of experience in the vineyard, I should like to suggest some guiding principles and point out a few of the problems you and I will face in the next decade:

1. There is an expression used by some colored people when referring to others of their racial background, that is, "She is colored just like I am." The mentally enslaved Negro who makes such a remark well knows hat you college students, your professors, and other leaders are subject to the same disrespect and indignities by the ignorant, poor, socially unaccepted white man, that he is. Only by achieving equality of opportunity for the lowest man on the totem pole, do we secure the rights of all of our people—white and colored alike.

2. Only by making democracy work in the United States, not tinkling cymbal and sounding brass, do we make secure our way of life. The people of the world have the choice between democracy and communism or possible annihilation. There is no question that all of us, regardless of the inequities, privation, and suffering we have so long endured in the United States, would choose first to live and next to live the democratic way of life. . . .In our struggle to secure equality of opportunity, personal security, respect for individual dignity, and rights of full citizenship we are making a heroic struggle not only for ourselves but, of greater importance, a struggle for the survival of the United States. America cannot hope that the uncommitted nations of

the world, or those controlled by dictatorship, will choose the democratic way if our failures to put into practice our pronounced belief in freedom continue to be heralded around the world. By destroying every vestige of discrimination at home, we make democracy secure at home and, in so doing, are the hope of the people of the world. Yes, the freedom riders and the sit-ins work not only to free themselves but also to make America free.

3. The capacity for peaceful, orderly change in America has kept this nation vigorous and alive. It is the hope for change which must motivate the masses of American Negroes. But despite all that has been accomplished, we are still suffering from racial and religious discrimination. It exists in education, employment, housing, and public accommodations—North, South, East, and West. Here and there individuals have been able to break through the barriers in the communities in which they reside. But, as you and I know, they are exceptions to the rule. . . .The great mass of colored people in the United States have had no such advantage. As a result we have been slow in developing even a small middle class. According to the census of 1960, only 13,056 nonwhites in Philadelphia and 1644 in Atlanta made over $6,000 in 1959.

The great mass of our people, discouraged by years of closed doors, have not accepted middle-class goals and values. For the past ten years, I have been a member of the Philadelphia Commission on Human Rights. We have a staff of twenty-nine persons, including eleven highly trained professionals, and a budget of close to $300,000. We do not receive in one year thirty complaints in discrimination in employment. Filing a complaint is meaningless to a man who has worn thin the soles of his shoes filing applications for work and then watched less skilled white applicants being employed. Our Commission has to send inspectors into the industries to count the number of colored employees, skilled and unskilled, and examine employment applications in order to ferret out the discrimination. We must subpoena the records when the employer is uncooperative and hold expensive, prolonged public hearings to throw the light of public opinion on the employment problem.

When the masses of Negroes upon whom lack of opportunity had imposed low horizons, limited aspirations and motivation, reflect consciously or unconsciously on these matters, they conclude it is not worthwhile to try to emerge into the middle class. The chance of succeeding is too slim to be worth the terrific effort. This attitude will not change by the masses' seeing, reading, or hearing about the limited number of Negroes who have emerged into the stream of American life. It will change only as the unceasing number of educated youths dedicate their lives not exclusively to making money but to convincing the Negro masses that the rewards of the American way of life are available to all who are willing to make sacrifices and to arousing the people in the communities in which they live to the acceptance of the Negro, the Puerto Rican, the Mexican, all the people of this heterogeneous nation into the mainstream of American life—into the churches, industries, and places of public accommodation, amusement, and culture.

4. The opportunities for unskilled labor, filled by mass migration in World War I and the employment of a million Negro workers in World War II in civilian jobs within four years, gave us an opportunity to prove ability to perform basic factory operations in a variety of businesses, in semiskilled and skilled capacities. Today, however, the demand is no longer for the unskilled or semiskilled workers; in the present industrial expansion in electronics, television, air-conditioning, spacecraft, and plastics, a worker is required to be highly skilled. Thus, the man or woman without skills today is destined to excessive or continuous periods of unemployment. Are you college students and alumnae prepared with the high degree of skill that employment requires today? In my professions, we call the secretaries "the prima donnas." A competent legal secretary demands and receives better pay than the average public school teacher. The shortage is so great that white law offices are seeking capable colored secretaries who know how to spell, can comprehend what they read, and understand the meaning of material dictated to them.

The freedom rides, sit-ins, boycotts are performing a service which history alone can fully evaluate. These activities have proven their effectiveness by the results you have seen in Georgia—where the University of Georgia has its first colored students; where the legislature adopted a local option law which permits localities to determine whether or not schools are to be desegregated; where by edict of the United States Supreme Court, the unit voting system has been broken, and as a result, for the first time in ninety-two years a Negro Senator has been elected to the Georgia State Legislature. Certainly much remains to be done in Georgia as well as all over the United States. But the momentum has opened the dike, and the hole, pouring out the forces of opposing desegregation, is constantly widening.

My concern is that you and I be prepared to live in the highly competitive world in which we will find ourselves as the walls of segregation come tumbling down. Will the few who secure the first top jobs remember the many who are still at the bottom of the ladder and continue to bring them to the top? Will we remember that our apparent security is dependent upon the degree of security enjoyed by all citizens of this country and the world, and thus concern ourselves with foreign affairs, world disarmament, or the plight of the deprived at home, in South America, Asia, and the world? Will we be determined to prepare ourselves with such excellence in skills needed in the atomic age that our talents will be sought after with more zeal than we can seek the opportunity to use them? In what degree we answer these questions will depend not only the freedom of Negroes in the United States but also the security of freedom to all the people of this nation and the world.

Edith S. Sampson (1901-   )

"Choose One Of Five."

Born in Pittsburgh, Pennsylvania on October 13, 1901 Edith S. Sampson was one of eight children. As an adult she worked during the day and took college classes at night. She attended the New York School of Social Work and the School of Social Services Administration at the University of Chicago. Mrs. Sampson received an LL.B. and an LL.M degree in 1925 and 1927 respectively from John Marshall Law School and Loyola University, Chicago. In 1925 John Marshall Law School honored her with an LL.D. degree. President Truman appointed Mrs. Sampson to the United States delegation to the United Nations in 1950 and twelve years later she became a member of the United States Citizens Committee for NATO. She has served successfully as a circuit court judge in Chicago thereby becoming the second black woman elected to the bench in the United States. This speech was presented at the 100th Annual Commencement at North Central College Naperville, Illinois on August 30, 1965.

Jayme Coleman Williams and McDonald Williams, ed., *The Negro Speaks: The Rhetoric of Contemporary Black Leaders*, (New York: Noble and Noble Publishers, Inc., 1970), pp. 41-45. *(See acknowledgement page iv).*

This degree that you have bestowed upon me out of your magnificent kindness is not just an honor. It's outright flattery—and I love it.

Recognizing that it's impossible adequately to express my gratitude, I shall take the coward's way out and not even try.

Let me, instead talk briefly to these graduates who have won their degrees the hard way instead of by the simple expedient of traveling from Chicago to Naperville.

You graduates have every right to expect penetrating words of profound wisdom from an LL.D. even when the doctorate is honorary.

You look for too much, of course, if you ask that I settle all affairs, both international and domestic, in anything under an hour. But I surely ought to be able to handle either one or the other of the side-by-side package without imposing too great a strain on your patience and your posteriors.

I should be able to untangle the enigma of Vietnam for you in ten minutes and solve the Dominican problem in another five. This would still give me, within a twenty-minute limit, ample time to pronounce with authority on the assorted crises in the UN, NATO, the Organization of American States, the Congo, Laos, Cambodia, Malaysia, Indonesia, India, and Pakistan.

Or if I were to talk about the domestic scene, I should be able to sum up for you my definitive solutions to the problems of interracial relations, poverty, urban renewal, mass transportation, education—both higher and lower—organized crime, juvenile delinquency, the balance of payments, the labor-management controversy, and what's to become of those dreadful people in Peyton Place.

If you wanted an analysis of the current state of art, literature, music, drama, and philosophy, you would naturally have to give me another ten minutes.

Unfortunately, though, I am going to have to disappoint you, and I can only hope that you survive the sharp shock of disillusion. The degree that I've been given, precious as it is to me, did not endow me with instant wisdom.

As a result, I've been forced to fall back on a substitute for the all-revealing address that is your due today.

It's worse than that, really. Compounding what is already an offense, I'm going to present to you a multiple-choice test—the last of your college career.

The only consolations that I can offer in presenting the test are that it involves no blue books, you may consult texts freely, the test is self-scoring, and you have a lifetime at your disposal now to complete it.

This exam will be proctored, though. The proctors will be two—the community in which you live and, hardest taskmaster of all, your inner self.

The question: What do you do with your college education now that you have it—and now that it is beginning to become obsolete even as you sit here?

Choose One Of Five Possible Answers:

Choice One: Put your diploma in a convenient drawer and close the drawer. Put whatever textbooks you've accumulated in a bookcase and close the bookcase. Put your mind to the dailiness of earning a satisfactory livelihood and close your mind.

I should warn you that it will take a bit of doing to follow this course with the rigor that it deserves.

You will have to take care not to read anything except, in the case of men, the sports pages or, in the case of women, columns of household hints.

You'll have to choose your friends with extreme care to make sure that you don't rub up against any stimulating personalities.

You'll have to build your own defenses against a world of complex realities that will insist on trying to intrude on you at the most inconvenient times.

But it can be done. I've known college graduates who have achieved it. They've wrapped themselves in an apathy so thick that they're in a position to say in all truth, "No opinion," to any Gallup or Roper pollster who might question them on any subject.

It's a choice that's available to you—choice one.

Choice Two: Go forth into that waiting world, carefully assess the prevailing opinions, and then conform.

Forget this theoretical nonsense they've been feeding you here at North Central. What do professors and assistants and associates and instructors know about the real world anyway? Academics, all of them.

You'll have your degree. That certifies you're educated. Let it go at that.

This choice gives you more latitude than choice one.

You can scan the whole of the daily newspaper, as long as you make certain it's a newspaper that agrees with you and all other right-thinking citizens on all critical issues.

You can keep *Time* or *Newsweek*; *Life* or *Look* on the coffee table.

You can subscribe to the *Reader's Digest* and had better read at least some of it for conversational purposes.

You are even permitted, if you take this choice, to buy two books a year as long as you make sure they're best sellers. Reading the books is optional.

You don't have to be nearly so selective in making friends if you go this route instead of the first one. Just avoid the kooks— although that's easier said than done when what prevailing opinion recognizes as unmistakable kooks come in bewildering variety. But with a little caution you can easily manage.

After all, about 80, perhaps 85 percent of the people with whom you'll come in contact fit nicely in this choice-two category. It isn't that their particularly talented at blending into the background. They are the background.

You, too, can be a pillar-of-society conformist. No strain, no pain.

Well, almost no pain. The anguish of those moments in your middle age when you lie sleepless at 2 a.m. or 3 and wonder what ever happened to all your bright ambitions of college days—that anguish and those moments don't count too much.

Most of the time you can be comfortable with choice two, and who could ask for more than that?

One footnote at this point: Don't worry that your college degree will set you apart and make it impossible for you to be a really thoroughgoing conformist.

That was a slight danger in my day, but it's none at all now.

Ever since people have come to recognize the dollars-and-cents value of a college diploma as a passport to employment, more and more people have been going to college. Only the bigoted, narrow- minded people hold a degree against a person today, and the ranks of the conformists are filled with those who have had even campus and even classroom exposure. B.A.s, B.S.s, masters, doctors—they can all live in the ticky-tacky houses.

Choice Three: Refuse to relax in the commoner forms of conformity. Find yourself, instead, a clique of the elite, an "in" group, and conform yourself to it.

You might imagine, from that bare description of this choice, that this would be a difficult thing to do. It isn't at all.

There are just two requisites.

First, you must have a specialty of your own, some one field— or, better, part of a field—in which you're expert. It might be something in the arts—music before Vivaldi, for instance, or the epic poetry of Afghanistan. On the whole, though, it's better if your specialty is a little more practical-intellectual but moneymaking.

Then to the specialty, whatever it is, you add a dedication to everything that is avant-garde and an amused contempt for everything else that isn't.

One thing you can't have if you go the third choice way—at least not today— and that's a conviction that human beings and the history they have made and are making are important. Nothing is important really—nothing, that is, except your one staked-out small field of specialization.

A James Reeb is beaten to death for daring to assert in action the dignity of man. A Mrs. Liuzzo is shot, killed after the Selma to Montgomery march. Too bad.

But someone suggests that *The Cabinet of Dr. Caligari* isn't such great shakes as a movie. This is monumental heresy. Tie him to the stake and put a torch to the faggots.

You must preserve the proper hierarchy of values, you see. If you join the sort of "in" group I have in mind, your reading becomes restricted again, I'm afraid.

You mustn't read the daily papers, or at a minimum, you mustn't admit it if you do. The Sunday *New York Times*, on occasion, can be tolerated, but no more than tolerated.

You may not read *Life, Look, Time, Newsweek*, or the *Reader's Digest*, not to mention such unmentionables as *Better Homes and Gardens* or *Family Circle*. Nothing more popular than *Scientific American*.

No best-sellers, of course—that goes without saying. It's much better to criticize Saul Bellow without having read *Herzog* all the way through, although you should read enough to be able to say it nauseated you so much you couldn't finish it.

This constriction of your reading is rather unfortunate in one way, really. You can't read things like the *New Republic*, or the *National Review*, or *Commentary*, or *Foreign Affairs*, or the *Bulletin of Atomic Scientists*, or the *Reporter*, or anything of that sort. Those all deal with political and social and economic matters, you see, and an "in" conformist who attached importance to such matters would be drummed out of the corps. Serves him right.

Choice Four. Choice four, though, offers an alternative for those who cannot erase their political-social-economic consciousness.

Join an extremist group.

There is real effort involved in this at the very beginning. You have to study the various groups that present themselves and make your initial commitment.

The beauty of this choice, though, is that, once you've made it, you can turn off your thinking and let yourself be carried by the forward surge of what is obviously a significant movement.

Say you link yourself to the far right.

Your enemies are immediately identified for you—Negroes, Jews, and communists. Communists are easy to recognize—they're all the people who don't agree with you.

You know immediately what to oppose—fluorine in the water supply, income taxes, aid to foreign nations, the Supreme Court, movements for mental health, and any squeamishness about dropping nuclear bombs at will or whim.

You know immediately what to support—anything that the leaders of your group find good and pleasing, although unfortunately they find little that's either.

Say you link yourself to the far left.

Your enemies are immediately identified for you—capitalists, the poor misled sheep of the middle class, and Fascists. Fascists are easy to recognize—they're all the people who don't agree with you.

You know immediately what to oppose—all business corporations with no exceptions, all Trotskyites, all deviationists, all revisionists, all efforts to help established governments resist communist revolt.

You know immediately what to support—anything that the leaders of your group find good and pleasing, which is what the men in Moscow have smiled upon for the day.

What is so attractive about choice four is that it requires no mental effort of you beyond the initial effort of making your selection. Yet it provides a wide-open emotional release that isn't possible with any of the first three choices.

With choice four you can convince yourself that every action you perform has world-molding significance. In sharp contrast to the choice-three people, choice-four people are convinced that everything is important because everything links somehow to the cause.

Choice Five: And then, finally, there's *choice five*. It's hard to state this one. About as close as I can come to it is this: Hang loose, but stay vibrantly alive.

This one's strenuous. This one's demanding.

Choice five would demand of you that you consider today's graduation no more than a pause to catch your breath before continuing the lifelong job of education.

It would demand of you that you be your own unique best self. And there is no higher demand than that.

Choice five entails wide-ranging reading and deep-probing thought. It calls for a contradictory thing—a mind that is constantly open to new facts that dictate change but at the same time is resolutely committed to what seems best at any given point of time.

It calls for human involvement, a compassionate concern for everyone of this fast-shrinking little planet of ours and for the generations to come.

It calls for the resolute rejection of all stereotypes and insists on the thoughtful examination of even the most widely held assumptions that are too easily taken for granted.

If only choice five involved only one thing or the other— thought or action—it would be ever so much easier. It doesn't though. It involves both.

And as if that weren't bad enough, this choice usually brings with it a certain amount of inner ache, because this way is a lonely way.

Those who make choice four are caught up on a wave of fervent enthusiasm that is all the more compelling because there's so little of the rational in it. They have the company of their Birchite brothers or their communist comrades.

Those who make choice three clump together with others of their kind to exchange small coins of comment about existentialism and Zen, the hilarious glories of Busby Berkeley movies, and the charm of Tiffany lampshades.

Those who make choice two are protected by the great crowd of which they've so willingly, gladly made themselves an anonymous part, no different from every other anonymous part. Those who make choice one deliberately dull their sensitivities. They are cud-chewing, content to join the boys at the bar on a Saturday night or the girls at the bridge table Wednesday afternoon. They vegetate.

But those who make choice five are never fully comfortable. They are nagged by their realization that they could be wrong.

They're prodded by their recognition that they've still so much more to learn and even more than that to understand.

They're made restless by their knowledge that no matter how much they do, there's still ever so much more left to be done.

Choice five people have to live constantly with an acceptance of the fact that there are no simple answers in this world because there are no simple questions.

This makes life exciting for them, challenging, at least intermittently rewarding. But comfortable? No.

I would not urge choice five on any of you graduates. It asks so much of you.

Any of the other four will see you through to age sixty or sixty- five, retirement, and a modest pension. They might easily do better than that and make you rich. In dollars, that is.

Five is there, though, one of the multiple choices on the test.

If any of you in this class of '65 makes the fifth choice, I wish you'd let me know about it. You I'd like to know better than I possibly can just by having made a speech here.

You I would treasure even above the LL.D with which North Central College has graciously honored me—and that, you can believe me, is saying a great deal.

IV

Introduction

Chapter four contains three speeches by prominent nineteenth century abolitionist leaders and three speeches by renowned twentieth century reformers. Each of these black males rendered a special contribution to the advancement of the African American people. The nineteenth century black men fought relentlessly for the abolition of slavery. The twentieth century black men are tenacious in their battle against the sickness of racism. Although the subject matter varies from one speech to the other the struggle for individual rights dominates all of the discourses.

The first speech by Dr. James McCune Smith is a call for the Christians of Great Britain to call upon the Christians of the United States to "desist from the sin of slaveholding." Smith perceives an irony when a United States legislator was "hooted and howled" at for submitting rights of petition in behalf of the slave yet at the same time "king-ridden, infidel France" cheered an abolitionist for his "measures for emancipation" for the enslaved French. At this time the only recourse for the African American was to celebrate the abolition of Slavery and the Slave trade in the French and British colonies.

The second speech is by the activist Samuel R. Ward. In this public speech at Faneuil Hall in Boston Ward set forth a scathing attack on the supporters of the Fugitive Slave Law and defied any of the slave catchers to apprehend him. His oration intended to signal the pro-slavery forces that militant black resistance would be the order of the day. As he said: "But we have come here to make a common oath upon a common altar that this bill shall never take effect." Ward protested the infamous law in several speeches and repeated over and over again that "we, the people, will never be human bipeds, to howl upon the track of the fugitive slave."

The third speech is by the famous black emancipator Frederick Douglass. To an audience of sociologists Douglass explains that the exodus of freed blacks from the South is justified. However he is of mixed feelings about the emigration because for many decades black men and women invested much of their labor in building the South. On the other hand, the white Southerner's exploitation of the black farmer under the crop-lien system was an evil and unfair practice. On that point Douglass agreed with the people leaving the South.

The fourth speech is by the famous black leader Booker T. Washington. This speech to the Women's New England Club in Boston gives the lie to the commonly held belief that Washington acquiesced readily to the demands of the white power structure. In this address he spoke openly about the inequities in public schools and in railway accommodations. These remarks were in response to the southerner Henry W. Grady who was spreading erroneous information in his successful speech "The New South." Washington mentioned also the lack of voting rights for blacks and the 10,000 blacks who had been lynched since emancipation. That was notably unusual language for Washington to utter.

In the fifth speech James Weldon Johnson discusses "Our Democracy and the Ballot" at a dinner to Congressman F.H. LaGuardia at the Hotel Pennsylvania, New York City, March 10, 1923. At the heart of Johnson's oration is the basic American principle "founded upon the fact that every American citizen through the ballot, is a ruler in his own right." Johnson, a member of the National Asssociation for the Advancement of Colored People became widely known as a true and dauntless leader ready to battle against the most difficult odds when it came to race relations. To educate his distinguished audience Johnson informed them of the ugly facts about the South: "And so we have it as an admitted and undisputed fact that there are upwards of four million Negroes in the South who are denied the right to vote but who in any of the great northern, mid-western or western states would be allowed to vote." The sixth speech is by Dr. Martin Luther King, Jr. in which he preached about his own eulogy. He instructed his audience that when he is eulogized not to refer to his many awards he won or where he went to school. He said he did not want a long funeral. The sermons should be short; no one is to talk too long. But he directed his audience to say that he tried to give his life serving others. He declared: "I want you to say that I tried to love and serve humanity." In the sermon King drew on the Scriptures for support. In that regard he developed his oration around the gospel of Mark in which James and John asked Jesus if they can sit by his side in his established kingdom. King addressed that request and said that we would be quick to condemn James and John. But King noted that before we condemn we should look to ourselves and see that we have the same selfish desires for recognition and importance. These selfish needs he referred to as the Drum Major Instinct. "If you want to say that I was a drum major," he instructed, "say that I was a drum major for justice: say that I was a drum major for peace; I was a drum major for righteousness." In brief, he wanted to be remembered as a drum major for human rights not for shallow recognition or importance.

JAMES McCUNE SMITH (1813-1865)

"The Abolition of Slavery and the Slave Trade In the French and British Colonies."

Intellectual, physician, and writer, Dr. James McCune Smith grew up in New York City. The son of a slave he owed his freedom to the State of New York Emancipation Act. When refused admission to American universities Smith entered the University of Glasgow in 1832 receiving the degrees of B.A. in 1835, M.A. in 1836, and M.D. in 1837. After graduation he worked in a hospital in Paris for a short time and then returned to the United States. In due time Smith bought property and opened a pharmacy in New York City. He is remembered more for his writings and his social activism and less for his medical practice. Dr. Smith's writings reflect a knowledge of the sciences, history, foreign languages, and classical literature. Much of his writing concerned supporting the equality of the black race. In reply to an attack upon blacks by John C. Calhoun, Smith wrote "The Influence of Climate upon Longevity" in *Hunt's Merchants' Magazine* in 1846. Thought to be the most scholarly black writer of his day, he accepted an appointment as professor of anthropology at Wilberforce University but failing health prevented his teaching. He died from heart disease in 1865. Dr. Smith delivered this speech to an antislavery society meeting. In New York City in 1838.

The Colored American, June 9, 1838.

Mr. President, Ladies and Gentlemen: I rise to offer a resolution expressive of our high satisfaction in the noble efforts of the abolitionists of Great Britain and France, who, although they are separated from us by the width of an ocean, and by distinct political institutions, are nevertheless united with us in sentiment and exertion in the sacred cause of immediate and universal emancipation.

With these two nations we are connected by ties of the closest amity, and enjoy greater reciprocal influence than with any others upon the globe. To these nations our struggle for independence gave the first impulse to the path of liberty, which, if they had trod with slower, they have trod with more consistent steps than we: for every step they have advanced, each measure they have gained, has been an advantage not only to themselves, but to all who are dependent on them. And whenever the people of Great Britain or of France have obtained any portion of civil liberty, their first exercise of it has been to extend the precious boon to their fellow subjects, held in the galling chains of West Indian slavery.

In the last century, the first Convention elected by the French people immediately abolished slavery in two French colonies: and in the present, the passing of the

British Reform Bill has rapidly been followed by the abolition of British West Indian slavery. France, indeed, set the first, the most glorious example, because liberty was conferred without stint of restriction, without any lengthened delay to sicken hope, or purgatorial state to blast expectation; it was sudden and entire; the man who had until yesterday toiled in the field, and had known no other incentive to labor than the cart-whip, was to-day raised to the dignity and privileges of a citizen of the republic; the woman who until yesterday had sobbed over her youngling and besought the grave to snatch it from the horror of existence to-day held it towards the skies and shrieked, "He is free!"

This example has proved most instructive, for when France again bent her neck to the iron yoke of a ruthless tyrant, and suffered her sons to be slaughtered at the altar of ambitious despotism, the men whom she had so suddenly liberated showed themselves worthy of their freedom; for, against the veterans of Europe's conqueror, against an armament sent out by the empire which overwhelmed Napoleon, amidst the loathing and scorn of a neighboring republic, and the cold and bitter neglect of all nations, they have maintained their freedom until now, when generous and consistent France inspired with the genius of modern abolitionism, by acknowledging the independence of Hayti, completes the triumph that revolutionary France began. France, then, has been the first to grant immediate and entire emancipation, and the first to acknowledge the right and capacity of a community of freedmen to rank among the nations of the earth. And although she (France) still holds 250,000 slaves in some of her dependencies, yet recent movements nearly akin to her pristine efforts promise these a speedy liberation.

Sir, this transaction is one of the most cheering that has occurred in the history of abolitionism. For we here find a legislative body, without any recurrence to the primary assemblies of the people, without being urged by petitions or bound by pledges, without being incited by the tales of horror that always accompany slavery— for it is a remarkable fact that the slaves of Catholics are better fed and better treated than those of Protestants: I say we find a legislative body without any of the ordinary inducements, at the first discussion of the subject, not only adopting the measure proposed by the most sanguine of the abolitionists, but actually desirous of advancing still further. This was a manifestation of principle at which we may blush as Americans, but rejoice as men: and unwilling as I am to utter any remark, or draw any comparison reflecting even the slightest discredit on

"My own, my native land"

yet there is something in the facts which, however humbling, may yet prove instructive. The very year that witnessed in our Hall of Representatives the appalling spectacle of a venerable man hooted and howled at when he sought even the rights to petition in behalf of the slave, the same year beheld the legislature of king-ridden, priest- ridden, and as some say, infidel France, cheering on an abolitionist in his measures for emancipation.

Mr. President, if we next turn our eyes toward Great Britain, on whose dominions the sun never sets, whilst they extend through every clime, we find her the neighbor of almost every nation, and therefore capable of influencing all: and this influence is regulated by those sound principles for which she is so justly distinguished, which are her shelter in the hour of danger and her glory in the day of prosperity. Sound as these principles are on all other questions, they are preeminently so on that question which we are this day met to forward. For if, unwittingly, the British people became deeply imbued in the blood guiltiness of slavery and the slave trade, yet as soon as they became aware of the enormity of the crime and possessed the power to remove it, they made signal and instantaneous atonement by the immediate emancipation of their 800,000 slaves. And this great movement was distinguished by none of the bitterness of a political contest, none of the selfishness of a political victory. And when the battle was over and the victory won, the men who had gained it—the dissenters of England and Scotland— still heard the clank of chains, the groans of men and the wails of women held in slavery by other nations. They heard these sounds and they felt the principles by which they had been recently been stirred still glow within them and expand their benevolence beyond the limits of a single empire: they felt the force of that sentiment uttered nearly a thousand years ago by an African slave. *"Homo sum humani nil alienum ama puto."* They felt that their country was the world, their countrymen mankind, and were urged by motives that they could not resist to make the attempt to disenthrall all their countrymen: and they bound themselves by solemn compact to begin a moral agitation that shall not cease until the last fetter shall fall from the last slave upon our earth.

They formed the British Society for the immediate and universal emancipation of slaves, and the consequent destruction of the slave trade throughout the world.

Sir, what are the means by which they hope to obtain so glorious a result? The means are simple, but with God's blessing they will prove efficient. With the bible in their hands, and its precepts for their guide, they are determined calmly, but earnestly and incessantly, to remonstrate with all slaveholders, and to beseech them to liberate their slaves.

Although at the present time their efforts are devoted to another and more appropriate object, the entire abolition of slavery, which yet lingers in their colonies under the name of apprenticeship, yet as soon as they have abolished the apprentice-ship system—and they will do so, even if it be but one hour sooner than its appointed expiration, yet they will obtain that hour, in order that the principles of immediate emancipation may, in their colonies, vanquish the chicanery of slavery in its very metamorphosis—then, sir, with the renewed zeal, the additional experience, and the force of the complete example which this victory will give them, they will bring all their energies to bear upon slavery as it exists in these States.

We may rejoice then, sir, in the present efforts of the British abolitionists on account of the principle for which they are made. It is a struggle for immediate instead of gradual emancipation.

Should the apprenticeship, which works so badly, be permitted to continue until 1840, the evils which have resulted, and the insurrections which might arise from it, would be, to the slaveholder, an argument against emancipation in any form, and to many friends of liberty an argument for very gradual emancipation. The position in which the British abolitionists are now placed must convince slaveholders that they must grant, and abolitionists that they must obtain immediate emancipation, else they will be forced to "fight their battles o'er again."

We may rejoice in these efforts on account of the renewed zeal which they will infuse into the abolition party of Great Britain.

One moral victory gained raises the mind to an eminence whence it perceives others that must be achieved, and inspires it with new energies for the struggle. Each step advanced has increased their zeal and enlarged their views.

The flame of abolitionism is no longer confined to the dissenters of Great Britain; it has even penetrated within the wall of the church established by law; and bishops of the Church of England have at length discovered that the advocacy of the cause of God's suffering poor is not inconsistent with apostolic order. Men of every rank and of every sect are gathering around the standard of abolition, the great principle from which the anxiety grows--that of loving all men—is, imperceptibly to themselves, diffusing its healing influence over the hostile parties for once united; dissenter and churchman, Protestant and Papist, standing on the broad platform of humanity and covered with the mantle of charity, are beginning to love one another whilst united to manifest their common love towards the crushed and bleeding slave.

And when the apprenticeship is abolished, this mass of mind, animated by the principle which now unites it, and in the exercise of the same, will devote its entire energies to the emancipation of our slaves. And the Christians of Great Britain will call upon those of these states, in one long and loud incessant series of remonstrances, entreating them to follow the British example.

Sir, I admire this method of remonstrance. Judging from those we have already received, they seems to be of the right tone, and calculated to effect much good. I deem the method of remonstrance right because it is warranted by the usages of nations in the past and at the present time. In our own time one government has freely remonstrated with another on the destruction of the African slave trade: why, then, may not one people—who are the source of all governmental power—remonstrate with another for the abolition of slavery! The people of these United States, at least that very large and respectable portion of them which constitutes the American Temperance Society, have remonstrated with the British people on the side of intemperance; have not the people of Great Britain an equal right to remonstrate with us on the equally heinous sin of slavery? But, sir, not only has remonstrance—in other words, moral interference—been sanctioned by common usage and our own practice, but British interference in our slave question has actually been solicited, and solicited, too, by all the good and the great of our land, who are at this moment receiving pecuniary assistance from a few of the British people for the abolition of American slavery by means of colonization. Can the good and the great complain then if other British subjects, once solicited by the same agent, see fit to strive for the self-same object by remonstrating with the slaveholder on the justice, safety and expediency of immediate emancipation?

But, sir, common usage may be wrong, the Temperance and even the Colonization Society may be wrong in sanctioning national interference in national sins. I still plead for the right of remonstrance on higher grounds than common usage, or the sanction of moral reforming associations. Christians are governed by the laws peculiar to the commonwealth of Christ, and which are independent of mere human laws imposed by human communities; the citizens of the Church Catholic of the Redeemer may be spread throughout many climes and subject to various forms of political government, but no difference in climes, no diversity in form of political creed can break the links which makes them fellow-citizens in Christ, or free them from obedience to the precepts of the Saviour. One of these precepts is, that they may rebuke one another in love: and another is, that they may exhort each other to "good works." Reposing on these precepts and obedient to them, the Christians of Britain have a right to call upon the Christians of these United States to desist from the sin of slaveholding.

SAMUEL RINGGOLD WARD (1817-1866 ca.)

"Speech On The Fugitive Slave Bill."

Samuel Ringgold Ward, an abolitionist and prominent leader-orator, was born a slave on the Eastern Shore of Maryland in October, 1817. He and his parents escaped slavery and traveled to the northern free states. Ward spent a large part of his life traveling throughout the northeastern states, Canada, and Great Britain speaking out against American slavery. Frederick Douglass, the lion of black abolitionism, said of Ward: "As an orator and thinker he was vastly superior, I thought to any of us." Ward died in Jamaica, West Indies in abject poverty in 1866. The following oration was delivered at Fanueil Hall, Boston on April 3, 1850.

This speech appeared in the *The Liberator*, April 5, 1850.

I am here to-night simply as a guest.   You have met here to speak of the sentiments of a Senator of your State whose remarks you have the honor to repudiate. In the course of the remarks of the gentleman who preceded me, he has done us the favor to make honorable mention of a Senator of my own State—Wm. H. Seward. [Three hearty cheers were given for Senator Seward.]

I thank you for this manifestation of approbation of a man who has always stood head and shoulders above his party, and who has never receded from his position on the question of slavery. It was my happiness to receive a letter from him a few days since, in which he said he never would swerve from his position as the friend of freedom. [Applause.]

To be sure, I agree not with Senator Seward in politics, but when an individual stands up for the rights of men against slaveholders, I care not for party distinctions. He is my brother. [Loud cheers.]

We have here much of common cause and interest in this matter. That infamous bill of Mr. Mason, of Virginia, proves itself to be like all other propositions presented by Southern men. It finds just enough of Northern dough- faces who are willing to pledge themselves, if you will pardon the uncouth language of a backwoodsman, to lick up the spittle of the slavocrats, and swear it is delicious. [Applause.]

You of the old Bay State—a State to which many of us are accustomed to look as to our fatherland, just as well look back to England as our mother country—you have a "Daniel who has come to judgment," only he don't come quite fast enough to the right kind of judgment.   [Tremendous enthusiasm.]   Daniel S. Dickinson represents some one, I suppose, in the State of New York; God knows he doesn't represent me. I can pledge you that our Daniel will stand cheek by jowl with your Daniel. [Cheers.] He was never known to surrender slavery, but always to surrender liberty.

The bill of which you most justly complain, concerning the surrender of fugitive slaves, is to apply alike to your State and to our States, if it shall ever apply at all. But we have come here to make a common oath upon a common altar, that that bill shall never take effect. [Applause.] Honorable Senators may record their names in its behalf, and it may have the sanction of the House of Representatives; but we, the people, who are superior to both Houses and the Executive, too [hear! hear!] we, the people, will never be human bipeds, to howl upon the track of the fugitive slave, even though led by the corrupt Daniel of your State, or the degraded one of ours. [Cheers.]

Though there are many attempts to get up compromises— and there is no term which I detest more than this, it is always the term which makes right yield to wrong; it has always been accursed since Eve made the first compromise with the devil. [Repeated rounds of applause.] I was saying, sir, that it is somewhat singular, and yet historically true, that whensoever these compromises are proposed, there are men of the North who seem to foresee that Northern men, who think their constituency will not look into these matters, will seek to do more than the South demands. They seek to prove to Northern men that all is right and all is fair; and this is the game Webster is attempting to play.

"Oh," says Webster, "the will of God has fixed that matter, we will not re-enact the will of God." Sir, you remember the time in 1841, '42, '43 and '44, when it was said that Texas could never be annexed. The design of such dealing was that you should believe it, and then, when you thought yourselves secure, they would spring the trap upon you. And now it is their wish to seduce you into the belief that slavery never will go there, and then the slaveholders will drive slavery there as fast as possible. I think that this is the most contemptible proposition of the whole, except the support of that bill which would attempt to make the whole North the slave-catchers of the South.

You will remember that the bill of Mr. Mason says nothing about color. Mr. Phillips, a man who I always loved [applause.], a man who taught me my horn-book on this subject of slavery, when I was a poor boy, has referred to Marshfield. There is a man who sometimes lives in Marshfield, and who has the reputation of having an honorable dark skin. Who knows but that some postmaster may have to sit upon the very gentleman whose character you have been discussing tonight? [Hear! hear!] "What is sauce for the goose is sauce for the gander." [Laughter.] If this bill is to relieve grievances, why not make an application to the immortal Daniel of Marshfield? [Applause.] There is no such thing as complexion mentioned. It is not only true that the colored men of Massachusetts—it is not only true that the fifty thousand colored men of New York may be taken—though I pledge you there is one, whose name is Sam Ward, who will never be taken alive. [Tremendous applause.] Not only is it true that the fifty thousand black men in New York may be taken, but any one else also can be captured. My friend Theodore Parker alluded to Ellen Crafts. I had the pleasure of taking tea with her, and accompanied her here tonight. She is far whiter than many who came here slave-catching. This line of distinction is so nice that you cannot tell who is white or black. As Alexander Pope used to say, "White and black soften and blend in so many thousand ways, that it is neither white nor black." [Loud plaudits.]

This is the question, Whether a man has a right to himself and his children, his hopes and his happiness, for this world and the world to come. That is a question which, according to this bill, may be decided by any backwoods postmaster in this State or any other. Oh, this is a monstrous proposition; and I do thank God that if the Slave Power has such demands to make on us, that the proposition has come now—now, that the people know what is being done—now that the public mind is turned toward this subject—now that they are trying to find what is the truth on this subject.

Sir, what must be the moral influence of this speech of Mr. Webster on the minds of young men, lawyers and others, here in the North? They turn their eyes towards Daniel Webster as towards a superior mind, and a legal and constitutional oracle. If they shall catch the spirit of this speech, its influence upon them and upon following generations will be so deeply corrupting that it never can be wiped out or purged.

I am thankful that this, my first entrance into Boston, and my first introduction to Faneuil Hall, gives me the pleasure and privilege of uniting my humble voice against the two Daniels, and of declaring, in behalf of our people, that if the fugitive slave is traced to our part of New York State, he shall have the law of Almighty God to protect him, the law which says, "Thous shalt not return unto the master the servant that is escaped unto thee, but he shall dwell with thee in thy gates, where it liketh him best." And if our postmasters cannot maintain their constitutional oaths, and cannot live without playing the pander to the slave-hunter, they need not live at all. Such crises as these leave us to the right of Revolution, and if need be, that right we will, at whatever cost, most sacredly maintain.

Frederick Douglass (1818 - 1895)

"The Negro Exodus From The Gulf States."

Editor, reformer, U.S. Diplomat, and spokesperson for the oppressed, Frederick Douglass was born a slave on the Eastern Shore of Maryland. At twenty-one he escaped to the free northern states. In time he became a paid lecturer for the Massachusetts Antislavery Society. From 1845 to 1847 he took a speaking tour through Great Britain, returned to the United States, edited and published The North Star in Rochester, New York and participated in reform work. As an elder statesman his wisdom and knowledge gained from a distinguished career benefited public policy. He died on February 20, 1895. This address was presented to the American Social Science Association in Saratoga Springs, New York on September 12, 1879.

This speech is reprinted from: Philip S. Foner, *The Life and Writings of Frederick Douglass*, v. 4, (New York: International Publishers, 1955), pp. 324-342. Permission granted by International Publishers Company.

The Negro, long deemed to be too indolent and stupid to discover and adopt any rational measure to secure and defend his rights as a man, may now be congratulated upon the telling contradiction which he has recently and strikingly given to this withering disparagement and reproach. He has discovered and adopted a measure which may assist very materially in the solution of some of the vital problems involved in his sudden elevation from slavery to freedom, and from chattelhood to manhood and citizenship. He has shown that Mississippi can originate more than one plan, and that there is a possible plan for the oppressed, as well as for the oppressor. He has not chosen to copy the example of his would-be enslavers. It is to his credit that he has steadily refused to resort to those extreme measures of repression and retaliation to which the cruel wrongs he has suffered might have tempted a less docile and forgiving race. He has not imitated the plan of the oppressed tenant, who sneaks in ambush and shoots his landlord, as in Ireland; nor the example of the Indian, who meets the invader of his hunting-ground with scalping knife and tomahawk; he has not learned his lesson from the freed serfs of Russia, and organized assassination against tyrant princes and nobles; nor has he copied the example of his own race in Santo Domingo, who taught their French oppressors by fire and sword the danger of goading too far the "energy that slumbers in the black man's arm."

On the contrary, he has adopted a simple, lawful and peaceable measure. It is emigration—the quiet withdrawal of his valuable bones and muscles from a condition of things which he considers no longer tolerable. Innocent as this remedy is for the manifold ills, which he has thus far borne with marvellous patience, fortitude, and forbearance, it is none the less significant and effective. Nothing has occurred since the abolition of slavery, which has excited a deeper interest among thoughtful men in all sections of the country, than has this Exodus. In the simple fact that a few thousand freedmen have deliberately laid down the shovel and the hoe, quitted the sugar and cotton fields of Mississippi and Louisiana, and sought homes in Kansas, and that thousands more are seriously meditating on following their example, the sober thinking minds of the South have discovered a new and startling peril to the welfare and civilization of that section of our country. Already apprehension and alarm have led to noisy and frantic efforts on the part of the South to arrest and put an end to what is considered a ruinous evil.

It cannot be denied that there is much reason for this apprehension. This Exodus has revealed to southern men the humiliating fact that the prosperity and civilization of the South are at the mercy of the despised and hated Negro. That it is for him, more than for any other, to say what shall be the future of the late Confederate States; that within their ample borders, he alone can stand between the contending powers of savage and civilized life; that the giving of withholding of his labor will bless or blast their beautiful country. Important as manual labor is everywhere, it is nowhere more important than in the more southern of the United States. Machinery may continue to do, as it has done, much of the work of the North, but the work of the South requires bone, sinew, and muscle of the strongest and most enduring kind for its performance. Labor in that section must know no pause. Her soil is prolific with life and energy. All the forces of nature, within her borders are wonderfully vigorous, persistent and active. Aided by an almost perpetual summer, abundantly supplied with heat and moisture, her soil readily and rapidly covers itself with extremely noxious weeds, dense forests and impenetrable jungles, natural hiding places for devouring wolves and loathsome reptiles. Only a few years of non-tillage would be required to give the sunny and fruitful South to the bats and owls of a desolate wilderness. From this condition, shocking for a southern man to contemplate, it is now seen that nothing less powerful than the naked iron arm of the Negro can save her. For him, as a southern laborer, there is no competitor or substitute. The thought of filling his place with any other variety of the human family will be found utterly impracticable. Neither Chinaman, German, Norwegian nor Swede can drive him from the sugar and cotton fields of Louisiana and Mississippi. They would certainly perish in the black bottoms of those states if they could be induced, which they cannot, to try the experiment. Nature itself in those states comes to the rescue of the Negro; fights his battles and enables him to exact conditions from those who would unfairly treat and oppress him. Besides being dependent upon the roughest and flintiest kind of labor, the climate of the South makes such labor uninviting and harshly repulsive to the white man. He dreads it, shrinks from it and refuses it. He shuns the burning sun of the fields, and seeks the shade of the verandas. On the contrary, the Negro walks, labors or sleeps in the sunlight unharmed. The standing apology for slavery was based upon a knowledge of this fact. It was said that the world must have cotton and sugar, and that only the Negro could supply this want, and that he could be induced to do it only under the "beneficent whip" of some bloodthirsty Legree. The last part of this argument has been happily disproved by the large crops of these productions since emancipation; but the first part of it stands firm, unassailed and unassailable. It served him well yea rs ago, when in the bitterest extremity of his destitution. But for it he would have perished when he dropped out of slavery. It saved him then and will save him again.

Emancipation came to him surrounded by exceedingly unfriendly circumstances. It was not the choice or consent of the people among whom he lived, but against a death struggle on their part to prevent it. His chains were broken in the tempest and whirlwind of civil war. Without food, without shelter, without land, without money, or friends, he, with his children, his sick, his aged and helpless, was turned loose and naked to the open sky. The announcement of his freedom was instantly followed by an order from his old master to quit his old quarters and to seek bread thereafter from the hands of those who had given him his freedom. A desperate extremity was this forced upon him at the outset of his freedom, and the world watched with humane anxiety to see what would become of him. His peril was imminent; starvation stared him in the face.

Even if climate, and other natural causes, did not protect the Negro from all competition in the labor market of the South, inevitable social causes would probably effect the same result. The slave system of that section left behind it, as in the nature of the case it must, manners, customs and conditions, to which free white laboring men will not be in haste to submit themselves and their families. They do not emigrate from the free North, where labor is respected, to a lately enslaved South, where labor has been whipped, chained and degraded for centuries. Naturally enough such emigration follows the lines of latitude in which they who compose it were born. Not from South to North, but from East to West "the course of empire takes its way." Hence, it is seen that the dependence of the planters, landowners and old master-class of the South upon the Negro, however galling and humiliating to Southern pride and power, is nearly complete and perfect. There is only one mode of escape for them, and that mode they will certainly not adopt. It is to take off their own coats, cease to whittle sticks and talk politics at the cross-roads, and go themselves to work in their broad and sunny fields of cotton and sugar. An invitation to do this is about as harsh and distasteful to all their inclinations as would be an invitation to step down into their graves. With the Negro, all this is different. Neither natural, artificial nor traditional causes stand in the way of the freedman to such labor in the South. Neither heat, nor the fever demon that lurks in the tangled and oozy swamps, affrights him, and he stands today the admitted author of whatever prosperity, beauty, and civilization are now possessed by the South. He is arbiter of her destiny.

This, then, is the high vantage ground of the Negro; he has labor, the South wants it, and must have it or perish. Since he is free he can now give it, or withhold it; use it where he is, or take it elsewhere, as he pleases. His labor made him a slave, and his labor can, if he will, make him free, comfortable and independent. It is more to him than either fire, sword, ballot-boxes, or bayonet. It touches the heart of the South through its pocket.

It will not be soon forgotten that, at the close of a five hours' speech by the late Senator Sumner, in which he advocated, with unequaled learning and eloquence, the enfranchisement of the freedmen, he was met in the senate with the argument that legislation at that point would be utterly superfluous; that the Negro was rapidly dying out and must inevitably and speedily disappear. Inhuman and shocking as was this consignment of millions of human beings to extinction, the extremity of the Negro, at that date, did not contradict but favored the prophecy. The policy of the old master-class, dictated by passion, pride and revenge, was then to make the freedom of the Negro a greater calamity to him, if possible, than had been his slavery. But happily, both for the old master-class, and the recently emancipated, there came, as there will come now, the sober, second thought. The old master-class then found that it had made a great mistake. It had driven away the means of its own support. It had destroyed the hands and left the mouths. It had starved the Negro and starved itself. Not even to gratify its own anger and resentment could it afford to allow its fields to go uncultivated, and its tables to go unsupplied with food. Hence the freedman, less from humanity than cupidity, less from choice than necessity, was speedily called back to labor and life. But now, after fourteen years of service, and fourteen years of separation from visible presence of slavery, during which he had shown both disposition and ability to supply the labor market of the South, and that he could so far better as a freeman than he ever did as a slave; that more cotton and sugar can be raised by the same hands under the inspiration of liberty and hope than can be raised under the indolance of bondage and the whip,—he is again, alas! in the deepest trouble,—without a home; again out under the open sky, with his wife and his little ones. He lines the sunny banks of the Mississippi, fluttering in rags and wretchedness; he stands mournfully imploring hard hearted steamboat captains to take him on board; while the friends of the emigration movement are diligently soliciting funds all over the North to help him away from his old home to the modern Canaan of Kansas.

THE CAUSE OF IT

Several causes have been assigned to this truly desperate and pitiable spectacle. Many of these are, upon their face, superficial, insufficient and ridiculous. Agents in political trickery and duplicity, who will never go straight to a point, when they can go crooked, explain the Exodus as a cunning scheme to force a certain nomination upon the Republican party in 1880. It does not appear how such an affect is to follow such a cause. For, if the Negroes are to leave the South, as the advocates of the Exodus tell us, and settle in the North, where all their rights are protected, the country need not trouble itself about securing a President whose chief recommendation is supposed to be his will and power to protect the Negro in the South; and the nomination is thus rendered unnecessary by the success of the measure which made it necessary. Again, we are told that greedy speculators in Kansas have adopted this plan to sell and increase the value of their land. This cannot be—men of this class are usually shrewd. They do not seek to sell land to those who have not money,—and they are too sharp to believe that they can increase the value of their property by inviting to its neighborhood a class of people against whom there is an intense and bitter popular prejudice. Malignant emissaries from the North, it is said, have been circulating among the freedmen, talking to them and deluding them with promises of the great things which will be done for them if they will only go to Kansas. Plainly enough thi s theory fails for the want of even the show of probable motive. The North can have no motive to cripple industry at the South, or elsewhere, in this country. If she were malignant enough, which she is not, she is not blind enough to her own interest to do any such thing. She sees and feels that an injury to any part of this country is an injury to the whole of it.

Again, it is said, that this Exodus is all the work of the defeated and disappointed demagogues, white and black, who have been hurled from place and power by the men of property and intelligence in the South. There may be some truth in this theory. Human nature is capable of resentment. It would not be strange if people who have been degraded and driven from place and power by brute force and by fraud, were to resent the outrage in any way they safely could. But it is still further said that the Exodus is peculiarly the works of Senator Windom. His resolution and speech in the Senate, last winter, are said to have set this black ball in motion, and much wrath has been poured out upon that humane Senator for his part in the movement. It need not be denied that there is truth in this allegation. Senator Windom's speech and resolution certainly did serve as a powerful stimulus to this emigration. Until he spoke there was no general stampede from the cotton and sugar plantations of Mississippi and Louisiana. There can be no doubt, either, that the freedmen received erroneous notions from some quarter what the Government was likely to do for them in the new country to which they are now going. They may have been told of "forty acres and a mule," and some of them may have believed and acted upon it. But it is manifest that the real cause of this extraordinary Exodus lies deeper down than any point touched by any of the causes thus far alleged. Political tricksters, land speculators, defeated office seekers, Northern malignants, speeches and resolutions in the Senate, unaided by other causes, could not, of themselves, have set such a multitudinous Exodus in motion. The colored race is a remarkably home- loving race. It has done little in the way of voluntary colonization. It shrinks from the untried and unknown. It thinks its own locality the best in the world. Of all the galling conditions to which the Negro was subjected in the days of his bondage, the worst was the liability of separation from home and friends. His love of home and his dread of change made him even partially content in slavery. He could endure the smart of the lash, worked to the utmost of his power, and be content till the thought of being sent away from the scenes of his childhood and youth was thrust upon his heart.

But argument is less needed upon this point than testimony. We have the story of the emigrants themselves, and if any can reveal the true cause of this Exodus they can. They have spoken and their story is before the country. It is a sad story, disgraceful and scandalous to our age and country. Much of their testimony has been given under the solemnity of an oath. They tell us with great unanimity that they are very badly treated at the South. The land owners, planters, and the old master-class generally, deal unfairly with them, having had their labor for nothing when they were slaves. These men, now they are free, endeavor by various devices to get it for next to nothing; work as hard, faithfully and constantly as they may, live as plainly and as sparingly as they may, they are not better off at the end of the year than at the beginning. They say that they are the dupes and victims of cunning and fraud in signing contracts which they cannot read and cannot fully understand; that they are compelled to trade at stores owned in whole or in part by their employers; and that they are paid with orders and not with money. They say that they have to pay double the value of nearly everything they buy; that they are compelled to pay a rental of ten dollars a year for an acre of ground that will not bring thirty dollars under the hammer; that land owners are in league to prevent land-owning by Negroes; that when they work the land on shares they barely make a living; that outside the towns and cities no provision is made for education, and, ground down as they are, they cannot themselves employ teachers to instruct their children; that they are not only the victims of fraud and cunning, but of violence and intimidation; that from their very poverty the temples of justice are not open to them; that the jury box is virtually closed; that the murder of a black man by a white man is followed by no conviction or punishment. They say further, that a crime for which a white man goes free a black man is severely punished; that impunity and encouragement are given by the wealthy and respectable classes to men of the baser sort who delight in midnight raids upon the defenceless (sic); that their ignorance of letters has put them at the mercy of men bent upon making their freedom a greater evil to them than was their slavery; that the law is the refuge of crime rather than of innocence; that even the old slave driver's whip has reappeared, and the inhuman and disgusting spectacle of the chain-gang is beginning to be seen; that the government of every Southern State is now in the hands of the old slave oligarchy; and that both departments of the National Government soon will be in the same hands. They believe that when the Government, State and National, shall be in the control of the old masters of the South, they will find means for reducing the freedmen to a condition analagous to slavery. They despair of any change for the better, declaring that everything is waxing worse for the Negro, and that his only means of safety is to leave the South.

It must be admitted, if this brief statement of complaints be only half true, the explanation of the Exodus and the justification of the persons composing it, are full and ample. The complaints they make against Southern society are such as every man of common honesty and humanity must wish ill founded; unhappily, however, there is nothing in the nature of these complaints to make them doubtful or surprising. The unjust conduct charged against the late slaveholders is eminently probable. It is an inheritance from the long exercise of irresponsible power by man over man. It is not a question of the natural inferiority of the Negro, or the color of his skin. Tyranny is the same proud and selfish thing everywhere, and with all races and colors. What the Negro is now suffering at the hands of his former master, the white emancipated serfs of Russia are now suffering from the lords and nobles by whom they were formerly held as slaves. In form and appearance the emancipation of the latter was upon better terms than in the case of the Negro. The Empire, unlike the Republic, gave the free serfs three acres of land—a start in the world. But the selection and bestowment of this land was unhappily confided to the care of the lords and nobles, their former masters. Thus the lamb was committed to the care of the wolf; hence the organized assassination now going on in that country, and it will be well for our Southern States if they escape a like fare. The world is slow to learn that no man can wrong his brother without doing a greater wrong to himself; something may, however, be learned from the lessons of alarm and consternation which are now written all over Russia.

But in contemplating this Exodus, it should be kept in mind that the way of an oppressed people from bondage to freedom is never smooth. There is ever in such transition much to overcome on both sides. Neither the master nor the emancipated slave can at once shake off the habits and manners of a long-established past condition. The form may be abolished, but the great spirit survives and lingers about the scenes of its former life. The slave brings into the new relations much of the dependence and servility of slavery, and the master brings much of his pride, selfishness and love of power. The influence of feudalism has not yet disappeared from Europe. Norman pride is still visible in England, though centuries have passed since the Saxon was the slave of the Norman; and long years must elapse before all traces of slavery shall disappear from our country. Suffering and hardships made the Saxon strong—and suffering and hardships will make the Anglo- African strong.

THE EXODUS AS A POLICY

Very evidently there are to be asked and answered many important questions, before the friends of humanity can be properly called upon to give their support to this emigration movement. A natural and primary inquiry is: What does it mean? How much ground is it meant to cover? Is the total removal of the whole five millions of colored people from the South contemplated? Or is it proposed to remove only a part? And if only a part, why a part and not the whole? A vindication of the rights of the many cannot be less important than the same to the few. If the few are to be removed because of the intolerable oppression which prevails in the South, why not the many also? If exodus is good for any, must it not be equally good for all? Then, if the whole five milliions are to leave the South, as a doomed country,—left as Lot left Sodom, or driven out as the Moors were driven out of Spain—there is next a question of ways and means to be considered. Has any definite estimate of the cost of this removal been made? How shall the one or two hundred millions of dollars which such removal would require be obtained? Shall it be appropriated by Congress, or voluntarily be contributed by the public? Manifestly, with such a debt upon the nation as the war for the Union has created, Congress is not likely to be in a hurry to make any such appropriation. It would much more willingly and readily enact the necessary legislation to protect the freedmen where they are than appropriate $200,000,000 to help them away to Kansas, or elsewhere in the North. But suppose, as already suggested, the matter shall not be left at all to Congress, but remitted to the voluntary contributions from the people. Then a swarm of Conways and Tandys must be employed to circulate over the country, hat in hand, soliciting and collecting these contributions; representing to the people, everywhere, thus the cause of the Negro is lost in the South; that his only hope and deliverance from a condition of things worse than slavery is,—removal to Kansas, or to some country outside the Southern States. Then, would such an arrangement, such an apostleship of despair, be beneficial or prejudicial to the cause of the freedman?

Precisely and plainly, this is a gesture of the migration movement which is open to serious objection. Voluntary, spontaneous, self- sustained emigration on the part of the freedmen may or may not be commendable. It is a matter with which they alone have to do. The public is not called upon to say or do anything for or against it; but when the public is called upon to take sides, declare its views, organize emigration societies, appoint and send out agents to make speeches and collect money,—to help the freedmen from the South,—it may very properly object. The public may not wish to be responsible for the measure, or for the disheartening doctrines by which the measure is supported. Objection may properly be made upon many grounds. It may well enough be said that the Negro question is not so desperate as the advocates of this Exodus would have the public believe; that there is still hope that the Negro will ultimately have his rights as a man, and be fully protected in the South; that in several of the old slave States his citizenship and his right to vote are already respected and protected; that the same, in time, will be secured for the Negro in the other States; that the world was not the work of a day; that even in free New England, all the evils generated by slavery did not disappear in a century after the abolition of the system, if, indeed, they have yet entirely disappeared.

Within the last forty years, a dark and shocking picture might be given of the persecution of the Negro and his friends, even in the now preeminently free State of Massachusetts. It is not more than twenty years ago that Boston supplied a pistol club, if not a rifle club, to break up an abolition meeting; and that one of her most eminent citizens had to be guarded to and from his house (Wendell Phillips) to escape the hand of mobocratic assassins, armed in the interest of slavery. The Negro on the Sound boats between New York and Boston, though a respected educated gentleman, was driven forward of the wheels, and must sleep, if he slept at all, upon the naked deck in the open air. Upon no condition except that of a servant or a slave could he be permitted to go into a cabin. All the handicrafts of New England were closed to him. The appearance of a black man in any workshop or ship yard, as a mechanic, would have scattered the whole gang of white hands at once. The poor Negro was not admitted into the factories to work, or as an apprentice to any trade. He was barber, waiter, white-washer and wood-sawer. All of what were called respectable employments, by a power superior to legal enactments, were denied him. But none of these things have moved the Negro from New England, and it is well for him that he has remained there. Bad as is the condition of the Negro today at the South, there was a time when it was flagrantly and imcomparably worse. A few years ago he had nothing; he did not have himself, his labor and his rights to dispose of as should best suit his own happiness. But he has now even more. He has standing in the supreme law of the land, in the Constitution of the United States, not to be changed or affected by any conjunction of circumstances likely to occur in the immediate or remote future. The Fourteenth Amendment makes him a citizen and the Fifteenth makes him a voter. With power behind him at work for him, and which cannot be taken from him, the Negro of the South may wisely bide his time.

The situation at this moment is exceptional and transient. The permanent powers of the Government are all on his side. What though for the moment the hand of violence strikes down the Negro's rights in the South? Those rights will revive, survive and flourish again. They are not the only people who have been in a moment of popular passion maltreated and driven from the polls. The Irish and Dutch have frequently been so treated; Boston, Baltimore and New York have been the scenes of this lawless violence but those scenes have now disappeared. A Hebrew may even now be rudely repulsed from the door of a hotel; but he will not on that account get up another Exodus, as he did three thousand years ago, but will quietly "put money in his purse" and bide his time, knowing that the rising tide of civilization will eventually float him, as it floats all other varieties of the human family, to whom floating in any condition is possible. Of one thing we may be certain (and it is a thing which is destined to be made very prominent not long hence), the Negro will either be counted at the polls, or not counted in the basis of representation. The South must let the Negro vote, or surrender its representation in Congress. The chosen horn of this dilemma will finally be to let the Negro vote, and vote unmolested. Let us have all the indignant and fiery declaration which the warm hearts of our youthful orators can pour out against Southern meanness, "White Leagues," "Bulldozers," and other "Dark Lantern" organizations, but let us have a little calm, clear reason as well. The latter is a safer guide than the former. On this great occasion we want light rather than heat; thought, rather than feeling; a comprehensive view and appreciation of what the Negro has already on his side, as well as the disadvantages against which he has thus far been compelled to struggle, and still has to struggle.

THE EXODUS ILL-TIMED

Without abating one jot of our horror and indignation at the outrages committed in some parts of the Southern States against the Negro, we cannot but regard the present agitation of an African Exodus from the South as ill-timed, and in some respects hurtful. We stand today at the beginning of a grand and beneficent reaction. There is a growing recognition of the duty and obligation of the American people to guard, protect and defend the personal and political rights of all the people of the States; to uphold the principles upon which rebellion was suppressed, slavery abolished, and the country saved from dismemberment and ruin. We see and feel today, as we have not seen and felt before, that the time for conciliation, and trusting to the honor of the late rebels and slaveholders, has passed. The President of the United States, himself, while still liberal, just and generous towards the South, has yet sounded a halt in that direction and has bravely, firmly and ably asserted the constitutional authority, to maintain the public peace in every State, in the Union, and upon every day in the year; and has maintained this ground against all the powers of House and Senate. We stand at the gateway of a marked and decided change in the statesmanship of our rulers. Every day brings fresh and increasing evidence that we are, and of right ought to be, a nation; that Confederate notions of the nature and powers of our Government ought to have perished in the rebellion which they supported; that they are anachronisms and superstitions, and no longer fit to be above ground. National ideas are springing up all around us; the oppressor of the Negro is seen to be the enemy of the peace, prosperity and honor of the country. The attempt to nullify the national election laws; to starve the officer where they could not destroy the office; to attack the national credit when they could not prevent successful resumption; to paralyze the Constitution where they could neither prevent nor set it aside, has all worked against the old slaveholding element, and in the interest of the Negro. They have made it evident that the sceptre of political power must soon pass from the party of reaction, resolution, rebellion and slavery, to the party of constitution, liberty and progress.

At a time like this, so full of hope and courage, it is unfortunate that a cry of despair should be raised in behalf of the colored people of the South; unfortunate that men are going over the country begging in the name of the poor colored man of the South, and telling the people that the Government has not power to enforce the Constitution and Laws in that section, and that there is no hope for the poor Negro, but to plant him in the new soil of Kansas and Nebraska. These men do the colored people in the South real damage. They give their enemies an advantage in the argument for the manhood and freedom. They assume the inability of the colored people of the South to take care of themselves. The country will be told of the hundreds who go to Kansas, but not of the thousands who stay in Mississippi and Louisiana. They will be told of the destitute who require material aid, but not of the multitude who are bravely sustaining themselves where they are. In Georgia, the Negroes are paying taxes upon six millions of dollars; in Louisiana upon forty or fifty millions, and upon unascertained sums elsewhere in the Southern States. Why should a people who have made such progress in the course of a few years now be humiliated and scandalized by Exodus agents, begging money to remove them from their home; especially at a time when every indication favors the position that the wrongs and hardships which they suffer are soon to be redressed?

IT SURRENDERS A GREAT PRINCIPLE

Besides the objections thus stated, it is manifest that the public and noisy advocacy of a general stampede of the colored people from the South to the North, is necessarily an abandonment of the great and paramount principle of protection of person and property in every State of the Union. It is an evasion of a solemn obligation and duty. The business of this nation is to protect its citizens where they are, not to transport them where they will not need protection. The best that can be said of this exodus in this respect is that it is an attempt to climb up some other than the right way; it is an expedient, a half-way measure, and tends to weaken in the public mind a sense of the absolute right, power and duty of the Government, inasmuch as it concedes, by implication at least, that on the soil of the South, the law of the land cannot command obedience; the ballot box cannot be kept pure; peaceable elections cannot be held; the Constitution cannot be enforced, and the lives and liberties of loyal and peaceable citizens cannot be protected. It is a surrender, a premature, disheartening surrender, since it would make freedom and free institutions depend upon migration rather than protection; by flight, rather than by right; by going into a strange land, rather than by staying on one's own. It leaves the whole question of equal rights on the soil of the South open and still to be settled, with the moral influence of Exodus against us; since it is a confession of the utter impracticability of equal rights and equal protection in any States, where those rights may be struck down by violence.

It does not appear that the friends of freedom should spend either time or talent in furtherance of this Exodus as a desirable measure either for the North or the South; for the blacks of the South or the whites of the North. If the people of this country cannot be protected in every State of this Union, the Government of the United States is shorn of its rightful dignity and power; the late rebellion has triumphed; the sovereignty of the nation is an empty name, and the power and authority in individual States is greater than the power and authority of the United States.

BETTER TO STAY THAN TO GO

While necessity often compels men to migrate; to leave their old homes and seek new ones; to sever old ties and create new ones; to do this the necessity should be obvious and imperative. It should be a last resort and only adopted after carefully considering what is against the measure as well as well as what is in favor of it. There are prodigal sons everywhere, who are ready to demand the portion of goods that would fall to them and betake themselves to a strange country. Something is ever lost in the process of migration, and much is sacrificed at home for what is gained abroad. A world of wisdom is in the saying of Mr. Emerson, "that those who made Rome worth going to stayed there." Three moves from house to house are said to be worse than a fire. That a rolling stone gathers no moss has passed into the world's wisdom. The colored people of the South, just beginning to accumulate a little property, and to lay the foundation of families, should not be in haste to sell that little and be off to the lands of the Mississippi. The habit of roaming from place to place in pursuit of better conditions of existence is by no means a good one. A man should never leave his home for a new one till he has earnestly endeavored to make his immediate surroundings accord with his wishes. The time and energy expended in wandering about from place to place, if employed in making him comfortable where he is, will in nine cases out of ten, prove the best investment. No people ever did much for themselves or for the world without the sense and inspiration of native land; of a fixed home; of familiar neighborhood, and common associations. The fact of being to the manor born has an elevating power upon the mind and heart of a man. It is a more cheerful thing to be able to say, "I was born here and know all the people." It cannot be doubted, that in so far as this Exodus tends to promote restlessness in the colored people of the South, to unsettle their feeling of home and to sacrifice positive advantages where they are, for fancied ones in Kansas or elsewhere, it is an evil. Some have sold their little homes at a sacrifice, their chickens, mules and pigs to follow the Exodus. Let it be understood that you are going, and you advertise the fact that your mule has lost half his value—for your staying with him makes half his value. Let the colored people of Georgia offer their six millions worth of property for sale, with the purpose to leave Georgia, and they will not realize half its value. Land is not worth much where there are no people to occupy it, and a mile is not worth much where there is no one to use it.

A MISTAKE AND A FAILURE

It may safely be asserted that, whether advocated and commended to favor on the ground that it will increase the political power of the Republican party, and thus help to make a solid North against a solid South; or upon the ground that it will increase the power and influence of the colored people as a political element, and enable them the better to protect their rights, and ensure their moral and social elevation, the Exodus will prove a disappointment, a mistake and a failure; because, as to strengthening the Republican party, the emigrants will go only to those states where the Republican party is strong and solid enough already without their votes; and in respect to the other part of the argument, it will fail, because it takes colored voters from a section of the country where they are sufficiently numerous to elect some of their number to places of honor and profit, and places them in a country where their proportion to other classes will be so small as not to be recognized as a political element, or entitled to be represented by one of themselves; and further, because, go where they will, they must, for a time, inevitably carry with them poverty, ignorance and other repulsive incidents inherited from their former conditions as slaves; a circumstance which is about as likely to make votes for Democrats as for Republicans, and to raise up bitter prejudices against them, as to raise up friends for them. No people can be much respected in this country, where all are eligible to office, that cannot point to any one of their class in an honorable, responsible position. In sending a few men to Congress, the Negroes of the South have done much to dispel prejudice and raise themselves in the estimation of the country and the world. By staying where they are they may be able to send abler, better and more effective representatives of their race to Congress, than it was possible for them to send at first, because of their want of education, and their recent liberation from bondage. In the South the Negro has at least the possibility of power; in the North he has no such possibility, and it is for him to say how well he can afford to part with this possible power.

But another argument in favor of this emigration is, that having a numerical superiority in Mississippi, Louisiana and South Carolina, and thereby possessing the ability to choose some of their own number to represent them in the state and nation, they are necessarily brought into antagonism with the white race, and invite the very political persecution of which they complain. So they are told that the best remedy for this persecution is to surrender the right and advantage given them by the Constitution and the Government, of electing men of color to office. They are not to overcome prejudice and persecution where it is, but to go where it is not; not to stand where they are, and demand the full constitutional protection which the Government is solemnly bound to give, but to go where the protection of the Government is not needed. Plainly enough this is an evasion of a solemn obligation and duty, an attempt to climb up some other way; a half-way measure, a makeshift, a miserable substitution of expediency for right. For an egg, it gives the Negro a stone. The dissemination of this doctrine by the agents of emigration cannot but do the cause of equal rights much harm. It lets the public mind down from the high ground of a great national duty to a miserable compromise, in which wrong surrenders nothing, and right everything. The South is not to repent its crimes, and submit to the Constitution in common with all other parts of the country, but such repentance and submission is to be conveniently made unnecessary by removing the temptation to commit violations of the Law and the Constitution. Men may be pardoned for refusing their assent to a measure supported upon a principle so unsound, subversive and pernicious. The nation should be held steadily to the high and paramount principle, that allegiance and protection are inseparable; that this Government is solemnly bound to protect and defend the lives and liberties of all its citizens, of whatever race or color, or of whatever political or religious opinion, and to do this in every State and territory within the American Union. Then, again, is there to be no stopping-place for the Negro? Suppose that by-and-by some "Sand Lot Orator" shall arise in Kansas, as in California, and take it into his head to stir up the mob against the Negro, as he stirred up the mob against the Chinese? What then? Must the Negro have another Exodus? Does not one Exodus invite another?

Plainly enough, the Exodus is less harmful in itself than are the arguments by which it is supported. The one is the result of a feeling of courage and despair; but the other comes of cool, selfish calculation. One is the result of honest despair, and appeals powerfully to the sympathies of men; the other is an appeal to our selfishness, which shrinks from doing right because the way is difficult.

THE SOUTH THE BEST MARKET FOR THE BLACK MAN'S LABOR

Not only is the South the best locality for the Negro on the ground of his political powers and possibilities, but it is best for him as a field of labor. He is there, as he is nowhere else, an absolute necessity. He has a monopoly of the labor market. His labor is the only labor which can successfully offer itself for sale in that market. This, with a little wisdom and firmness, will enable him to sell his labor there on terms more favorable to himself than he can elsewhere. As there are no competitors or substitutes, he can demand living prices with the certainty that the demand will be complied with. Exodus would deprive him of this advantage. It would take him from a country where the land owners and planters must have his labor or allow their fields to go untilled and their purses unsupplied with cash; to a country where the land owners are able and proud to do their own work, and do not need to hire hands except for limited periods at certain seasons of the year. The effect of this will be to send the Negro to the towns and cities to compete with white labor. With what result, let the past tell. They will be crowded into lanes and alleys, cellars and garrets, poorly provided with the necessaries of life, and will gradually die out. The Negro, as already intimated, is preeminently a Southern man. He is so both in constitution and habits, in body as well as mind. He will not only take with him to the North, Southern modes of labor, but Southern modes of life. The careless and improvident habits of the South cannot be set aside in a generation. If they are adhered to in the North, in the fierce winds and snows of Kansas and Nebraska, the emigration must be large to keep up their numbers. It would appear, therefore, that neither the laws of politics, labor nor climate favor this Exodus. It does not conform to the laws of healthy emigration which proceeds not from South to North, not from heat to cold, but from East to West, and in climates to which the emigrants are more or less adapted and accustomed.

THE NORTH GATE OF THE SOUTH MUST BE KEPT OPEN

As an assertion of power by a people hitherto held in bitter contempt; as an emphatic and stinging protest against high-handed, greedy and shameless injustice to the weak and defenseless; as a means of opening the blind eyes of oppressors to their folly and peril, the Exodus has done valuable service. Whether it has accomplished all of which it is capable in this particular direction for the present, is a question which may well be considered. With a moderate degree of intelligent leadership among the laboring class at the South, properly handling the justice of their cause, and wisely using the Exodus example, they can easily exact better terms for their labor than ever before. Exodus is medicine not food; it is for disease not health; it is not to be taken from choice, but necessity. In anything like a normal condition of things the South is the best place for the Negro. Nowhere else is there for him a promise of a happier future. Let him stay if he can, and save both the South and himself to civilization. While, however, it may be the highest wisdom under the circumstances for the freedmen to stay where they are, no encouragement should be given to any measures of coercion to keep them there. The American people are bound, if they are or can be bound to anything, to keep the North gate of the South open to black and white, and to all the people. The time to assert a right, Webster says, is when it is called in question. If it is attempted by force or fraud to compel the colored people to stay, then they should by all means go; go quickly, and die, if need be, in the attempt. Thus far and to this extent any man may be an emigrationist. In no case must the Negro be "bottled up" or "caged up." He must be left free, like every other American citizen, to choose his own habitation, and to go where he shall like. Though it may not be for his interest to leave the South, his right and power to leave it may be his best means of making it possible for him to stay there in peace. Woe to the oppressed and destitute of all countries and races if the rich and powerful are to decide when and where they shall go or stay. The deserving hired man gets his wages increased when he can tell his employer that he can get better wages elsewhere. And when all hope is gone from the hearts of the laboring classes of the old world, they can come across the sea to the new. If they could not do that their crushed hearts would break under increasing burdens. The right to emigrate is one of the most useful and precious of all rights. But not only to the oppressed, to the oppressor also, is the free use of this right necessary. To attempt to keep these freedmen in the South, who are spirited enough to understand the risks and hardships of emigration, would involve great possible danger to all concerned. Ignorant and cowardly as the Negro may be, he has been known to fight bravely for his liberty. He went down to Harper's Ferry with John Brown, and fought as bravely and died as nobly as any. There have been Nathaniel Turners and Denmark Veseys among them in the United States, Joseph Cinques, Madison Washingtons and Tillmans on the sea, and Toussaint L'Ouvertures on land. Even his enemies, during the late war, had to confess that the Negro is a good fighter, when once in a fight. If he runs, it is only as all men will run, when they are whipped.

This is not time to trifle with the rights of men. All Europe today is studded with the material for a wild conflagration. Every day brings us news of plots and conspiracies against oppressive power. An able writer in the *North American Review* for July, himself a Nihilist, in a powerful article defends the extremest measures of his party, and shows that the treatment of the emancipated peasants by the government and landed aristocracy of Russia is very similar to that now practised towards the freedmen by the landed aristocracy of the South. Like causes will produce like effects, the world over. It will not be wise for the Southern slaveholders and their successors to shape their policy upon the presumption that the Negro's cowardice or forbearance has not limit. The fever of freedom is already in the Negro's blood. He is not just what he was fourteen years ago. To forcibly dam up the stream of emigration would be a measure of extreme madness as well as oppression. It would be exposing the heart of the oppressor to the pistol and dagger, and his home to fire and pillage. The cry of "Land and Liberty," the watchword of the Nihilistic party in Russia, has a music in it sweet to the ear of all oppressed peoples, and well it shall be for the landholders of the South if they shall learn wisdom in time and adopt such a course of just treatment towards the landless laborers of the South in the future as shall make this popular watchword uncontagious and unknown among their laborers, and further stampede to the North wholly unknown, indescribable and impossible.

BOOKER T. WASHINGTON (1856-1915).

"Address Delivered before Women's New England Club Boston, Jan. 27, 1889."

Educator and reformer, Booker Taliaferro Washington was born a slave on a plantation in Virginia in 1856 and he died on November 13, 1915. Determined to secure an education he attended Hampton Institute in Virginia. At Hampton Institute he belonged to the debate team and spent long hours studying speech. After graduation he went on to become the first president of Tuskegee Institute in Alabama. In time he became one of the most celebrated black men whose fame spanned the late nineteenth and early twentieth centuries. A popular spokesperson for blacks, he received during his career thousands of requests to speak. Consequently he had to be selective in accepting the invitations. One essayist wrote of Washington: "He practiced what he preached: courage, self-reliance, integrity, humility, dignity, and consideration for his fellow man." Another essayist denounced him as an accommodationist toward the South.

A duplicate copy of the handwritten manuscript can be obtained from The *BTW Papers*, The Library of Congress, Manuscript Division, Washington, D.C. 20540.

What is the actual condition of the 6,500,000 Negroes who inhabit the Southern States, and who for 250 years through no fault of their own and by the expressed or implied consent of all people, were deprived of the fruits of their labors and kept in abject ignorance, is a question that should often touch the heart of every American citizen? Starting 25 years ago, without a foot of land, without a hoe, without a horse, and unused to self-guidance and habits of economy, his mind befogged with ignorance and superstition, could you have expected him to have traveled very far in the direction of intelligence, wealth and independence? And yet he has made progress, says Dr. Haygood, that has been unequalled by that of any other people on the face of the globe in the same length of time. While there has been this almost marvelous progress, I fear we often overlook the magnitude of the work to be done because of the immense number of people to be reached, because of their extreme poverty and ignorance and the disadvantage of an acquired race prejudice. With this in view, I wish to spend a few minutes in speaking to you about my people, as I have actually seen their condition in the heart of the South during the last eight years. I know that you want the facts whether they are encouraging or discouraging.

(As to numbers,) Good authorities put the number of colored people now in the South alone at 6,000,000. In many of the counties of Alabama, and other Southern states they outnumber the whites — six to one, and if you would find the masses and know their real condition, you must leave the town and railroads and go into the interior, on the larger cotton plantations. In most cases the whites have left the country and moved into town, leaving the masses of colored people to themselves. Five sixths of these people live on rented land and mortgage their crops and stock for the food on which to live from day to day, and upon the money value of food, is charged an average of 25 percent interest. Four-fifths of these are today in debt—because of their own ignorance their lack of economy, and they are being forced to go into debt for the food on which to keep their bodies alive during the first year of freedom. Starting in debt; being charged an interest on the value of food which was and is still impossible for them to pay, his indebtedness in many cases has overlapped and increased from year to year, until it has fastened its iron claws upon the business amd moral life of the people to an extent that is appalling and the worst of it is, that in many cases the people have lost hope of bettering their condition, and consequently do only enough work to keep body and soul together. As a result of this system, with few exceptions, we find land poorly cultivated, houses and fences going to wreck, livestock poorly cared for, and a "tumble down" air generally. Understand, my remarks apply mainly to rural districts. The moral lessons of such a life are the worst.

During slavery the colored man reasoned this way: my body belongs to master, and taking master's chickens to feed master's body is not stealing. The practice thus started has to some extent been handed to this generation, and when pressed and cramped on every side by this horrible mortgage system, even to get food to keep life in his children, you must not be surprised if he breaks the command—"Thou shalt not steal." Four-fifths of the families live in small, one roomed cabins. Can you wonder that the morals of a people, whose mother, father, brothers, sisters, kindred, strangers, young and old, numbering sometimes ten or twelve, eat, cook, and sleep in the same room, are not all that they should be?

In the country districts the public schools are kept open on an average of 3 1/2 months in the year. The state is able to build no school-houses, and as the people themselves are unable to build them, the school is usually taught in the wreck of a log cabin, or under a bush arbor. The average country teacher is often unable to write his own name correctly and it not unfrequently occurs that there are scholars that know more than their teachers and often too those teachers are as weak morally, as mentally. For moral, religious, and intellectual life, these masses are dependent for guidance on their teachers and preachers, and the number of preachers is legion. They are even more ill fitted for their work than the teachers. One church near Tuskegee has a total membership of 200, and 18 are preachers. The character of many of them is represented by one of whom it is said that while he was at work in the cotton field in the middle of July, he suddenly stopped, looked up to heaven and said, "Lord, de work is so hard, de cotton is so greasy, and de Sun am so hot, dat I believe dis darky am called to Preach." In name these people are certainly religious, but its manifestation consists largely in emotion, and they are dreadfully wanting in real practical Christianity. In fact it is hard for a hungry man to be a good Christian. The denominational prejudice is so strong that it works a great injury to the schools and the moral life generally. It is often more important for one to be a Methodist or Baptist than to be a helpful follower of Christ. It is worth attention to note that while a very large proportion of the colored people are church members, Christians in name, bring about equally divided between Baptist and Methodist denominations; the mere fact of such membership is misleading and is no evidence that a large proportion of these people are not just as far from real Christian truth as taught by Christ as any people found in Japan or Africa.

In other words a large number of my people without knowing it are Christian heathen and demand as much missionary's effort as the heathen of foreign fields, but to return to education. Each colored child in Alabama will receive for its education this year 81c from the state, each child in Massachusetts about $15.00. Sixty percent of the colored children in the South attended no school last year. 2,000,000 voters of the South can not read the ballots they have the right to cast. Of the total negro population South of Mason and Dixon's line, one fourth can perhaps read in a way, but I do not hesitate to say that the number who have enough education to make it of potential effect in shaping and strengthening their moral and religious life, in order to withstand temptation and stand on their own feet as helpful forces in American life is not 10 percent of the whole population.

Now as to the wrongs growing out of prejudice you see in the newspapers that the negro is murdered often without a cause, that is true; that he is often deprived of political franchise, that is true, that on public highways he is often made to pay for first class accommodations, then forced to accept second class fare, that is true; But this question of race prejudice is rather an uncertain quantity. Let Negro students enter a Southern white school, if the Negro remains, the school will break up. Let a Negro Mechanic enter a northern factory as a laborer, and if the Negro remains, the factory will break up. As stubborn and unreasonable as this race prejudice is, no one can keep his eyes open without noticing from year to year a gratifying improvement. The fact is that a large proportion of the American people have for so long a time almost unconsciously associated the Negro with slavery, subjugation, poverty, filth and ignorance that it is hard to separate him in our minds from these conditions, and we find even Pat as he comes from Ireland, even before 1he learns the name of the president of the United States before he had or has time to change his shirt, begins to speak of "dirty Negroes."

Trying as this question is, it is by no means the principal or most weighty part of the problem. Human nature, I find much the same the world over. The poor Irishman or Jew is discriminated against until he gets property, intelligence and moral backbone then he ceases to be an Irishman or a Jew, and becomes a full-fledged American citizen.

It is interesting to note what form this prejudice exhibits itself, and to what extent it is disappearing. It is rather hard to understand why Southern white people do not object to sitting by the side of a colored person in a street car, and yet if there are some persons who change from a horse car to a steam car the white person will object to being in the same coach with the negro even though they are thirty feet apart.

Notwithstanding the eloquence of the late Mr. Grady and newspaper misstatements, the facts are, that in every one of the Gulf states, the Negro is forced to ride in Railroad coaches that are inferior in every way, to those given the whites, and they are made to pay the same fare that the whites pay. In many cases, the colored people are compelled to ride in the smoking car, and when this is not the case, one half of the smoking car is partitioned off for the colored people and even in this case the door leading from one room to the other is about as often open as shut. And here I would add that it is not the separation that we complain of, but the unequality of the accommodations. But even in this matter of public accommodation, there is an encouraging change. Ten years ago the same unjust discrimination was made in Virginia, W. Va. and North Carolina, but at present such discrimination is almost unknown in these states and the reformation is gradually working its way farther south. The situation was forcibly explained a short time ago, when I myself riding through Georgia in a first class car and one of the passengers asked why a Negro was permitted in that car. The conductor replied that he got into the coaches in North Carolina and it was hard to get him out after crossing the Georgia line. So far as concerns the Gulf states, the Negro is completely at the mercy of the white man in the state courts. The eloquent Mr. Grady disposes of this whole subject in this well sounded sentence: "And in every court," says he "the Negro criminal strikes the colored juror from the panel that the white man may judge his case." Now it would not, perhaps, have sounded so well yet it would have been the simple truth, if Mr. Grady had said that in the whole of Georgia & Alabama, and other southern states not a negro juror is allowed to sit in the jury box in state courts. And while on that subject Mr. Grady might have added even at the risk of spoiling his rhetoric, the information, that since freedom there have been at least ten thousand colored men in the South murdered by white men, and yet with perhaps a single exception, the record at no court shows that a single white man has ever been hanged for these murders. These are but a few examples of his eloquence versus the facts. If time would admit an analysis of Mr. Grady's speech I would reveal other equally untrue statements. The practice of lynching colored people is one of the curses of the south. This is usually resorted to when there is a charge of rape. In the midst of excitement when there is no time or disposition to inquire into the facts, some poor Negro is swung up to a tree and made to suffer for a crime which in five cases out of ten was committed if committed at all, by someone else. Then if the friends of this unfortunate Negro, in their excitement show any signs of indignation and anger and gather in knots to discuss the matter it is telegraphed all over the country that the Negroes are rising and troops must be sent to suppress them. A more docile, gentle, law- abiding people, I do not believe are to be found in the world. But even this barbarous mode of attempting to administer justice is being more and more condemned by the southern press, and we are sure that a healthy change in public sentiment is being wrought.

What I shall say regarding the political condition of the Negro, I shall confine to the Gulf states. In the first place, the Southern people in private conversation do not attempt to hide the fact that they regularly and systematically resort to means to nullify the colored vote that they are resolved in every case where the colored vote is large enough to have a controlling influence in an election, to see that the colored vote is not counted. Force in the form of shot-guns-Ku-Klux-Klan is now rarely resorted to, but the vote is quietly and persistently thrown from the ballot-box or is not counted. This practice has been so effectually used for so long a time, that is safe to say that not more than one-fifth of the colored voters ever attempt to vote in the state, and national elections. So discouraged have they become. But if you ask is not each political party required by law to be represented at the ballot-box by a judge. In answer, it should be remembered that the whole election machinery is in the hands of the whites, and it is very convenient to fulfil that part of the law by appointing as a judge to represent the republican party, some colored man who can neither read nor write. In the districts where the colored people outnumber the whites their [sic] the colored people have the least chance for expressing themselves politically.

(At this point in the handwritten manuscript a page is missing.)

can, by virtue of his superior knowledge of the chemistry of the soil, knowledge of improved tools and best breeds, raise 50 bushels of corn to the acre, while his white neighbor raises only thirty, and the white man will come to the black man to learn. Further they will sit down on the same seat and talk about it; (the value of trades.)

The negro will not be respected as a man until his business side as well as the moral And religious side is developed, and here comes the value of *illegible word* trial training. Trades Unions at the north exclude colored mechanics. These unions are gradually working their way south. Heretofore the negro has had a monopoly of the trades. In building a million dollar city Hall in Richmond Va. recently, not a negro was permitted to lay brick. Before the war a large number of colored boys were apprenticed by their masters to learn trades. The apprentice system is dying out, and the negro as a mechanic, or he will go to the wall. The industrial schools meet this demand, and furnish at the same time, the best moral training. At the Tuskegee Normal School, we have 400 students, half of them young men, and the demand to learn trades along with the 4 years literary course is much greater than we can supply. We have recently completed a three and a half story building. The bricks for the building were made by our students, several of whom get enough knowledge of brick masonry to enable them to go into any town or city in Alabama and make an independent living as a brickmaker. The sawing of the lumber was by the students, and more than one man has learned to handle a steam saw. The brick laying, plastering and painting and carpentry were done also by the students. This building cost $6000 and in its construction we taught enough students trades to average one mechanic for each $1000 entering into the cost of the building. This gain is in addition to the permanent use of the building for a dormitory. We are needing another building and can make six thousand dollars do the same amount of good. While the boys did this work, the girls made and laundered their clothes and in that way were taught sewing and laundering. This illustrates in some degree, the plan and scope of the industrial work at Tuskegee. Nothing tends more to develop moral back-bone than Industrial training. During its eight years existence the Tuskegee school has sent out many class room and mechanical teachers. Yes more than 100 young men and women. The moral and uplifting influence exerted for each of these teachers, in the communities where they teach is almost beyond calculation. I wish you could go, as I have gone, into one of these cotton districts, where all is discouragement and demoralization resulting from debt, mortgaging, renting, and lack of school advantages, and then go there two or three years later, and see the change that I have seen, wrought by one of those teachers. I have in mind one of our girls who went three years ago into a community where everything was just as dark and discouraging as anything I have mentioned. She began her work by calling the people together in weekly meetings. In these meetings she told them how to stop renting and mortgaging and begin buying the houses. She told them how they could have their money and build a school house, and prolong the school term. If you were to go there today you would see hope and encouragement beaming from every eye, you would find them buying little farms and instead of the wreck of a log cabin, a neat comfortable framed school- house, and the school term lasting 7 months instead of three. All this they have done without a dollars out-side aid—only they have had someone to show them *how* to *help themselves*. And herein lies the solution of this vexed Southern problem. This bringing a race from darkness into light—and putting it on its feet. I do not believe that there is any missionary work in the world that gives such satisfactory results in so short a time for the money spent. We do not ask direct help for the masses but help to enable such institutions as Tuskegee to send teachers as leaders and guides into every community. The one good thing that the negro got out of slavery was the power of hard work. He works now, but he does not know how to use the results of his labor. The Tuskegee School under no denominational control, with its 640 acres of land, 12 industries, $1,000,000 in property, with 27 teachers is trying to prepare 400 young men and women to do the same kind of work that I have attempted to describe.

JAMES WELDON JOHNSON (1871-1938)

"Our Democracy And The Ballot."

Poet, songwriter, anthologist, and U.S. Diplomat, James Weldon Johnson was born in Jacksonville, Florida and educated at Atlanta and Columbia Universities. He was the first black admitted to the Florida bar. He served as American consul to Venezuela and Nicaragua in 1903-1912. A charter member of the NAACP (National Association for the Advancement of Colored People) he served as its secretary from 1905-1930. He taught at Fisk University and at New York University. His autobiography Along This Way was published in 1930. A composer he collaborated on many songs with his brother. Like the editor and publisher Ida Wells-Barnett (q.v.) who waged her own personal battle against lynching Johnson carried on also an intense campaign against that same crime while with the NAACP. This speech was presented on March 10, 1923 at a dinner in the Hotel Pennsylvania in New York City honoring then Congressman Fiorella LaGuardia.

Reprinted with the kind permission of The Associated Publishers, Inc., 1407 14th Street, N.W. Washington, D.C. 20005-3704.

It is one of the commonplaces of American thought that we have a democracy based upon the free will of the governed. The popular idea of the strength of this democracy is that it is founded upon the fact that every American citizen through the ballot, is a ruler in his own right; that every citizen of age and outside of jail and the insane asylum has the undisputed right to determine through his vote by what laws he shall be governed and by whom these laws shall be enforced.

I could be cynical and flippant and illustrate in how many ways this popular idea is a fiction, but it is not my purpose to deal in *cleverisms*. I wish to bring to your attention seriously a situation, a condition, which not only runs counter to the popular conception of democracy in America but which runs counter to the fundamental law upon which that democracy rests and which, in addition, is a negation of our principles of government and a menace to our institutions.

Without any waste of words, I come directly to a condition which exists in that section of our country which we call "the South," where millions of American citizens are denied both the right to vote and the privilege of qualifying themselves to vote. I refer to the wholesale disfranchisement of Negro citizens. There is no need at this time of going minutely into the methods employed to bring about this condition or into the reasons given as justification for those methods. Neither am I called upon to give proof of my general statement that millions of Negro citizens in the South are disfranchised. It is no secret. There are the published records of state constitutional conventions in which the whole subject is set forth with brutal frankness. The purpose of the state constitutional conventions is stated over and over again, that purpose being to exclude from the right of franchise the Negro, however literate, and to include the white man, however literate.

The press of the South, public men in public utterances, and representatives of those states in Congress, have not only admitted these facts but have boasted of them. And so we have it as an admitted and undisputed fact that there are upwards of four million Negroes in the South who are denied the right to vote but who in any of the great northern, mid-western or western states would be allowed to vote or would at least have the privilege of qualifying themselves to vote.

Now, nothing is further from me than the intention to discuss this question either from an anti-South point of view or from a pro-Negro point of view. It is my intention to put it before you purely as an American question, a question in which is involved the political life of the whole country.

Let us first consider this situation as a violation, not merely a violation but a defiance, of the Constitution of the United States. The Fourteenth and Fifteenth Amendments to the Constitution taken together express so plainly that a grammar school boy can understand it that the Negro is created a citizen of the United States and that as such he is entitled to all rights of every other citizen and that those rights, specifically among them the right to vote, shall not be denied or abridged by the United States or by any state. This is the expressed meaning of the amendments in spite of all the sophistry and fallacious pretense which have been invoked by the courts to overcome it.

There are some, perhaps even here, who feel that it is no more serious a matter to violate or defy one amendment to the constitution than another. Such persons will have in mind the Eighteenth Amendment. This is true in a strictly legal sense, but any sort of analysis will show that violation of the two Civil War Amendments strikes deeper. As important as the Eighteenth Amendment may be, it is not fundamental; it contains no grant or rights to the citizen nor any requirement of service from him. It is rather a sort of welfare regulation for his personal conduct and for his general moral uplift.

But the two Civil War Amendments are grants of citizenship rights and a guarantee of protection in those rights, and therefore their observation is fundamental and vital not only to the citizen but to the integrity of the government.

We may next consider it as a question of political franchise equality between the states. We need not here go into a list of figures. A few examples will strike the difference:

In the election of 1920 it took 82,492 votes in Mississippi to elect two senators and eight representatives. In Kansas it took 570,220 votes to elect exactly the same representation. Another illustration from the statistics of the same election shows that one vote in Louisiana has fifteen times the political power of one vote in Kansas.

In the Congressional elections of 1918 the total vote for the ten representatives from the state of Alabama was 62,345, while the total vote for the ten representatives in Congress from Minnesota was 299,127, and the total vote in Iowa, which has ten representatives, was 316,377.

In the Presidential elections of 1916 the states of Alabama, Arkansas, Georgia, Louisiana, Mississippi, North Carolina, South Carolina, Tennessee, Texas and Virginia cast a total vote for the Presidential candidates of 1,870,209. In Congress these states have a total of 104 representatives and 126 votes in the electoral college. The State of New York alone cast a total vote for Presidential candidates of 1,706,354, a vote within 170,000 of all the votes cast by the above states, and yet New York has only 43 representatives and 45 votes in the electoral college.

What becomes of our democracy when such conditions of inequality as these can be brought about through chicanery, the open violation of the law and defiance of the Constitution?

But the question naturally arises, What if there is violation of certain clauses of the Constitution; what if there is an inequality of political power among the states? All this may be justified by necessity.

In fact, the justification is constantly offered. The justification goes back and makes a long story. It is grounded in memories of the Reconstruction period. Although most of those who were actors during that period have long since died, and although there is a new South and a new Negro, the argument is still made that the Negro is ignorant, the Negro is illiterate, the Negro is venal, the Negro is inferior, and, therefore, for the preservation of civilized government in the South, he must be debarred from the polls. This argument does not take into account the fact that the restrictions are not against ignorance, illiteracy and venality, because by the very practices by which intelligent, decent Negroes are debarred, ignorant and illiterate white men are included.

In this pronounced desire on the part of the South for an enlightened franchise sincere, and what has been the result of these practices during the past forty years? What has been the effect socially, intellectually, and politically, on the South? In all three of these vital phases of life the South is, of all sections of the country, at the bottom. Socially, it is that section of the country where public opinion allows it to remain the only spot in the civilized world—no, more than that, we may count in the blackest spots of Africa and the most unfrequented islands of the sea—it is a section where public opinion allows it to remain the only spot on earth where a human being may be publicly burned at the stake. And what about its intellectual and political life? As to intellectual life I can do nothing better than to quote from Mr. H.L. Mencken, himself a Southerner. In speaking of the intellectual life of the South, Mr. Mencken says:

> It is, indeed, amazing to contemplate so vast a
> vacuity. One thinks of the interstellar spaces, of
> the colossal reaches of the now mythical ether.
> One could throw into the South France, Germany and
> Italy, and still have room for the British Isles.
> And yet, for all its size and all its wealth and
> all the 'progress' it babbles of, it is almost as
> sterile, artistically, intellectually, culturally,
> as the Sahara Desert. . . If the whole of the late
> Confederacy were to be engulfed by a tidal wave
> tomorrow, the effect on the civilized minority of
> men in the world would be but little greater than
> that of a flood on the Yang-tse-kiang. It would be
> impossible in all history to match so complete a
> drying-up of a civilization. In all that section
> there is not a single poet, not a serious
> historian, not a creditable composer, not a critic
> good or bad, not a dramatist dead or alive.

In a word, it may be said that this whole section where, at the cost of the defiance of the Constitution, the perversion of law, the stultification of men's consciousness, injustice and violence upon a weaker group, the 'purity' of the ballot has been preserved and the right to vote restricted to only lineal survivors of Lothrop Stoddard's mystical Nordic supermen—that intellectually it is dead and politically it is rotten.

If this experiment in super-democracy had resulted in one one-hundredth of what was promised, there might be justification for it, but the result has been to make the South a section not only in which Negroes are denied the right to vote, but one in which white men dare not express their honest political opinions. Talk about the political corruption through the buying of votes, here is political corruption which makes a white man fear to express a divergent political opinion. The actual and total result of this practice has been not only the disfranchisement of the Negro but the disfranchisement of the white man. The figures which I quoted a few moments ago proved that not only Negroes are denied the right to vote but white men fail to exercise it; and the latter condition is directly dependent upon the former.

The whole condition is intolerable and should be abolished. It has failed to justify itself even upon the grounds which it is claimed made it necessary. Its results and its tendencies make it more dangerous and more damaging than anything which might result from an ignorant and illiterate electorate. How this iniquity might be abolished is, however, another story.

I said that I did not intend to present this subject either as anti-South or pro-Negro, and I repeat that I have not wished to speak with anything that approached bitterness toward the South. Indeed, I consider the condition of the South unfortunate, more than unfortunate. The South is in a state of superstition which makes it see ghosts and bogeymen, ghosts which are the creation of its own mental processes.

With a free vote in the South the specter of Negro domination would vanish into thin air. There would naturally follow a breaking up of the South into two parties. There would be political light, political discussion, the right to differences of opinion, and the Negro vote would naturally divide itself. No other procedure would be probable. The idea of a solid party, a minority party at that, is inconceivable.

But perhaps the South will not see the light. Then, I believe, in the interest of the whole country, steps should be taken to compel compliance with the Constitution, and that should be done through the enforcement of the Fourteenth Amendment, which calls for a reduction in representation in proportion to the number of citizens in any state denied the right to vote.

And now I cannot sit down after all without saying one word for the group of which I am a member.

The Negro in the matter of the ballot demands only that he should be given the right as an American citizen to vote under the identical qualifications required of other citizens. He cares not how high those qualifications are made—whether they include the ability to read and write, or the possession of five hundred dollars, or a knowledge of the Einstein Theory—just so long as these qualifications are impartially demanded of white men and black men.

In this controversy over which have been waged battles of words and battles of blood, where does the Negro himself stand?

The Negro in the matter of the ballot demands only that he be given his right as an American citizen. He is justified in making this demand because of his undoubted Americanism, an Americanism which began when he first set foot on the shores of this country more than three hundred years ago, antedating even the Pilgrim Fathers; an Americanism which has woven him into the woof and warp of the country and which has impelled him to play his part in every war in which the country has been engaged, from the Revolution down to the late World War.

Through his whole history of this country he has worked with patience, and in spite of discouragement he has never turned his back on the light. Whatever may be his shortcoming, however slow may have been his progress, however disappointing may have been his achievments, he has never consciously sought the backward path. He has always kept his fact to the light and continued to struggle forward and upward in spite of obstacles, making his humble contributions to the common prosperity and glory of our land. And it is his land. With conscious pride the Negro can say:

> This land is ours by right of birth,
> This land is ours by right of toil;
> We helped to turn its virgin earth,
> Our sweat is in its fruitful soil.
> Where once the tangled forest stood—
> Where flourished once rank weed and thorn,—
> Behold the path-traced, peaceful wood,
> The cotton white, the yellow corn.
>
> To gain these fruits that have been earned,
> To hold these fields that have been won,
> Our arms have strained, our backs have burned
> Bent bare beneath a ruthless sun.
>
> That banner which is now the type
> Of victory on field and flood—
> Remember, its first crimson stripe
> Was dyed by Attucks' willing blood.
>
> And never yet has come the cry—
> When that fair flag has been assailed—
> For men to do, for men to die,
> That we have faltered or have failed.

The Negro stands as the supreme test of the civilization, the Christianity and the common decency of the American people. It is upon the answer demanded of America today by the Negro that there depends the fulfillment or the failure of democracy in America. I believe that the answer will be the right and just answer. I believe that the spirit in which American Democracy was founded, though often turned aside and often thwarted, can never be defeated or destroyed but that ultimately it will triumph.

If American Democracy cannot stand the test of giving to any citizen who measures up to the qualifications required of others the full rights and privileges of American citizenship then we had just as well abandon that democracy in name as in deed. If the Constitution of the United States cannot extend the arm of protection around the weakest and humblest of American citizens as around the strongest and proudest, then it is not worth the paper it is written on.

MARTIN LUTHER KING, JR. (1929-1968)

"The Drum Major Instinct."

United States Baptist Minister, author, and social reformer, Dr. Martin Luther King, Jr. received the 1964 Nobel Peace Prize for his leadership of the nonviolent struggle for social equality. Born in Atlanta, Georgia on January 15, 1929, King later attended Morehouse College and took the A.B. in 1948, a B.D. in 1951 from Crozier Theological Seminary, and a Ph.D. in 1955 from Boston University. He came to national attention in 1956 as a result of leading a boycott of the public buses in Montgomery, Alabama to protest racial segregation. Dr. King played a major role in several civil rights demonstrations and became a compelling orator whose voice resonated with a revivalist's enthusiasm. His books contain his rationale for the philosophy of nonviolence that he espoused. On April 4, 1968 he was shot to death in Memphis, Tennessee.

Sermon printed with the kind permission of the Martin Luther King, Jr.. Center for Nonviolent Social Change, Inc., Atlanta, Georgia 30312.

This morning I would like to use as a subject from which to preach "The Drum Major Instinct," and our text for the morning is taken from a very familiar passage in the tenth chapter as recorded by Saint Mark, beginning with the thirty fifth verse of that chapter, we read these words: "And James and John the sons of Zebedee came unto him saying, 'Master, we would that thou shouldest do for us whatsoever we shall desire.' And he said unto them, 'What would ye that I should do for you?' And they said unto him, 'Grant unto us that we may sit one on the right hand, and the other on thy left hand in thy glory.' 'But Jesus said unto them,' Ye know not what ye ask. Can ye drink of the cup that I drink of and be baptized with the baptism that I am baptized with all shall ye be baptized. But to sit on my right hand and my left hand is not mine to give, but it shall be given to them for whom it is prepared."

And then Jesus goes on toward the end of the passage to say, "But so shall it not be among you, but whosoever of you will be the chiefest, shall be servant of all." The setting is clear. James and John are making a specific request of the Master. They had dreamed, as most Hebrews dreamed, of a coming king of Israel who would set Jerusalem free. And establish his kingdom on Mount Zion, and in rightousness rule the world. And they thought of Jesus as this kind of king, and they were thinking of that day when Jesus would reign supreme as this new king of Israel. And they were saying now, 'you establish your kingdom, let one of us sit on the right hand, and the other on the left hand of your throne.'

Now very quickly, we would automatically condemn James and John, and we would say they were selfish. Why would they make such a selfish request? But before we condemn them too quickly, let us look calmly and honestly at ourselves, and we will discover that we too have those same basic desires for recognition, for importance, that same desire for attention, that same desire to be first. Of course the other disciples got mad with James and John, and you could understand why, but we must understand that we have some of the same James and John qualities. And there is, deep down within all of us, an instinct. It's a kind of drum major instinct - a desire to be out front, a desire to lead the parade, a desire to be first. And it is something that runs a whole gamut of life.

And so before we condemn them, let us see that we all have the drum major instinct. We all want to be important, to surpass others, to achieve distinction, to lead the parade. Alfred Adler, the great psychoanalyst, contends that this is the dominant impulse. Sigmund Freud used to contend that sex was the dominant impulse, and Adler came up with a new argument saying that this quest for recognition, this desire for attention, this desire for distinction is the major impulse, the basic drive for human life - this drum major instinct.

And you know, we begin early to ask life to put us first. Our first cry as a baby was a bid for attention. And all through childhood the drum major impulse or instinct is a major obsession. Children ask life to grant them first place. They are little bundles of ego. And they have innately the drum major impulse, or the drum major instinct.

Now in adult life, we still have it, and we really never get by it. We like to do something good. And you know, we liked to be praised for it. Now if you don't believe that, you just go on living life, and you will discover very soon that you like to be praised. Everybody likes it, as a matter of fact. And somehow this warm glow we feel when we are praised, or when our name is in print, is something of the vitamin A to our ego. Nobody is unhappy when they are praised, even if they know they don't deserve it, and even if they don't believe it. The only unhappy people about praise is when that praise is going too much toward somebody else. But everybody likes to be praised because of this real drum major instinct.

Now the presence of the drum major instinct is why so many people are joiners. You know there are some people who just join everything. And it's really a quest for attention, and recognition, and importance. And they get names that give them that impression. So you get your groups, and they become the grand patron, and the little fellow who is henpecked at home needs a chance to be the most worthy of the most worthy of something. It is the drum major impulse and longing that runs the gamut of human life. And so we see it everywhere, this quest for recognition. And we join things, over-join really, that we think that we will find that recognition in.

Now the presence of this instinct explains why we are so often taken by advertisers. You know these gentlemen of massive verbal persuasion. And they have a way of saying things to you that kind of gets you into buying. In order to be a man of distinction, you must drink this whiskey. In order to make your neighbors envious, you must drive this type of car. In order to be lovely to love, you must wear this kind of lipstick or this kind of perfume. And you know, before you know it, you're just buying that stuff. That's the way advertisers do it.

I got a letter the other day. It was a new magazine coming out. And it opened up. "Dear Dr. King, as you are on many mailing lists, and you are categorized as highly intelligent, progressive, a lover of the arts, and the sciences, and I know you will want to read what I have to say." Of course I did. After you said all of that and explained me so exactly, of course I wanted to read it.

But very seriously, it goes through life, the drum major instinct is real. And you know what else it causes to happen? It often causes us to live above our means. It's nothing but the drum major instinct. Do you ever see people buy cars that they can't even begin to buy in terms of their income? You've seen people riding around in Cadillacs and Chryslers who don't earn enough to have a good T-Model Ford. But it feeds a repressed ego.

You know economists tell us that your automobile should not cost more than half of your annual income. So if you're making an income of five thousand dollars, you car shouldn't cost more than twenty-five hundred. That's just good economics. And if it's a family of two, and both members of the family make ten thousand dollars, they would have to make out with one car. That would be good economics, although it's often inconvenient. But so often...haven't you seen people making five thousand dollars a year and driving a car that cost six thousand? And they wonder why their ends never meet. That's a fact.

Now the economists also say that your house shouldn't cost more, if you're buying a house, it shouldn't cost more than twice your income. That's based on the economy, and how you should make ends meet. So, if you have an income of five thousand dollars, it's kind of difficult in this society. But say it's a family with an income of ten thousand dollars, the house shouldn't cost more than twenty thousand. But I've seen folk making ten thousand dollars, living in a forty and fifty thousand dollar house. And you know they just barely make it. They get a check every month somewhere, and they spend all of that out before it comes in, never have anything to put away for rainy days.

But now the problem is, it is the drum major instinct. And you know, you see people over and over again, with the drum major instinct taking them over. And they just live their lives trying to out do the Joneses. They got to get this coat because this particular coat is a little better, and a little better looking than Mary's coat. And I got to drive this car because its something about this car. I know a man who used to live in a thirty-five thousand dollar house. And other people started building thirty- five thousand dollar houses, so he built a seventy-five thousand dollar house, and he built a hundred thousand dollar house. And I don't know where he's going to end up if he's going to live his life trying to keep up with the Joneses.

There comes a time that the drum major instinct can become destructive. And that's where I want to move now. I want to move to the point of saying that if this instinct is not harnessed, it becomes a very dangerous, pernicious instinct. For instance, if it isn't harnessed, it causes one's personality to become distorted. I guess that's the most damaging aspect of it - what it does to the personality. If it isn't harnessed, you will end up day in and day out trying to deal with your ego problem by boasting.

Have you ever heard people that you know - and I'm sure you've met them - that really becomes sickening because they just sit up all the time talking about themselves. And they just boast, and boast, and boast, and that's the person who has not harnessed the drum major instinct.

And then it does other things to the personality. It causes you to lie about who you know sometimes. There are some people who are influence peddlers. And in their attempt to deal with the drum major instinct, they have to try to identify to so-called big name people. And if you're not careful, they will make you think they know somebody that they don't really know. They know them well, they sip tea with them. And they...this and that. That...that happens to people.

And the other thing is that it causes one to engage ultimately in activities that are merely used to get attention. Criminologists tell us that some people are driven to crime because of this drum major instinct. They don't feel that they are getting enough attention through the normal channels of social behavior, and so they turn to antisocial behavior in order to get attention in order to feel important. And so they get the gun. And before they know it they rob the bank in a quest for recognition, in a quest for importance.

And then the final great tragedy of the distorted personality is the fact that when one fails to harness this instinct, he ends up trying to push others down in order to push himself up. And whenever you do that, you engage in some of the most vicious activities. You will spread evil, vicious, lying gossip on people, because you are trying to pull them down in order to push yourself up.

And the great issue of life is to harness the drum major instinct. Now the other problem is when you don't harness the drum major instinct, this uncontrolled aspect of it, is that it leads, to snobbish exclusivism. Now you know, this is the danger or social clubs, and fraternities. I'm in a fraternity; I'm in two or three. For sororities, and all of these, I'm not talking against them, I'm saying it's the danger. The danger is that they can become forces of classism and exclusivism where somehow you get a degree of satisfaction because you are in something exclusive, and that's fulfilling something, you know. And I'm in this fraternity, and it's the best fraternity in the world and everybody can't get in this fraternity. So it ends up you know, a very exclusive kind of thing.

And you know, that can happen with the church. I've know churches get in that bind sometimes. I've been to churches you know, and they say, "We have so many doctors and so many school teachers, and so many lawyers and so many businessmen in our church." And that's fine, because doctors need to go to church, and lawyers and businessmen, teachers - they ought to be in church. But they say that as if the other people don't count. And the church is the place where a doctor ought to forget that he's a doctor. The church is the one place that the school teacher ought to forget the degree one has behind her name. The church is the one place where the lawyer ought to forget that he's a lawyer. And any church that violates the 'whosoever will, let him come' doctrine is a dead, cold church, and nothing but a little social club with a thin veneer of religiosity.

When the church is true to its nature, it says, "Whosoever will, let him come." And it does not propose to satisfy the perverted uses of the drum major instinct. It's the one place where everybody should be the same standing before a common master and saviour. And a recognition grows out of this - that all men are brothers because they are children of a common father.

The drum major instinct can lead to exclusivism in one's thinking, and can lead one to feel that because he has some training, he's a little better than the person that doesn't or because he has some economic security, that he's a little better than the person who doesn't have it. And that's the uncontrolled, perverted use of the drum major instinct.

Now the other thing is that it leads to tragic - and we've seen it happen so often - tragic race prejudice. Many have written about this problem - Lillian Smith used to say it beautifully in some of her books. And she would say it to the point of getting men and women to see the source of the problem. Do you know that a lot of the race problem grows out of the drum major instinct? A need that some people have to feel superior. A need that some people have that they are first, and to feel that their white skin ordained them to be first. And they have said it over and over again in ways that we see with our eyes. In fact, not too long ago, a man down in Mississippi said that God was a charter member of the White Citizens Council. And so God being the charter member means that everybody who's in that has a kind of divinity, a kind of superiority.

And think of what has happened in history as a result of this perverted use of the drum major instinct. It has led to the most tragic prejudice, the most tragic expressions of man's inhumanity to man.

I always try to do a little converting when I'm in jail. And when we were in jail in Birmingham the other day, the white wardens all enjoyed coming around the cell to talk about the race problem. And they were showing us where we were so wrong demonstrating. And they were showing us where segregation was so right. And they were showing us where intermarriage was so wrong. So I would get to preaching, and we would get to talking - calmly, because they wanted to talk about it. And then we got down one day to the point - that was the second or third day - to talk about where they lived, and how much they were earning. And when those brothers told me what they were earning, I said now, "You know what? You ought to be marching with us. You're just as poor as Negroes." And I said, "You are put in the position of supporting your oppressor. Because through prejudice and blindness, you fail to see that the same forces that oppress Negroes in American society oppress poor white people. And all you are living is the satisfaction of your skin being white, and the drum major instinct of thinking that you are somebody big because you are white and you're so poor you can't send your children to school. You ought to be out here marching with everyone of us every time we have a march."

Now that's a fact. That the poor white has been put into this position - where through blindness and prejudice, he is forced to support his oppressors, and the only thing he has going for him is the false feeling that he is superior because his skin is white. And can't hardly eat and make ends meet week in and week out.

And not only does this thing go into the racial struggle, it goes into the struggle between nations. And I submit to you this morning that what is wrong in the world today is the nations of the world are engaged in a bitter colossal contest for supremacy. And if something doesn't happen to stop this trend I'm sorely afraid that we won't be here to talk about Jesus Christ and about God and about brotherhood too many more years. If somebody doesn't bring an end to this suicidal thrust that we see in the world today, none of us are going to be around because somebody's going to make the mistake through our senseless blundering or dropping a nuclear bomb somewhere, and then another one is going to drop. And don't let anybody fool you, this can happen within a matter of seconds. They have twenty- megaton bombs in Russia right now that can destroy a city as big as New York in three seconds with everybody wiped away, and every building. And we can do the same thing in Russia and China.

But this is where we are drifting, and we are drifting there, because nations are caught up with the drum major instinct. I must be first. I must be supreme. Our nation must rule the world. And I am sad to say that the nation in which we live is the supreme culprit. And I'm going to continue to say it to America, because I love this country too much to see the drift that it has taken.

God didn't call America to do what she's doing in the world now. God didn't call America to engage in a senseless, unjust war, (such) as the war in Vietnam. And we are criminals in the war. We have committed more war crimes almost than any nation in the world, and I'm going to continue to say it. And we won't stop it because of our pride and our arrogance as a nation.

But God has a way of even putting nations in their place. The God that I worship has a way of saying, "Don't play with me." He has a way of saying as the God of the Old Testament used to say to the Hebrews, "Don't play with me Israel. Don't play with me Babylon. Be still and know that I am God. And if you don't stop your reckless course, I'll rise up and break the backbone of your power." And that can happen to America. Every now and then I go back and read Gibbons' *Decline and Fall of the Roman Empire*. And when I come and look at America, I say to myself, the parallels are frightening.

And we have perverted the drum major instinct. But let me rush on to my conclusion, because I want to see what Jesus was really saying. What was the answer that Jesus gave these men? It's very interesting. One would have a thought that Jesus would have said "You are out of your place. You are selfish. Why would you raise such a question?"

But that isn't what Jesus did. He did something altogether different. He said in substance. 'Oh, I see, you want to be first. You want to be great. You want to be important. You want to be significant. Well you ought to be. If you're going to be my disciple, you must be.' But he reordered priorities. And he said, "Yes, don't give up this instinct. It's a good instinct if you use it right. It's a good instinct if you don't distort and pervert it. Don't give it up. Keep feeling the need for being first. But I want you to be first in love, I want you to be first in moral excellence. I want you to be first in generosity. That is what I want you to do." And he transformed the situation by giving a new definition of greatness. And you know how he said it? He said now, "Brethren, I can't give you greatness. And really, I can't make you first." This is what Jesus said to James and John. "You must earn it. True greatness comes not by favoritism, but by fitness. And the right hand and the left are not mine to give, they belong to those who are prepared."

And so Jesus gave us a new norm of greatness. If you want to be important - wonderful. If you want to be recognized - wonderful. If you want to be great - wonderful. But recognize that he who is greatest among you shall be your servant. That's your new definition of greatness. And this morning, the thing that I like about it...by giving that definition of greatness, it means that everybody can be great.

Because everybody can serve. You don't have to make your subject and verb agree to serve. You don't have to know about Plato and Aristotle to serve. You don't have to know the second theory of thermodynamics in physics to serve. You only need a heart full of grace. A soul generated by love. And you can be that servant.

I know a man and I just want to talk about him a minute, and maybe you will discover who I'm talking about as I go down the way, because he was a great one. And he just went about serving. He was born in an obscure village, the child of a poor peasant woman. And then he grew up in still another obscure village where he worked as a carpenter until he was thirty years old. Then for three years, he just got on his feet, and he was an itinerant preacher. And then he went about doing some things. He didn't have much. He never wrote a book. He never held office. He never owned a house. He never went to college. He never visited a big city. He never went two hundred miles from where he was born. He did none of the usual things that the world would associate with greatness. He had no credentials but himself.

He was thirty-three when the tide of public opinion turned against him. They called him a rabble-rouser. They called him a troublemaker. They said he was an agitator. He practiced civil disobedience; he broke injunctions. And so he was turned over to his enemies, and went through the mockery of a trial. And the irony of it all is that his friends turned him over to them. One of his closest friends denied him. Another of his friends turned him over to his enemies. And while he was dying, the people who killed him gambled for his clothing, the only possession that he had in the world. When he was dead, he was buried in a borrowed tomb, through the pity of a friend.

Nineteen centuries have come and gone, and today, he stands as the most influential figure that ever entered human history. All of the armies that ever marched, all the navies that ever sailed, all the parliaments that ever sat, and all the kings that ever reigned put together have not affected the life of man on this earth as much as that one solitary life. His name may be a familiar one. But today I can hear them talking about him. Every now and then somebody says, "He's king of kings." And again I can hear somebody saying, "He's lord of lords." Somewhere else I can hear somebody saying, "Christ there is no east or west." And they go on and talk about..."In him there's no north and south, but one great fellowship of love throughout the whole wide world." He didn't have anything. He just went around serving, and doing good.

This morning, you can be on his right hand and his left hand if you serve. It's the only way in.

Every now and then I guess we all think realistically about the day when we will be victimized with what is life's final common denominator - that something we call death. We all think about it. And every now and then I think about my own death, and I think about my own funeral. And I don't think of it in a morbid sense. Every now and then I ask myself, "What is it that I would want said?" And I leave the word to you this morning.

If any of you are around when I have to meet my day, I don't want a long funeral. And if you get somebody to deliver my eulogy, tell them not to talk too long. Every now and then I wonder what I would want them to say. Tell them not to mention that I have a Nobel Peace Prize, that isn't important. Tell them not to mention that I have three or four hundred other awards, that's not important. Tell him not to mention where I went to school.

I'd like somebody to mention that day, that Martin Luther King, Jr. tried to give his life serving others. I'd like for somebody to say that day, that Martin Luther King, Jr. tried to love somebody. I want you to say that day, that I tried to be right on the war question. I want you to be able to say that day, that I did try to feed the hungry. And I want you to be able to say, on that day, that I did try, in my life, to clothe those who were naked. I want you to say, on that day, that I did try, in my life to visit those who were in prison. I want you to say that I tried to love and serve humanity. Yes, if you want to say that I was a drum major, say that I was a drum major for justice: say that I was drum major for peace; I was a drum major for righteousness. And all of the shallow things will not matter. I won't have any money to leave behind. I won't have the fine and luxurious things of life to leave behind. But I just want to leave a committed life behind.

And that's all I want to say...if I can help somebody as I pass along, if I can cheer somebody with a word or song, if I can show somebody he's travelling wrong, then my living will not be in vain. If I can do my duty as a Christian ought, if I can bring salvation to a world once wrought, if I can spread the message as the master taught then my living will not be in vain.

Yes, Jesus, I want to be on your right side or your left side, not for any selfish reason. I want to be on your right or your best side, not in terms of some political kingdom or ambition, but I just want to be there in love and in justice and in truth and in commitment to others, so that we can make of this old world a new world.

V

Introduction

This chapter includes six speeches by Mexican American males. These Mexican American leader-orators became vocal during the twentieth century to articulate the frustrations and needs of their people. Outspoken advocates of equal rights for the Mexican American—also known as Chicanos— they sought their constitutionally guaranteed freedoms by learning how to be sucessful in an Anglo-controlled society. They earned college degrees, they became politicians, they organized unions, and they proselytized activists from the public at large. Each speaker was driven by a deep-seated need to bring equality and justice to his less-privileged brothers and sisters. These Mexican American males achieved many of their accomplishments through the effective use of oratory.

The first speech is by the liberal politician Henry Gonzales who accused the Chicano leadership of MAYO, (the Mexican American Youth Organization) of reverse racism. Gonzales criticized the leaders of the youth group for their "passions that may be obscure." He stated that the people in charge are confused and "they want to promote and exacerbate fears that already exist." Gonzales warned that "It is not possible to pursue a just cause with unjust tactics." In his conclusion he told the Chicano activists: "It is not possible to expect sympathy or justice from those whom you threaten with hatred and destruction and it is self-deluding to think that there is no alternative to inviting violence." In spite of his liberalism Gonzales was unabashedly critical of the young Chicano activists.

The second speech is by the educator and poet Sabine Ulibarri. Ulibarri's central concern in this discourse is the frustration experienced by the Chicano pupil in the Anglo classroom. He knew how the student faced the language barrier, the "female-dominated classroom," the suspicious classmates, and the need to be someone "very special, a star, a hero, in order to win." Ulibarri's piece sent a message to the educator that valuable resources are lost when the non-Anglo student is forced into a state of loneliness by the Anglo educational system.

The third speech is by Cesar Chavez. This public discourse intended to give support and hope to the workers of the Economy Furniture Company. The employees had been without a contract for two and a half years. Chavez traveled to Austin, Texas to give an inspirational message to the men and women of that Furniture company. In one place in his address he said: "From this day on we're going to make progress. We're going to be dealt with as human beings. We're going to have our place under the sun— under the Texas sun. And we're going to be counted—as equals." At the close of his speech Chavez implored his people to obtain an education. He said it made possible the one way to deal with discrimination and other obstacles in the way of their advancement.

The fourth speech "Social Revolution in the Southwest" is by Rodolfo "Corky" Gonzales. This talk at the University of Denver is a description of the social tranformation that was beginning to take place at the time of Gonzales' talk. He mentioned several instances of student involvement and said: "And I think as I talk across the universities and as I talk across the country I find that the young people, the young radical is willing to move. He's rejecting, he's rejecting this society because he knows it's rotten." To illustrate his point that the Chicano as well as the radical college student intended to change society he remarked: "He's not the Chicano at the back of the church with his hat in his hand, saying his name is 'John Miller' instead of Jaramillo, to be accepted." The new, young, proud Chicano Gonzales said was "going to start identifying with who he is, what he is, and what his purpose in life is."

The fifth speech is by Jose Gutierrez entitled "The Chicano and Education." Gutierrez's speech is akin to a sociological treatise, in that, many of his ideas are descriptions of the way the Anglo's have treated the Mexican American. For example, he mentioned how history has been distorted, how nativism has created negative attitudes, and how the Anglo has an erroneous perception of the Chicano. At one point he said the educational system of the public schools "pushed out" young Chicanos. He queried: "How can we remain in a school that refuses to give you any kind of dignity; in fact takes steps to destroy you completely when you are six and seven years old." Gutierrez concluded his oration with a notably realistic statement: "We're talking about La Raza Unida, about the Gringo and soon. It may make us feel good, temporarily, but that's not reality, baby. You've got to work and work hard! You've got to help carry the load of others who may be weaker, who may have already pushed so hard and so long that they need some aid."

The sixth speech is by Henry Cisneros. Cisnero's public discourse is a message to America about its future. He addresses a number of topics that are crucial to our swiftly changing nation. He refers to social trends, the aging population, and ethnic minorities. One special point in the speech is Cisnero's discussion of "The Community as Focal Point" in which people are beginning to perceive that if they are "going to have a good life" then they are going to have to center on "community settings." He labels this "Amenity Planning." It is the enhancement of a community's cultural life, the visual arts, and music and other performing arts. It is the revitalization of "dying downtowns" by attracting new businesses, enhancing residents's lives, and producing excellence in the design of parks, streets, and neighborhoods.

Cisneros concludes his speech by noting that it is not a matter of whether or not a city will do these things for its improvement, but it is a matter of how it will be done.

n.b. As for the accents for Spanish words I wish to adopt the same practice as the authors of *A War On Words: Chicano Protest in the 1960's and 1970's*, Greenwood Press, 1985, professors John C. Hammerback, Richard J. Jensen, and Jose Angel Gutierrez. Those writers stated on pages 7-8 of their work: "Authors and publishers have been notoriously inconsistent and occasionally incorrect in their use of accents for Spanish words. This inconsistency creates confusion for some readers. Moreover, whether Spanish words are accented or not, those readers familiar with Spanish will be likely to know correct pronunciation while those unfamiliar will not. Therefore, we have decided not to accent Spanish words in this book." I will not accent Spanish words in this book.

Henry Barbarosa Gonzalez (1916-   )

"Reverse Racism."

Congressman and lawyer Henry Gonzalez was born in San Antonio, Texas on May 3, 1916 and he attended the San Antonio public schools. After attending San Antonio Junior College he took a degree at the University of Texas at Austin. In 1943 he graduated from St. Mary's University School of Law with an LL.B degree. Following a period of working at a variety of jobs he entered politics in 1950. He held positions on the San Antonio City council and the Texas State Senate—the first Mexican American Senator in 110 years. He has always been an outspoken champion of equal rights for all minorities. In 1961 he took a seat in the United States House of Representatives and has been regularly reelected to that position. In spite of his liberalism he has been unabashedly critical of Chicano activists. In that regard he is considered by many Mexican Americans as conservative.

The *Congressional Record* of April 28, 1969.

It is virtually impossible for any man of reason, intelligence and sensitivity not to see every day the destructive and corrosive effects of racism. It is virtually impossible for a man who has seen and acknowledges the existence of racism and its terrible results not to fight against it.

Racism is based on feelings that are beyond my power to fathom; it is fear, hatred and prejudice combined into a poison that divides men who under their skin are identical; it causes some to believe that they are superior to others; simply because they are one thing and others are not; and racism has given us all a burden of dishonor, guilt and grief.

The passions of racial hatred have been fanned high by fanatics and demagogues long since gone, but the poisons they disseminated remain with us still. Who can forget the contorted, hateful faces of people attacking innocent children who sought nothing more than to obtain equal educational opportunity, to enter schools freely without regard to the color of their skin? And who can forget the shameful defiance of law by George Wallace's stand in the doors of a great university, or the deadly riots at the University of Mississippi? And who can forget the fire hoses of Birmingham? Who among us did not feel shame on the day of the incident at Selma bridge? The passions that fueled those incidents, and that have bombed schools and churches, and that have created night riders and slick demagogues are with us still. The fears that created Jim Crow are still around, and we are burdened yet with the disaster that frightened *Plessy vs. Ferguson;* dozens of court decisions and hundreds of judicial orders have yet to erase the stain that decision placed on our legal system.

There is in physics a series of laws having to do with motion. There is a law of inertia which states that a mass that is headed in a given direction is inclined to continue in that direction until its force is spent or some superior force deflects or overcomes it. There is another law that states that for a given force there is an equal and opposite force; for every action there is an equal and opposite reaction. In the laws of civilizations gone by we can observe these same kinds of phenomena; and injustice will continue until its force is spent or until society rectifies it; and an injustice on one side may lead to another injustice on the other. Even as the poisons of racism are with us still, though its legal foundations be destroyed an gone for all time to come, so too can racism produce an equally deadly, opposite poison that can be called reverse racism. I say it can produce that opposite effect, for the law of politics are not so precise as the laws of physics; in social interaction there are no immutable laws. It is true that inertia exists in political and social systems, much as it does in physics, but an opposite action, a reaction, will occur only when the force of inertia is so great that only legitimate force can change it.

I beleive that we are attacking the forces of hate and bigotry, and I believe that however slowly and painfully we may be doing it, our country is overcoming the forces of racism. I believe that the racism is spent, or very nearly so, and that it is possible that justice in this land can be achieved within legitimate means.

I do not believe that violence is necessary to obtain justice, and I do not believe that hatred is necessary either; I do not believe that there is any reason why despair should be so great that reverse racism can be justified. Yet reverse racism, and reverse racists exist and their voices are loud, if largely unheard.

No man ought to either practice or condone racism; every man ought to condemn it. Neither should any man practice or condone reverse racism.

Those who would divide our country along racial lines because they are fearful and filled with hatred are wrong, but those who would divide the races out of a desire for revenge, or out of some hidden fear, are equally wrong. Any man, regardless of his ambitions, regardless of his aims, is committing an error and a crime against humanity if he resorts to the tactics of racism. If Bilbo's racism was wrong—and I believe it was—then so are the brown Bilbos of today.

Fifteen years ago as a member of the City Council of the city of San Antonio, Texas, I asked my fellow Council members to strike down ordinances and regulations that segregated the public faciilities of the city, so as to end an evil that ought never to have existed to begin with. That Council complied, because it agreed with me that it was time for reason to at long last have its day. Eleven years ago I stood almost alone in the Senate of the State of Texas to ask my colleagues to vote against a series of bills that were designed to perpetuate segregation, contrary to the law of the land. I saw the beginnings then of a powerful reaction to racist politics and I begged my colleagues to remember: "If we fear long enough, we hate. And if we hate long enough, we fight." I still believe this to be true. Since then there has been vast progress in Texas. I did not know how to describe to you the oppression that I felt then; but I can tell you that the atmosphere today is like a different world. Injustices we still have aplenty, but no longer is there a spirit of blatant resistance to just redress of just grievance. Yet despite this change in the general atmosphere, despite the far healthier tenor of public debate and public action today, I felt compelled almost exactly a year ago to address the United States House of Representatives on the continuing and alarming practice of race politics, and what I chose to call the politics of desperation.

There are those in Texas today—and I suppose elsewhere as well—who believe that the only way that the problems of the poor, and the problems of ethnic minorities, will be solved, is by forcing some kind of confrontation. This confrontation can be economic, or it can be direct and personal, but whatever form it may take, the object is to state in the most forceful possible terms what is wrong, and to demand immediate and complete corrective action. This tactic leaves no room for debate and often no room for negotiation, however reasonable that might be. It is the tactic of drawing a line and saying that it is the point where one system ends and another begins. This may not sound unreasonable in itself, and in fact the tactics of confrontation may have a place in political life. But the problem is that this deliberate and very often sudden confrontation might or might not be reasonable, and the demands presented might or might not be legitimate. The fact is that the tactic deliberately attempts to eliminate alternatives to violence, and it is therefore risky at best and at worst it can lead to disaster. This sort of politics is only one step removed from rebellion.

When the politics of race are added to the politics of confrontation, the makings of tragedy are abundantly clear. Race politics is itself highly unstable, and the same is true of the politics of confrontation. When the potent mixtures of long held passions are met on a hard line, but with justice obscured or perhaps lost in the midst of slogans, then great and perhaps irreparable damage can result.

There are those in Texas who believe that reverse racism can be mixed with the politics of confrontation, and that the result will be justice—or if not justice at least revenge. One cannot be certain whether the new racists want justice or revenge; only one thing is certain and that is that you cannot have both.

Probably the leading exponent of the new racism in Texas is the current president of the Mexican-American Youth Organization. This young man is filled with passions that may be obscure even to himself; he is ready to accuse anyone who does not help him of being a "turncoat" and anyone who opposes him of having "gringo tendencies" and concludes that most of the citizens of Texas are racists. Indeed, if he is opposed, he says, "...within a few years, I will no longer try to work with anybody." He is not certain of what he wants, except that he does not want to "assimilate into this gringo society in Texas." He wants to be "Mexicano" but not "Mexican." He wants to expose and eliminate "gringos," and by that he means killing if "it doesn't work." Of course, I am told that this young man never meant to make such threats, though he clearly uttered them. But those who utter threats and who clearly mean them, must be prepared to be challenged. And I do not believe that anyone who claims any position of responsibility, or anyone who pretends to leadership can make threats of killing and still be expected to be responsible.

This young man and his followers have attempted to find settings in Texas to practice their militance, and in particular to test out their theory of confrontation.

They distribute literature that is replete with hatred, and which builds on the supposed romance of revolution; too often one finds a photo of Juarez running alongside a photo of Che Guevara in MAYO literature. It would be hard to find a broader appeal than that to build a myth based on Guevara. They print such patent nonsense as "there is no bad luck, just bad gringos." They like to label enemies: "If you label yourself a gringo then you're one of the enemy." They give the overall impression that anyone the MAYO leadeship disapproves of is either a gringo or has "gringo tendencies" or is a "turncoat." Only one thing counts to them: loyalty to la raza above all else, and MAYO next. Of course they reserve the right to judge who is loyal and who is not.

Filling people with the bright phrases of revolution and the ugly phrases of race hate, MAYO seeks to find a confrontation. They sought it at Del Rio, Texas on Palm Sunday, but did not find it. Some of them sought it at Denver that same weekend, but did not find it. When they do, they have every likelihood of doing great harm to themselves and the cause they are supposedly trying to advance. The fuel of tension and the flame of passion make a dangerous mix.

I do not favor repression, because I do not believe that order is something that can be forced, at least not in an open and free society. I believe that there is enough good will and enough determination in this country that justice will prevail, and without resort to violence on one side or the other.

The young racists want to promote and exacerbate fears that already exist; they want to destroy what they perceive as an equilibrium, or a stalemate, that militates against their perception of justice. I do not think they will succeed. I believe that most Americans believe, as I do, and as Sandburg did, that:

Across the bitter years and howling winters
The deathless dream will be the strongest
The dream of equity will win.

This is no land of cynics, and it is no land of demagogues; it is a land wherein I believe reason can prevail; if it cannot succeed here, it can succeed nowhere.

I oppose this new racism because it is wrong, because it threatens to destroy that good will, that sense of justice that alone can bring ultimate and lasting justice for all of us. This new racism threatens divisions that cannot be soon healed, and threatens to end whatever hope there may be—and I think that hope is considerable—of peaceful progress toward one country, indivisible, with liberty and justice for all.

I do not want to see Texas riots and burned buildings; and I do not want to see men beaten, men killed, and fear rampant. I have seen it happen in other cities; I have seen fear and hate and violence destroy that essential impetus toward full justice. I have seen the ugliness of division and violence. I do not want to see it again, and I do not want again to have to fight against blind unreasoning intolerance. It is not necessary and it is not inevitable.

But the fruit of racism is not prejudice, fear and distrust. There can be no benefit from it, no matter how you color it with romance, or the new techniques of confrontation. There can only be tragedy from it. If MAYO gets its confrontation, it will not "crush any gringo who gets in (the) way."—"squashing him like a beetle"— and it will not "kick the door down." It will only find itself beaten in the end, and with it, the hopes of many innocent people who follow their false banner.

The new racists, if they succeed in their divisive efforts, will in the end only unloose destructive forces that may take generations to control, for those who plumb the well-springs of hate and break the dams of passion always learn too late that passions and hatreds are far easier to open than they are to close. It is not possible to pursue a just cause with unjust tactics, and it is not possible to justify cruel and deceitful actions by the end hoped for. It is not possible to expect sympathy or justice from those whom you threaten with hatred and destruction and it is self-deluding to think that there is no alternative to inviting violence.

I stand for justice, and I stand for classless, raceless policies. I stand for action, and I stand for freedom. I stand against violence, racism, and anyone or anything that threatens our ability in this land to govern ourselves as a free people.

Sabine R. Ulibarri (1919-   )

"The Word Was Made Flesh: Spanish in The   Classroom."

A professor of Modern and Classical Languages at the University of New Mexico Sabine Ulibarri presented the following address to the Cabinet Committee Hearings on Mexican American Affairs in El Paso, Texas in October, 1967. Ulibarri's opening statement in the speech is indicative of the central problem vis-a-vis the Anglo and the Chicano. "The language, the Word," he exclaimed, "carries within it the history, the culture, the traditions, the very life of a people, the flesh. Language is people." The imperative asserts Ulibarri is that the Chicano child be taught about "his own culture, his own history, his own contribution to the life-stream of his country." In addition, Ulibarri is known for his collections of stories *My Grandma Smoked Cigars,* 1978 and *First Encounters*, 1982.

Reprinted with the kind permission of the author.

In the beginning was the Word. And the Word was made flesh. It was so in the beginning, and it is so today. The language, the Word, carries within it the history, the culture, the traditions, the very life of the people, the flesh. Language is people. We cannot even conceive of a people without a language, or a language without a people. The two are one and the same. To know one is to know the other.

It is all a matter of language. It is a matter of economics. It is a matter of urban versus rural societies. Hispano children speak Spanish. Most of them are poor. Many of them live in the country. Many have recently moved to the city. Consequently, they are predestined to failure, frustration and academic fatigue in our national public schools.

The Hispano child begins with a handicap the very first day he shows up in the first grade. English is the language of the classroom. He speaks no English, or he speaks inadequate English. The whole program is designed to make him an Anglo. He doesn't want to become an Anglo, or he doesn't know how. He comes from a father-dominated home and finds himself in a female-dominated classroom. the Anglo concepts and values that govern and prevail are unintelligible to him. In all likelihood he comes from a low social and economic class, and there he is in Anglo middle class environment. Much too frequently he is fresh out of the country, and the city in general, and the school in particular, might just as well be in another planet. He probably feels very uncomfortable in the unfamiliar clothes he is wearing. He looks about him. The teacher, far from representing a mother image, must seem to him a remote and awe-inspiring creature, the children around him so friendly with one another and so much at ease, look at him with suspicion. There is nothing in the atmosphere from which he can draw any comfort. Everything he sees is foreign. The climate of sound is confusing, and frightening. The Hispano kid, Jose Perez finds himself in a hostile environment indeed. He will never, ever, forget this day, and this day will influence everything he does from then on. So the very first day in school, before he comes up to bat, he has two strikes against him. Before the coin is tossed, he has a penalty of a hundred yards against him. He has to be something very special, a star, a hero, in order to win.

Amazingly enough, he does much better in the primary grades that one would expect. It is later when he gets into deep trouble. In the primary grades the language of the classrooms is primarily what the linguists call "sign language," that is, the kind of language a dog would understand: "stand up," "sit down," "go to the blackboard," "open your books," "let's sing." The Hispano kid falls behind in the first grade, but not too much; his intuition and native intelligence keep him afloat.

Each successive year he falls farther behind, and as time goes on, as the language becomes more abstract and more transparent, the gap of deficiency becomes wider and wider—until he becomes a drop-out. We hear a great deal about the high school drop-out. We are going to hear more and more about the university drop-out. Imagine if you will the young Hispano with his high school diploma in his hot little hand who appears at the university. He's highly motivated, eager and full of illusions. He has been more successful than most. His family is very proud of him. He is going to be somebody. Then comes the shock. He finds out. He doesn't know how to read! His teachers never taught him how to read. How could they? They didn't know Spanish. They didn't understand his culture. No teacher can teach a second language effectively without knowing the native language of her students and understanding their culture. So the kid is suspended. No one can blame him if he feels cheated, betrayed and frustrated. He earned the high school diploma in good faith, and he put in more than the normal effort to earn it. And a valuable asset to our society is lost in anger and despair.

Above all the Hispano should be educated in his own culture, his own history, his own contribution to the life- stream of his country. An American citizen of Jewish extraction, who is proud of being a Jew, is worth more to himself, to his people and to the United States than one who is not. An Hispano who doesn't speak Spanish must choke on his chile.

Cesar Estrada Chavez (1927-   )

"Chavez in Austin, Texas."

Social activist and union organizer Cesar Chavez was born to a poor Mexican American family on their farm near Yuma, Arizona on March 31, 1927. Similar to many other southwestern farm families during the depression of the 1930's the Chavez family lost their land and were forced to become migrants working from harvest to harvest. Chavez spent his childhood in migrant worker camps. During that time he attended nearly thirty different schools. Eventually he reached the seventh grade. He served two years in the United States Navy during World War II. Out of the service he joined with farm worker organizers and became a volunteer with Community Service Organizations (CSO). From CSO he learned organizing and leadership skills. In 1954 after years of organizing and establishing chapters he became a paid CSO organizer. In September 1965 Chavez took a fledgling union of 1700 members into a grape strike in Delano, California. From that strike he received national prominence. The strike referred to as la causa was based on two principals: nonviolence and national liberal support. His strike actions often produced positive results for his workers. His union headquarters operates out of *La Paz* in Keene, California where he is working to reverse the trend against his unions and unionism in general. Chavez delivered this speech in Montopolis Community Center, Austin TX on February 6, 1971.

Reprinted from "The Rhetoric of La Raza" by Robert Tice, Unpublished Mss. Chicano Research Collection. Hayden Library. Arizona State University, 1971.

Muchisimas gracias, Senador Bernal, hermanas y hermanos. De repente es necesario hablar en dos idiomas y se me hace que ahora es una ocasion de estas. De manera que lo voy a tener que hacer es...si cuando hablaban del ingles y espanol preguntaba un senor que si cual era la diferencia. Y le digo que la diferencia era simple; que la idioma ingles es para los negocios, es para hacer negocios. Y la idioma espanol es la idoma de los angeles y tambien se us para enamorar. Les voy a resentar los negocios primero y luego termino con lo, con lo mas bueno.[1]

Friends, sisters and brothers, honored guests, I'm extremely pleased to be here in Austin and in Texas. I've heard so much of the warm Texas hospitality, and let me tell you that I really know what you mean when you say, when we hear in California about the Texas hospitality (a hearty "Right on!" from the audience). I think that everyone that I've come in contact to, with in this day and a half has been extremely gracious, and courteous and friendly. The only thing that I heard there's a newspaper in Dallas that didn't like the idea of my coming here or being honored (by the Texas legislature) and so ...but that's only one against millions since I've been here.

We're here to visit with you and we're here to share with you. But we're here mainly because there's a job to be done. We're here because we want to see Lencho Hernandez, Pancho Ramirez, *companero* (comrade) "Cowboy" Salcedo—all the strikers in Economy Furniture—to get a contract. And we're here to plan...and we're going to do our share in the boycott. We're now boycotting in sixty- five cities across the land, and when I get back to Delano I'm going to ask our boycotters to also include in their list all of the Economy Furniture labels so they won't be bought at the Montgomery Ward stores.

And I'm asking you to do a couple of things: First of all, don't buy at Montgomery Wards until they give up that scab furniture. And secondly, don't eat tacos. But if you need tacos, don't eat lettuce. But if you can't give up the lettuce in the tacos, then don't eat tacos and enchiladas for the duration!

We think that it's high time that these men and women who've been suffering now for two and a half years have a union. It's outright disgraceful that this employer, one employer is able to give, to hold people back from having their rightful place in society by having a union. It's high time that not only in Texas but in California— everywhere across this land—that workers should not be made to suffer for two and a half years for the right, to get the right that was given them, not by the employer, not by any legislation—by inherent right. They were born with the right to be able to join unions or union of their choice. And in this case, the people at Economy Furniture have been waiting for two and a half years. And I ask all of you, sisters and brothers, that from now on begin doing the job on Montgomery Ward and the other stores that sell the furniture. Tell them you're not going to buy *ni siquiera un carreto de hilo* [2] until they give up the furniture.

Anyway, we know things that the owners of the Economy Furniture don't know. We know that they've lost! We know that they've lost; it's just a matter of signing the contract. See, they don't realize that because the boycott is so powerful. The boycott is one of the most powerful weapons that poor people and people who struggle for justice have in this world. It's so powerful because it's really nothing more than the extension of love from one human being to the other. It makes it possible for people in the east coast and in California and in other places, in Texas, in Austin, and all over the world to help one another in a very direct way. And in the case of Economy Furniture by not buying at Montgomery Ward, but of buying that scab furnitue. In the case of the lettuce workers, of course, by giving up lettuce. You see, once you get that: Once you get the idea of a boycott in motion, in track, and it begins to function on its own, nothing in this good earth will stop it—except a signed contract.

I visited with Lencho and Pancho and Cowboy and the other leaders in the strike. I visited with them. I went to the picket line. I went to their office. I went to the picket shack and I went to their homes. And, you know, it reminds me so much of Delano. So much. The office, their office that they have. So much like Delano. And you see really why you might speak with envy because people that have been fighting for two and a half years must have a same kind of spirit. And they, they can destroy, and they can, and they can harass and they can imprison and they can do all sorts of things. But the spirit they will never destroy. And it's the spirit of our people that's speaking loudly today.

There's so many good people that must be thanked: the resolutions that were passed in the house and the senate; the resolution that was passed at the county, by the county commissioners (Bexar County, Texas); all of you good people here and last night at the airport.

And I think that we're getting together really because we accept that we've had it. *Ya basta* (That's enough!) From this day on we're going to make progress. We're going to be dealt with as human beings. We're going to have our place under the sun—under the Texas sun. And we're going to be counted—as equals. With no, with no offense to the present governors of the various southwestern states, I'm making a prediction that before the decade of the Seventies is over we're going to have a Chicano in one of those governors' seats. And when that day comes, when that day comes, we're not going to stop there. We'll want to go on to Washington too.

I'd like to mention a friend of yours and a friend of ours and a friend of our movement. *This* man who served us so faithful and so well and that's one of the reasons, I guess, he lost. We met him in Washington, in Delano, and we met him in Coachella (Coachella Valley, California). He was marching with us in 120-degree weather. A great, a great man, Senator Yarborough is here (Former U.S. Senator Ralph Yarborough of Texas, who received a standing ovation). He's a good man and a kind man. You know, I feel, I don't feel as secure now since he had to leave Washington. So it's going to be up to...if you don't want him in Texas, let us have him in California. We'll do something with him over there.

You know, the development of the power of the boycott is so garbled because it is extension of love from one individual to the other, and it creates a chain reaction that has tremendous consequences—good. It reminds me of a couple of stories: As the progress of the boycott in the grape went on and on, you know, for almost five years some very beautiful things happened. I could stand here and tell you for a whole day of many of the stories, but I'd like to tell you two short stories to illustrate to you what it means. Remember during the boycotting of grapes in Washington, D.C. there's a family there who's been very partial to our movement, a lady and a man with young children who used to speak of the grape boycott and the *campasino* movement in California almost daily at the dinner table. And one day the mother was out in the store shopping with one of her—a four-year-old girl. And they were pushing a cart down the aisle and they came upon this huge display of table grapes. And the little girl stopped and the mother was going to go by. And the little girl stopped and pulled her mother's dress and she said, "Mommy, when can I have some boycotts?"

And the other one is...I was in New York not long ago, and I was asked to speak at the, at the...cathedral, the large cathedral in New York. And I was coming into the, in the lobby to go into the cathedral. And we met this young couple with young kids. And he told me a little story that had taken place that morning. He got the kids up and said, "Look, we have to go to the cathedral and we're going to have to go hear Cesar Chavez speak." He asked the six-year- old kid, "Do you know who Cesar Chavez is?" And the little boy said, "Sure, who wouldn't? He invented grapes."

You know, one of the things we have to be very careful ourselves is that as we struggle for our own raza and as we do our thing to protect ourselves, we have to constantly think that there are also other people. Not necessarily Chicanos who are in our same condition or even worse. And many immigrant groups have come to this country and have pulled themselves by their own bootstraps and have forgotten about the next guy that was behind them. And so nothing really big was accomplished. But if we can turn that, if we can turn that around a little bit and bring ourselves up by our own bootstraps and then turn around and give our hand to our brother—whether it be black or Chinese or Japanese or Filipino, it doesn't really mattter. If we can do that then think that we're going to be the lasting glory of our own race and of our own country.

A while ago, while I was having another meeting at Lencho's house I talked to, to a black fellow who came to talk to me. And he was saying that was there anything we could do to begin to create a coalition to help one another. He said roughly there are twenty or thirty percent black and twenty or thirty per cent Chicanos. And then we need, what? ten per cent more, and we can get them from the students, so we'll have a majority. So, of course, I thought it was a great idea. It's easier to fight with the majority on your side than to be a minority; you know how it is to be a minority anyway.

I want to tell you one, one more thing: The International Upholsterer's Union is a good union. It's a clean union. It's a union that's been here with Lencho and the other strikers for two and a half years. Very few unions want to take on a losing fight, or what seems to be losing in the beginning. But it's also their contribution and their understanding that the fight to organize Economy Furniture is not really a fight to organize a single union in one locality, but it goes beyond that. You let those people at Economy Furniture get their contract and all of the organized plants in the area are going to get contracts. And it's going to be the beginning of, of a big drive among the Chicanos to get themselves organized into their own union.

Friends, let me close by just saying that we know that when human beings are concerned for one another; that the thing that all of us want when we're concerned for one another is to build and not to destroy. And we're concerned really for the dignity of man. We're saying that we're concerned not only for the guy that makes the headlines or the guy that has the money or the guy that has the good word. But we're concerned for the least of our own brothers. And we're concerned for human dignity. We're concerned for everyone and particularly concerned for the poor. And it's at this point then that I think that we realize that to do, to struggle and to struggle very hard and to want to change things so we can get justice and dignity for our people.

I think it means also we're concerned about, about the whole question of how we do it. Either we want a total victory or we want a half-baked victory. And I think all of us want a lasting, total victory. And I think the only way to get it is by working hard, understanding what we're doing. *Con capricho* (With firmness). Never give up. And I think doing it non-violently is going to really, really make the difference.

So you see, the power structure loves nothing better than to put you behind the eightball. Nothing better than to have you defending yourself instead of defending your people. And we have a, we have a, an agreement in our own movement that the movement shold be big enough, big enough so that it's never going to be defending things that are not right even though it may be someone in the leadership position of the movement. And secondly, should be small enough to take care of the smallest of the smallest problem that the least member might have. And I think that these are guidelines that one has to set for himself. If not, then it becomes a mass movement that tends to look just above people's heads and tends to count social security numbers instead of names, instead of living and breathing human beings.

One of our biggest problems today in America is that as organizations get big they get immobile because they stop being individual-oriented groups and they have become mass- oriented. And mass orientation sometimes tends to take away the very important, very important ingredient—you've got to be with people if your'e going to win.

I want to thank you very much for being here, and I want to say a few words in Spanish.

Todos sabemos, todos sabemos y Reconocemos la necesidad de unirnos porque en la union esta la fuerza, como dice un dicho mexicano. Hon hay, ustedes imagininse en el mundo, somos, aqui estamos seres humanos, reconocemos la necesidad de organizarnos. Hay que...la necesidad de organizacion es tan reconoscible que hasta las hormiguetas nunca andan salas, siempre andan en boncho ?verdad?

Dejenme platicarles un cuento que dice tambien la necesidad de organizacion. He platican que por alla en Mexico habia unos senoras que eran arrieros y que dia iban dos amigos uno, dos arrieros caminando por una vereda ?entienden espanol? Caminando por una vereda y uno de ellos era muy listo con el azote. El azote es un "whip" ?verdad? Y alli en esos contonrnos, en esos pueblitos. Era tanta la fama que todos las gentes que lo airaban lo adoraban porque era muy bueno para el azote. Iban caminando el y otro muchacho y este muchacho que iba con el iba tratando de sacar a ver de que tamano era,loiba testeando como decimos nosotros aca con mitad espanol...y cuando pasaron asi por un nopal alli donde iban por una lomita, le dice el muchacho al senor este le dice, mire senor, ustred que es muy bueno para el azote ?porque no corta esta tuna? Esta saco el azote ye cuando se arrimo a la tuna, le pego con el azote a la tune y la corto como si humiera sido con un cuchillo. Y luego la tuna asi en la vereda, asi la levanto. Y para esto el senor qua iba con el pues se quedo viendo pues se quedo bien sorprendido, se quedo muy admirado.

Caminaron por poco y llegaron a un arbol que estaba una rama asi enfrente y al pasar les iba a tumbar el sombrero. Dice, mire senor, usted que es tan bueno para el azote ?porque no corta esta rama? Pues saco el senor, cuando se iba arrimande alli, saco el azote y tumbo la rama, la corto con el azote y pues ya pasaron ?verdad? Pues esto le causo grand admiracion al senor; ya no hallaba que hacer. Iban caminando y ahi paso asi una mosca asi volando, y dice !mire aqui a mosca! El senor saco el azote y le corto la cabeza y para esto ya se quedo el hombre que no sabia ni que decir; se quedo tan sorprendido que ya no podia ni hablar.

Siguieron andando un rato, y para esto paso una avispa. Y dice, mira ahi va una avispa peguele, Y el senor saco el azote ye se encamino a pegarle a la avispa y luego se detuvo. Dice, mira, a esas no, dice porque ellas estan organizadas si le pegoa una se me echan todos encima. Y entonces asi debe de ser con nosotros. Un mal en contra de uno de los nuestros es un mal en contra de todos nosotros. Yo me acuerdo no hace mucho tiempo en California cuando trabajabamos como mi gratorios, se quebraba el carro—eran carros viejitos en aquel entonces estabamos mucho mas jovenes que hoy. Y se quebraba el carro a la orilla del camino y no pasaban ni diez minutos y el primer carro de mexicanos que pasaba se paraba, y ni tenian ni un mexicano en esos lugares. Y ahora hermanos, entre mas grandes se hacen, los carros y mas grandes las carreteras mas aprisa corren los mexicanos en los carros y menos atencion ponen a sus hermanos.

Tenemos que empezar a cambiar; si deveras creemos por nuestra raza; el que es buen juez comienza por su casa empieza. Si deveras creemos en nuestra raza, entonces comenzar a hacer tales cuales. Com quien pensaba que anos ?quien pensaria veinte anos atras que hoy en la moderna ibamos a mandar a mi papa y a mi mama a una "rest home" porque ya estan viejites? !Nunca! Era una verguenza hacerlo. Nos quedabamos con ellos porque es parte de la familia, es parta de la unidad, de la seguridad de la familia mexicana y mas y mas la gente, como dice, no mira, todavia tiene sesenta anos—setenta y cinco—hay que mandarlo a un "old men's home" a este hombre. Una persona que me dice que quiera a su raza pero desprecia a su padre no me puede convencer que deveras quiere a su raza.

Porque una persona que no puede ni llevar a su mama cuando todo es porque tiene que ir a trabajar porque si no trabaja no garra dinero y si no garra dinero la television de color y el carro y el "vote." No me pueden decir que, que tienen mucho carino por su raza. Porque es la unidad basica y si no tenemos tiempo para nuestra madre, entonces ?comos vamos a tener tiempo para los demas?

Son los ideales que comienzan a cambiar. Y mientras no cambiemos y no paremos y examinemos ?porque esos ideales cambian? No porque nosotros estemos cambiando sino porque la presion sobre nosotros. Si lo que sucede aqui es de que hay lo que nombramos la presion en este pais es tremenda del...no tienen que hacer super consumidores para poder vivir. Si vamos a una tienda a comprar una cajetilla de cigarros, llevamos cinco dolares mal, mal, mal que tengamos que salir, vamos a gastar tres o cuatro dolares. No teniamos que gastar pero lo gastamos. Porque ahi tienen los dulces alli abajo con muchas luces; todo lo que venden con luces y colores, aunque no necesite uno, va y lo compra porque en la mente le estan poniendo a uno que lo tiene que comprar aunque no quiera. Si tiene uno un carro del "1970" ya quiere uno; viejo, compreme un "71" porque mi comadre ya compro uno del "71'"

De manera que cuantas presiones comienzan a tener impacto en nuestros ideales y en nuestros valores. Mientras no cambiemos eso vamos a ser vintimas de lo que criticamos. Ya para terminar, a mi se me hace que uno de los mejores trabajos que se esta haciendo es con la juventud. Los jovenes estan llenos de idealismo, llenos de fuerza; pueden trabajar dia y moche y no estan decepcionados si son ellos los wue van a comenzar a guiar. Son ellos los que tenemos que darles el aporjo pa' que nos puedan guiar. Y de todos lados nos llegan recordatorios ?verdad? Yo tengo un nino que tiene doce anos y trae el pelo, a mi se me hace que esta muy largo; y pues les dije pues cortate el pelo; y me dice, no yo no me lo quiero cortar. Y le dije, pues yo no le hablaba asi a mi papa ?verdad? Y entonces comence a tratar de buscarle manera y entonces dijo mire ?como le gustaria si comiera lechuga? Y alli se acobo la cosa.

La necesidad por la educacion es una necesidad basica y por tanto si no entonces nos atascamos como un grupo. De manera que el pleito para componer a todo el sistema que existe que esta contrario a nuestro...a nuestros constumbres, que esta contrario a lo que nos han ensenado y a lo que pensamos ser; el asunto de como nos educan y las discriminaciones y muchas veces los problemas que pasamos como ninos, a pasan nuestros ninos porque asunto de educacion no esta adecuada, no esta hecha a tal manera que vaya a tratar con nuestros propios problemas de antecedencia, de raza y en fin hay que cambiarlos. Si no lost cambiamos va a pasar lo que paso en Mexico una, un chiste que me platican. Alla en, durante la epoca del Presidente Cardenas se hizo una campana tremeda para educar a todo mundo. Todo nino que taba analfabeta de iba a educar y comenzo el gobierno a organizar escuelas por todos lugares de Mexico. Pero un lugar, alla un pueblecito en la sierra que se les olvido. Y cuando los residentes alli en las campillas miraron que, pos, que el gobierno los habia olvidado, ellos se pusieron a hacer una escuelita de adobe. Y luego buscaron a ver quien iba a ser la progesora y habia una nina de catorce anos que habia ido al dos anos de escuela "so" la pusieron de progfesora. Ya tenia como pos ya como unos seis meses con los nonos, cuando el gobierno en Mexico, en la capital, se dio cuente de que estaba esa escuelita alli, y mando a un, a un inspector federal de educacion que fuera a ver que estaba pasando en la escuelita. Cuando llego el inspector federal a la escuelita esa entro y dijo, senorita, yo soy inspector federal de educacion y como hay costumre alla salga se para afuera porque quiero hacerle un examen a los ninos a ver que had aprendido. Pues la senorita se salio para afuera y dice el profesor este, este inspector, les dice a los ninos, miren, voy a hacerles un examen sobre la historia de Mexico a ver que han aprendido. Habia como unos treinta ninos alli donde dice miren ?quien de ustedes me puede decir quien fue el que le quemo los pies a Cuauhtemoc? Y todos...se quedo serio, nadien respondio. Dijo bueno diganme ?quien le queno los pies a Cuauhtemoc? Y se miraron uno al otro y nadien respondia. Al fin un, un nino alli mas atrevido se paro y dice, mire, Senor inspector, yo le quiero asegurar a usted que aqui somes muy pobres pero somos muy honrados asi es de que nadie de nosotros le quemamos los pies a Cuauhtemoc. Y entonces para la educacion nuestra no queremos que pase esto. Tenemos que saber quien la quemo lost pies a Cuauhtemoc.

3

Muchisimas gracias. !Que Dios los bendiga!

Footnotes

1 Thank you, Senator Bernal (Texas Senator Joe Bernal of San Antonio, who introduced Chavez), sisters and brothers. Suddenly it is necessary to speak in two languages, and it appears that now is such an occasion. So we must use both languages—English and Spanish. A man was asking what difference there was between them and I said, "English is the language of business; Spanish is the language for angels and people in love." I'll start with business and end with the better part.

2 not even a spool of thread

3 We all know and recognize the need for unity. And as a Mexican saying goers, "In unity there is strength." We recognize the need for organizing ourselves. Even little red ants are never alone, always in a bunch.

Let me relate a Mexican anecdote about two men, two cowboys walking on a path. And one was recognized in the surrounding towns as being very good with a whip. The man with him was testing him. As they passed a cactus plant he challenged the other to use his whip to cut off the fruit (called tuna) of the cactus. He did so as though he were using a knife. The companion was impressed. As they passed a tree the companion challenged the man to cut off a branch with his whip; the man did a clean job of it. And this caused a great reaction in the other cowboy. They walked some more and a fly passed by. Being challenged again, the man cut off the fly's head. The companion—left speechless—really didn't know what to do any longer when a bee came and he said, "There, get that bee!" The whip handler thought a minute and said, "No, they're very organized; if I harm it I'll have thousands of its kind on me soon." So then that is how we ought to think: a wrong doing against any one of us is a wrong doing against all of us.

I remember back in California, working as migrants; we were young then. Our car would give out. And as we waited on the roadside, if a car with Mexicans came they would stop immediately to help us poor Mexicans. But now with cars so new and big the Mexicans will rush by not noticing his brother in trouble.

We must change, really begin to look out for our raza. Charity begins at home. For instance, who'd ever have dreamed that one would even consider sending Mama or Papa to a nursing home because they're old? Never! Shameful! Because we have family unity and love as Mexicans. A person who claims love for his raza but does not love his father can't convince me he loves his people. A woman who can't take in and take care of her mother because she has to work because she wants a color TV or a new car can't tell me she'll be able to love her raza. Because if we have no love for our mother how can we love anyone else?

Those ideals are changing. And that's not because we are changing but because the pressure's on us. The pressures in this country are tremendous; it is seeking to make super-consumers of us in order to live. The rat race. My wife wants to change her 1970 model car because my godmother has a 1971 car. All these pressures are having an impact on our ideals and values. As long as we let it, we'be victims of what we criticize.

Now that I'm going to finish, I must say that one of the best jobs being done is by youth. They are strong and can work day and night. They're not disappointed in knowng they are tomorrow's leaders. They need our encouragement and support. We get reminders from all over: My twelve-year-old son had his hair too long, I thought. He said he didn't want to cut it. I said I didn't speak that way to my father. When I just could not get to him, he asked, "How would you like it if I ate lettuce?" The discussion ended.

Education is a basic and important need. If we have no education we are stuck—spinning our wheels—as a group. All this existing system that is contrary to our traditions and customs—that is contrary to what or how we think of being—can be fought only with education. The way we are educated, the discrimination, the problems we have as children is because our education is not adequate. Our education is not enough to deal withour problems of ancestry and raza. If we don't learn to educate ourselves something may happen like what took place in Mexico during President Cardenas' term:

It's a joke they tell me about—there was a tremendous campaign to educate the people. Every child of age was to be educated; schools were organized. But they forgot a small place up in the mountains. And when the authorities found out there was no school, they built one of adobe. They found a fourteen-year-old girl, who had two years of schooling, for the teacher. When the governmental authorities heard of this they sent out an inspector to the little place in the mountains. When he arrived he identified himself and asked the teacher to leave the classroom so he might examine the pupils as to their learning. The federal man told the nearly thirty children that he was going to test them on Mexican history: "Who can tell me who burned Cuauhtemoc's feet?" No one answered. Upon the inspector's insistence one boy stood up and said, "Listen, Mr. Inspector, we are very poor but we are very honest, I guarantee you none of us burned Cuauhtemoc's feet!" We must know everything; we must know who burned Cuauhtemoc's feet! Thank you. May God bless you.

Rodolfo "Corky" Gonzales (1929-   )

"Social Revolution in the Southwest."

Community organizer, political activist, and Mexican American leader Rodolfo "Corky" Gonzales was born in the Mexican barrio of Denver, Colorado in 1929. A high school graduate of the Denver public school system Gonzales soon took an interest in boxing and became a Golden Gloves champion winning sixty-five of his seventy-five fights. In time he became active in politics and rose to district captain in democratic politics in Denver. In addition, he was coordinator for Colorado Viva Kennedy campaign for President and later he became Chair of a local anti-poverty program. Gonzales instituted the Chicano Youth Liberation conferences which helped to define goals for Mexican American youths. In 1970 he started the Colorado Raza Unida party (RUP). Concerned with self-determination and nationalism Gonzales's imaginative poem *Yo Soy Joaquin* has become a centerpiece of Chicano pride, especially among young people. The poem has been printed in anthologies, performed or recited on the stage, quoted by several writers, and analyzed extensively. *Yo Soy Joaquin is* "Corky" Gonzales's significant contribution to Mexican American culture. Gonzales presented this speech at the University of Colorado on November 20, 1967.

From "The Rhetoric of La Raza" by Robert Tice, Unpublished Mss. Reprinted with the kind permission of the staff of the Chicano Research Collection. Hayden Library. Arizona State University, 1971.

I'm not so used to sitting down while I speak, and I'm pretty sure Mr. Tijerina would rather be in action when he speaks. But it's also nice to be here and want to welcome all of you and. . .

My subject for the night is "Social Revolution in the Southwest." And I think that looking out among you that I can see some familiar faces of those people who have considered themselves revolutionists in a spirit. And you might want to know in what fashion this revolution is taking place and why it's taking place. And if you really want to know why, I'll give you some reasons of why it is taking place and why it's going to come to a more positive head.

First of all, we just have to look at the overall situation across the United States, and especially across the Southwest, for the Mexican American, Spanish American people. And realize that the Southwest is very much like one of the colonies that have been colonized by England, by some of the European countries and those places that are economically colonized or militarily taken over by the United States of America.

We have the same economic problems of those under- developed countries, and we suffer from the same type of exploitation and political strangulation. And because of this, you have a new cry for militancy and a new move. And in doing this we start to evaluate what this society is all about. And we start to point to the defects; we start to point to the real errors in a society that our leadership in the past, including many of us who have wandered through a maze of looking for the right answers to tell the people, the right answers for ourselves. And we come to grips with ourselves and realize that the old methods are passe; the involvement in politics in two political bodies that are stagnant, that are status quo have nothing to offer us.

A Democratic Party that offers a fine philosophy and then doesn't live up to it; a Democratic Party that produces George Wallaces and Connallys from Texas and produced the different bigots that operate in a political world under the guise of these great, tremendous philosophies left down by some of the real progressive legislators of our time.

So, we look at this and we realize that the only thing we can gain from the Democratic Party, in most cases, is to become involved with a status quo party that is willing to use us, willing to give us double-talk, willing to give us window-dressing and appointments and patronage. But this does not change the social problems of the poor. It does not change the social problems of different ethnic and minority groups.

The Republican Party is sterile, has nothing to offer, and they have money to deal with. And they have the same kind of a patronizing offer of jobs for one or two and nothing of progressive changes for the rest of the people.

So we evaluated this and looked around and started to inform and started studying the economics of our Southwest and realize how we've been HAD. And how we've been USED. And we start to want to make some changes.

And how are we going to make these changes? We had to start from the very bottom. It's true that most revolutions are usually started from the middle class, and we think that the middle class of this society is also revolting against its own society. That's why you have young radicals who are rejecting the war that they didn't make, rejecting the draft that is, so far as they're concerned, unfavorable, illegal, and they're rejecting the very morals, or lack of morals, in a society that is supposed to present all these beautiful answers to decent living and to fair practice and to democracy and equality and all these fine words that you read from your Constitution, your Bill of Rights.

All this fine talk that comes out of the double-talking mouths of politicians. And you hear these words and the whole society across this country does not believe a politician. You don't believe L.B.J. because you know he won't rat on Bobby Baker. You know that the industrialists in this country are making millions of dollars out of the Viet Nam war. That even the whole economy of this nation is balanced on that war, when that money utilized for war could be utilized for progress, could be utilized for housing, could be utilized for medical care and education for all people without any concern of race, creed or color or ethnic group. Instead it's utilized because there are people that are power-hungry and money-hungry and they're willing to make their dollar. It doesn't matter how much of the blood is stained on it or whose blood it is.

And I think that when we recognize the hypocrisy of our country's political nature that you're going to reject it because politicians are not elected by the majority of the people in this country or the electorate. They are elected by a minority that is mesmerized and hypnotized by a high- priced, Madison Avenue technique, TV, until most people are punch-drunk when they go into a voting booth. Not only that, the candidates elected are, either have to be rich to be independent or they are bought by private industry and big business. Therefore, the laws and legislation of our country are not made for the people, by the people. They are made by lobbyists who are hired by the industries, hired by business people. And those civil rights laws that do come out of our legislatures are so riddled with amendments that they're not worth the paper they're written on. Because those laws do not change the engrained racist attitudes that this educational system teaches to our young people, teaches to the Anglo, teaches to our people. And because of this attitude—and I can point to many examples and maybe you read your own books and look at them—you realize that for us, or for we the people with the Spanish names who are considered foreigners (when there are too many of us around) by easterners who didn't know we existed here this side of the Mississippi, don't realize the history. And those westerners who are here already have the attitudes, the traditional attitudes that the southern whites have about the black man. And therefore we have this to battle with.

And where do all these attitudes come from? They come from the educational system, from your mass media, from the story structure from movies and TV that place the Mexican American in a second-class category or in a villainous category. The man with the moustache usually symbolizes the guy with a nife in his pocket or the guy hiding behind a tree or coming out "Don't I know you from somewheres?" with a big rifle in his hand. He's usually the bandit or if it's in SHIP OF FOOLS he's the pimp or the prostitute. If it's in THE DIRTY DOZEN he's now the cowardly Chicano that's gotta crawl up that rope like a speed demon because he's afraid he can't get up, he can't cut it.

And yet, the only time we're afforded any of the real contributions we give this nation and we gave this nation is when we die overseas for somebody else's battle. When we die, you know, in the movie scripts for the Anglo captain, then we're heroes. When we die for unjust and unholy wars that are created by the administration, by the business people and military complex, then we are heroes. We're afforded, you know, medals; we're given credit for being part of our great nation. And then we look back and realize what has happened to us.

And the revolution is going to start because young people are now starting to evaluate exactly how they've been oppressed, exactly how they've been exploited, exactly how thay have been HAD. And how their people were too kind, too good, and too warm-hearted to open their arms to the raging hordes of people that come across the Mississippi that had no knowledge of the mining industry, had no knowledge of the farming industry, had no knowledge of the ranching industry. And yet were taught, and all the techniques that were here were already here and were *given* to these Anglo oppressors and aggressors. And the young people are starting to realize that they are not a conquered people and nobody, NOBODY really knows anything about the Treaty of Guadalupe-Hidalgo.

I think Mr. Tijerina has taken on a tremendous battle, but he has it based on international law and he has it based on legality and facts. And it points to a very, very stark reality that none of our young people have learned who they are, can identify with anything but the Anglo success image, and therefore he'd have to reject what he is and commit ethnic suicide and sometimes it's escapist to gain a degree to escape from the misfortunes and the tragedy of a defeated people. And therefore, he doesn't have to identify with defeat as seen in the eyes of this society. He can identify with success and the better things of life. But he also must, or is expected to commit ethnic suicide to do it.

And I say that there's no right for any nation, for any people or any society to destroy a culture, to destroy a people. We see that day in and day out. Economically the majority Anglo controls the economics, controls the employment doors. And then wants to make all the decisions. When there is money that comes in to, say the War on Poverty, say Labor Department training program, *they* make the decisions. They're the Big Brother that hands down the ideas. They come into our communities to try and organize us, and they create more problems than if they stayed out of our community, went back to their middle- class society and taught them something about living, something about life.

And we have been sort of disturbed because our leadership is kind of confused. We've all been confused and looking for the direction and the way. And the direction does not lie, does not lie through picketing and demonstrating any more. We have tried the due processes of going through laws to gain redress and police brutality and legal and legitimate legislation to try to put it across, to change differences, to change the migrant labor laws, to change the different laws that affect us. And what has happened? We run up against brick walls.

It doesn't matter when a so-called "liberal" candidate sponsors raising the minimum, the minimum income, or the minimum wage from a dollar and a quarter to a dollar thirty- five and think he's giving us something. Because a man that's not working doesn't care if it's three dollars and sixty cents if he can't get a job.

And this is what happens in the Southwest. I don't know of any Anglos that find it very hard to be hired in the Southwest. And yet the natural resources of our people, the people who are here and part of the earth find it very difficult to find a job on the same level. Because they immediately point to technology, skills and all these different qualifications even to go out and shovel sand for the state highway department. The different requirements or tests that have nothing to do with the job you're going to do, have nothing to do with the type of work that you can do, have nothing to do with your actual capability of doing the work. But is nothing but a restriction and a barrier to one group from the other. A complete, a complete control by an Anglo society that has turned its back on the culture that exists here.

Now this is a nation of tourists. The people go all over. They go to Italy, to look in on little Italian villages and to enjoy the culture and rub shoulders with tradition. They go to Mexico to look at little villages and look at the people and the architecture and the art. And they come back and they're cultured because they can say "manana" and "si, si" and a few things like this, you know. Then they come here, right in their own country and they destroy culture. They destroy a whole nation of people. You know, if you live in a country club area of Denver and you can speak Spanish, you're cultured. If you live down on Armour Street, you a Mexican. And this is the difference. (Applause)

Now when you start evaluating what all the contradictions of our country are. What you're taught in the school that is right and what is wrong. And then you go out into real life and you find out exactly that it's a lie. Because in your school system you've been taught that the only successful image is an Anglo image because that's the only successful man. Whether it be Custer who just got shot down again (he's off the TV) but they're going to make a hero out of him because he had yellow hair. And we all know that he was exposed as a psycho, as a ego-maniac, and as a fraud. Now he comes back because he is this image and they try to develop him as a hero-image again.

Now this myth has to be destroyed. And we have to destroy it. And I think that the young people of this nation should start realizing that the people that they're really fighting are the Establishment, is the Society, is the System. And you have to look at it and realize that it is completely contradictory to itself.

That they teach, they teach us that the only image of success is Anglo, so that our young kids can become Anglos and become patriotically brainwashed to go die and show their *machismo* (which our people do by gaining more medal of honors, congressional medal of honors than any other ethnic group, who die double the proportion of their numbers in the armed forces so that they do have this guts.) But we have to direct that guts into a revolution— here where the battle really is, not over there to kill other people that are protesting or revolting for their own self-determination. We have to start self-determination here at home. And how do we do it? We have to destroy a myth. A myth that is taught to us by the school system, by the biggest financial combine and brainwashing machine in the history of our nation and in the history of the world.

Now, one of the other things that is taught in this educational system is that if you have money, you're a success. And it doesn't make a difference whether you're a cheat or a liar or a hypocrite or a coward. As long as you have money in this society you are recognized as a success. So that as the poor people go to school and try to identify with success, they're going to reject their homes; they're going to reject the places they live; they're going to reject the values that their forefathers or their fathers and mothers are giving them. They're going to reject their culture and their language because this is not Success. And Money is Success. Love of human beings, love of each other is not important. The only thing is "Make that fast buck."

And everybody gets wound up making this fast buck so much that he forgets what life is all about. He forgets what love is all about. Even a process of complete extermination of himself, driving himself toward neurosis (sterilization of the soul is what I call it) and, I think, only to gain a fat stomach, to make sure he has two cars in his garage, that he keeps his house bigger and better than his next door neighbor's and his grass is cut shorter. He doesn't give a damn about his next door neighbor or the man across the street or anybody else as long as they don't confuse or rather disrupt the crease he's putting on the sofa from his behind watching the TV. And he doesn't want his TV program disrupted. Because he's going to sit there like a drone and a fat slob and forget about the rest of the world as long as he keeps his belly full, as long as he *thinks* he's educating his children who are going to go and learn something. (And I hope they're learning more than he did. I hope they're learning that he is responsible for the society that exists today.)

And I think as I talk across the universities and as I talk across the country I find that the young people, the young radical is willing to move. He's rejecting, he's rejecting this society because he knows it's rotten. And he's not rejecting it because a young, or an old, or a middle-aged Mexican sits up here and tells you, "This society is rotten." Because I'm not part of your society. I don't want to BE that part of your society. I want to eat steak and *frijoles* and *chili verde* at the same time. but I don't want to have to live the kind of life that's being lived by your society.

And what are your own experts telling you about this society? What are your young writers, your intellects telling you? When a man reaches the real pinnacle of intellectual achievement, he rejects this society. He doesn't accept it. He realizes what it is. And I think that this has to be engrained. Not only into the middle- class radicals who are coming away from their society, but we have to teach our young people who are the first ones to be brainwashed by this machine. We have to teach them what the economic strangulation is. How they're politically exploited. How they are mistreated.

And now the young Anglo who's taking part in the anti- draft movement, the young Anglo who's taking part in the struggle against the phony institutions like the CIA. These people are starting to begin to realize what the police state is all about. What we've been suffering for centuries, you're just learning about right now when you go out on that picket line. (Applause)

There must be a tremendous fear going through the hearts of the people who love to be policemen. They can't cut it any other way. But they can get identity, they can get a uniform, a badge and get authority because they can't cut it on the outside field and get this kind of position. And the type of person that's drawn to a police force is usually not "love thy neighbor" type. He's looking for a place where he can exert this force, he can, he can exert this superiority that he feels he has, this authority.

I saw a picture in the FREE MOVEMENT newspaper and I saw a young, slender Anglo student being held by four massive policemen: one guy had a billyclub against his throat, one guy had his arm bent backward this way, and the other guy had him by both shoulder blades. And I just wondered to myself, how much fear and cowardness, how much insecurity do those four big slobs have that one of these can't handle this one young kid? And have enough respect for him and make the kid respect him that they can have a meeting of the minds, and if the boy is wrong he's going to be arrested, right. And if he's not wrong he's got a right to speak his piece. But why? It takes four, you see. But you're just learning about it. Sometimes it take ten and twelve cops to do up a Chicano down at Curtis Park or to do up a Chicano down on Armour Street. Or to do up a Chicano down on Lincoln. You see, it takes ten and twelve, it takes the whole riot squad and they all come down and get their licks in.

But you're just learning about it now. We've been bleeding. And we've been getting angry. And we've been, our people have been brainwashed by the media. They want to be conventional; they don't say that this is wrong. They don't want to be labeled "communists" or "radicals" or "un-American." They don't want to be labeled anything because they are very patriotic and proud of their country. So what happens? We have to teach them not to be blind in their loyalties, to find out, to evaluate.

And let them tell you that the young students across this nation, not so many in our western universities; it seems that the urther east we get from the border line the more conservative some of our graduates get, meaning those of my name, my name and other names that are Spanish. But we find some of the students out of Cal State, out of San Jose University, out of UCLA, out of the University of New Mexico. Young kids are writing revolutionary songs. Young kids that are going to be the new intelligentsia or a real revolution are coming forth, just like their doing in the black revolution. Young kids that are not subjected to inferiority complexes that their fathers knew. Nor the beatings on street corners like we knew. Young kids who know what their rights are and are not going to accept a second-class status.

And these young people are going to have to have a new direction. And that new direction is going to be to destroy, to destroy a system that is rotten. We say, when you say that, when you say "destroy" then you mean complete anarchism. I don't mean that. Why doesn't everybody, like they tell us about being un-American, why don't they live up to their Constitution? Why don't they glorify Thomas Paine instead of George Washington? 'Cause they don't have enough guts for the truth. You know there's a big difference. Why don't they tell you the real history in your history books? Why do they make Sam Houston a hero of the Alamo? They say he was an American. He was a Mexican. He was a traitor. He swore allegiance to Mexico. For a Mexican land-grant to develop the area. And Travis and Bowie were mercenaries. They weren't heroes.

You better start learning about who our people were. You better start learning about what is happening across the country, and we're going to teach our people in the *barrios*, where they're mean enough to fight, not just be weak. And re-direct their attitudes and their directions toward the real revolutionary thought instead of going outside and showing their *machismo* and blasting each other in some alley, on some street because they're mad and mean and they know there's revolution in them but they don't know where to go.

We're going to teach them where to go. We're going to teach them about this system, the economic problems. We're going to teach them about the legislation that is rotten and corrupt. We're going to teach them about the politicians that are using our people. We're going to teach them about the welfare system that perpetuates itself in order to keep people in bondage. We're going to teach them about the different government finance programs that take our best leadership and rob us of our leadership. We're going to teach them how not to starve, but how to live. And this is a big difference.

We're going to teach them about the fact that a guaranteed income of the armed forces is not the most heroic thing to do. That if this school system can teach them how to be patriotic and how to die for this country— and it doesn't matter what the reason is—we're going to teach them how to die in the *barrios* for a real reason and a real cause.

And you're going to see the Mexican American will be fighting a revolution entirely different than you've ever seen in this country because you have people that have guts and courage. You have people that show it overseas. And you have people that will be selected because they love their own people. And when they learn about the directions they won't be blasting each other. They'll be picking the right spots. And they won't be burning their own houses down nor their brothers' houses down. There's going to be a selectivity that you've never seen before.

And they're looking for methods, they're looking for strategies. And the strategies are coming about. And there are new young, militant people all across the Southwest. You don't read about them. Rap Brown might burp in Maryland and you get a headline. But they don't want to let a nationalism set in for the Mexican American, Spanish American. Because they know that if the world of Tijerina, if the words of radicals, if the statements that we say here tonight are spread across the news media and are identified with by young Mexican Americans, Spanish Americans in the *barrios*. If it's identified with and they feel it's information that they've been looking for, then they'd probably have the strongest force they've ever fought against.

Because we're the last. We've been here the longest of anybody. This is our land. This is our country. And let me tell you this: We have still not completely been absorbed by this society. By this monstrous new creation. I don't call it a modern culture 'cause there's no culture in this society. It's just a society. The values are mixed up and corrupted because you contradict or rather this society contradicts everything it does. It comes in here and it gives the money. It gives you OEO grants to help you become educated. The minute you try to become educated the way YOU want to be educated in the land of the free, then certain limitations are placed on you. And the CIA is part of your organizations. And if you don't allow the CIA to come in and brainwash you, then you're suspended from this school. Right? (Over Applause) And this is what takes place in a society that contradicts itself from day to day and adds a statement as it's made.

We say, and we've watched our own leadership. You know, the Anglo society doesn't have an exclusive right to horses' asses. We have our horses' asses too. And we have to point them out and wipe them out. We have to obliviate them. If it's economically we're going to stop buying from them. But we're going to teach them that what they gain from us they bring back and help the people to grow. Help our own people to educate themselves. Help our own people for their own self-determination.

We know and we have to point to this: there is a tremendous nationalism in our people even though they say there is factionalism, the fight. Of course, when thirty Anglos go up for one job it's "competition." When two Mexicans go up for one job "they're fighting each other." You see, that's the difference. When you do it, it's all right, meaning the Anglo society. When we do it, you know, it's not competition, we're killing each other off. When we make a sort of top-level position immediately we're considered leaders, you know. And they create our leaders for us. And this, again, is because they want to make the decisions in everything that's done.

And we will start making our own decisions. We will make our own mistakes. And if they're wrong we'll suffer from them. We can't do any worse than we've done with your leadership. 'Cause your leadership has corrupted us. Your leadership in a city where we face a society is where our young people become involved in crime. The *campesino*, the men, the *caballeros* from the *ranchitos*, the migrant laborers, the villagers, the people from the mountain villages. What do they bring to the city and this society? They bring honesty. If nothing else they bring a purity that can never be matched. And what does this society and this city do to them? Why do we end up on the bottom of the ladder economically? Why do we end up on the top of the ladder in the juvenile courts and in the phony institutions? It's because we are the oppressed. And this is where society destroys us.

And I think that our young people better start evaluating this. And those who go to the life of crime are not following the footsteps of our culture. They are following the footsteps of this society that produces ghettos and crimes, discrimination and prejudice and phony legislation. And contradictions that nobody can stomach anymore. And I think when we start evaluating this and we start telling our young people, "This is it. This is the way it is." Because we want to set a nationalism into our young people that they can identify who we are. That they can identify with Tierra Amarilla as a battlecry symbolic of *machismo* and a right to self-determination. That we can identify the *huelga* in California as a new move for economic betterment. That we can identify the different statements and philosophies of a new breed of people that are willing to put their life on the line and their head on the line and call a spade a "spade."

And as I said before it doesn't matter what color a man is. He can still be a sellout. Santa Ana was a Mexican and he sold Mexico out. Batista was a Cuban, he sold all of Cuba out. And Trujillo was a Dominican and he sold out the Dominican Republic. And Franco is a Spaniard and he strangled the freedom of all Spaniards. He's a dictator. This doesn't mean that if there's a Gonzales, a Trujillo, a Santa Ana that's a despot that he's going to be accepted. This is the thing we have to start teaching our young people. Because even if these top leadership buy the Establishment then they are the enemies. And this is what we have to teach. This is what we have to say.

And there is a revolution brewing. It's not amazing and it's not impossible. Because as I said, the minimum wage has usually been the hand that kept the sleeping in line and keeps him sleeping. And then along comes the OEO to try and keep him sleeping more. And then along come a fifteen dollar, a five dollar raise in Social Security to keep him sleeping more. But let me tell you that a minimum wage—I'll say it again—does not mean a damn thing to the guy that doesn't have a job. And there's no employment for him. What does he care about a minimum wage? He wants food in his belly, he wants his children fed and educated. And there is possibility of revolution.

If a hundred and twenty cities can go up in flame in one summer, what can the new conditioned, experienced people that took part in that be planning for next summer? What new plans and ideas do they have? What did they learn from it? They learned a lot. And as the black revolution starts, this is the one thing: the *mexicano* could not identify very well with picketing. He didn't want to be conspicuous. He didn't want to be, you know, a bad show. So he didn't like that. So we found only a certain portion would do it. It was still negative to him. It was still something he rejected. But let me tell you that the young cats across the Southwest are really identifying with the violence in the black movement. They're really identifying with Action 'cause this represents a *machismo* that can come out of the *barrios*.

And I talked with a group of East L.A. boys. For some five hours they kept me and we talked about strategies, we talked about avenues. And they want to use the legitimate, they want to use the pressures, they want to change different things, they want equality. But they're mean and bad enough to burn the whole town down if it don't come about. And that's the difference. He's not the Chicano at the back of the church with his hat in his hand, saying his name is "John Miller" instead of Jaramillo, to be accepted. He's now a young, proud Chicano that's going to start identifying with who he is, what he is and what his purpose in life is.

And I think this is important. As some people say, what's in the bag for you? And the bag is creativeness. If you are creative you'll join the revolution, 'cause you're going to change something. You're going to mold a whole new future. And it's worth twenty or three thousand times more than sitting making that crease in front of the sofa, in front of the TV. And I'd rather be out in the front line of the revolution than hiding in a closet. Thank you very much.

Jose Angel Gutierrez (1944-   )

"The Chicano and Education."

Organizer, activist, judge, and educator Jose Angel Gutierrez was born into an upper-class Mexican immigrant family in Crystal City, Texas in 1944. At the age of twelve Jose Angel's father died forcing the family into farm work around Crystal City. He attended school in Crystal City and distinguished himself in high school as a champion debater and student body president. He obtained a B.S. in political science from Texas Arts and Industries University at Kingsville. In 1968 Gutierrez took an M.A. in political science at St. Mary's University in San Antonio. In 1976 he completed a Ph.D. at the University of Texas at Austin. While a student at St. Mary's Gutierrez and some companions organized the Mexican American Youth Organization (MAYO) as an agency to bring about social change. Soon he became a member of the city council of Crystal City and a member of the school board. In 1970 he and a group of Mexican Americans created a political organization La Raza Unida. After prolonged political activity he took teaching positions first at Colegio Cesar Chavez in Mount Angel, Oregon and later he became Associate Professor in Social Sciences at Western Oregon State College in Monmouth. Gutierrez delivered this speech to La Raza Unida Party in San Antonio Texas on May 4, 1970.

From "The Rhetoric of La Raza" by Robert Tice, Unpublished Mss. Reprinted with the kind permission of the staff of the Chicano Research Collection. Hayden Library. Arizona State University, 1971.

Es bonito saber que lo aprecen a uno, pero es mas bonito saber que a uno le hacen prequentas, y lo mantenan el pueblo en una forma que uno se debia de tratar como iqual. Como demonstraciones se anque se crerar mucho el corazon am veces nos yega al corazon asta aqui ariba y nos hecha perder muchos de nosotros. Mucho cuidado.[1]

Se trata de poyitos, se displumo. No se vaja a meter la idea que ende ceara el guyo canta.[2] No, this is very much of a surprise that we have quite a large turnout. I see some fine people in the audience. There is President Jernigan, Vice President Rhode, some other people that I am not familiar with the faces. I have been removed from A&I for some time, I am glad that you are all with us, *especialmente mis hermanoes que estan aqui. Aber se podemos aprender un poquito y ayuudar a pensar un poquito mas claro tambien.[3]*

It is surprising, to repeat it again, that we have such a turnout. Perhaps some of you that worked so hard in trying to get me to come and arranging the facilities and the wonderful hospitality so far should remember that perhaps it's best to get all your posters torn down, be denied radio time and be denied your space in your ad in the Kingsville RECORD. This is the way your get a large turnout.

I wanted to discuss about three areas in the topic of the Chicano and education. In these three main areas are a little historical documentation to exploit the myth that we are ahistorical, that we have no history — apena naciemos ayer[4]— that we just began our campaign just a few months ago. And I would like to explain the role that economics play into education, and then give a little explanation of what little contact I've had with people involved in making the educational issue for Chicanos a major portion of the Chicano movement as a whole.

You know, we have been treated and discussed, analyzed, studied for quite a long time, and presently we're the favorite of the social scientists and the foundations. They like to know what kind of suntan lotion we use, or is it natural? They'd like to know why the accent that we have is not quaint like LBJ or Lady Bird's (President and Mrs. Lyndon Johnson), or the late dear President Kennedy and other notables that we have who also speak in a funny way. But that's quaint, that is very, oh, you could say they have much finesse because they're able to handle their accents in a very polished and intellectual way, sort of sophisticated. But when it comes to the Chicano, you know, we have a problem with our tongue — somehow it's different you know. Sera por el chile.[5]

In the process of so much study we have discovered and it is printed in many, many books — some of which you are quite familiar with. Dr. Madsen and his book THE MEXICAN AMERICANS OF SOUTH TEXAS, Lydia Heller and her book on Mexican American youth and even some of our brothers. . . Julian Samora and his book about forgotten Americans and many, many others who . . . Latin Americans in Texas and on and on and on . . . with a whole host of materials that are available that reflect the discoveries or the conclusions of all these studies. And most of these studies are what Dr. Romano, uno de los meros guyos at Berkeley de nuestra raza,6 calls "social science fiction" because we can take the case of myself and many of you who are here, who have worked on many projects together. You know *la raza* is supposed to be less ambitiously motivated and underachieving and non-goal oriented and all this other jargon that is thrown about that only social scientists understand, and the only thing we know is that no valemos, es lo que decien, no damos el ancho.[7]

It's quite perplexing or quite ironic that in the one breath they say all that and in the other breath, you know, you get accused of doing too much, you organize La Raza Unida, you work on MAYO, you lecture, you do that. They don't say your ambitious. They don't say your're energetic. They don't say you're very, you know gung-ho. They think you're a trouble maker, you know. You deviate. You know there is something wrong with you. You care too much, you know. This is what has been the major fallacy, or one of them, in the treatment of Chicanos by people doing research and writing books; and this — keep in mind that after the research is published — this is the same material that is used to formulate policies by institutions such as this one, such as welfare system, such as the churches, such as the foundations, such as the Boy Scouts. Many, many things are affected by the writings of these social scientists because we have a big thing about people with credentials who go on to college who somehow survive and manage to keep on to graduate school and acquire your silver stars and bronze stars for valor, purple hearts for injuries and so on. Then you're worth listening to 'cause obviously you had enough courage and enough perseverance to through all that and do something in writing, put it down, and obviously you must have something on the ball. And this is what then we receive in terms of policy.

This is why, you know, we get such crazy notions that we should not give welfare to women who are with men, that they should be by themselves in order to qualify. Because obviously we're just promoting illegitimate kinds of relationships, and we're promoting all kinds of promiscuity. And this is the same kind of notion that will get into an institution — particularly in education — both the secondary schools, junior high and elementary grades and even universities where they say there aren't very many qualified Chicanos to give jobs.

This is why this university, while it may have approximately thirty-two per cent Chicanos in the student body, has Chicanos on the staff, on its faculty that you can count on this hand and have one finger left over. Actually there are eleven people here. I grossly distorted the fact because it's eleven out of 278, and I don't think that's too much of a distortion. And besides, the one that we do have here, four of them are in what they do the best job at and are capable of and that is in Spanish. Obviously, every Chicano has got to know Spanish! This is why in secondary schools any Chicano that comes out of college, whether he gets a degree in physical education or a degree in biology, is either coaching and is given Spanish to teach.

Well, anyway, I'm delaying. . . The point that I wanted to make is that the policy that is coming out of institutions is based on the findings of social scientists who not only have distorted and grossly made and invented new myths, *menteres,*[8] and stereotypes, *cruidids, que uno tiene.*[9] But they also made us creatures that are apolitical and timeless, somehow just suspended there, you know. We're incapable of any kind of thing that would change the society. *El destino, tu sabes nos tiene acuachos en el vetable no mas. Y decien que nos gusta, por eso somos chaparos.*[10] And they also said that we were just born yesterday.

You know, I can remember this is particularly the case with the good liberal groups, for example THE TEXAS OBSERVER — the liberal magazine that has been accused of even being Communist, not by us of course. We think it's full of crap! These people in 1963 when Crystal City first came into notoriety had big headlines that said, "The Sleeping Giant is Awakening." They had this picture of this giant like the person in Jonathan Swift's book GULLIVER and all these little pegs around him with chains se estavan revantando. El gigantato se tava levantando.[11] And they explained that this was the beginning in Crystal City. Well, se paso el tiempo,[12]and I guess we must have discovered tranquilizers or something because in 1969 uvo una marcha chincotuda[13] in Del Rio and habia como tres mil chiquaspatas ayi asiendo un poco rido y protesta.[14] And again THE TEXAS OBSERVER — in light of this tremendous outpouring of Chicanos into the streets to make La Raza Unida more than a slogan but a reality, to join their brothers there in Del Rio. Again the headline came, "The Sleeping Giant is Awakening." So I guess he went to sleep for another six years.

This is how we get our history not only distorted and erased but even rewritten. So that we are made ahistorical, that we just don't have anything at all, that somehow we've been here and nobody has discovered us not even Columbus. And this and tiny other things have led into an attitude by the dominant group — let's be kind tonight, Anglos— that has a name to go with a long, long time in history. It's called "nativism" movement. Some of you have read of the Know-Nothing Party; these people did not take after us because they didn't know about Chicanos due to the fact that there are people who live in Connecticut who think that Texas is still part of Mexico. They are correct basically but the political reality is just not that. Anyway, they were anti-Irish and anti- Catholic. So, you know, we picked up a little bit of that later on, or rather we got the hell later on because we're still very much Catholic. These people, it seemed like a little track record, that every decade they would switch. First it was the Irish; then they (sic) were the Germans. In fact, good old Benjamin Franklin, the man we read very much about as being one of the founding fathers, was very much a Gringo in his time — except he wasn't taking on Chicanos, he was against the Germans, and very much in the fashion of what is said today in the public schools and the philosophy that permeates the education department here. He said that the language of German should be prohibited because it was un-American. He did not like the idea of German newspapers circulating because he couldn't understand them. That was somehow subversive. And that they should be good Americans of they wanted to sit in the legislature. And this is what the beef was all about. Germans were getting elected into positions of political representation. So we have quite a number of characters involved.

Woodrow Wilson was another character who not only in addition to being president of the Unites States also had some very strong ideas about what constituted a good American. He said that any body in this country that had any loyalty to a particular ethnic group was un-American or was not a good American. You hear this today, si comes tacos, si te gusta Augustin Ramirez, si creases que erea[15] Chicano then you're basically un-American. Even though like fools we're getting killed in Vietnam, the guys are being super-patriots, we're still basically un-American.

So you see, out of this nativism thing that hit every root that is coming to this country we also are a part of this. So we're not exclusive, we haven't been discriminated because we're the only ones left now. Everybody's got it at one time or another. So some people in the social sciences developed some theories about this. They say, well you know, this is very typical; I guess it's just common human nature that somebody different comes along you would like to look at his peculiarities and make comments about them. Try to make him different; try to make him more like you. That is all fine and dandy. And they devised about three different ideologies that have had great effect of impact on the American mind; that is the notion of the melting pot, the notion of cultural pluralism and the notion of even secession, some people should break away.

The black movement of a guy by the name of Rose and a guy by the name of Garvey, who wanted to create a black nation not only here in the United States but outside of the United States. And currently in the Chicano movement there is some talk about *creating* Aztlan, and right now it is in the psychological stage. We feel that we are already a nation *en espirito y en realidad queremos a . . .bajo el concepto del ser Aztlan.* [16]   So these three things have caused us some particular pain; because here in the state of Texas it was a strict demand that we conform. And I'm jumping history a little bit. This was after the war, after the Mexican War and it was the United States who declared war on Mexico and not the other way around.

Well anyway, out of that same age, fear — after the war — fear of Mexicans because we were lazy, we were ingorant, we could not take care of Texas, nor California, nor New Mexico, nor Arizona, nor Utah, nor Montana. You know, we were just incapable and we were not suited for government. And this notion of "manifest destiny" got thrown about, and this was a key phrase that was used during the period of social darwinism. Darwin was the one who talked about "survival of the fittest," which is romanticized by many as being, you know, a way to prove that you are a superman. And this is the big notion behind what Hitler did in Germany in trying to prove the superiority of the Aryans, the Germans. And this got twisted around because basically it's just a very animalistic kind of concept como lost animales[17] Survival of the fittest, *el perro mas grande, el marrano mas trumpudo aguarado la mascorca.[18]*   Out of this came Manifest Destiny.

This was President Polk, another of our ex-Presidents, a fine man—had he lived today he probably would have been my best friend—had the idea that since they were so good at bringing democracy in the United States and having such a fine system that it was the white man's burden, you know, to extend the United States from the Atlantic to the Pacific and to the North Pole and to the South Pole. This was their Manifest Destiny; *el destino de eyos no era andar el vetable, era de ser el   mero bueno.* [19]   It is very easy to adhere to that conclusion. We all think we've got something going pretty good. Personally you like the way you look, you like the way you stand, you like the way you talk, and so on. So this cat just figured that he was so good and that the country was in such fine shape that it ought to be extended over to all the South and Latin American countries.

This is where we became the objects, you know, of being foreign, being alien, being unwanted and being conquered. And what happened to them in the process was that they got very fearful of strangers and customs that were alien to them, but they rationalized it by saying it was not any good. And they put the value on the wrong thing; they were superior culturally, linguistically, strength, wealth and in the form of government they could devise, and so on. So they began the process of cultural genocide. And this is what we still have today. The reason why our parents today and many people who are in this audience and around this building have a very low English formal educational attainment. This is not by accident. This is in the program designed for Chicanos for a long time, in fact, it is still here in the schools today; like in many other schools. Now I know that I am picking on A&I a bit, but it is my school and I feel somewhat bad that corrections have been slow in coming along — although they have been coming.

You don't have the services for these thirty-two per cent Chicanos of which approximately seventy per cent are all getting into the educational field. Any kind of planned curriculum that would arm them with the tools to teach other *Chicanitos* (diminutive for Chicanos) — maybe even their own kids — and let's say bilingual education or bicultural programs or education, Chicano studies and this kind of stuff.

This is tantamount to the cruel attitude that goes on into our public schools of pushing out eighty per cent of all Chicano students in this state; because we are not dropouts, we are ushed out. How can we remain in a school that refuses to give you any kind of dignity or any kind of identity; in fact take steps to destroy you completely when you are six and seven years old, and it's a thirty-five year-old-average aged person who is picking on that kid? Making him suffer the psychological trauma of peeing in his pants because he can't say properly, "May I be excused?" and he says, "Please be excused?" or "Can I be excused?" Or being embarrassed because you have the nerve to bring those ridiculous-looking *tortillas* y chorizo para la escuela? Que realaga, vato.[20] And even further, to tell you when you're sitting there at age eleven, twelve, thirteen, fourteen, fifteen, sixteen you still are the son of Santa Ana who killed those glorious heroes at the Alamo. Somehow it's just like the cowboys and Indians all over again. Everytime the good guys and Gringos win, they're good guys, victorious, you know. But everytime we, like the Indians, do something we're the masochists.

You see the way history is written: just like in the comic books. And this is the way it's still protrayed on television and 20th Century-Fox. You don't believe me? Go see *Butch Cassidy and the Sundance Kid*; nobody else but two super-human Gringos could take on the whole armies of South America. And even with some of our dear friends — the people with the long hair and so on, drug culture and freaks — they too are not devoid of all this mental illness. 'Cause you see *Easy Rider*; you know that whole easy ride was made possible by a dumb Chicano pusher who couldn't even have the sense to sell the drug at a good price and take a trip himself.

This carries on into the secondary schools when the Chicanos begin to socially interact with the people they have recess with; the same people that sometimes referred to them as "Mexicans" and "greasers" and so on. But any of the names didn't have any meaning; they still enjoyed activities on both sides, enjoyed each other's company, playing with each other. And then they realized there were young males and young females; and, oh boy, they soon realized that Chicanos must have a separate standard of beauty. It was inconceivable to have Chicanas elected as the most beautiful girl. And perhaps she could move her fingers; they're good haciendo tortillas,[21] maybe one of them could be a twirler.

So the same thing carried over into the scholarships. Obviously Chicanos didn't have enough here (in the head); they were meant for field work and the few that did, well, those were "different" Mexicans. They were Joe and Pete, you know; Fred, Mary; they were good All-American types. They were going to succeed; they had those qualities; they had ambition; they wanted to improve themselves, pull themselves out by their own bootstraps. They had a goal in mind: they wanted to be better than their parents; they wanted to get educated. But then they were also denied entrance into being the most representative of your school, or even competing in the forensic interscholastic league.

But some people managed to survive. But all of us remember and know these things are fact. It wasn't long ago that this change began taking place in the schools, both secondary and colleges when Chicanos began entering in great numbers so that they had to shift from a popular and democratic procedure of election of all those things to a more restrictive school of elitist kind of procedure that is very anti-democratic. Teachers then got into the selection of cheerleaders, twirlers. Teachers got into the selection of who was scholastically adept so they could join the honor society; and the outside judges were brought in to determine who should be Miss Crystal City or Miss Carrizo Springs Schools. And then, of course, the counselors and the administrators determine who would be the Chicanos who should be given the opportunity to participate in speech and given the opportunity to go and debate and maybe even participate in the Pan American United Nations model, you know.

So this burst the bubble in many of the Chicanos' heads because what they were reading in books — of what was supposed to be — was not what they were doing day to day; and they learned that that kind of behavior is described as hypocrisy, described as lying, described as cheating. And we didn't like it; it still goes on. Because it leaves you deeply scarred in the mind. It makes you very bitter, very upset, very angry and you want to change those things NOW. But then you are accused of being too impatient, too militant. And "change comes about slow. You have got to wait. Every group, every minority group has had to work to get to where they're at." Somehow they excuse themselves of any guilt. This is the historical kind of thing that we have experienced, and I'll give you some specific cases that came just from the Chicano movement for education and these are just some general comments:

This has been our personal history; what we are experiencing. This is why we have such a tremendous push- out rate. The schools are not attractive to us. The schools are not the place to be if you want to be comfortable. Schools are not the place to go and look for models and people who can inspire you. In other words, school is a fake; there is nothing there for real. So many Chicanos get turned off, but some make it despite of all the odds. Another problem that plagues us — or those few who made it — is the fact that we have economics that gets into the picture (sic).

Most of us, at one time or another, lived in rural areas where there was very little money; most of the school districts have a low tax base. There is not enough money for this or for that, and the priorities determined by the state department of education determined by the federal government somehow excluded us. And it wasn't until recently that the Office of Education opened up the Spanish speaking division and began developing the bilingual education program and subsidizing schools, colleges and even high schools through programs like NYC, who now are allocated some money, the Work-Study program and career opportunities and different things like this. But the economics that I have talked about were the built-in economic problems that we had; we have been pushed into a subservient role of providing services. We're the ones who go out and get the cherries and strawberries that go along with your ice cream sundaes and your Post Toasties in the morning, and the one that takes care of the beef steaks that you eat at your Sunday barbecue. This guy is out on Tuesday at five o'clock in the morning checking the cattle and picking the lettuce that is served here — even though it's non-union; it's picked by unions but shipped non -union. Chicanos have been doing tremendous amounts of work.

In fact, during the Thirties with the great repatriation movement of moving Chicanos that were already here back into Mexico; Chicanos who came here much in the fashion of the people who came from Europe where they put tags on them because they didn't know English. They didn't know anything that was going on. They would ship them across the country to work in railroads, mines and so on. This is how Chicanos ended up in Omaha, Kansas City, Michigan, Lansing, Chicago steel mills, Detroit, Milwaukee, even Canada, Connecticut. We worked in all those things also; this is not mentioned.

We are made to believe that we somehow exist just in the Southwest, and yet the fact remains that the third largest concentration of Chicanos is found in Michigan — very far removed from the Southwest. And some metropolitan areas in the Midwest like Chicago and Milwaukee have more people than perhaps we have in the state of new Mexico, depending which half you take.

So we had to move, consequently interrupt the educational program. We've had to value survival above education, which isn't a bad idea because it was bad enough trying to survive inside the educational system coupled with the survival outside in the daily world. So we became migrants, moving in our annual vacation back and forth looking for a way to make a living, and we became segregated in our schools because we came in late and the people who stayed there year round couldn't pass on a nine-month basis. Can you imagine what migrants would be able to do in six months that he is home?

So there were some challenges around 1958 of the segregation suits that were filed in places like Hondo and Del Rio, Uvalde, Crystal City, maybe even down here. I'm sure of it. So that the segregation was eliminated but then we still remained migrants. So now today we have a very legal and very proper segregation and it's called the "Migrant Program." You know, we have migrant elementary schools, migrant junior high schools, migrant schools where they have their own basketball teams, their own football teams, their own bands and their own special curriculum and so on.

So now many of these kids look around and they say, "Vato, soy muy grande, si soy Chicano, vato."[22] So now it's worse. It's bad enough in some places being Mexican, trying to live with that, and now adding another label of being a migrant. That is yet worse than being a Mexican; you get to stay after school later, you know; you go to school longer; you don't do the same kind of things that everybody else does. So you're somehow worse off in this image that is in the minds of those kids. So we certainly have a problem that derives from our particular economic basis. It's very uncomfortable to live with.

More and more frequently Chicanos are getting out of agriculture, but that does not alleviate the situation in schools because we have some school districts and some colleges who for their own reason will refuse to hire of incorporate into their program or even think of bringing a program that would offer financial aid of say the nature of Work-Study, you know, to offer Chicanos and blacks and other minorities. And sometimes these people through carelessness will not have enough people there, and they will have their programs terminated. Or they will mismanage some sort of fund so that there is not enough. And this causes an extreme amount of difficulty for the Chicano who spends a tremendous amount of time getting himself psyched up trying to get into college and then get gutted on an economic kind of program.

This is why also Chicanos in many places — particularly A&I and Pan American-wanted to get removed and uncommitted to the activities of civil rights nature. *El Chicano no quere coperar con el movimento* [23] because their families have sacrificed a great deal to get him here. And then of course we've got all these kind of restrictions that if you engage in any kind of civil disobedience your loan might be terminated; you might be expelled from school and so on. So you live with a threat, you know. You have to go through the mold. You have to go through the assembly line. You can't raise questions of how come there is only one course that helps Chicanos and just barely because it's taught by a monolingual in your school? Or you can't raise questions of how come the Chicano Studies Department — it's not even a department — doesn't have any money? How come they don't hire more Chicanos here? 'Cause then you're placing yourself in jeopardy. It's not that these people are not interested, not committed.

I think if there was some way you could actually take a poll of every Chicano in this school, of these 32 per cent an overwhelming majority are interested in making the thing better. But given the circumstances they would rather just cool it and wait till they get out. This is economic; we're people. *No mas que amos estados tan ambriados que garamos un vesito y lochupamos, y lo chupamos, yo lo metamos en los ovacos paque no lo agaren.* [24]

This is not bad. This is not envidia (envy). This is survival. That is what it's all about because just now, recently have movements gotten so widespread support that now we feel comfortable that we have the support. *Podemos ablar de carnalismo, y los camaradas, lo hermanos Del Rio necessitan ayuda, aya vamos. Si matan uno nuestro en Brownsville aya estamos, Protestamos en Harlingen, San Benito, Kingsville. Si viene Chavez (Cesar Chavez of Delano, Calif.) vamos con el. Si viene Gonzales (Rodolfo Gonzales of Denver, Colo.) vamos con el. Si viene el Doctor Garcia (Hector Garcias of Corpus Christi, Texas) vamos con el.* [25] And this is the present day thing that is coming about. *No vamos crearnos de las mantieras que no hechan; que somos envidioso, y que no degamos que un Americano suba. Esas son mantieras, son invenciones de los que no quieren ver progreso del mejicano.*[26] And this is where I get into the specifics about the advice given to us that the only way you people can do well is to get educated; that's he key. With a college education, it doesn't matter, you know, what your are, what you last name is, "If you've got a degree you can make it on your own." Bullshit! Chicanos have been trying to get in — and I don't know why — into the American educational system for a hell of a long time. This marching in the streets, picketing, signs, civil disobedience, as far as I know, were here in San Antonio as early as 1929.

You know that there were over 30,000 Chicano parents and teachers, students that were walking and stopping traffic in San Antonio, downtown San Antonio because the schools that Chicanos had were not only segregated, but a school *que no tiene ni calentadores, y los hombres tienen que ir a esconderse, dal la espalde a la escuela pder orinarse porque no avia nomas para las mujeres. No tienen libros; no tienen nada.*[27] They were talking about education; they wanted the same kind of education as everybody else in terms of resources, money, personnel, who understood and cared and were some of them.

They followed the leadership of a man called Eluterio Escobar, who just passed away last year, and that movement lasted until the schools were built and heat was put in and there was an effort made to recruit among the community those Chicanos from Mexico who had educational attainment from that system to come in as teacher aids.

As early as then this business of community involvement and total personal participation was already in our Chicano movement. In the Forties and Fifties the GI Forum and the LULAC were getting organized; and still today very strongly advocate education as one of the major objectives of every Chicano. They set up scholarships. They pushed all the veterans, Chicanos — and there's a lot of them — to get into and take advantage of the GI Bill. So we had to pay a pretty price; by going to war and killing other people who we didn't even know. We somehow mistakingly think that this is the way to come back and qualify to build a house or be able to get money to go to college. That's a hell of a price to pay!

In the Sixties, even in this community, school strikes by junior high kids, mind you, and believe me there's much talk about Communist infiltrators who come in from Cuba on every weekend Braniff flight to agitate the kids. It's very difficult to agitate, you know, a sixth grader or a seventh grader or an eighth grader unless he knows what your're talking about, unless you really get it together. And just like I didn't know what I was saying by saying "la niggasoota (nigger shooter) may I please cused?" I thought that was the name of a john, that was the name for the john. That still goes on today.

So we got something together; there is no generation gap between the Chicanos. In fact, the older a Chicano is the closer together he is with the youth because he has a lifetime of experience of frustration and pain; and the kids are much brighter today, it doesn't take them long to catch on. They know what our problem is, and our problem is not us — as we are frequently referred to; the Spanish speaking problem, the problem of the language barrier of the problem of the Mexican people. We don't have any problem. If something, we've got tremendous things we can aid people who do have the problems, the mono-lingual, the mono-cultural, you know, who are very much deprived. Even though they think they are the greatest thing since sliced bread!

You cannot claim or put the blame on outside agitators or subversive influences when you have over thirty-nine schools throughout the state and different parts in every geographical corner you can find — if you can find corners in this state — who have experienced one sort of school strike or school boycott and about 100 others who have experienced some sort of disorder on behalf of Chicano students. And I'm glad that they are being very disorderly. It is about time that we demand changes. For too long we have been under the attitude we should ask and the changes would come about and we should be patient.

But if they are erasing our history and if they are re- writing our history we don't know how long we have to wait. We think we've just been waiting since yesterday, but if we know our history we've been waiting for generations. And this is criminal to ave in this town in 1960 a 4.4 grade level of attainment among Chicanos twenty-five years and older; 2.3 grade level in Zavala County; 1.8 in LaSalle County — 1.4, excuse me — 1.8 that was in 1950 in Zavala County. Half a grade point level of progress in a decade. At that rate we could expect to graduate out of junior high school in mid next century. And so schools have been shut down; and of course we could not tolerate that kind of disorder, we must follow procedure. "You must talk to your teacher, talk to your counselor, talk to your principal, talk to your superintendent, talk to your school board and they will take care of the problem." But it hasn't happened.

You hear that there is no literature available that will reflect at least somewhat accurately the historical contributions of Chicanos, blacks, Indians and other people other than whites. You know, you would think that's the only people that exist in the Southwest if you pick up any kind of book. They just don't make them; they haven't been written yet. There's no bilingual materials, and we can't buy them from Mexico because it's prohibited by the federal government to invest any kind of money of the United States government in Mexico.

We can't have a national school program, we can't have an additional counselor, we can't have an assistant principal or instructional supervisor, you know why? Because they're trying to save a little tax money. They do have those categories available, but they're using them up by placing somebody in that slot, they're using up the teacher unit.

"You can't have Chicano studies, that's reverse racism. What, what possible contribution could that make to history? What value is it to study Chicano music and art? There is no such thing. What do you mean sociology and economics of Chicanos and blacks? We can't find qualified Mexican Americans; we can't identify them. They're just not coming out of school. They're not getting PhD.'s. We don't have enough money to pay what it takes to get somebody down here. Our budget is already written."

All these things, you know, that are just excuses, just postponing what changes should be made. But you know why they don't make them? Because they call themselves educators and administrators. Since they're giving the definition there is nothing you can question. All we have is the consequences of that kind of policy and that kind of activity on their behalf. And if that is the way we should judge them, then they're non-educators; they're very piss- poor administrators because they haven't given us a thing. They have failed miserably with us. And we can't be made to blame for that, for the consequence of that. We cannot possible understand, you know, what *zenophobia* is, or *lexocentric*. We've never been taught the word. *Pero en espano decimos yo mastico chicle, me duele el celebro.* [28]   You translate those words into English that a little five- year-old *Chicanito* says or *una viehita Chicanita de sesenat y nuever anos dece* [29] and you find it comparable to a pre-schooler Anglo who will say "I am masticating" or "My cerebellum hurts."

No one is going to tell you that the "ez" at the end of Fernandez, Martinez, Gonzalez is just the same thing as if you were saying Johnson, Frederickson, Martinson, Dickinson and so on. Son of Dicki, son of Martin, the son of Gonzalo; "ez" is the son of. Nobody tells you words like almauda, algodon, alfombra, alambre[30] are words that come from the Arabic heritage we have in our past. They go back I don't know how many centuries, and we still see them today. *Molcajete, chile* — all those words — our knowledge and other languages. La Lingua de los Indios, de nuestros padres Aztecas[31] we still use today. And we were generous even to let some of the people use some of our words like barbecue, rodeo and *chapateras,* chaps you know. We don't mind; we know we've got a good thing going. And if you don't think so, why do you think that every record that comes out by the Baja Marimba band and the Tijuana Brass makes the top ten? How come every one of these modern homes that is built has architecture very influenced by Spanish and Indian architecture? When you walk in, the people — because of their ignorance, because of their callous attitude — will have *un olcajete que uno use en muestra casa como senicero.* [32]   They don't buy Chicano rugs in Mexico to put on the floor; they put them on the wall to look at. *Se enchan porque tenemos muchos ninos y eyos compran pildoras para comprar un air conditioner or un carro,* [33]   or to afford a pedigree boxer or a swimming pool — something much more precious than a human life!

These are the contradictions that now in the omission in instruction has caused Chicanos to begin thinking that perhaps we might as well resign ourselves that *nadien mas va ser el hale no mas que el Chicano.* [34]   So we better get it together and get the Chicano studies going. The other people are incapable of even finding this information; obviously they haven't done it. And if they are not incapable they are not interested. So we'll take the job; *tenemos un espalda muy ancha para garar la carga.* [35]

So now in the Seventies we see the tremendous demand for Chicano Studies. All it means is; just leave us alone and we'll take care of ourselves. We'll find out what it is we need to know. And this is what we're saying in that the bulk of the Chicano movement is interested in education. Because we know that while it may be necessary to disrupt and be disorderly in order to obtain the justice that is necessary, we also have the responsibility of rebuilding and presenting solutions. And this is what you are doing here in this university. And that's what I did when coming here to this university: to learn it. And I did learn, and I am very grateful that I was afforded this opportunity — not by the people here — but by the society that is too good and too rich to put a man in office to allow people who don't give a damn about it to destroy it.

Como (as) Chicanos we can't let them have it all. So we've got to have engineers; we've got to have accountants and administrators. I'm very proud of A&I for having Mr. Salinas as assistant to the president (Manuel Salinas of Kingsville). Perhaps one day he will become a Chicano president, perhaps the first in the state of Texas. We need him; we need all kinds of people. But we need also to be very sincere about our rhetoric. We're talking about La Raza Unida, about the Gringo and so on. It may make us feel good, temporarily, but that's not reality, baby. You've got to work and work hard! You've got to help carry the load of others who may be weaker, who may have already pushed so hard and so long that they need some aid.

So whether you're a janitor or whether you work in the cafeteria — or you don't work — or you're just getting out of school, we all got to get it together and try to make some sense out of this nonsense and some order out of the chaos that we have been subjected to and been part of for too long.

This is the message that I wanted to talk about. I know that I've dragged it out quite a bit but now it's your turn. You're certainly welcome to equal time.

!VIVA LA RAZA! (Speaker used raised fist symbol) and said: Incidentally, *muchos decin que eso lo laventamos de los hermanos negros; antonces avia un revolucunario muy famoso Emiliano Zapata que en esa mano cargaba una carabina.*[36]

Footnotes

1 It is good to know that one is appreciated, but it is better to know that one is asked questions and that the town maintains one in the form that one is supposed to be —as an equal. No matter how much the heart wants to sometimes, the heart comes up to here and spoils many of us. Be careful.

2 We are dealing with baby chicks; they lose their feathers. Don't let the idea get in that wherever the rooster wants to, he can sing.

3 Especially my brothers that are here, Let's see if we can learn a little and help ourselves think a little clearer also.

4 we were just born yesterday.

5 it must be because of the hot pepper.

6 one of the big guys of our raza at Berkeley. (Octavio I. Romano-V).

7 we are not worth anything, that is what they say, we don't measure up.

8 lies.

9 peculiarities that we have.

10 destiny, you know, has us bent over the vegetables no   more. And they say we like it, that is why we are so short.

11 they were breaking. the giant was getting up.

12 time went by.

13 there was a gigantic march (March 30, 1969).

14 there were about 3000 Chicanos there making noise and protesting.

15 if you eat tacos, if you like Augustin Ramirez, if you believe you are a Chicano.

16 in spirit and in reality we want to . . . under the   concept of being Aztlan.

17 like the animals.

18 the biggest dog, the hog with the biggest snout got the ear of corn.

19 their destiny is not to pick the vegetable, but to be the boss.

20 tortillas with sausage to school? What a shame, man.

21 making tortillas,

22 "Man, I'm real great, I'm not even a Chicano."

23 The Chicano does not want to cooperate with the movement

24 It's just we have been so hungry . . . and I don't say   it with shame, we have been so hungry that we get a bone   and suck it and suck it, and then we put it in our   armpit.

25 We can talk of brotherhood and friends, and if our   brothers in Del Rio need help we go there. If they kill   one of ours in Brownsville we are there. We protest in   Harlingen, San Benito, Kingsville. If Chavez comes we are with him. If Gonzalez comes we are with him. If   Dr. Garcia comes we are with him.

26 Those are lies. We are not going to believe the lies   they tell us; that we are envious, that we do not let a   white advance. Those are lies, inventions of those who do not want to see the Mexican progress.

27 that had no heaters, and the men had to hide, turn their   backs to the school to urinate because there were facilities only for the women. They had no books; they had nothing.

28 But in Spanish, it's like saying I am masticating, my   cerebellum hurts.

29 an old 69-year-old lady says

30 pillow, cotton, carpet, wire

31 The language of the Indians, of our Aztec fathers

32 a molcajete that one uses in our homes as an ash tray.

33 They get angry because we have so many children and they buy pills so they can buy an air conditioner or a car

34 no one but the Chicano will do the job.

35 we have wide shoulders to carry the load.

36 Some say that we picked it up from our black brothers;   there was a very famous revolutionary Emiliano Zapata who carried a rifle in his hand.

Henry G. Cisneros (1948-   )

"Doing More For More: Hispanic Issues For
Texas And The Nation."

Born in a west side Mexican barrio of San Antonio, Texas Henry Cisneros
attended the city's parochial school system. He took his A.B degree and an M.A. in
urban planning at Texas A & M University. In 1971 he became the youngest White
House Fellow in U.S. History. In that regard he served as an assistant to the secretary
of Health, Education, and Welfare. Subsequently, he earned another M.A. in public
administration from Harvard University. He received the Ph.D. degree from George
Washington University and then returned to San Antonio to teach government at the
University of Texas. In 1975 he ran and won a seat on the city council. In 1981
Cisneros became Mayor of San Antonio. He ran again in 1983, 1985, and 1987 and
was successful each time. Inasmuch as his fifty dollar a week salary as mayor is
insufficient he teaches at Trinity University and his wife works. Cisneros presented
this speech at the Independent Sector Annual Meeting in Houston, TX on October 25,
1988.

Reprinted with the kind permission of the author.

A philosopher who has worked most recently at the American Enterprise
Institute, a fellow named Michael Novak, has written a number of books, including
The Spirit of Democratic Capitalism. He has evolved into a thinking about what he
calls the "mediating institutions" in the society. His views present broad opportunities and unusual roles for organizations and institutions represented here.

As a mayor, I can clearly see that most of the problems that we face in our cities
require not the efforts of government, not the self-reliance of individuals acting alone,
but a whole series of intermediary or mediating institutions. Novak says that the
present partisan philosophy is just out of touch with the real need. D e m o c r a t s
tend to think in terms of big government, alphabet soup bureaucracies. Republicans
have tended to think in terms of the individual's solving problems alone. In fact, both
of these are really outdated concepts. A whole new matrix of interrelated institutions
and networks or institutions is what is called for. And that, more than anything else,
I think, captures the idea of what the independent Sector is all about.

I'll talk with you today about the future. It is a future that I'd like to address in
several ways: the social trends and demographics of our nation's future, some of the
economic and technological issues of our future, and a sense of political and
governance questions. Then we can see what these trends mean for your institutions
and the organizations that you manage that are so important to our country.

First, I am convinced that the dominant feature of our times is change. This change is massive in its scale, almost impossible to document. How pervasive is change in the manner in which it touches our lives? A constant flow of new products and the latest technology are consistently infused into our daily lives. These are manifest in the daily routine from the starting of an automobile to the checking out of groceries at the grocery store, using the latest state-of-the-art laser technology.

It's a change that is rapid in its pace. What we hear on the evening's news is likely to have a different cast by the time we hear it in tomorrow morning's broadcast. And it's a change that, ironically, is permanent. That is to say, it is a constant, relentless, feature of our world. And anyone whose personality requires that things stand still in order to understand them—a kind of Polaroid snapshot of the world to comprehend it and understand it— is going to be ill-suited for the reality of the dimensions of this change.

When I first became a City Council member in San Antonio, I used to think in those frames of mind—project management, beginning-to-finish—hoping that when we completed a project, the whole world would stop for a second and bask in the accomplishment that I regarded it to be. I can't tell you the disappointment when nobody stopped at all. The train just kept right on moving. And I have discovered since that it requires a temperamental adjustment, a personality adjustment, to handle relentless and constant change.

Some of the great changes sweeping across the landscape of our country will touch your organizations, the assumptions of your work, and the requirements for how you will adjust your own personal thinking and the mind-set of these institutions.

SOCIAL TRENDS

To me, the most serious social development of the next decade, and certainly of the next century, is the juxtaposition of two demographic realities. One is the aging of traditional populations, the other, the growth of ethnic minorities.

Aging Populations

In 1990, the census will show for the first time in American history that we will have more Americans over 65 years of age than teenagers. The United States population will continue to grow older as the median population age continues to rise. And frankly, we haven't seen the end of this trend.

As the Baby Boomers of my generation reach 55 and 60 and 65, in the years 2000 to 2010, we will see an unprecedented number of people in the pre-retirement years—

and then into retirement status. So there will be growing concerns about issues of generational equity.

To the degree society fails to provide income security and a sense of quality of life for that greater-than-ever number in advancing age, the entire society will pay the price for the fear and insecurity that is associated with that age group. I have seen this in my own city. We have had movements supporting Proposition 13-type capping of taxes, largely initiated by retiree populations. It is serious in that these populations seem to be saying, "As long as we are income-insecure, we can't afford to go with you and ride with you and support you, on matters related to building new schools, or basic new infrastructure, or investing in bond issues, or sustaining property tax increases."

It suggests not only an aging in the population mix but several attitudes of retrenchment as well, with respect to the American future and the willingness to invest in that future. There are very serious questions beyond the more traditional issues of health care and Social Security and other that have been mentioned.

Ethnic Minorities

Now, the changes described above become particularly serious when they are juxtaposed against the other demographic reality, which is the growth of ethnic minorities in our society, particularly Blacks and Hispanics. It's not an accident that the Mayors of Chicago or Philadelphia or Newark or Baltimore or Atlanta or Los Angeles are Black. Nor is it an accident that the mayors of Miami or Denver are Hispanic. Nor is it an accident that women have put together coalitions that include large support groups of Blacks and Hispanics in Houston or in Dallas or in San Diego or in other American cities. These are not chance events. They are reflective of fundamental new demographics in America's cities.

In the 1950s Carl Stokes was elected mayor of Cleveland. That was a historic achievement, a historic moment—that a northern city would elect a Black mayor. Today, it is more the rule than the exception, and I suspect this will continue into the next decade and the year 2000.

But far more important than what is happening in cities— because this could be dismissed by the society as enclaves of demographic change that are not indicative of the society as a whole—are new data showing what this means for the country.

The California State Library System—which is the overarching, guiding institution for about 1200 libraries in the state of California—initiated an analysis asking the question, "How do we help guide the libraries of California for the cultural traits and attributes of the expected new demographics of the year 2000?"

Keep in mind that the year 2000 is a few short years from now and that 2000 is not a stopping point. We tend to look at these statistics and freeze frame them in the year 2000, forgetting that whatever demographics move us to 2000 are going to accelerate by 2005 and 2010. So to plan for the moment, rather than for the dynamic that runs through it, is repeating the mistake that described earlier about how to think about change.

According to the Rand Corporation's analysis conducted for the California State Library System, in the year 2000, California will be the largest state in America. The second largest state after California will be New York. California's population will be 27 million and New York's will be about 17 million, to give a feel for the order of magnitude there. California in the year 2000 will be 40 percent Hispanic, Asian, and Black. Not some central city, but the massive, entire state that is California.

San Francisco County will be 65 percent minority, the largest of which will be Asian. Los Angeles County (not the city of LA) will have a population of 8 million, 60 percent of which will be minority, the largest percent, Hispanic. Even Orange County, traditional center of conservative population, will be 40 percent minority, the largest percent, Hispanic. In rural areas like Imperial Valley, of the 73 percent minority, the largest portion will be Hispanic. the "Latinization of America" will be defined more specifically in a later section of this presentation.

The most stunning statistic to come from the library study was that in the year 2000, 92 percent of the people of California will live in counties that are at least 30 percent minority. Thirty percent is a significant number. With a minority of almost one-third, we begin to see the effect upon the cultural feel of the community. Ninety-two percent of Californians will live in such counties in the year 2000.

It seems this whole question of ethnic transformation is no longer a question of doing right by someone else, exhibiting Judeo-Christian compassion, observing civil rights, or upholding constitutional ideals. It becomes an issue of how American functions, and how America, not to put too strong a phrase on it, "survives."

Because, you see, to the degree that the majority of these minorities just described—at least Blacks and Hispanics—live in the lower rungs of the economic ladder, we will not be able as a society to carry the burden of an underclass that is that large, relegated to a status of lesser productibility, lesser literacy, lesser citizenship. The simple fact of the matter is that no country operating in the very tough competition in which we will function in the next century will be able to function carrying 10 or 15 or 20 million people in a permanent underclass. It won't work.

The Prime Minister of Japan said several years ago that he was not worried about America's competing in the next century with Japan, because, he said, "America is a polyglot nation—too many Blacks and Hispanics." And he was properly criticized for that statement. But, frankly, he could have altered it only slightly and probably been correct. America will not be able to compete with the Japanese in the new and emerging industries, nor with northern Europeans for that matter, unless it addresses the educational needs and the productivity needs of those large Black and Hispanic populations. So, this whole question of the juxtaposition of the aging of traditional populations and the growth of minority populations is an issue that must be at the forefront of the concerns of every American in service. Oh, I suspect it's possible to live a good life and never worry about this question—in suburban enclaves, shopping malls, or new cities in suburban modes. But it is not possible to be in service to this country and its ideals and its goals and its future and its prosperity and be unaware of these issues.

Now it so happens that there's a kind of silver lining in this cloud, because, while traditional populations are aging, the economy still continues to grow—more slowly than before, but nevertheless it grows. There will be jobs. If those large minority populations are matched to those new jobs, this economic engine that is American society works again. But it will take investment in skills, investment in education and human capital in order for that to work. This presents probably the most critical domestic, security, and survival questions for the year 2000.

Continuing Needs

Another social trend that will continue to affect your work includes the continued increase in single parent families. There will be more children in crisis—due to poverty, child abuse, and suicide. We will see an increased focus on illiteracy. We will reshape traditional medical systems, as the costs of delivery and medical services drive traditional methods out of the reach of many Americans. AIDS will continue to be a critical question, and drug abuse will be increasingly visible. And, education will be the front burner question for many Americans who want to do something significant for the future of the society.

That means creating in schools a climate of high expectations for all students, not just for the most advantaged—to set a national standard by which it is unacceptable to perpetuate failure in the schools, as so many school systems tend to do today. We need special emphasis on preschool and early education. Nutritional deficiencies or disadvantaged children must be overcome enroute to creating the environment in which learning can take place.

We need to work together—public sector and private sector, schools and businesses, and the mediating institutions that you represent—to create effective schools where there are clear instructional goals and high expectations; and where the principal provides strong leadership of the kind that is entrepreneur creating an effective school. We need a school where achievement data are used to create clear targets of accomplishment. All of these will be part of the social setting in which your organizations will go forward into the 1990's and beyond.

ECONOMIC AND TECHNOLOGICAL TRENDS

There's a second set of themes that are economic and technological trends. Now what makes the situation that I've described earlier a little dicey is that it happens to match a period in American history when growth has slowed. We're losing some of the jobs that created the stable middle class that was so essential to accomplishing the American dream in the 1950s and 1960s and the 1970s.

Today the prosperity of our country becomes ever more dependent upon the economic strength of other nations. That doesn't mean that we're absolutely losing in the competition with other countries. We're still growing, in terms of our GNP and our production levels. But, if you recently read Paul Kennedy's book, *The Rise and Fall of the Great Powers*—which was very difficult for me to read because it was so heavily economically historical—he paints this picture: it's not necessary that this country slip in terms of its absolute production; rather, what happens is that others become stronger and we lose in percentage terms. That is what he sees happening to America.

There's no doubt that the Japanese will take larger shares than they have. And the Europeans, after 1992, functioning as a European community, will take larger shares than they have. So the United States will suffer some percentage declines. Whatever our GNP percentage was on the world chart, it will be lower in the 1990s. That's not a pessimistic forecast; it's a statement of fact. We are in a new set of relationships. As a result, we're going to see more jobs going offshore—jobs to Korea, Singapore, and Taiwan. Now you have the NICS—the newly industrializing countries in Asia, Thailand, Malaysia and Indonesia—taking a share of jobs. So it's a whole new ballgame, and it's going to affect our jobs.

What concerns me about that is the implication for what we might call the American Class Structure, an almost un- American idea. We don't think in terms of classes. But unless real attention is given to this question of how our economy unfolds, we are going to gravitate toward a society that is more polarized along income lines.

This is not the doing of government. A cutting of social programs didn't do this. It's more intrinsic to our economy, although government could have been a greater factor in redressing this direction over the last few years.

The Human Factor

Data for last year show that one-fifth of Americans, 20 percent of the U.S. population, earned 43 percent of the nation's income. This is the largest percentage since the end of World War II, for that 20 percent to earn almost half the income. The bottom 20 percent earned only 4.7 percent of the national income, which is the smallest percentage for the lowest one-fifth in 25 years. So there is a polarization occurring. I referred earlier to the creation of a permanent underclass; that's what threatens to happen if these trends toward income polarization continue.

Given that the new jobs being created require greater knowledge of mathematics, science, and quantitative methods, what we face is a wider chasm between those who are technologically competent and those who will be relegated to a kind of bystander status in this new economy.

When the latter occurs, the number of children in poverty will grow. Homelessness will continue to persist. We will find new challenges in pay equity issues, as the bottom rungs of the society simply cannot live on the pay structure that they have. And, as more women work in this new economy, because it is simply impossible to function with a single wage earner in the home, we'll find more demands for child care, flexible hours in the workplace, and many other such family related concerns.

POLITICAL AND GOVERNMENTAL TRENDS

A third trend and creation of this future is political and governmental. I expect, for example, that we'll see the continued development of a conservative mood in the country. It's an interesting phenomenon. I don't know what explains it, except that it's in part related to the demographics that were described earlier. A larger percentage of the populations is living to advance years and, frankly, they become fearful as that occurs—fearful about income security. The politics of fear are always the most effective, and the mood will be one that lends itself to that, I think, as we go into the next century.

One aspect of this politics of conservativism is that we're not going to see new programs at the Federal level. Frankly, I don't think it matters who's President in 1989 or 1993. Neither candidate will be in a position to start a whole host of new local services or urban programs; it's just not possible. The deficit is running at over $100 billion. We have a need for a level of defense spending, at least to suffice in negotiations with the Soviets.

Decentralization

The simple fact is that we're going to see a continuation of the trend toward decentralization of responsibilities to state and local government. And, as a mayor of a city, I'll tell you that local governments just do not have the resources to respond to the range of problems that we confront. Continued cuts in governmental funding of human services, matched to public pressure to solve the federal budget deficit, will create an environment in which many problems will go unresolved or responsibility for them will fall to organizations such as those that you represent. It is a simple statement of fact that this mediating sector— organizations and institutions in service—must play a larger role in addressing many of these social questions as we go into the next century.

The Community as Focal Point

Now another dimension that I think will occur as we watch this dencentralization is the business of cities' becoming the focal point for American life. And that means not just in the kind of negative terms that I've been describing today—epidemics of teenage pregnancies and problems related to illiteracy and other things—but also in creating a positive quality of life.

A new sphere of activity is operating at city hall. It's related to the fact that more and more Americans are finding that if they're going to have a good life, it's going to be within community settings. That field is called "Amenity Planning." And I suspect that as we go forward into the next decade, we're going to see a greater emphasis on amenity planning—cultural planning, the visual arts, music and other performing arts—enriching a community, attracting new business and enhancing residents' lives. This change will also play a role in attracting revenues to a community, as cultural districts revitalize dying downtowns.

The greening of America's cities—parks and open spaces—provides recreation, supports neighborhood identities, warehouses and riverwalks (such as the one we're so proud to present in San Antonio). Animation (a strategy of bringing liveliness to whole communities), bringing in millions of dollars, enhancing local pride with street festivals and ethnic celebrations; all of these act as a bridge for unity. Animation fills with profitable crowds downtown areas that once were deserted central business districts. Neighborhoods and their preservation bring out a cultural reward, enhancing civic pride of people in low income areas. Ethnic districts with their rich heritage can become a financial asset to many communities.

Excellence in design, concept competitions, focusing attention on the importance of community aesthetics on everything from parking lots to creating city vistas, and design competitions on new public buildings and public art, create images for communities as unique places. Each community has a definable character, recognized and separate from other places. That character is enhanced by and reflected in museums, libraries, and historical societies. Also, interpretive centers, planetariums, sidewalk exhibits of local archaeology, and educational centers have their own unique qualities. This can be accomplished through working with local universities to locate everything from small business incubators and continuing education centers in cities. All of this will be the responsibility of local communities.

The federal government is not going to be in a position to do these things; state governments for the most part are not. So again, one of the principal themes of this era is going to be the decentralization of responsibility for the quality of life in which we live. And we will either make these things happen in communities, or they will not exist. These things are possible even in hard times.

We witness Pittsburgh, converting itself from the tired, grimy center of the coal and steel business in the 1950's and the 1960's to a city that Rand McNally has characterized as one of the most livable cities in America today. The manner in which it has revitalized its downtown, forged relationships with Carnegie Mellon University, revitalized the climate of small business entrepreneurship—these things are possible. We see them in Pittsburgh. We see them in Boston, where the waterfront redevelopment has spread to the downtown as a whole.

Rejuvenation has also taken place in Baltimore and in Atlanta, which asserted for itself a role as an international city and created, then, a bonafide national focal point. Or Indianapolis—whose own residents called the place "India no place" a few years ago—today has simply asserted a new role for itself, using the amateur sports and the efforts of the Eli Lilly Foundation to put millions and millions of dollars into the community. They have also added a pro basketball team, the Indiana Pacers, and pro football team, Indianapolis Colts.

So this theme then, of decentralization, which includes local involvement and local commitment by foundations and mediating institutions such as yours, will be a very important theme in our lives and the life of our country over the next few years.

LATINIZATION OF AMERICA

The other theme that I think is going to be important is what might be called the "Latinization of America." that doesn't mean that America is going to become a Latin country, although our Latin population will be larger than that of many countries that are 100 percent Spanish speaking. but it does mean that this is one of the big stories of the next century—one could say this decade or the next decade, but I choose to talk about it in terms of about the year 2000—because I think there will be an irrevocable momentum to that particular demographic change by the year 2000. It's a wonderful, wonderful thing to see the American fabric have room for one more dimension—the warmth and richness that is the Hispanic culture.

This is a phenomenon, partly because the numbers are so significant that Hispanics will make up the largest ethnic minority in America by the year 2000; most demographers agree. Though it has the fastest growing trend in absolute numbers of people, the population mass in and of itself is not the story. The combination of numbers, though there is significance in where those numbers happen to be, creates a kind of multiplier effect.

When you are 20 percent of the American population of California—with California as important as it is to America—that's an extraordinary multiplication of influence. Twenty percent of Texans—and Texas could be close to the second largest state in the country by the year 2000—constitutes an extraordinary influence. Florida, one of the fastest growing states in America in the last 20 years, already has a governor named Bob Martinez. And the Mayor of Miami is Xavier L. Suarez. Hialeah has a population of 74 percent Cuban. In New York City, there are 1.4 million Puerto Ricans. Chicago's residents include 500,000 Hispanics. Arizona and New Mexico are 36 percent Hispanic. The Mayor of Denver, Colorado is Federico Pena.

There are places that prove to me these are national phenomena, though the strength tends to be significant in certain places such as those I've described. Please keep in mind the states that I've just mentioned, and think of presidential politics and large delegations—Florida, Texas, California, New York, and Illinois—and then add to that growing states like Arizona and Colorado.

National Scene

What makes it a national story is the extent to which there are Hispanic communities in states that we don't think of as having any Hispanic significance. I was surprised when the Mayor of St. Paul, Minnesota, after a speaking engagement at Macalester College, asked me to join him campaigning. I couldn't imagine how in the world I could help him campaigning in St. Paul, until he took me to Our Lady of Guadalupe Church on the city's west side to a group of 500 Hispanics whom he was courting in the particular election.

Witness the efforts of the Concilio for the Spanish Speaking in Seattle, where a young man named Ricardo Sanchez has run a good strong race for he City Council. Or observe a meeting in Michigan of Hispanic elected officials, expecting to meet in a coffee shop, and instead finding over 200 elected and appointed officials from the State of Michigan and Michigan local communities in Flint, and Saginaw, and Lansing, who are Hispanic.

See a young man be elected to the state legislature from Gary, Indiana and East Chicago, Indiana, where the Hispanic community is particularly strong. We know that there are 100,000 Hispanics each in New Jersey, Connecticut, and Pennsylvania (where the Philadelphia growth is very significant politically, as it is in northern New Jersey). So this is a national phenomenon which is going to be important just on the basis of numbers.

It will also be important because of the new sophistication in Hispanic advocacy organizations like the National Council of La Raza, headed Raul Yzaguirre. But very importantly, there's the Southwest Voter Registration and Education Project, until recently headed by the late Willie Velasquez, which changed voter registration patterns and voter education throughout the southwestern United States, thus creating an entirely new politics in the Southwest.

Three thousand Hispanic elected officials in America— half of them in Texas, an incubator of talent—are serving on school boards, county commissions, and city councils. These people, in turn, rise to the legislature, to the state senate, and to the Congress. And in time, we will see—in Texas, California, New Mexico, Arizona, and Colorado—governors and senators and persons who are able to lead the politics of the southwestern United States in significant and contributory ways.

The Mexican American Legal Defense and Education Fund, which is a member organization of Independent Sector, is litigating right now in Los Angeles to change the makeup of the Board of Supervisors of Los Angeles County, where there are four Supervisors governing eight million people. Each Supervisor has greater responsibility than four Congressmen.

Los Angeles County has a budget larger than that of 42 states in America. Yet despite the size of the Hispanic population, not a single member of the Board of Supervisors is Hispanic. So, with these groups joined by the Justice Department, which acknowledges the inequity of the situation, litigation begins to change the status. The new sophistication is impressive today in organizations which used to be competitive, backbiting, envious, and divisive. Very sophisticated political strategies and leadership emerge from such organizations in the Hispanic community. That's a second reason for what I think will be an explosive, awakening, prideful strength.

Affirmation of Culture

The third reason is the most important—that Hispanics themselves are asserting the truth about their role in this country, and Americans are willing to listen. It's a wonderful story of pride and history of people whose roots in the southwestern United States stem literally from the bloodlines of the Aztecs. The dark skin, the dark hair and the facial features are all attributable to those civilizations in Tenochtitlan, which was the center of the Aztec empire, in what is now Mexico City.

Advanced forms of astronomy, medicine, and architecture existed when the Spaniards arrived in the 1500s. Descendents of those bold and noble Spaniards literally burned their ships in the harbors of Vera Cruz as they began their trek across what is now Mexico and the United States. So it is not an accident that we have names of cities all over our country that bear the Hispanic heritage. Senora de los Angeles de la Purisima Concepcion is the modern city of Los Angeles. The state of Colorado, taking the Spanish word for red, is named after the red sunsets they found there. Or la nevada is the snowfall whose namesake is the modern state of Nevada. Montana was the mountainous region that is today the state of Montana. Or numerous other places that bear the evidence of these people who walked in search of glory and evangelized throughout the southwestern United States—like San Francisco or Santa Fe or San Antonio. Or the modern heroes of the civil rights fights are a wonderful story of assertion of truth of people who have fought this country's wars and won more medals for bravery han any other ethnic group per capita.

I learn new facts all the time. The average number of young men lost in the Vietnam war by schools across America was about ten per major school in the country. I was at San Antonio's Edgewood High School last night, where they lost 57 in the Vietnam era, because of the patriotism that runs so deeply in the spirit of the Hispanic community.

The images are changing from that of the peon who's sitting with his tequila resting against a cactus to a father who is training his sons and daughters to be doctors and engineers and technologists...from the fetching young lady with the rose in her mouth, leaning against the cantina wall, to the mother who stands proudly before the pictures of her four sons, each wearing the uniform of a different branch of the Armed Services of the United States--that image will change ever more into the next century, as the culturalization process continues.

It's not an accident, I suppose, that the Miami Sound Machine has some of the top hits on top 40 radio. Nor was it chance that "La Bamba" was one of the most popular movies of the summer of 1987. Nor is it mere circumstance that Arquitectonica, as one of the hottest architectural firms in the country, is changing not only the skyline of Miami; it is sought all over the United States. Nor is it happenstance that people of both sexes melt to the music of Julio Iglesias. Nor is it mere chance that nachos, perhaps the greatest indication of a cultural beachhead, outsell hot dogs at the Chicago Cubs' baseball games.

My point is that this is a phenomenon. It's nothing to be afraid of, but it requires the understanding of how to harness that raw energy of the immigrants once again to revitalize and rejuvenate the country.

CONCLUSION

Those are a number of themes that I think characterize our mutual progress forward—themes for government, business, the individual, and, very importantly, those mediating institutions you lead. Corporate support for basic human care needs must grow in the years ahead. The way in which we're going to deal with drug and alcohol abuse, domestic violence, child abuse, and other basic questions—these confront our society.

Education is too important to leave to a handful of school boards and professional educators. It is at the heart of whether or not this American ideal goes forward. And so investing in education is, again, a joint endeavor. That is why we will see more corporations involved in Adopt- a-School programs and others such as the one that exists in Boston, called the Boston Compact; or in Baltimore, the Baltimore Commonwealth Agreement. Or we see in my own city the San Antonio Education Partnership, where we put together a coalition of businesses, colleges, schools, and community organizations simply to invest in the future of our children. The effort requires the involvement of everyone in society.

It means increased corporate encouragement of volunteerism among employees and contributions of noncash gifts in kind with mediating institutions, such as yours, steering all of that energy and all of those resources in the most productive way. As a mayor, I can tell you that we have all kinds of offers from corporations, but frequently they meet the advertising needs of the company and not necessarily what needs to be done in the city.

So, what it takes is organizations that have the capability to steer gently, not to look a gift horse in the mouth, but to somehow guide and rein him in the right direction to achieve the maximum impact. This includes building parks for children in the central city, setting up programs in schools, investing in literacy, dealing with teenage pregnancy, or helping the senior citizens (whom we have to make secure, less they become a force in retarding goals for the future). Whether it be harnessing volunteers from among senior citizens or retirees or getting corporations and government to prepare older workers for service in retirement—all of that effort in the society requires the kinds of institutions that Independent Sector supports.

These realities of demographic change and economic transformation are the American story of the 1900s and the year 2000. It's not a question of whether, it's only a question of how we prepare to meet them head on and remain consistent to the most basic American ideals.

And the most basic ideals are those that we teach to children when they come to school for the first time. Too young to understand the words, they trust us, and they memorize, "...One nation under God, indivisible, with liberty and justice for all." We mean one nation—not privileged suburbs juxtaposed against burned out inner cities, reservations for a permanent underclass. We are talking about one nation—not rust belt against sun belt.

We refer to one nation under God—a God who can see into the home of the manufacturing worker rendered obsolete by a transforming economy, the home of the senior citizens afraid to step outside of their walled and barred existence (even to get the Social Security check or to walk to the corner store). This is a God who can see into the junkie heavens, the shooting galleries, who can see into the home of the battered spouse. One nation, indivisible—not one which has been rent asunder into Black and White, not rent asunder by selfishness or polarization. One nation under God, indivisible, with liberty and justice for all. Not just for those who were born with the right color of skin or the right color of hair, who speak with the right accent, went to the right school, grew up in the right neighborhoods, have the right last name— that's not what we teach them. We teach them one nation, under God, indivisible, with liberty and justice for all.

Those ideas, it seems to me, are fundamental to the makeup of our country. Without them, people are relegated to a permanent structured, rigid class society, which is unacceptable to us. Without them, people have no reason to invest in the future. Without them, everyone wants everything now and no sacrifice, because there's not promise of a better future. Those ideals are essential to the American idea. If government cannot provide them because of fiscal and economic realities, if demographics, make this harder, what all that means is that Americans of goodwill, such as those of you in this room and the institutions you represent, must rise to the occasion. It is on this question that the makeup, and the complexion, and the prosperity of our country into the next century will depend.

VI

Introduction

This chapter includes six speeches by Mexican American females. No other influences were so strong in shaping the thoughts of these women than their Mexican heritage and their relationship with the land. That becomes evident as we see how the speeches reflect the serious concern these women have for the uplifting of the Chicano and their preservation of tradition. These enlightened females have dedicated themselves to improve the condition of their people by dedicating themselves to a crusade for equality and respecting past values. To achieve their goals the approach of the speakers vary. While some speakers express their views from the rostrum at the meeting hall, another communicates her feelings by way of an interview. Some chose the narration as a device to convey their thoughts and others sent their grievances to the highest government official in Washington in a collection of speeches.

The first speech by Lydia Aguirre describes the full meaning of the name Chicano. Aguirre defines the Chicano and then disqualified the stereoptypes that surround the name. She informed her audience about the proud and resourceful leaders of the movement. She reminded her listeners that the Chicano is bilingual as well as involved in every level of society. The Mexican American is not a simple, ignorant, migrant worker. She told her listeners: "We are doctors, university professors, lawyers and congressmen as well as farm laborers, maids, housewives, plumbers, mailmen and engineers." She stated that the social activist displayed courage fighting racism which is so widespread in an America that "seems unable to tolerate differentness." Aguirre closed her speech by demanding the right to be a first-class citizen in the United States.   The second speech is a by an activist Nita Jo Gonzales Aleman. Aleman surveyed the successful protest activities of 1969 and 1970 in California, Texas, and Colorado in her discourse. It represented her way of connecting the protests with a declaration of Aztlan, that is, the Mexican Americans are a great and proud people. As she mentioned the social activism all over the southwest she reasserted Chicano power. Her determination is shown in the following goals: "A step-by-step plan to restore my people's dignity and the individualism our ancestors once relished." Again she added: "[N]o longer are the youth of la raza going to humbly accept the indignities and psychological destruction of our people." She ended her speech by saying that with this nationalistic approach people were beginning to find solutions to problems that "confront and have surrounded us for generations."

The third piece is an interview with folksinger Joan Baez. Ms. Baez covered several topics in the interview. She talked about her public school experiences, the judicial system, nonviolence, minorities, and people's use of power. In the areas touched upon she revealed her sensitivity toward others, and, how she viewed the world around her. She declared that she did not categorize herself with any special group but she wished to be identified "more with humanity as a whole." She admired Cesar Chavez: "he may provide the best example of strong nonviolent action." Of minorities she said: "I would never want to see a good Mexican become a good American. I would rather that he become a brother in the brotherhood of man." The judicial system, she observed, was one that did not promote justice, but kept order. It would appear that the concerns that meant so much to Ms. Baez in the Sixties are just as important to her today.

The fourth speech is by Valentina Valdes. Her discourse is a description of the relationship between the Hispanic children and the Anglo Americans, especially in the public school systems. She related to her audience how humiliated she had been when the school children would whisper or make jokes about the way she spoke. In short, the mocking caused the Mexican American school child to be ashamed to use their own language. The tragedy in all of this ridicule is that it leads to a people's "denial of culture, language and history." It makes them ashamed of who they are even to the point of saying the name Jose as "Joe." When Ms. Valdes and others saw that the Chicano was beginning to deemphasize culture and language "An agricultural cooperative was started...The purpose of it is to bring back some of the good old ways of working together and also to inject some hope into our oppressed people." The aim was to become self-sufficent by working communaly.

The fifth speech is by Jovita Gonzales. Mrs. Gonzales' discourse is a sentimental piece that pays tribute to the dying out of a certain part of Mexican folk-lore—the wandering and independent vaquero. The vaquero loved freedom and the open prairie and held a dislike for law and restraint. The vaquero disappeared because the large cattle companies began purchasing the ranges in the latter half of the last century. When the barbwire and the cattle empires appeared the vaquero, disappeared. Mrs. Gonzales said that to understand Mexican folk-lore is to understand the spirit and the soul of the Mexican people.

The sixth and final discourse in this chapter is "Rancho Buena Vista" by Fermina Guerra. Mrs. Guerra's narration is an authentic depiction of life on the frontier during the 1800's. As the Mexican American settlers were trying to establish homesteads they had to face dangers of floods, marauding Indians, and confrontations with the much feared Texas Rangers. "Rancho Buena Vista" reveals the hard- working and strong-willed character of these people who tolerated hardships and natural disasters to make a decent life for themselves. Her piece shatters stereotypes of the lazy good-for-nothing Mexican.

Lydia R. Aguirre

"The Meaning of the Chicano Movement."

Lydia Aguirre has invested much of her life in the Social Work profession. At the time of this discourse (1973) she served as a member of the faculty of the University of Texas at El Paso teaching in the college's Social Work Program.

Reprinted from *Social Casework*, May 1971, pp. 259-261 with the kind permission of the publisher, *Family Service America*.

Let me start by saying that the Chicano is an extremely diversified "individual." We are as heterogeneous as our history. Without that background of history, it is difficult to understand us. No somos Mexicanos. We are citizens of the United States with cultural ties to Mexico and in some instances to Spain, but, within our ties of language and culture, we have developed a culture that is neither Spanish nor Mexican. *Entre nosotros habemos quien habla un espanol puro, pero tambien entre nosotros habemos los "batos" que no pueden conseguir "jale" por la razon que sea.*

We are bilingual. We are doctors, university professors, lawyers, and congressmen as well as farm laborers, maids, housewives, plumbers, mailmen, and engineers. There are some Mexican-Americans who are tio- tacos, those who ride the fence and cuando se les aprieta el cinto, nos dan en la torre. But then, there are some Mexican Americans who would readily turn Chicano when they are scratched a little. By that I mean when they understand the true value of this our diversified Chicano movement.

About the term Chicano," I cannot as yet give you a scholarly explanation. From my adolescence in Edinburg, Texas, I remember Chicano as a   derogatory term applied only by us, who we then insisted should be called Mexican- Americans. We demanded that we be classified as Caucasian. Chicano was a term used self-consciously and degradingly only by ourselves. In his columns in the Los Angeles Times, Ruben Salazar attempted to define the term. In one column he wrote, "A Chicano is a Mexican-American with a non-Anglo image of himself...actually the word Chicano is as difficult to define as 'soul'" In Another instance, he wrote, "For those who like simplistic answers Chicano can be defined as short for Mexicano. For those who prefer complicated answers it has been suggested that Chicano may have come from the word Chihuahua—the name of a Mexican state bordering on the United States. Getting trickier this version contends that Mexicans who migrated to Texas call themselves Chicanos." In a third reference he said, "Chicanos then are merely fighting to become 'American.' Yes, but with a Chicano outlook."

As I understand the word "Chicano" in the Chicano movement, it is this: if there is no lowest of the low and no highest of the high and each will wear the label of Chicano with pride, he will have personal respect and with it dignidad y unidad con hermanos Chicanos. He will be proud to assume his heritage guaranteed in the Treaty of Guadalupe-Hidalgo and proud to use the language and customs that are his by heritage, treaty, and corazon. Chicano power simply means that in the finding of identity—that is, a right to be as he is, not Mexcican, not Spanish, not speaking either a "pure" English or a "pure" Spanish, but as he is, a product of a Spanish-Mexican-Indian heritage and an Anglo-Saxon (American, or, as Mexico says, Estado Unidense) influence—he will unite with his brothers in heritage. As he has pride and unity, so will he lose his self-consciousness and self-degradation and thereby will gain status and power.

Collectively, the Chicano in unity can influence the social systems, that have perpetuated social injustices. Some say we are in the midst of a social revolution. I prefer to state that we are in the midst of a renaissance. We challenge the educational system to recognize our "differentness." We challenge ourselves to be proud of this differentness. We challenge the educational system to teach Hispanic history, to teach bilingually, and to give us adequate schools where students are largely Chicano. We demand not to be segregated. We demand that others recognize our differentness and work within that differentness rather than make the Chicano suppress his Chicanismo and adopt Anglo-Saxon ideals.

We demand that our side of the story be old. From this demand grew the Ruben Salazar Memorial Scholarship Foundation. Ruben Salazar dared to speak the truth. His voice was silenced when he was killed in Los Angeles in the line of duty, covering the 1970 Chicano Moratorium for his paper. Through the mass communications scholarships we are offering, we hope to educate young people in television, radio, and journalism to continue Ruben Salazar's message. Needless to say, the present mass media sometimes distort the truth. What may really be a justified confrontation on a social injustice can be reported as a riotous disruption.

Some of us feel that we need parallel institutions to have real justice. The Ruben Salazar Memorial foundation has a long-range goal of establishing or sponsoring a daily newspaper. Later on, who knows—perhaps even Chicano radio and television!

We continue being so terribly diversified, yet we have so many cultural values that unite us. Each area has problems unique to that area. Northern new Mexico is rural and communal. The people there are fighting for their lands and grazing and water rights. Urban areas fight both discrimination and racism. Racism is so difficult to fight because it is so intangible and difficult to pinpoint. Yet it is all around us.

Take, for example, El Paso. People with Spanish surnames number almost half of the population of El Paso. Yet we have very few businessmen proportionately. If we look at executive positions of the major companies, we are lucky to find a sprinkling of Spanish surnames. Many of our educated young people have to leave this community to find jobs. I personally know several young people who looked diligently for jobs for months and either left town or took a menial job. Last week, however, I received a call from an Anglo-Saxon young lady friend of mine who found a good job after only three days of looking in a city strange to her. Were the former just unfortunate incidents and was the latter a fortunate incident?

In approaching the problems facing us, the Chicano uses different methods. Each in his own way is striving to achieve human dignity, self-respect, and just equality. Some Chicanos (and I include myself) attempt to effect change within established systems, and if that does not work, attempt to establish parallel systems. Hence, we have separate newspapers, Chicano conferences, businesses. We attempt to change the educational system to better meet our needs. We demand justice in courts and police within the established order. Other Chicanos prefer isolationism or brown separatism. These are in the minority. Very few would want a separate nation.

Others, particularly in New Mexico, who brought from Spain and continued the system of an agrarian, communal society into this century, want a return to that system which in that climate and region is almost imperative to survival. It is interesting to note that the Pueblo Indian who lived in that region when the Spaniards arrived had a similar system already in operation.

In our search for identity, we are researching and I feel, perhaps creating the concept of Aztlan. Supposedly, we are descendants, through our Indian heritage, of the native peoples of the Southwest. The Aztlan people had a civilization that is still with us in a modified form through Mexican-Spanish influences. Aztlan lives in any land where a Chicano lives: in his mind and heart and in the land he walks. The emblem used extensively in Chicano circles is a black Aztec eagle on a red background.

Carnalismo, a feeling or an allegiance that permeates the movement, means a type of brotherhood within members of La Raza characterized by depth of feeling and allegiance to other carnales. It is the type of feeling and allegiance that many blood relatives have for one another. Once a Chicano is your carnal he will stand with you through thick or thin.

In social work circles (I am a social worker by training), we are looking at the aspects of the Chicano (Mexican-American) family that are conducive to mental health. We are attempting to break the stereotypes associated with the Chicano family and show the Chicano family with its healthful components as well as with its harmful components. We are looking at the extended family and at the social welfare institutions that penalize the Chicano for preserving these family ties. In a sense, our culture has retained the "People orientation" lost to many in our materialistic society.

One of our leaders in the movement has been Cesar Chavez with his organization of farm workers. His is a nonviolent movement. From the frustration of the strikes originated the Teatro Campesino (in Delano, California in 1965). Out of the need for laughter, the strikers began a fast-paced, almost slapstick style of comedy mimicking those pertinent to the strikers: the patron, the contractor, the scab, and so forth. It is now a tremendously effective mode of showing the problems faced by Chicanos. It is raw; it is realistic; it is life itself!

Reies Lopez Tijerina is another leader. His leadership is primarily in Tierra Amarilla in New Mexico. He is a land-grant spokesman, although presently imprisoned for destroying federal property in one of the national forests. Tijerina is a native of southern Texas. He saw his father run off his land in a most humiliating fashion. He was from humble origins, and he drifted around in farm camps. He was an extremely eloquent, fiery speaker for his Alianza, fighting for return of lands to land grantees and communal rights, but, most important, for full recognition of the Treaty of Guadalupe-Hidalgo. Ranchers have distorted laws in this area to suit their needs.

Rodolfo "Corky" Gonzalez from Colorado has been a leader in the migratory labor area. He is an ex-boxer, lecturer, poet, political activist, and community organizer, as well as a businessman and philanthropist. He is presently president and director of the Crusade for Justice, a Chicano civil rights organization in Denver. His poem, "Yo Soy Joaquin," should be required reading for everyone. Joaquin's first words poignantly describe the anguish of the Chicano who is confused and lost in the Anglo society.

Jose Angel Gutierrez of Crystal City, Texas, is a young man who is devoting his most capable energies toward establishing a base of political power in Texas. Chicanos who have become disillusioned with both political parties have created a third party, La Raza Unida.

The Mexican press was a strong ally to the Mexican- Americans who fought injustices during and after World War II. We are still fighting these injustices, but now with a better self-concept, with a sustaining and lasting dedication and determination, and with more sophisticated and greater manpower. The dedication is courageous and contagious. We are fighting the vast racism that is rampant in our country and that seems unable to tolerate differentness. We are fighting for the right to be as we are—Chicanos. And within our culture we demand the right to be first-class citizens within this our United States.

Por mi Raza habla el Espiritu.

Nita Jo Gonzales Aleman (1950-   )

"Through the Curtain of Discontent A Face Emerges."

Social activist and writer Nita Jo Gonzales Aleman was twenty years old when she presented the following diatribe. In this public discourse she directs her bitter comments at the oppressive Anglo or Caucasian. Here Aleman presents "El Plan Espiritu De Aztlan." Aztlan means a great and proud nation.

Signs proclaiming BLACK POWER, CHICANO POWER, POWER TO THE PEOPLE, NATIONALISM, REVOLUTION and INSURRECTION are samples of what has erupted from coast to coast and sea to sea as the world's youth declares itself human. And through the curtain of discontent that surrounds our country's schools, campuses and slum areas, a face emerges. The face of a too-long-silent race, a face whose brown windows quietly reveal a heritage three hundred years old; a face whose humble expression vividly confesses twenty thousand years of existence, a brown face that lays claim to the fact that we are a *mestizo* race. Indian mother and Spanish father brought forth a breed of *mestizos* known to the mentality of this society as a hyphenated citizen; the label reads MEXICAN-AMERICAN. We, the new breed of *mestizos*, would be the "niggers" in a land that we nursed and coddled, watching, protecting, even at the cost of the blood of our wives, husbands, sons and daughters, with the hope and justification that our grandchildren would benefit from the fruit our lives and labor would reap from *mi tierra* (my land).

Then the white sea of maggots came and tore the yet unweaned child from my *raza's* (race) bosom, and on its valleys, mountains and plains flew a foreign body, a body of red, white and blue. But that has passed, and progress has lengthened the life span and enabled the busy housewife to give more time to her church activities. Now man, a white man, has claimed the moon god for the good old U.S.A. Yet in the fields, the mines and the factories children of Zapata, Villa, Quetemoc and Che crave a glass of milk or a piece of bread. And in the hearts and souls of the second, third and fourth generation Chicano a continual anger seethes, a growth of bitterness and sometimes hate for the government and the people who shove us under the mat only to call us out to sell Fritos or to die to save a *gringo* major in a war where promises and treaties are silenced by machine gun fire, the smell of death and cries of anguish.

As the earth continues its revolution around the sun, science prepares for man's first step on Mars, local police brush up on their riot procedures and Chicanos throughout the Southwest venture into a new era of movement. As my *raza* glances back over the scenes at the close of Act I, we recall the march of three thousand migrant workers from Delano to Sacramento, California—a march that emphasized the rights denied to the migrant worker. Demands were made- -demand for better housing, better wages and the freedom to be a Chicano, a man. Fifteen thousand Chicanos march together at a Los Angeles Blow Out. Fifteen thousand walk out to dramatize that we are no longer second-class citizens who own nothing but a name, a language, a heritage- -our keys to the doors of economy, education, individualism and equality.

Thirty are arrested in Del Rio, Texas, for exercising their right to the freedom of speech, a right that we are asked to respect, a right that the present-day law enforcers do not uphold. And so one week later two thousand Chicanos respond to the Establishment's blunder by demonstrating that our *raza* has had enough, and cries of "Ya basta" ("We've had enough") still linger in the atmosphere.

A walkout of West High School students in Denver followed by a confrontation with the police set the stage, and four days and four nights belong to the Chicano community. During that short period of time, a Chicano *barrio* dated to lift its head face-to-face with its oppressor.

The last of March, 1969, and the beginning of April were witnesses to the harmony of the voices and *gritos* (yells) which at one time or another proclaimed to the city fathers "Chicano Power." They were heard together with chants of "Unidos venceremos" ("United we shall overcome"), letting the sound of their proclamation ring across the Southwest. From the *barrio*, the school and the campus, eighteen hundred representatives from all Chicano youth organizations heard the call for unity and eighteen hundred came when the Crusade for Justice sponsored the first Chicano Youth Liberation Conference. After four days of constant discussion, deliberation, songs, dances and *actos*, eighteen hundred joined forces and announced to the oppressors of our people that *Aztlan* (the name given to the land north of Mexico by the Aztecs) would live again in "El Plan Espiritu de Aztlan." ("The Spiritual Plan of Aztlan").

> Mi Raza declares to you, "Columbia," our preamble
> of independence.

EL PLAN ESPIRITU DE AZTLAN

In the Spirit of a new People that is conscious not only of its proud historical heritage, but also of the Brutal "Gringo" invasion of our territory, we, the Chicano inhabitants and civilizers of the Northern land of their birth and concentrating the determination of our people of the sun, Declare that the call of our blood is our Power, our responsibility, and our inevitable destiny.

We are Free and Sovereign to determine those tasks which are justly called for by our house, our land, the sweat of our brows, and by our hearts. Aztlan belongs to those that plant the seeds, water the fields and gather the crops, and not the foreign Europeans. We do not recognize capricious frontiers on the Bronze Continent.

Brotherhood unites us, and love for our brothers makes us a people whose time has come and who struggles against the Foreigner "gavacho" who exploits our riches and destroys our culture. With our heart in our hands and our hands in the soil, we Declare the Independence of our Mestizo Nation, We are a union of Free Pueblos. We are Aztlan.

Por la Raza Todo
Fuera de la Raza Nada

The above declaration is supplemented by a step-by-step plan to restore my people's dignity and the individualism our ancestors once relished. The first step of *El Plan* is nationalism. Our *jefitos* and *jefitas* (parents) held onto the old way, saving our raza's traditions and values of life from total destruction by the technical, competitive society now in existence. But no longer are the youth of *la raza* going to humbly accept the indignities and psychological destruction of our people.

Elementary school children, as well as students in secondary schools and colleges, are now demanding that the history and heritage of our people be taught in their schools. We are demanding that the Treaty of Guadalupe be upheld and bilingual education be put into effect, not just on a college or high school level, but from the very start of formal education.

We no longer wish to feel that we can't speak our mother tongue in school for fear of expulsion and that we are inferior because the teacher is "culturally deprived" and is unable to pronounce our names correctly. Chicanos everywhere are now beginning to stir as our self-identity is being restored.

Food co-ops, cultural centers and our own newspapers are the tools young Chicanos are using to bring about a change in their lives across the Southwest. Through these devices the Chicano organizations of Aztlan hope to become economically independent of this society. We hope to build an economy of our own that will bring life back into our economically drained communities. We toil for a future where our families, who move with the crops for survival, will find the means necessary to sustain life on land of their own; a future in which *la raza* will not be forced from the frying pan into the fire, moving out of the migrant stream into a rat-infested *barrio*.

When our people make the move to the city, we do not have the technical skill to make a living for our families. We are, therefore, forced into a position where we must receive assistance from the city welfare office. But though our people must receive welfare payments or some form of governmental assistance to survive, we will not be treated as though we are animals. We insist that such assistance is a "right" and not a "privilege."

Too often the city fathers decide that our children will be bused to other schools in the hope that they will assimilate into this "good society." But it is definitely assured that those "underprivileged" children will be unable to keep up with children who have had the advantage of rat-free homes, modern schools, highly up-to-date books and qualified teachers. We demand that our schools be rehabilitated; that the money now spent for busing be used for refurnishing *barrio* schools, hiring Chicano teachers and supplying our school libraries with books relating to *la raza*.

September 16, Mexican Independence Day, was celebrated this year in Denver by a crowd of more than eight thousand, and more than four thousand Chicanos walked out of their schools to bring to the attention of our oppressors that as long as this country and this government refuse to let us breathe, we will take it upon ourselves to struggle to the surface of this "melting pot."

In this manner we are beginning to find our own solutions to the problems that confront and have surrounded us for generations. We submit that our answer to the racism of this society is nationalism. A nationalism that is not of necessity exclusive, but that does let us set our own definitions and our own priorities. A nationalism that strives to be self-sufficient without being imperialistic or exploitative. A nationalism that is named *Aztlan*.

Joan Baez (1941-)

"Thoughts On A Sunday Afternoon."

Folksinger, political activist, and songwriter, Joan Baez was born in Staten Island, New York on 9 January 1941. She grew up in a number of college towns because both parents were educators. As a child she showed great musical talent and learned to play the guitar successfully at twelve years of age. She developed a strong social conscience and began her career as a folksinger because she was influenced by the social criticism of many folk songs, her own personal experiences with racial prejudice, and her Quaker upbringing.

Joan Baez overwhelmed her audience with her beautifully clear voice when she made her first professional appearance at the 1959 Newport Folk Festival. Soon she had a nationwide following. She has participated in numerous rallies and demonstrations for equal rights for African Americans and farm workers. She marched with Dr. Martin Luther King, Jr. and held benefits for Cesar Chavez. Her deep concern for world peace led to her founding the Institute for the Study of Nonviolence in 1965 and Humanitas International in 1979.

From *The Chicanos: Mexican American Voices* by Edward W. Ludwig. Copyright (c) 1971 by Edward W. Ludwig. Reprinted by permission of Viking Penguin, a division of Penguin Books USA, Inc.

I have been asked if I think of myself as a Mexican or a Chicano or as being dark-skinned. This is a difficult question for me to answer, since for the past ten years of my life I have made a point of not categorizing myself. I have refused to accept the title of singer, for instance. I have not particularly identified myself with any special group, but more with humanity as a whole.

I've always thought brown is beautiful, and every chance I've had to get into the sun I've done so, because I like being brown.

When I entered junior high school there was prejudice against brown prople. It took me a couple of years to realize that my being brown was why I did not make friends easily.

I have never really regarded myself as Mexican or English. My father was Mexican and was born in Pueblo, Mexico. On my mother's side there was English and a dash of Irish. I never thought of myself as an English girl, and not too much as a Mexican. I feel distant from the cause of any particular minority group in the sense that when I throw myself into "the cause," it is that of mankind. I have never felt I should work just with browns or just with blacks or just with whites.

In the same way, my husband David, who is in prison, has not wanted to involve himself only with political prisoners. When he was in Safford, a federal prison, about half of the prisoners were Mexicans. After he had finally got them involved in "the cause," they reached a point where they too felt that they were participating in the struggle of all persecuted people.

I know that color made a difference in junior high school. I think I find difficulty in talking about this because I never felt I was badly discriminated against. When I was in junior high my father was a professor at a university, and although I look very Mexican I did not speak Spanish. I felt that Mexican kids were getting a dirty deal, but I did not feel that I was. When my father first came to Stanford, one of the top professors there would hardly speak to him. My father really had to struggle to break through that barrier.

I remember a story my parents told me. In a little town in New York State somebody called me "nigger" because they had never seen anyone as dark as I was. I said, "You ought to see me in the summertime." I loved dark-colored skin.

Once somebody called me a dirty Mexican, and a student asked my teacher, "Is she a Mexican?"

My teacher, attempting to defend me said, "Joan is the very highest breed of Spanish."

I said, "What do you mean, the very highest breed of Spanish? I'm a Mexican." I made a big point of saying I was a Mexican.

Probably the worst place in my childhood, so far as prejudice is concerned, was southern California. For about a year my younger sister did not want to play with me or be seen with me. She tagged after my older sister, who was fair.

But I've put that thought out of my mind—perhaps because it's unpleasant, but also because I have now done all right for myself. Maybe I feel guilty about my success and don't like to harp on the times I have sensed prejudice in people.

There's a theory that people who have known struggle— minority-group people—may have become more sensitive, especially in their music or writing, than most white middle-class Americans.

I have a feeling that probably this isn't true. Ira Sandperl, my friend and co-worker is a Jew. At times some other people get very righteous about how much their group has suffered. But Ira said, for example, "Four thousand years we have suffered, and look what we are doing in Israel now—bombing Arabs."

I don't know what creates sensitivity in people, but it pops up in very odd places.

Is it possible for us to be nonviolent in a violent world?

Yes, I think it is possible and necessary for us to be nonviolently active everywhere. Of course, nonviolence offers no guarantees. But the curious thing is that people who do violence don't receive any guarantees either.

Statistics show that you have a much better chance of coming out alive in a nonviolent battle.

Too many people are hanging onto the old idea of violence. All that violence has done is to destroy people, but we are too terrified to try something different. Cesar Chavez may provide the best example of strong nonviolent action, and I am sure he does not offer any guarantees.

In the Institute for the Study of Nonviolence, we do not have any special training for the practice of nonviolence. We do not have a tactical approach. To root yourself in nonviolence and to be a nonviolent soldier means that you make a decision to go out into the world to confront evil and organize against it, and at the same time make the decision not to do harm to people.

Our approach at the Institute is more on a level of what you and I are going to do to make a change in our lives. Basically, how do we break down the nation-state— which also means breaking down smaller nationalistic groups?

It is assumed that deprived groups should have what everybody else has. But in this society if all the browns and blacks had what the whites have, we would be in an even more hideous situation than we are in now. If they got into the stream of what is now America, then they, too, would be exploiting others, say, in Latin America, Vietnam, Africa. America as a nation is the most destructive force in the world today. In the search for equality our vision must go farther than just wanting what other people have and what we have been deprived of.

In short, I would never want to see a good Mexican become a good American. I would rather that he become a brother in the brotherhood of man.

Browns and blacks are the targets of the most vicious attacks by the state because minorities are the easiest to manipulate. They are the brunt because America needs them. America needs a brunt to go on doing what she does in the world and at home. One of the tragedies of war is that the poor people of every nationality are the ones that carry most of the guns, fight, suffer, and die.

These people who are kept in ignorance and poverty will grab anything that comes to them. If they are educated as to what the nation is really like, it will be easier for them to resist what is offered. ut we have to offer them alternatives that do not yet exist. Until we can offer them something that looks like a real alternative as a way of life, we can do little, and they, less. In a sense, you can say that this is what our work is all about—trying to create that alternative.

It is very difficult to live in a society like this. I think it is up to everyone to help find this alternative. The beautiful thing about Chavez is that he is working with poor people and together they are trying to make something out of nothing. He is building something in spite of America. I feel that the sooner we become color-blind the better it is going to be. And while we attempt to become color-blind, white people should stop destroying brown and black people. I don't think that an alternative can be found within the governmental institutions we have now, because when a person enters the system he has to pledge himself to the nation-state. In the nation-state when we talk about defense we are talking *not about defense of people but about defense of land.* Because the nation-state emphasizes the importance of land, people have to die to protect land. The most expendable things turns out to be human life.

Obviously, it is not possible to find human alternatives within the existing judicial system. The judicial system is not there to promote justice. It is there to keep order. This is exactly why my husband is in prison. Prison is somewhere to put people whom society is afraid to have walking around the streets. True, there are some good people working in the system who try to do some good things. Anytime there is a good judge, I am happy because of him; and anytime there is a lawyer who fights for someone deprived, I am happy. But the system operates primarily to prevent resistance.

What my husband David is saying when he talks about draft resistance is, "Claim your life." Say an absolute "No" to that system and then try to build a different basis for action.

What I am most aware of is people's concept of power. Power is something everyone has, and yet few people in this society truly believe they have power. If the people (not the politicians) could feel in themselves a genuine sense of power, they could behave in a very different way. They would not have to throw rocks. A lot of radicals are really into violence, and, so far as I am concerned, violence is reactionary. In fact, there is a contradiction in terms when we say "violent revolutionary," because revolution means change, and violence is a reversion to a former pattern.

When one raises his fist and shouts "Power," it appears to me he does this because he thinks somebody else has power and he wants to take it for himself. But if he assumes that he is born with power, he doesn't feel the need to grasp it away from someone else. There is enough to go around when we recognize our own power.

To me, what is worth building and organizing is the power of love.

I don't think our alternative can be found within the present educational system. I think the educational system we have now should be replaced. In the context of this society, education would always end up being the same—it would wind up being nationalism.

The basic issues in all of life are never met in the existing educational system. How do you relate to God, no God, sex, drugs, truth, openness, honesty, fear, parents, etc? And finally, how are you going to treat other people? Are you going to kill people or are you not going to kill people? You can not discuss that in school because it is taken for granted that you will kill people. They call it defending your country, but it means killing people. Most of us do not see ourselves involved in the process of murder, but we very much are.

Revolution to me would mean people recognizing the sanctity of human life, and that's the revolution that has never happened. There have been lots of revolutions— people throwing over the government and taking other people's property. But all the good that comes out of a violent revolution comes in spite of the violence.

If we could learn to fight in a different way—get different weapons—then we could really have a chance to win. But for the first time since time began, men would have to recognize that there s only one thing that is really sacred, and that thing is life.

Valentina Valdes (1949-   )

"Viva La Causa! Viva La Raza."

Born in Denver, Colorado and raised in San Luis, Colorado Valentina Valdes attended San Luis Public School and Lincoln High School. Concerned over the conditions of the Mexican American she went to work for an agricultural cooperative after she graduated from high school. She was twenty-one years old at the time she submitted this discourse to the publishing house on the problem of growing up as a Chicano in America.

Reprinted with permission of Macmillan Publishing Company from *Manifesto Addressed to the President of the United States from the Youth of America,* edited by Alan Rinzler. Copyright (c) 1970 by Macmillan Publishing Company.

When I first went to school, I didn't know a word of English, but in the little Colorado village where I lived everybody was Chicano. So I had Chicano teachers all through grade school and learning English from them wasn't that hard for me. Up until the third grade we could speak Spanish freely. I had a third grade teacher who would have us go up in front of the class to tell stories, recite poems or sing songs. Most of the kids would speak in Spanish and she would even tell us some stories in Spanish. But after the third grade, if anyone was heard speaking Spanish on the school grounds, he was taken to the principal's office.

I know of a family that moved from a small village in New Mexico, where practically everybody including the teacher spoke Spanish, to a bigger city. When their little boy started school, he didn't speak a word of English and the teacher didn't know Spanish. The little boy used to tell his father that he could see the teacher's lips moving but didn't understand what she was saying. Because he could not understand or learn anything, he didn't want to go to school any more. The members of his family would try to walk him halfway to school, but when he was almost there he would turn around and go back home crying. Finally, the family sent one of its older girls to school with him, to translate what the teacher was saying. But that was no solution.

At the end of 1968 in Albuquerque, New Mexico, a survey was made of Chicanos starting school. One mother told how when her little boy started school, he didn't understand English. When he spoke in Spanish the teacher hit his hand and he grew to have an inferiority complex. It was hard for him to learn. When he didn't learn, he was sent to a school for the retarded. But he wasn't born retarded, they made him that way.

These stories show how society creates dropouts—who are really forced-outs. Besides not being taught in our own language, we don't learn anything about our culture or history. All we learn about in school is Dick, Sally and Jane, or Mr. White and Mrs. Jones, who have blond hair and blue eyes. And Kit Carson, Davy Crockett and Daniel Boone, the famous Indian murderers. We are taught that Joaquin Murietta, Pancho Villa and Emiliano Zapata were bandits, even though they were fighting with and for the poor against the rich, like Robin Hood, except that they were also fighting for the true liberation of our raza (race). Emiliano Zapata made the most beautiful and true statement: *"La tierra es de todos como el aire, el agua la luz y el calor del sol. Y tienen derecho a ella los que la trabajan con sus propias manos."* "The land is of everyone like the air, the water and the light and the heat of the sun. And those who work the land with their own hands have a right to it."

They don't teach us anything about the Laws of the Indies, which once prevailed in what is now the Southwest. They don't teach us about the Treaty of Guadalupe Hidalgo— which ended the so-called Mexican-American War in which the United States took all our land—and how it said that the United States must respect the land grants issued by Spain and Mexico, as well as the culture of the Spanish-speaking people living on these lands. They don't teach us about our Indian ancestry and culture, except to say that the Indians were "savages."

In school other kids who are whiter than you make fun of the color of your skin. This is what happened to me, until I began to hate my color and began to wish that I was whiter. So what happens when we are old enough to wear makeup? We put on tons and tons of white makeup. Then we're not satisfied with this, so we dye or bleach our beautiful black hair red or blond to look more Anglo. Why does all this come about? Because we don't learn anything about the beautiful culture our Indian ancestors left us.

Our fathers adopted a lot of that culture—many things, from the way people used to work communally down to *tortillas* (our bread). I remember that all the kids who took lunch to school, including me, would never take *tortillas* or *frijoles* (beans). It was shameful to take these things. If someone brought *tortillas* or *frijoles*, the other kids would whisper and make fun of him (even though they themelves ate these foods at home) until he would never want to take Mexican food for lunch again. In the lunch room they would never serve tortillas, chile, or beans, even though the school was 99 percent Chicano. But now that the businessmen have found out that they can make money out of this delicious Mexican food, there are Mexican food stands and *taco* houses all over the place. All this is very effective for the Anglo government. Not letting us learn in our own language is very bad; we get so used to being ashamed of speaking our language that even if we know how to speak it, or understand it, we don't want to use it. This usually happens in the big cities. It gets so bad that we are even ashamed to pronounce our last names as they should be pronounced, and our first names always get translated. You don't say your name like it should be said, but you pronounce it like an Anglo name. Joe for Jose, Galigoose for Gallegos.

This denial of culture, language and history is very bad for our people. But, worse, our everyday life is bad. Jobs are hard to find and our people are hungry; more than half of them in northern New Mexico earn an income below the official poverty level. All this goes back to the Treaty of Guadalupe Hidalgo.

After that treaty was signed, and in spite of all the promises in it, the people were cheated out of their land in every way from trickery to just plain armed robbery. For instance, some Texans would offer a crop of beans to the people (who didn't know English) for the small service of making an X on a paper. That paper would be a document for their land ownership, and so they lost it. People would lose their land for not paying the taxes demanded by the United States government—when they had never known land taxation before and all the new American laws were published only in English. There were so many kinds of robbery. In 1832 more than 580,000 acres of land in just one grant belonged to the heirs of Tierra Amarilla, New Mexico. By 1969 the heirs had only 10,000 acres left. In another grant, that of San Joaquin, the heirs held about 500,000 acres in 1806. Today they have only 1,411.

The communal lands were all eaten up by the National Forest. The forest service now charges people to graze their animals, cut wood, fish or hunt deer on the land they once used freely. They could take as many cows as needed to graze there; today many people kill or sell their animals because they cannot afford the fees. The lumber companies get almost all the wood and the people can't afford to build.

In rural villages like Tierra Amarilla, New Mexico, a Chicano graduating from high school finds there is nothing for him to do. The only jobs available are the jobs the rich Anglo rancher or the Anglo government give, like working on roads or dams. Then there are the Chicano teachers and cops, who are mostly *lambes* (boot-lickers); once they get into the world of money, they say "I made it, why can't you?" and they don't give a damn about the rest of their own people—they even ignore or snub them. They don't give a damn about their *raza* or culture. So most boys join the military and go to fight dirty wars, or they go to another state to find work. Girls leave for the city to work as waitresses or scrubwomen. Young married couples leave their homes and go to the city.

The people once had a beautiful way of living. People used the common lands as they needed, with no fences and no friction among neighbors. Whenever a family needed wood to build a house, all the neighbors would go with the family to the *sierra* to get as much as they needed, without any authorities telling them anything. When they returned, the neighbors would then help the family build the house.

If a family needed meat, the men would go deer hunting or fishing and get what they needed without any trouble. When the hot weather came and it was too warm for the sheep to wear their winter coats, the people would sheer off the wool to make blankets, jackets and socks for the winter. People were not stingy either. When they killed a cow, a pig or a sheep, they would invite two or three neighbors to help do the butchering. After they finished, the neighbors would be sure to get a good share of the animal that was killed. This is the way they worked, and a family was always sure to have meat in the house. When relatives or friends came to visit, they were always received well and were welcome to stay as long as they wished; the longer they stayed, the happier everybody was.

When it was time to plant, about nine, ten or more families would get their workhorses together and would go help one neighbor to plow and plant many acres of land. Then they would go to another house, and another, until the whole village was planted. For the weeding and harvest they would work the same way; and with the crops of the harvest they would trade with nearby villages and among themselves for the different things grown (like beans, potatoes and wheat for peaches, chile and tomatoes).

But life has changed; people have gotten used to the American way of life. Still, the people here in Tierra Amarilla, as well as in other small villages, have held onto a lot of their culture and language. I was raised in a small village something like this and little kids learned to speak in Spanish. When I was about fourteen we moved to a big city, and there most Chicano kids didn't speak in Spanish—they didn't even understand it; the younger they were, the less they understood Spanish. After living in the city for two years, whenever I heard a little boy or girl speaking Spanish, I felt like crying and hugging them.

Yes, life is different now; when relatives or friends go to visit people and stay over a week or two, people begin to wonder when their visitors are going to leave. The food in the house is getting less and less and a job doesn't support so many people. When people kill an animal, instead of sharing it with their neighbors, like their ancestors did, they hide it so it will last longer for the family. If a family doesn't have any animals (and there are many who don't), then they just don't eat meat because meat is too expensive to buy from the store. The only way they can eat meat is if they go deer hunting, and if they hunt out of season, they may be in danger. If a Forest Ranger catches them, they could get ten years in jail. But it is all right if a Texan comes to get elk during the hunting season, even if he only takes the head for his trophy room and leaves the rest of the meat to rot.

All these things have made many of our people angry and ready to fight for their rights. In other parts of the United States, it is mostly the youths who are involved in the Movement. But in northern New Mexico the older people are the ones who know the culture and history and who have been most interested in *La Causa* (The Cause). These are the people who formed the Alianza Federal de los Pueblos Libres, of which Reis Lopez Tijerina is the leader. He has awakened many people inside the state as well as outside. There are new youth organizations too, but they have many problems. One very strong young man in *La Causa* started a group here in northern New Mexico last year. Then he had to leave the state because he couldn't pay his bills and he couldn't find a job here. The enemy knows how to divide us and weaken us.

But people go on trying. An agricultural cooperative was started in Tierra Amarilla by some young people. The purpose of it is to bring back some of the good old ways of working together and also to inject some hope into our oppressed people. The land on which the crops are planted and equipment also were lent by some Chicanos. The harvest is being divided among them and the volunteer workers, according to the needs of the family. Volunteers have come from all over the United States to help make this dream of working communally again and becoming self-sufficient real.

This is what we want: To run our own lives. To have the *sierra*, with its beautiful high green grass now going to waste, belong to the people again. To graze our animals like we used to, without any fences. To be able to go to the *sierra* freely to hunt deer or fish without anyone telling us what to do. To be able to go into the *sierra* and cut wood as needed.

We want good doctors and medical clinics that really want to cure people, not like the present doctors, who only care about money.

We are sick and tired of being considered "inferior" to the rich white race, and of white people telling us that our bronze race is ugly, ignorant, superstitious and lazy, and that our Indian ancestors were "savages."

We want to rule our own schools. We want to be taught in Spanish by good Chicano teachers who know as well as love and are proud of our Indian and Spanish heritage, culture and history.

Viva La Causa! Viva La Raza, our people! *Tierra o Muerte* -the famous cry of the Zapatistas in the Mexican Revolution—Land or Death!

Jovita Gonzalez (1904-   )

"Folk-Lore of the Texas-Mexican Vaquero"

Born January 18, 1904 in Roma, Texas folklorist, writer, and teacher Jovita Gonzalez received her education "in Texas institutions of higher learning." She taught high school Spanish in Corpus Christi and St. Mary's Hall in San Antonio. She has published extensively in the *Texas Folklore Society Journal* and made significant contributions to southwest folklore. In 1936 she served as president of the Texas Folklore Society. She and her husband Edmundo Mireles expressed an interest in teaching Spanish in the primary grades. Consequently, they published a series of nine textbooks on that subject.

Reprinted from *Texas and Southwestern Lore,* Number VI, 1927, pp. 7-9 with kind the kind permission of the Publications of the Texas Folklore Society.

It is hardly conceivable that in this era of publicity and in this Texas, where every phase of ranching has been more or less popularized, there should exist unknown to the vast majority of Texans and other Americans an extraordinary type of range man. Such, nevertheless, is a fact. Moreover, this distinct and unfamiliar man of the range has been in Texas for nearly two centuries. Texas born and Texas bred, he is considered even by many of those who know him—superficially—as an undesirable alien. He is a product of the state, and loves Texas as his country; yet to Anglo-Americans of a few years' stay in the state he is an outcast. On one side, he descends from the first Americans, the Indians; on the other, his ancestry can be traced to the Spanish adventurer and conquistador. From the mingling of these two races a unique type has resulted, possessing not only salient characteristics of both but also certain peculiar traits created by the natural environment and surroundings in which he lives. This composite type is the vaquero of the Texas-Mexican frontier.*

First, his inherited traits will be considered. From his Indian ancestor he has inherited a love for freedom and the open prairie, a dislike for law and restraint, a plaintive melancholy that permeates all his actions, and a fatalistic tendency that makes him see the hand of fate guiding and mastering all his efforts. *"Suerte y Mortaja del cielo bajan"* ("Fortune and Death come from above") seems to be his motto in life. When misfortune assails him, the only answer to his problem is a shrug of the shoulder and a *"Si es mi suerte que le voy a hacer?"* ("It is fate: what can I do about it?")

From the Spaniard comes a courteous attitude toward women (especially before he is married), a daring spirit of adventure, and a deep rooted love for beauty, particularly music and singing. From the same source he has also inherited a sincere religious feeling, which, mingled with pagan superstitions and beliefs, has added flavor and color to the legends and other forms of folk-lore of the borderland.

Living far from all contact with civilization, he is naturally suspicious of all innovations and newcomers. Every new invention introduced is a check to his freedom. An old vaquero told me once of what to him was paradise: the open prairies with no fences to hinder the roaming of the cattle and the wanderings of the cowboys. "Cuando vino el alambre, vino el hambre." ("With the coming of barbwire, came hunger.") In spite of his pessimism, the vaquero is a poet at heart. He sees the beauty of the sage- brush in bloom; the singing of the mocking bird on clear moonlight nights invites him to sing—not songs of joy and happiness but plaintive melodies of unrequited love and tragedies, Like all people who live in close touch with Nature, he understands all the creatures of the woods and interprets them in his fanciful way.

As has already been stated, the vaquero is at heart a religious man; all the wonders of Nature he attributes to a super-natural power. All goodness and beauty come from the Virgin Mary and are part of her. A beautiful sunset is her smile; the blue sky is the blue of her mantle; the rainbow is formed by the tears that she sheds for sinners.

The folk-lore of the Mexican vaquero has the combined charm of the Andalusian lore as told by Fernan Caballero and the quaintness and simplicity of the Indian myth. To understand it is to understand the spirit and the soul of the Mexican people.

* The vaquero is not the aristocratic, landed proprietor of the borderland, but the wandering cowboy whose only possessions are his horse, an unlimited store of legends and traditions, and the love for his *chata,* by which name the Spanish-American cowboy, whether Mexican vaquero or Argentinian gaucho, calls his sweetheart.

Fermina Guerra

"Rancho Buena Vista."

Born in the area of Laredo, Texas Fermina Guerra is a descendant of the settlers of the Rio Grande border. She studied at the University of Texas and while there wrote a master's thesis in which she describes the ways of life and the traditions of the people of the Rancho Buena Vista. Guerra focuses on their rugged indiviudalism and their struggle with the natural environment.

Reprinted from "Rancho Buena Vista: Its Ways of Life and Traditions" by Fermina Guerra, in *Texian Stomping Grounds,* Publications of the Texas Folklore Society Number XVII, 1941, pp. 59-77.

In the extreme northeastern part of Webb County, fifty miles from Laredo and twenty-one miles from Encinal, lies the Buena Vista Ranch. It is not large as ranches go, only about three thousand acres; but it has its share in the traditions of the ranch country.

The land is typical brush country. There is an abundance of prickly pear and other forms of cactus. Mesquite grass abounds, and in the lower places, foxtail and other tall grasses grow. In early times, the plains for twenty miles around were covered breast-high with *zacate de bestia* (hay for animals), but all this tall grass is gone now. The hardy bunch grasses best survive droughts and overgrazing.

The country is broken by many gravel hills, and the slopes are covered with fragments of petrified wood. From them a grotto twenty-five feet in length has been erected at the ranch home.

A stone's throw west of the ranch house flows a creek, generally a mere trickle of water interspersed with *esteros,* deep pools. In time of flood it overflows to cover a half-mile-wide valley and brings destruction in its wake. It rises in the high land to the south and empties into Nueces River, eighteen miles to the north. Near its source, it is called El Pato (Duck), in its middle course, La Becerra (Heifer Calf), and near its mouth, La Parida, this last name meaning a female—perhaps a cow, perhaps a woman—with a newborn offspring.

The country is, comparatively speaking, newly settled. There had been ranches and towns along the Rio Grande since 1755, but in 1869, when Don Justo Guerra and his two sons, Florencio and Carmen, brought their herds of sheep and goats across the Rio Grande at Laredo, the country to the north was largely virgin land. There were not even resident Indians. Arrowheads and other Indian relics abound today, but the only Indians were raiding parties from farther north. The three Guerras came out to the Becerra Ranch, then owned by Casimiro Benavidez. At that time there were only four ranches in the region—El Pato, La Becerra, El Nido, and La Parida. Of them, only La Becerra remains.

After the Civil War broke out and the Southern ports were blockaded, the only outlet for cotton was through Mexico. One of the cotton roads from San Antonio to the Rio Grande was hacked out through the brush six miles north of La Becerra Ranch. The opening through the brush, now grass- covered, and the marks that the wide iron tires of the ox carts left on flint rocks in their path can yet be seen. While the guns of war thundered far away and ox carts rumbled across the Becerra, Don Justo Guerra, his wife, and their sons saw their herds increase. Ranching was the sole occupation of the country, and for most of the Border ranchers the war was as far away as the operations of Bismarck in Germany. At the brandings, all the rancheros working in cooperation, the *orejanos* —the "slick ears," or mavericks—were held until the cow hunts were over. Then there was a roping contest, a kind of fiesta, at which the best ropers kept for their own the wild, unclaimed animals on hich they contested. Sheep and wool, however, for a long time were the chief products of the ranchers of this part of Texas.

Shortly after the close of the Civil War, Florencio Guerra married Josefa Flores from Laredo. He established himself farther down the creek at a natural rock ford. The banks were higher here, the creek deeper, the land more fertile. He named the place Buena Vista (Good View). Meanwhile, the country was being settled, and it became necessary to establish legal claim in the land under the Texas homestead law.

So much for the establishment of the Rancho Buena Vista. In time a school was built near the ranch house. Without presuming to domain or wealth, Buena Vista became a kind of social headquarters for the country around it. Yet the ways of life on it were characteristic of the ways of life on scores of other Mexican ranches between the Nueces and the Rio Grande, in the brush country of Texas—and also in the border country of Mexico. The traditions pertaining to Buena Vista that have been told over and over among the children and grandchildren of Florencio Guerra and his wife, Josefa Flores, are the kind of traditions to be heard all up and down the border country.

Some of them, perhaps a majority of them, treat of actual happenings, and are folklore only in that they are traditional and that they are hardly important enough for history. The stories are of Indians, floods, captives, sheepherders, buried treasure, violent death, happenings when the bishop came or the wool went to town. When a fire burns on a winter night or when it is raining and the water in Becerra Creek is high, people at Buena Vista tell and hear these traditions of the land.

HIGH WATER

Ever-present in the minds of ranch people is the question of water. The foremost topic of conversation among them is the condition of the range, the prospect of rain, the water of the tanks. This part of the country has never found good well water to pump up with windmills, and tanks are depended on for stock water.

In the old days there were no tanks. The cattle watered at the two or three creeks in the country. In time of drouth they were driven by the eighteen miles to the Nueces River. There was never trouble over water rights. Through the years these ranchmen kept the peace among themselves; the struggle with nature occupied their chief energies. The first fence went up in 1891. Don Florencio's son, Donato, used to go out of his way before and after school to watch the fence-building operations being carried on by the Callaghan Ranch hands, who were erecting a fence between Vista Ranch and theirs.

Three times in the history of Buena Vista Ranch, La Becerra Creek has been half a mile wide—1878, 1903 and 1937. Of course, the oldest flood is the most romantic. Don Justo and his wife were still living then, old and set in their ways. Their ranch house was of mesqite poles and adobe, thatched with grass and set on the very banks of La Becerra Creek.

One day it started to rain; torrents poured down. As the creek began to rise and there was no abatement of the downpour, the other members of the family grew frightened. Not Don Justo. He had seen rain before; nothing ever came of it. But the rain poured all night and a second day; the creek continued to rise.

Now it was up to the corral, adjoining the house. No matter; it would go down presently. A second night, and a third day, the rain continued pouring. At dusk on the third day, the water began to enter the house. A young matron, wife of Don Carmen, holding her child in her arms, told her husband to take her to higher ground. She feared remaining in the house another night with that constantly rising water. Gladly enough, he complied. Before leaving, he begged his aged father and mother to accompany him, but they laughed. "You will get all wet for nothing," they said. "We have a roof over our heads. What if there is a little water in the house?"

But the young mother set out for the hill to the east. Before she reached it, she was obliged to swim to save herself and child, her husband aiding her. The rain was still pouring so hard that they got lost in the brush, but they went on eastward.

Eventually they found themselves on a well-known hill. Don Florencio's ranch was just a mile to the northwest. The mother asked her husband to go down there and ask for some dry clothing for the baby, as the night was cold and it was still raining hard. Willingly enough, Don Carmen set out.

On reaching the house, he told Don Florencio what had happened at the upper ranch. Hurriedly the latter saddled his best horse and set out to see what he could do to persuade his parents to leave their house and take to the hills. The water was not so high at Buena Vista, though it was at the door of the main house.

About daybreak, he reached the shore opposite his parents' ranch. there was a raging torrent between him and them. From afar off, barely to be seen among the treetops, he could discern the roof of the house and two people perched on it. He could hardly hear their feeble cries, so great was the distance.

Like most ranchmen of his time, Don Florencio could not swim. He depended upon his horse to carry him across the streams. This task his present mount refused to perform. Time after time he forced the animal into the water, only to have it turn back. At length he returned to his own ranch for a fresh mount. This horse, too, refused to venture out into the flood. So Florencio was forced to flounder at the edge of the current and watch those faraway forms, fearing to see them disappear from sight. But towards evening, the waters began to recede, and the next day he was able to go out and rescue the exhausted old people from their predicament.

The flood of 1903 was unusual in that no rain accompanied it. One hot, sunny morning Don Florencio noticed what appeared to be a cloud of mist rising rapidly from the bushes south of the house along the creek. It was coming fast, with a rushing sound. Suddenly he realized that a wall of water, far wider than the creek banks, was bearing down upon him. One of his laborers was down the creek bed driving some goats to higher ground. Racing his horse, he hurried to get within calling distance of the man, Carlos. The laborer saw Don Florencio and heard his call, but not realizing that the danger was so close, went leisurely on with his work. Suddenly the turbulent water was upon him, and he was borned along with it as it swirled among the bushes. Fortunately, after his first fright, he was able to collect his wits sufficiently to grasp at an overhanging limb and so save his life.

The flood of 1937 was more prosaic: the creek itself did no particular damage, but the water destroyed all but three tanks in a radius of twenty miles and left the range worse off than before the rain.

Such is the life of the ranchmen of Southwest Texas; drouth and flood too much water or not enough, then, now, and always.

INDIANS

Indians were not regular residents of the country, and no one knew from what tribe they came. It was generally believed that they were runaways from the Indian territory far to the north, for they were often dressed as white men and at first deceived their victims. By 1875 nearly all the Indians had been gathered into reservations by the U.S. Government, but it was customary to allow a few at a time to leave the reservation for the purpose of hunting. These would band together at some distance from the reservations and make forays to the south, where there were no soldiers to stop them.

Such bands occasionally made their way into the territory about Buena Vista Ranch. Don Florencio, in his boyhood, lived in constant fear of the Indians and often caused his father to laugh at him because he professed to have heard their whistling or cries in the brush or to have seen the dust sent up by their horses' hoofs.

The reports were not always figments of the imagination. Indians did come sometimes and had to be driven away. The oldest houses had apertures in the walls, *troneras*, about four by twenty inches within the house and about three inches square on the outside, that gave opportunity for the besieged settler to fire in several directions without being in danger from Indian arrows. The whole countryside abounds in arrowheads. In a morning's walk one may pick up a hundred points of all sizes, ranging from delicate bird points to heavy arrowheads three inches or more in length.

The Indians came, though, chiefly to steal horses. They generally illed only in case of resistance. Don Florencio and his brother had worked too hard in getting their horses, to stand by idly while Indians drove them away. So one day when a band came upon them on the range—it was about 1877—Don Carmen and Don Florencio fired upon the band. The Indians had a number of horses with them; in return they fired a volley of arrows and several pistols, and Don Carmen's horse fell. His brother leaned down and lifted him to his own mount and then turned to fire at the Indians again. But the firing had startled the horses into flight, and the Indians took after them.

The fleeing horses ran toward the Buena Vista ranch house. From afar off one of the boys saw them coming and recognized Indians in pursuit. He climbed up on the horse shed to see better. On came the horses. Just south of the ranch they swerved away toward the creek, at the edge of which old Marcos, the *pastor*, was herding the goats.

The boy began shouting to the women in the house below:
"Here come the Indians chasing horses!"
"They are coming here!"
"Now they are going to cross the creek south!"
"There are Marcos and the goats!"
"Now the Indians see Marcos!"
"He is stopping them! He is talking with them! They are quarreling!"
"Marcos is coming this way!"
"One of the Indians is aiming an arrow at him!"
"He's hit! The Indians are running on away down the creek after the horses! I think Marcos is dead!"

And he was. That visit was the last that the Indians made to Buena Vista Ranch.

Although the Indians did have firearms at the time, they used arrows on many occasions. They had used both pistols and arrows in the encounter earlier in the day, but on passing by the ranch, they killed Marcos with an arrow. They saw no need of wasting their ammunition.

LA CAUTIVA

Three miles south of Buena Vista Ranch was the ranch of Antonia Hinojosa, *la cautiva*. She was a romantic figure in the region, a former captive of the Indians. As a young woman she had lived in the Mexican state of Chihuahua. She had married young and had an infant son.

One day she went down to a creek nearer her hut to wash clothes and took her infant along. While she was there, a band of roving Indians from across the border came upon her and her child. They captured her, and cutting the ears off her son, left him lying on the creek bank. She never saw him again.

For a number of years she lived among the Indians, at length becoming the wife of one of them. By him she had a daughter, Lola. But she longed to escape. In a battle between tribes she was taken by the enemy and separated from her daughter. The Indian man grieved for her and told Lola the Spanish name of her mother and urged her to seek her if anything happened to him. Then it happened that Lola's Indian father was killed in a personal fight with another brave. In some way Lola escaped and got cut off from the Indians and grew up among white people. She never ceased searching for her mother, but it was many years before she found her.

Meanwhile, the mother, Antonia Hinojosa, had been released by the Indians because the United States Government made them give up all their captives. She came to La Becerra Creek and took up a homestead. She lived alone and had not even a laborer to help her.

She made bags out of cowhides to carry away the earth she painstakingly dug out of the burrow pit of her tank; that little tank is still to be seen on her ranch.

Her ranch house was of stone, brought from the bed of La Becerra Creek. The stones are now part of a modern house on the neighboring ranch of Cesario Benavidez.

Once, during the Indian raids, she closed up her horses in her corral and herself mounted guard upon them day and night. When the Indians arrived, she stood her ground so that they left her unmolested.

Through a long life she had many trials and adventures. But she prospered. One of her laborers was the ill-fated victim of Justo Manta, the "badman" of the region. At length, when she was a feeble old woman, her daughter learned of her whereabouts. Lola was about sixty years old at the time and lived in Austin. She came alone to her mother's ranch, and thus they lived together for a few years.

The daughter decided to return to Austin, but she left word with friends and neighbors that they should advise her immediately if Antonia fell ill. Several years passed before the call came. Upon receiving word of her illness, Lola set out from Austin posthaste. But Antonia, being one hundred and five years old, did not live till her daughter arrived. Lola heard of her mother's death when she reached a ranch about five miles away.

The shock was too great for the aged traveler; she was unable to continue her journey. Soon she herself died, and the two are buried side by side on the ranch of "La Cautiva."

VISITS OF THE MISSIONARIES

Ranch people of the early days were generally inclined toward a virile piety. Throughout south Texas, missionary priests visited the ranches at least once a year. Their task was not a difficult one, as far as religious instruction was concerned, for every vaquero, shepherd, sheepshearer, ranch owner, ranch woman and child knew the basic tenets of the Catholic religion, could recite the prayers, sing the hymns, and take an intelligent interest in the services.

At Buena Vista, the visit of Father Antonio Serra was an occurrence of great importance. Weddings were performed, baptism administered, Mass celebrated, the sick visited, and consolation given to the bereaved. After the erection of the schoolhouse, the services were held there.

Days before the missionary was due to arrive, all the women of the surrounding ranches had made preparations for the great day. The visit of the missionary was of social interest as well as of religious significance. The occasion was one for feasting and gayety. The Guerra ranch was always the meeting place for the people, because of its central location and the fact that the stone schoolhouse was the best available place in which to hold the services.

A day or two before the missionary's arrival, the women gathered to help with the preparations. The best room, the best bed, the best kitchen utensils, and the best food were set apart for the missionary. Everything was bustle and hurry. For not only was the missionary to be fed and housed, but the people from all nearby ranches were to be entertained. Families arrived in wagons, on horseback, in buggies, or on foot to be present when the missionary arrived. They were fed and camped in the ranch enclosure.

After the padre had been welcomed, he first heard confessions. Then Mass was celebrated. During Mass all except the very young children received the Eucharist. This morning service, which invariably included a sermon, was lengthy. Nor was the padre able to take such rest during the day. Always there were infants to be baptized, children and adults to be catechized, and, of course, it would have been most unusual if no young couples presented themselves to have their marriage blessed. Evening found the zealous priest with his congregation for the recitation of the Rosary, the 'Ave Maria's' interspersed with devotional hymns.

If the yearly visit of the priest was an occasion of rejoicing, the visit of the bishop was an event for superb celebration. He came only once every four or five years. Sometimes, in the absence of roads, he had to be guided by some vaquero. In the earlier days he traveled on horseback, accompanied by one or two priests, or even alone. Later on he traveled in a stage coach with something of a retinue. He usually came in the spring, and then the enclosure at Buena Vista was made a bower of flowers. The ranchmen formed an escort to meet him at the arroyo. Over the ranch enclosure was a great white arch, under which he and his party and the escort passed. Children with baskets of flowers stood along the way, strewing it with flowers. But often they were so wonder- struck that they forgot to distribute the flowers.

Amusing things were always happening even at the most solemn times. On one occasion, a very respectable matron, Senora Panchita Alegria, who was busy in the kitchen helping prepare the meat for the bishop, heard the school bell ringing to call the people to greet His Excellency. She rushed out with everyone else to receive his blessing. This blessing is administered by the bishop to each individual separately. One approaches him, kneels, kisses the ring which the bishop has been given by the Pope, and then receives the blessing.

When Senora Alegria had thus knelt and received the blessing, the bishop looked at her and smiled.

"Are you going to kill me now?" he inquired, "or wait until later in the day?"

With astonishment and chagrin, the startled matron realized that she still held gripped firmly in her hand the big butcher knife with which she had been cutting the meat.

TIO PEDRO AND THE RANGERS

Tio Pedro, a cousin of Don Florencio, had established himself on a small ranch to the north of Buena Vista. He was a peaceful man with a wife and two children. He worked hard and managed to gather together a stock of cattle and several good horses.

It happened that on one occasion three Mexican thieves stole some of his horses. He missed the animals almost immediately and began to search for them. After traveling for a little while through the brush, he saw their tracks in the dust and set out after the thieves. He came upon them about dusk as they were preparing their evening meal. Dismounting from the horse, he shouted to them to surrender his animals. Instead, they opened fire. He returned their fire, and one of the thieves fell dead. The others fled.

Much perturbed over what he had done, he traveled back to the ranch, where he arranged for the burial of the dead man. Then he went down to Cotulla and gave himself up to the authorities for trial. He was relesased on bond. At the time of his trial he was cleared. Returning to the ranch, he took up his peaceful life again.

A few months later, two Texas Rangers presented themselves at Buena Vista Ranch. These men were the terror of the Mexican ranch country. It was generally believed that they shot first and asked questions afterwards. They were very civil and asked for Don Pedro Fulano, who had killed a horse thief in defense of his rights.

Don Florencio asked why the Rangers were seeking him. They laughingly replied that they had never seen a Mexican brave enough to stand up for his rights and would like to set eyes on one. As they were passing through the country on their rounds, this seemed a good opportunity to do so.

The tale did not ring true to Don Florencio. It was about dinner time; so he asked the strangers to remain for the meal offering to take them over afterward. Much to his surprise, they stayed and chatted in a friendly way over the meal.

But Don Florenico was worried. Calling aside his young son, he said, "Saddle a horse, Donato, and ride to the ranch of Tio Pedro. Tell him the "rinches" are here asking about the killing of the horse thief, and though they don't seem unfriendly, I want to warn him."

Donato sped away unmolested. When he reached Tio Pedro and gave his message, the man was between two fires. He had been tried and acquitted of his crime, but tales he had heard of the "rinches" made him fear they they would pay little attention to the laws of the country if they had the inclination otherwise.

For a while he stood in thought. Then he said to his wife, "I don't know these men. Maybe they mean no harm. but once they catch me, if they are out to get me, I will stand no chance of escaping. I'd better go now while I am free."

Immediately he saddled a horse and rode away. Weeks later, after the Rangers had gone, his family received word from him saying he had reached safe haven in Old Mexico and for them to sell the property and join him.

This they did, and crumbling walls now attest to the terror of the "rinches" that lived in the hearts of even honest men.

HUMOROUS TALES

Gabina Ortegon, an old nurse, was with the family in 1882. That year was terribly cold. There was ice everywhere for days at a time. Early in the mornings Gabina would sally forth seeking little sticks to start the fire in the *bracero* (brazier) that she used to warm her frozen fingers and the toes of her charges.

One bitterly cold morning she had difficulty finding her fagots; they were covered with ice. Shivering with the cold, she at length reached the ranch house again and painstakingly started her little fire. She put some of the frozen fagots near the blaze so the ice might melt from them before she put them in the fire. As she sat there warming her fingers, she started in surprise. Surely her eyes were plaing her tricks. She rubbed them hurriedly and looked again. It was true! Her little frozen sticks were curling, writhing, lifting heads, crawling away! They were frozen snakes that she had picked up under the bushes along the creek!

About the same time Antonio Guerra, a relative of the family, found a stray horse. He rode the beast for a while, expecting to find the owner. As time passed, he decided to sell the animal and went to a judge of his acquaintance.

"May I sell this horse?" he asked the judge.

"Certainly," the judge replied. "Why do you ask such a foolish question?"

Antonio did not reply, but went and duly sold the horse. The buyer did not fare so well as Antonio had done. In a few months, the owner appeared and claimed the animal. Antonio Guerra was hailed into court on the charge of selling stolen goods.

"But I had permission to sell him," he insisted. "This very judge gave me permission to sell him." "Yes," the judge replied, "but I thought the horse was yours." "Well," Antonio replied with a twinkle in his eye, "I did not need your permission to sell what is my own. But I did need to sell someone else's animal."

On another occasion, this same Antonio caused the women folk at Buena Vista a very uncomfortable half-day. It was in the early eighties when the Indian tales were still rife. Old Marcos had not been dead so many years, killed by an Indian arrow, and 'La Cautiva,' with her tales of Indian captives, was living just over the way.

As was their custom, the women went out at daybreak one morning to do the washing in La Becerra Creek. While they were busily at work, Antonio conceived the notion of frightening them. He got an old pair of chaps out of the horse-shed. They had fringes on them and were stiff with age. He put one leg of the chivarras upon his head, and at a distance it looked like a war bonnet. Carefully, he crawled among the underbrush across the creek; suddenly, he poked his head out between two branches in full sight and gave a blood-chilling yell. The startled women got a glimpse of the fearful war bonnet and fled up the creek, tearing through brush like mad.

It happened that there was a little gulch a little way up the creek, well hidden by the undergrowth. Into this the frightened women plunged. It was ten or fifteen feet deep, but, luckily, they broke no bones in their fall. there they lay, terrified for their lives for hours.

Antonio immediately repented of what he had done and began to call for them to come our of hiding, but in their terror they mistook his voice for that of Indians, hot on their trail. At length one of them recognized his voice, and they came back, too shaken to be angry.

'Tia' Juana was the heroine of another humorous incident. One morning the men were out near the corrals getting ready for the day's work when a javelina came wandering across the clearing. No one was armed; so one of the men called to Juana, who was near the horse-shed, to bring something with which to kill the animal. As the arms were not there, she did not know what to take to them, till one shouted to bring a lasso. She came around the end of the shed swinging it as she came, only to find the javelina between her and the man.

"Throw it, Juana!" they cried, and hardly taking aim, she let fly. To her utter astonishment, she lassoed the animal. She was more frightened than the animal was, to be sure, but she brought it up standing and became the heroine of the day.

Buena Vista ranch was always ready to try new things. Today, the modern oil range is in the kitchen; an enormous mechanical refrigerator furnishes ice cream and other frozen dainties for the table; there is running water in the bathroom, a radio in the living room, a modern high- powered car at the door. in 1899, Don Florencio was just as ready to welcome new-fangled things. At that time, Don Susano was traveling the country demonstrating the marvelous new phonograph. And he was invited to the ranch. The machine was a queer looking box equipped with several sets of head phones. All the family and neighbors from miles around gathered in the stone house. It had been built of blocks from the bed of La Becerra Creek in 1882. The walls are eighteen inches thick and as strong today as ever. Many additions have been made to the building, but in those days it was the 'ranch house' and stood as a white, shining landmark. Arrived in this fortress, the guests were seated in a circle, each with a pair of audiophones clamped to his head. Don Susano solemnly played his collection of wax recordings, still more solemnly collected a coin from each guest, and a new group gathered about the new machine.

As soon as ice was manufactured in Laredo, Don Florencio had it hauled out to the ranch on special occasions and buried in pits lined with grass. In large, old-fashioned, wooden freezers the women folk made ice cream, a queer dessert to be favored by an old ranchman of Indian-fighting days.

CURES AND INCANTATIONS

All ranches have their favorite cures and remedies, and so has Buena Vista. Chief among the remedies have always been those for snakebite. One remedy was to put *cuajo* (rennet) in milk and immerse the bitten place in the liquid. The *cuajo* was supposed to draw out the poison. Another method of treating snakebite was to immerse the limb in a hole of thin mud, also supposed to draw out the poison.

In old days rabies was prevalent in coyotes, just as now. Once Don Florencio lassoed a rabid coyote and found himself in a predicament, for the animal endeavored to attack the horse on which he was mounted. He was forced to outrun the animal and drag it to death.

In those days the only remedy for the bite of a rabid animal was a prompt burning out of the wound with a red-hot iron. The treatment left a deep and serious burn, but it saved the life of the individual. One person, Victor Flores, bitten by a rabid coyote, was thus treated by a man named Paz Benavidez who had been a captive among the Indians.

In old times, too, there lived on a neighboring ranch a negress noted for her powers as a *curandera*. She cured one of the children of fits, another of *ojo* (evil eye) and others of many kinds of illnesses. She was a midwife and in later years moved to Laredo, where she was well and favorably known as a practical nurse among even the wealthiest American and Mexican families. She is still living and is estimated to be 115 years old.

Once a great cloud rose in the south and threatened the ranch. It was black, and boiling up the sky at a terrific rate. A young girl who was present at the house cried out that she knew an incantation that would part the cloud and save the ranch from destruction. She ran into the kitchen and grasped a huge knife. Rushing into the yard, she pointed it toward the heavens and began to form a huge cross. As she brought the knife downward, the cloud parted, half going to the east and half to the west, leaving the ranch untouched.

BURIED TREASURE

There are many tales of buried treasure told of the ranches near Buean Vista. On the ranch itself there was never anything buried; a large and fast-growing family kept every cent well in use. Don Florencio used to say: "Dicen que donde hay dinero, arde; pues, donde no hay, arde mas." The play on words loses its flavor upon translation, but the saying may be rendered thus: "They say that where money is, it burns; well, where it isn't it burns one more."

At the Trevino ranch in the neighborhood is an old strong box without a lid that has a history. The box is of heavy wrought iron, now much rusted, more than one-fourth of an inch in thickness. It is about a foot wide, fourteen inches deep, and nearly two feet long. In the eighties the Trevinos, like various other ranch families, had a town house at Laredo. As they spent most of their time at the ranch, they left the town house in care of servants for months at a time.

On one occasion, after an absence of several months, they went to town to stay for a few weeks. Upon their arrival, they found their home closed and the servants gone. After much trouble, they forced an entrance. What was their surprise to find one corner of the floor ripped up, earth scattered about, a hole in the ground, and this iron strong box, rusty as now, lying on the floor empty. No one ever found any trace of the servants. What they found can only be conjectured, but the box remains today, a silent witness that something was there.

When the eldest daughter of Don Florencio grew to womanhood, she lived for a time at the Chihuahua Ranch, east of Buena Vista. While there, she had a shepherd among her servants called Simon Prieto. He came from nowhere, penniless and without pack. She gave him work at fifteen dollars a month and board. He told her to save the money for him from month to month and he would collect it when he wished to go to Laredo 'sometime.' He worked on the ranch for about a year and left the place not once during the time.

One evening he came to the ranch house and showed Dona Simona and old Mexican silver dollar that he said he had found in the *monte*. It was tarnished and covered with earth. A few days later, he brought in another, then a third, and a fourth.

Upon the appearance of the fourth dollar, Dona Simona said, "Simon, you have found a cache of money off in the brush somewhere. Don't be a fool; bring it in where I can care for it for you. If you don't, some other wandering shepherd will come and rob you of what you have found."

The man declared that he had found no cache, only those four dollars. Simona let the declaration pass. After all, the money was his, and if he wished to lose it, the worry was his, not hers. A few weeks later, in the spring of 1900, one of Simona's children fell ill, and she had to depart for Laredo, expecting to be gone for a few days. She was gone several months. She had left hurriedly and had not paid her servants. When she returned, she found Simon Prieta gone. He had taken a horse and a rifle from the ranch, but no money. At a ranch to the south he had stopped and bought provisions and cartridges for the gun and paid with the money from a well-filled purse. He never appeared to collect his year's wages. How did a poor shepherd get so much money, save through a cache of buried coin?

Long before, between 1882 and 1892, there lived on another ranch near the Chihuahua an old couple named Buitron. He was a doddering old soul who left the management of affairs to his wife, a miserly woman who hoarded every penny that came their way. They had herds of goats, sheep, and cattle upon which they realized money every year. After buying meager provisions and still more meager clothing, she hid the remaining money somewhere on the ranch, but she would never tell her husband where the money was hidden. She promised year after year to do so. "When I come to die," she would say, "I'll tell you where the money is, but not before."

For fifteen years or more the two lived thus frugally. Suddenly, the old woman died one night of a colic and had no opportunity to reveal the hiding place of her life savings. The old man spent all the remaining years of his life digging around the house, trying to find the money, and all to no avail. He had the chimney torn down and the kitchen demolished; he had the door-yard honeycombed with excavations.

But he never found a penny. To this day the money lies buried somewhere on the ranch.

At La Parida, a few miles to the north, is an abandoned ranch. About the year 1902, two Americans came out past the ranch just north of Buena Vista with a map. They asked numerous questions and went rolling on their way. A few days later they returned and passed out of the country as they had come.

The owner of the ranch was curious about them and followed the buggy tracks. They led him to the abandoned ranch house of La Parida. About three feet east of the doorway there had been for many years a large flat boulder lying on a hewn-off mesquite stump. At the edge of this boulder was a deep hole. Lying on the upturned earth nearby was a large box made of the heartwood of mesquite. And in the dust at the bottom of the box were still the round marks of coins. So the treasure had flown.

THE TRASQUILAS

In the early days of the Buena Vista Ranch there were few cattle. All of the ranchmen kept herds of sheep guarded by *pastores*. The grass was lush, the range was unfenced and there was a good market for the wool. Shearing was done twice a year, in April and September. Itinerant sheep-shearers came to each ranch in turn, bringing their own entourage, including a sturdy woman cook, whom they always called "Madre."

It was amusing to hear them at meal time calling out. "Madre" this, and "Madre" that, to the bustling woman who attended to their wants.

The ranchmen marveled at their skill and at their attention to their work. There was no siesta in the heat of the day; there was no stop for *merienda* in the afternoon. Furthermore, their dexterity with the flying shears was a thing to watch with awe. A good workman would shear a hundred sheep a day. When twenty such men were at work in the sheep-shearing sheds, the bleating of the sheep, the snipping of the shears, the joking voices of the workers, and the warning cry of "Golpe," as a sheared sheep was released to go bounding out of the shed, blended to make an uproar foreign to the usual somnolent scene. This cry of "Golpe" was a signal given by a shearer when he finished shearing a sheep and let it loose. It was a warning to the other shearers to be ready to dodge, for the sheep would make its way blindly into the pen and might stumble into anything in its path.

Besides the shearers, there were men to carry the wool and men to pack it. This packing was done with the help of a tall wooden rack on which jute sacks were stretched. One man filled the sack; another tramped the wool into it with his feet so that each sack might hold as much as possible.

When the shearing and packing were done, Don Florencio and his sons loaded the wool into ox carts and made their trip to Laredo, where wholesale wool dealers bought his wool.

Here he bought provisions. Early in his married life he established here, too, a town house. At first he built a tiny place of mesquite poles, thatched with straw; later, he built a stone house; then, one of lumber, big and rambling. Now, this, too, has been replaced by a twelve- room brick dwelling, modern in every detail.

Here at Laredo his ten children were born; here, and at the ranch, he and his wife spent their busy days. But the ranch held the center of their affections. He asked his children to bury him there.

A stone's throw behind the ranch house one may see his grave.

VII

Introduction

Chapter seven includes speeches by White American females which span the nineteenth and twentieth centuries. Three discourses address American slavery—a major concern of the nineteenth century women activists. Those women made positive contributions to the abolition of slavery even though anti and some pro-slavery advocates attempted to stifle all female involvement in public affairs. The other three orations illustrate the wide variety of issues that concern the speakers—ethics in government, woman suffrage, and youth as an asset of free societies. Not a sedentary observer of social, political, and economic problems the American woman has been active consistently in the quest to secure for herself and others their guaranteed birthright in America.

The first speech by Susan C. Cabot was presented at an American Antislavery meeting in New York City in 1855. Her opening remarks were a series of excuses she doubtless had heard from people regarding the question of slavery. One typical comment was: "I make a rule of forgetting the slaves as far as I can. What is the use of dwelling upon what you cannot help?" Disturbed by this show of indifference to human bondage she alluded to Jesus Christ's admonition that we are expected "to bear one another's burdens." Her comments which criticized the unsympathetic are reminiscent of the oft-heard remark: "I do not wish to get involved."

The second speech is by the renowned Susan B. Anthony. In this presentation in March of 1884 before the United States Senate's Select Committee on Woman Suffrage Anthony argued for a floor vote on woman's suffrage. In this most eloquent plea to the Senate committee on woman's suffrage Anthony made two points: 1) Our Government has fundamental principles guaranteeing "perfect equality to all the people." 2) It would be a more impartial and equitable society if all its citizens could vote. The address was the first time the question of whether or not women should have the right to vote was brought before the Senate. Unfortunately the Senate voted on the measure and it was defeated. Success finally came on June 4, 1919 when Congress approved the nineteenth amendment to the Constitution and submitted it to the States for ratification.

The third speech in this chapter "Epistle to the Clergy of the Southern States" is by Sarah M. Grimke a Southern aristocrat turned abolitionist. After Sarah and Angelina were allotted slaves by their mother both sisters emancipated their black charges. Subsequently Sarah attempted in this discourse to inveigle the Southern ministers to persuade "the minds of a vast proportion of the Christian community," to free their slaves because they "regard you (the minister of Gospel) as the channel through which divine knowledge must flow." A deeply religious woman Sarah's speech is sprinkled throughout with Biblical allusions. In this regard she criticized the clergy as well as the church. To the clergy she said: "What an appalling spectacle do we now present! With one hand we clasp the cross of Christ, and with the other grasp the neck of the down-trodden slave!" To the church she said: "And this is the sin which the Church is fostering in her bosom—This is the leprosy over which she is casting the mantle of charity, to hide, if possible, the "putrefying sores."

The fourth speech is by a woman whose life transcended the nineteenth and twentieth centuries—Eleanor Roosevelt. Mrs. Roosevelt's ideas in this speech are directed toward young people. Her main focus is that youth is a valuable "asset of free societies" because invariably it guarantees the renewal of vital energy from generation to generation. When she warns youth about "ruling oligarchies" she observes: "A tyrant can never tell who is for him or against him because he cannot enter the secret heart of any man." Her advice to the young people in attendance was that "we must use our heads in an active campaign to expose the propaganda designed to divide us, and to promote the unity and cooperation of free people." She informed the youth that they, at that moment in time had the chance to help their generation face problems with "responsiblity and realism."

The fifth speech is by Geraldine A. Ferraro who took the Reagan Administration to task for its abuse of power. Her speech on ethics pointed to some politicians as she states that "More than ever before, we are right to ask for higher standards from the people who make and enforce our laws." Ferraro went on to say that we should be doing some ethical soul-searching. We need to debate these questions in public and in private. She told the graduates they would need an ethical framework to allow their "success to blossom." She told the graduates they had learned the skills of how to make this world a better place—a world of humanity and compassion.

The sixth speech is by Julie R. Kidd, a high school student from Frewsburg, New York. Ms. Kidd has been deeply affected by the plight of the homeless in the streets of our nation. Her address focuses on the need to remedy this national disgrace. She reminds the reader of the message of Dr. King who proclaimed that the principle of love must be manifest in all our lives. Ms. Kidd would have us apply Dr. King's manifesto to the problem of the homeless.

Susan C. Cabot

"What Have We, As Individuals, To Do With Slavery?"

Suffragist and antislavery activist Susan Cabot delivered the following speech to the American Antislavery Society's Annual Meeting in 1855. Disturbed by the public's rationalizations and disinterest for American slavery Cabot alludes to Jesus Christ's admonition that we are "to bear one another's burdens." This speech is from *Anti-Slavery Tracts*. No. 15.

Speech courtesy of Oberlin College Library Special Collections

'I wish you would not distress me by continually talking about the slaves. I do not consider the subject as belonging either to you or me; it is for the south, and not for the north. The southerners must do their work, and we must do ours. I make a rule of forgetting the slaves as far as I can. What is the use of dwelling upon what you cannot help? It only unfits one for doing anything. For my own part, I find quite enough for my time and thoughts in feeling and acting for those at my very door, whose wants and necessities require all one's spare hours; and were I to take up the slave question, I hardly know what would become of me. No; this work is beyond my powers; it would be only a waste of time and feeling to attempt it. At all events, I cannot bear it; it only makes me nervous, and no good comes of dwelling upon it.' These words, or their meaning, are often uttered to those who allude to the subject of slavery in their intercourse with friends; but they do not always carry conviction with them, even when those to whom they are addressed are conscious that the speaker is one who is devoted to charitable thoughts and deeds, and earnestly striving to take their full share of the duties which Christianity lays upon her disciples; but we lament the more for this very reason that they should be uttered, because we think them at variance with that very charity which calls upon us to overcome all things. It may seem foolish or presumptuous to attempt to confute them, and we would not strive to do this in the way of argument; but in presenting another, and what seems to us a more satisfactory view of the subject, we may hope, as "in water face answereth to face, so the heart of man to man," that we may by this appeal excite sympathy and interest in what seems to us a more just and Christian way of looking at the subject.

In reply to the remarks we have cited, we would say that our interest for the slave springs from the same source as our interest for the poor; we cannot say, My heart shall flow out for the white woman, and not for the black, for the free woman, and not for the bond. The sense of justice and of right does not stop to inquire how far, or how long, or upon what objects she shall exercise her divine power; but, like the widow with her flask of oil, pours out upon him who stands in need, and finds in proportion as this is done, so is the supply. In how few words are we told in this simple story to trust in right doing! When we undertake to fix the boundary of our hearts, and say how far, or how long, or for whom they shall move us to act, it shows we have not put our confidence in Him who has made them to beat; it is the questioning of the divine power to mistrust them in this way. While we are intent upon doing the right thing, the urn will fill without our care; for we know not at best how it is that we are able to remove mountains, excepting by our trust in the divine word.

Those who are troubled and made nervous by the discussion of slavery, and wish never to hear about it are not put into this state because they have no feeling for the slave, but because they find it necessary to work with a distinct idea that they must accomplish something, as they show when you ask them to give money to buy one of these poor sufferers. How willingly they will do this! And yet in their hearts they may have been wanting in that true sympathy which, in the sight of God, makes this purchase a dreadful comment on the relation of his children one to the other.

'Why,' we are asked, 'do you say we may have been wanting in true sympathy for the slaves?' Because we believe a true sympathy for their condition would leave no desire to criticize any sincere efforts to help them out of their despair, but would gladly join in the work, with the prayer that God would order it for the right.

When we feel called upon to do something, the nerves take their appointed place, and give us the power to accomplish what we desire to do; and then they become sources of pleasure, and not of pain. To bear one another's burdens came from the lips of Jesus. Did not his life show us how to do this? When he calls the leper to him, had not his heart overflowed with love and compassion and the thought that this too is a child of God, would he not have felt nervous, and questioned the prudence and propriety of touching him?

The circumstances of the complexion and conformation of the slaves, added to their long history of degradation, influences unconsciously, we think, the feelings and judgment of those who do not sympathize with the advocates of their cause. These objectors find it easy enough to see the mistakes that are made in the means used, and in the mode of doing the work. Doubtless there is some ground for these objections, so keenly perceived; but we think the tares in this field can safely be left. When some delicate woman, brought up in the refinements of life, visits the hovel of the poor drunkard, and sees the object of her charity so disfigured that hardly a trace of humanity is left, she, all the more, longs to bring back the soul to this degraded temple, that it may again assert its origin. Her heart does not grow cold by criticism, but burns with a new desire, at the sight of this ruin, to do something to restore this fallen one. But this poor creature is white; hence her ears are quick to hear any suggestions to break the sinful chains that bind him to the earth. She does not ask herself to what country he belongs; she knows he is a child of God, and that is enough. But the poor negro whose dark skin we are unaccustomed to, whose chains are riveted by the hand of the white man, whose degradation is compelled by the avarice of selfishness, must be pleaded for, must be reasoned about, before we can penetrate the prejudice that hardens the heart against him—a prejudice which blinds the eye of justice, and makes us forget that this too is a child of God; and one whom, could the curtain be raised, perhaps we should see nearer the throne of grace than, in our short-sightedness, we imagined. By whose fiat did this dark skin come into the world? Are we to question the wisdom of his existence? Are we to judge the Almighty?

If the question were put, whether, if the three millions of slaves were white instead of black, there would not be more sympathy for those who take their part, and less criticism upon their imperfect measures, there are many who would say, 'Yes,' and add, 'naturally enough we do prefer white to black; we have a right to our preference, and no one has a right to interfere with it.' We would not infringe upon the rights of any one; respect for the rights of all being the groundwork of our interest in the slave. It is our preference, our choice, which guides us in our efforts for the emancipation of the slave; but it is not a choice of color, so much as of morality. We do not condemn this preference of any one; but when a matter of taste oversteps its legitimate bounds, and influences our judgment of right and wrong, encroaching upon the integrity of our hearts, bribing our consciences, and ruling our lives, then we are giving up gold for dross, the permanent for the transient, the corruptible for the incorruptible. Would the fugitive slave law, that forces men and women to break away from their honest calling and the fireside of their cherished homes have been received with such patriotic consideration had these fugitives a white skin instead of a black one? This new aspect of the system of slavery, this new manifestation of its reckless power, has a tongue for itself; it needs no comment. The 2d of June, 1854, has not yet quite faded out of the memory of those who, perhaps then for the first time, were made conscious of what stuff slavery is made.

But our object is not now to call up the horrors of slavery, in order to make apparent the view we have of it; it is simply to show our relation to it as Christians that we speak of it. We have said that one difference between those who do and those who do not advocate the cause of the slave is that the latter are influenced by the fact that their actions in this regard need the incentive of apparent results. One of their arguments against any action is that they see no good in it; 'What is the use of talking, if you do nothing? How are your lectures and your speeches going to affect the slave? There he is still in bondage, and will continue to be so for all your words.' It may be so; but, could this be proved, it would not shake the friend of the slave from his purpose of cleaning his skirts of the sin of slavery by his constant protest against it, and his determination to do all that in him lies to overthrow it this being a necessary and natural expression of his allegiance to justice, and of his sympathy with humanity. We do not acknowledge as a consistent Christian him whose actions in the moral world are influenced by the idea of success, as a necessary condition of his efforts for the right. He shows a skepticism in the power of right. He works not as children, in the love of obedience to the perfect standard set up in our hearts, which we must obey, to become rebels. He would put himself in the place of the divine law that he may come to a shorter method of accomplishing the work. For a time, in the eye of the world, he may succeed; but He that knows the end from the beginning sees with a clearer eye. It is from the starting point of right, and not of calculation that the abolitionist sets out upon his work of reform. His mind is not weakened or troubled by the many stumbling blocks in his way, nor is he moved from his purpose because misunderstood. When we are in earnest, we are unmindful of casualties. If the ground we have taken is a false one, if there is in it any contradiction to the simple precepts of Jesus, anything of variance with his life, then should it be abandoned; but not till then. It may be supposed from what we have said that we are indifferent to results; not at all; but we leave them in the hands of God.

There must arise in the mind of every one who uses his faculties consciously some idea of the object he has chosen as most worthy of the use of his powers; but it comes before his mind as the result of the work of time, with which he personally has nothing to do, any further than a strict adherence to what he conceives to be the right thing at the time requires. The artist who first conceives the idea of the cathedral glowing in all the splendor of his aspiring soul, solemnized with the desire of making a place of worship fitting the Most High is not deterred from devoting all his thoughts to the carrying out his conception from the fact that he shall never see it realized; he still feels a sacred obligation to be true to his idea; he still retains his temple of worship within.

With these views, it is natural that the advocate of the slave should be opposed to those who try to forget him, who think it not their affair to interfere with his condition, who treat the attempt to restore him to the place God assigned him as Quixotic. Those who so feel are considered the common sense part of society, the rational—practical. We have attempted to show how we differ from them, and why; and we think we have the vantage ground, from the fact that we have espoused the cause in question. The interest which induces one to adopt any subject (supposing the mind tolerably fair) helps him to understand and see more quickly its claims; it renders him clear sighted to its vulnerable points, that he may guard against them. We cannot do justice to any subject till we have loved it; it is this "hunger of the heart" which is essential to put in motion the will, and which gives sight to the understanding.

When our philanthropy is influenced by our taste it shows that it springs not from the highest source, and is liable to fail when its refreshing waters are most needed for the parched lips which plead for it; but when this happens, we are apt to think the fault is in the object and not in ourselves. This is a failure we can avoid, as we have before intimated, by starting from the highest point, from that source of living waters which is a well ever springing up, that we may always trust in. Those who are simply guided by their taste and their sensitiveness in their works of philanthropy naturally avoid all contact with slavery. The fact of the color and degraded condition of the slave repels them. This seems to us as a form of atheism. It may seem a harsh judgment; but surely, if we believe that we are all children of God, and that he is no respecter of persons; it is great presumption for us to discard as unfit for our sympathy any portion of his family; and by indulging in this selfish selection we are doing homage to ourselves rather than to Him. This exclusive feeling carried out would gradually estrange us from an impartial Being; our hearts would grow hard; and, in the midst of our rejoicing amongst our chosen friends, some hour might come when there might appear a fiery hand, that would write in burning characters that the days of such a philanthropy were numbered. It seems more fitting for Christians to take their feast at the common table of humanity, where neither complexion nor country can interfere with our belief that we are all children of God, all learners in the great school of life which is the preparation for a higher existence.

The advocates of the slave are called people of one idea. But this one idea—what is it? It is an idea that includes all others, for its aim is to overthrow a system which takes in and covers all the immoralities and sins that man can work upon the fair face of God's earth. Let one sin be mentioned which does not, almost of necessity, spring from the atheistic root of slavery! From the time when Joseph was cast into the pit by his brothers down to the present hour, its poisonous root has sent forth its shoots; and her, in this so called land of freedom, it flourishes in the plantations, and is exhibited on the auction block. We are longing and looking for the hour when the sin that has sold our brothers shall, through much sorrowing and many tears, be so repented of that on bended knee and in deep humiliation we shall ask pardon for our great iniquity. May this Joseph be the prefigurement of our better spirit, of our allegiance to the highest law of right. Let us take all that we have, and make a pilgrimage in the search for what we have lost, till we find ourselves again in the arms of truth and justice. We have done this great sin in the sight of Heaven; let us pray to be released from its weary bondage that our souls may be refreshed by peace of conscience. Let this slavery become a history to be told to our grandchildren, taking its place with that record of sins of which the floods of heaven were opened to destroy all likeness from the face of the earth. Let us pray for that mercy which shall allow us an ark of safety in the integrity of our determination: that we may rise above these dark waters which threaten to destroy the life of our souls.

Susan B. Anthony (1820-1906)

"For The Women Suffrage Amendment."

A pioneer in the women's suffrage movement Susan B. Anthony was born in Adams, Massachusetts on February 15, 1820. Her relentless agitation prepared the way for the adoption of the 19th amendment (August 18, 1920) to the federal constitution. After teaching school and organizing temperance societies she dedicated her life to the antislavery movement and women's rights. She collaborated with Elizabeth Cady Stanton and published in New York a liberal weekly entitled The Revolution (1868-1870). Some critics believed her public speaking inferior to her contemporaries. But her strengths according to one writer "lay in her strong organizational abilities, logical precision in framing arguments, and keen lobbying skills." A dedicated activist Susan Anthony was a driving force behind the suffrage Movement. She died in Rochester, New York on March 13, 1906

The following speech is from: Select Committee on Woman Suffrage, United States Senate, March 7, 1884. Printed as part of the debate on the woman suffrage amendment, January 25, 1887. Congressional Record, 40th Cong., 2nd Sess., vol 18, pt. I, pp. 998-1002. The first two-thirds of Miss Anthony's statement is reproduced here.

Mr. Chairman and Gentlemen: Mrs. Spencer said that I would make an argument. I do not propose to do so, because I take it for granted that the members of this committee that we have all the argument on our side, and such an argument would be simply a series of platitudes and maxims of government. The theory of this Government from the beginning has been perfect equality to all the people. That is shown by every one of the fundamental principles, which I need not stop to repeat. Such being the theory, the application would be, of course, that all persons not having forfeited their right to representation in the Government should be possessed of it at the age of twenty- one. But instead of adopting a practice in conformity with the theory of our Government, we began by saying that all men of property were the people of the nation upon whom the Constitution conferred equality of rights. The next step was that all white men were the people to whom should be practically applied the fundamental theories. There we halt to-day and stand at a deadlock, so far as the application of our theory may go. We women have been standing before the American public for thirty years, asking the men to take yet one step further and extend the practical application of the theory of equality of rights to all the people to the other half of the people—the women. That is all that I stand here to-day to attempt to demand.

Of course, I take it for granted that the committee are in sympathy at least with the reports of the Judiciary Committee presented both in the Senate and the House. I remember that after the adoption of the fourteenth and fifteenth amendments Senator EDMUNDS reported on the petition of the ten-thousand foreign born citizens of Rhode Island who were denied equality of rights in Rhode Island simply because of their foreign birth; and in that report held that the amendments were enacted and attached to the Constitution simply for men of color, and therefore that their provisions could not be so concerned as to bring within their purview the men of foreign birth in Rhode Island. Then the House Committee on the Judiciary, with Judge Bingham, of Ohio., at its head, made a similar report upon our petitions, holding that because those amendments were made essentially with the black men in view, therefore their provisions could not be extended to the women citizens of this country or to any class except men citizens of color.

I voted in the State of New York in 1872 under the construction of those amendments, which we felt to be the true one, that all persons born in the United States, or any State thereof, and under the jurisdiction of the United States, were citizens, and entitled to equality of rights, and that no State could deprive them of their equality of rights. I found three young men, inspectors of election, who were simple enough to read the Constitution and understand it in accordance with what was the letter and what should have been its spirit. Then, as you will remember, I was prosecuted by the officers of the Federal Court, and the cause was carried through the different courts in the State of New York, in the northern district, and at last I was brought to trial at Canandaigua.

When Mr. Justice Hunt was brought from the supreme bench to sit upon that trial, he wrested my case from the hands of the jury altogether, after having listened three days to testimony, and brought in a verdict himself of guilty, denying to my counsel even the poor privilege of having the jury polled. Through all that trial when I, as a citizen of the United States, as a citizen of the State of New York and city of Rochester, as a person who had done something at least that might have entitled her to a voice in speaking for herself and for her class, in all that trial I not only was denied my right to testify as to whether I voted or not, but there was not one single woman's voice to be heard nor to be considered, except as witnesses, save when it came to the judge asking, "Has the prisoner anything to say why sentence should not be pronounced?" Neither as judge, nor as attorney, nor as jury was I allowed any person who could be legitimately called my peer to speak for me.

Then, as you will remember, Mr. Justice Hunt not only pronounced the verdict of guilty, but a sentence of a $100 fine and costs of prosecution. I said to him, "May it please your Honor, I do not propose to pay it"; and I never have paid it, and I never shall. I asked your honorable bodies of Congress the next year—in 1874—to pass a resolution to remit that fine. Both Houses refused it; the committees reported against it; though through Benjamin F. Butler, in the House, and a member of your committee, and Matthew H. Carpenter, in the Senate, there were plenty of precedents brought forward to show that in cases of multitudes of men fines had been remitted. I state this merely to show the need of woman to speak for herself, to be as judge, to be as juror.

Mr. Justice Hunt in his opinion stated that suffrage was a fundamental right, and therefore a right that belonged to the State. It seemed to me that was just as much of a retroversion of the theory of what is right in our Government as there could possibly be. Then, after the decision in my case came that of Mrs. Minor, of Missouri. She prosecuted the officers there for denying her the right to vote. She carried her case up to your Supreme Court, and the Supreme Court answered her the same way; that the amendments were made for black men; that their provisions could not protect women, that the Constitution of the United States has no voters of its own.

Mrs. SPENCER. And you remember Judge Carter's decision in my case.

Miss ANTHONY. Mr. Carter said that women are citizens and may be qualified, &c., but that it requires some sort of legislation to give them the right to vote.

The Congress of the United States notwithstanding, and the Supreme Court of the United States notwithstanding, with all deference and respect, I differ with them all, and know that I am right and that they are wrong. The Constitution of the United States as it protects me. If I could get a practical application of the Constitution it would protect me and all women in the enjoyment of perfect equality of rights everywhere under the shadow of the American flag.

I do not come to you to petition for special legislation, or for any more amendments to the Constitution, because I think they are unnecessary, but because you say there is not in the Constitution enough to protect me. Therefore I ask that you, true to your own theory and assertion, should go forward to make more constitution.

Let me remind you that in the case of all other classes of citizens under the shadow of our flag you have been true to the theory that taxation and representation are inseparable. Indians not taxed are not counted in the basis of representation and are allowed to vote they are taxed; never before. In my State of New York, and in nearly all the States, the members of the State militia, hundreds and thousands of men, are exempted from taxation on property; in my state to the value of $800, and in most of the States to a value in that neighborhood. While such a member of the militia lives, receives his salary, and is able to earn money, he is exempted; but when he dies the assessor puts his widow's name down upon the assessor's list, and the tax-collector never fails to call upon the widow and make her pay the full tax upon her property.

In most of the States clergymen are exempted. In my State of New York they are exempted on property to the value of $1500. As long as the clergyman lives and receives his fat salary, or his lean one, as the case may be, he is exempted on that amount of property; but when the breath leaves the body of the clergyman, and the widow is left without any income, or without any means of support, the State comes in and taxes the widow.

So it is with regard to all black men. In the State of New York up to the day of the passage of the fifteenth amendment, black men who were willing to remain without reporting themselves worth as much as $250, and thereby to remain exercising the right to vote, never had their names put on the assessor's list; they were passed by, while, if the poorest colored woman owned fifty feet of real estate, a little cabin anywhere, that colored woman's name was always on the assessor's list, and she was compelled to pay her tax. While Frederick Douglass lived in my State he was never allowed to vote until he could show himself worth the requisite $250; and when he did vote in New York, he voted not because he was a man, not because he was a citizen of the United States, but simply because he was worth the requisite amount of money. In Connecticut both black men and black women were exempted from taxation prior to the adoption of the fifteenth amendment.

The law was amended in 1848, by which black men were thus exempted, and black women followed the same rule in that State. That, I believe, is the only State where black women were exempted from taxation under the law. When the fourteenth and fifteenth amendments were attached to the Constitution they carried to the black man of Connecticut the boon of the ballot as well as the burden of taxation, whereas they carried to the black woman of Connecticut the burden of taxation, but no ballot by which to protect her property. I know a colored woman in New Haven, Conn., worth $50,000, and she never paid a penny of taxation until the ratification of the fifteenth amendment. From that day on she is compelled to pay a heavy tax on that amount of property.

Mrs. SPENCER. Is it because she is a citizen? Please explain.

Miss ANTHONY. Because she is black.

Mrs. SPENCER. Is it because the fourteenth and fifteenth amendments made women citizens?

Miss ANTHONY. Certainly, because it declared the black people citizens.

Gentlemen, you have before you various propositions of amendment to the Federal Constitution. One is for the election of President by the vote of the people direct. Of course women are not people.

Senator EDMUNDS. Angels.

Miss ANTHONY. I wish you, gentlemen, would look down there and see the myriads that are there. We want to help them and lift them up. That is exactly the trouble with you, gentlemen; you are forever looking at your own wives, your own mothers, your own sisters, and your own daughters, and they are well cared for and protected; but only look down to the struggling masses of women who have no one to protect them. If you would look down there the question would be solved; but the difficulty is that you think only of those who are doing well. We are not speaking for ourselves, but for those who can not speak for themselves. We are speaking for the doomed as much as you, Senator EDMUNDS, used to speak for the doomed on the plantations of the South.

Amendments have been proposed to put God in the Constitution and to keep God out of the Constitution. All sorts of propositions to amend the Constitution have been made; but I ask that you allow no other amendment to be called the sixteenth but that which shall put into the hands of one-half of the entire people of the nation the right to express their opinion as to how the Constitution shall be amended henceforth. Women have the right to say whether we shall have God in the Constitution as well as men. Women have a right to say whether we shall have a national law or an amendment to the Constitution prohibiting the importation or manufacture of alcoholic liquors. We have a right to have our opinions counted on every possible question concerning the public welfare.

You ask us why we do not get this right to vote first in the school districts, and on school questions, or the question of liquor license. It has been shown very clearly why we need something more than that. You have good enough laws to-day in every State in this Union for the suppression of what are termed the social vices; for the suppression of the grog-shops, the gambling houses, the brothels, the obscene shows. There is plenty of legislation in every State in this Union for their suppression if it could be executed. Why is the Government, why are the States and the cities, unable to execute those laws? Simply because there is a large balance of power in every city that does not want those laws executed. Consequently both parties must alike cater to that balance of political power to vote for it, and, consequently, the party that can not get into power.

What we ask of you is that you will make of the women of the cities a balance of political power, so that when a mayor, a member of the common council, a supervisor, a justice of the peace, a district attorney, a judge on the bench even, shall go before the people of that city as a candidate for the suffrages of the people he shall not only be compelled to look to the men who frequent the grog- shops, the brothels, and the gambling houses, who will vote for him if he is not in favor of executing the law, but that he shall have to look to the mothers, the sisters, the wives, the daughters of those deluded men to see what they will do if he does not execute the law.

We want to make of ourselves a balance of political power. What we need is the power to execute the laws. We have got laws enough. Let me give you one little fact in regard to my own city of Rochester. You all know how that wonderful whip called the temperance crusade roused the whisky ring. It caused the whisky force to concentrate itself more strongly at the ballot-box than ever before, so that when the report in the spring of 1874 went over the country the result was that the whisky ring was triumphant, and that the whisky ticket was elected more largely than ever before. Senator Thurman will remember how it was in his own State of Ohio. Everybody knows that if my friends, Mrs. ex-Governor Wallace, Mrs. Allen, and all the women of the great West could have gone to the ballot-box at those municipal elections and voted for candidates, no such result would have occurred; while you refused by the laws of the State to the women the right to have their opinions counted; every rum-seller, every drunkard, every pauper even from the poor-house, and every criminal outside of the State's prison came out on election day to express his opinion and have it counted.

The next result of that political event was that the ring demanded new legislation to protect the whisky traffic everywhere. In my city the women did not crusade the streets, but they said they would help the men to execute the law. They held meetings, sent out committees, and had testimony secured against every man who had violated the law, and when the board of excise held its meeting those women assembled, three or four hundred, in the church one morning, and marched in a solid body to the common council chamber where the board of excise was sitting. As one rum- seller after another brought in his petition for a renewal of license, who had violated the law, those women presented the testimony against him. The law of the State of New York is that no man shall have a renewal who has violated the law. But in not one case did that board refuse to grant a renewal of license because of the testimony which those women presented, and at the close of the sitting it was found that twelve hundred more licenses had been granted than ever before in the history of the State. Then the defeated women said they would have those men punished according to law.

Again they retained an attorney and appointed committees to investigate all over the city. They got the proper officer to prosecute every rum-seller. I was at their meeting. One woman reported that the office in every city refused to prosecute the liquor dealer who had violated the law. Why? Because if he should do so he would lose the votes of all the employes (sic) of certain shops on that street, if another he would lose the votes of the railroad employes, and if another he would lose the German vote, if another the Irish vote, and so on. I said to those women what I say to you, and what I know to be true to-day, that if the women of the city of Rochester had held the power of the ballot in their hands they would have been a great political balance of power.

The last report was from District Attorney Raines. The women complained of a certain lager-beer-garden keeper. Said the district attorney, "Ladies, you are right, this man is violating the law, everybody knows it, but if I should prosecute him I would lose the entire German vote." Said I, "Ladies, do you not see that if the women of the city of Rochester had the right to vote District Attorney Raines would have been compelled to have stopped and counted, weighed and measured? He would have said, 'If I prosecute that lager-beer German I shall lose the 5,000 German votes of this city, but if I fail to prosecute him and execute the laws I shall lose the votes of 20,000 women.'"

Do you not see, gentlemen, that so long as you put the power of the ballot in the hands of every possible man, rich, poor, drunk, sober, educated, ignorant, outside of the State's prison, to make and unmake, not only every law and lawmaker, but every office-holder who has to do with the executing of the law, and take the power from the hands of the women of the nation, the mothers, you put the long arm of the lever, as we call it in mechanics, in the hands of the whisky power and make it utterly impossible for regulation of sobriety to be maintained in our community? The first step towards social regulation and good society in towns, cities, and villages is the ballot in the hands of the mothers of those places. I appeal to you especially in this matter.

I do not know what you think about the proper sphere of women. It matters little what any of us think about it. We shall each and every individual find our own proper sphere if we are left to act in freedom; but my opinion is that when the whole arena of politics and government is thrown open to women they will endeavor to do very much as they do in their homes; that the men will look after the greenback theory of the hard-money theory, that you will look after free-trade or tariff, and the women will do the home housekeeping of the government, which is to take care of the moral government and the social regulation of our home department.

It seems to me that we have the power of government outside to shape and control circumstances, but that the inside power, the government housekeeping, is powerless, and is compelled to accept whatever conditions or circumstances shall be granted.

Therefore I do not ask for liquor suffrage alone, nor for school suffrage alone, because that would amount to nothing. We must be able to have a voice in the election not only of every law-maker, but of every one who has to do either with the making or the executing of the laws.

Then you ask why we do not get suffrage by the popular- vote method, State by State? I answer, because there is no reason why I, for instance, should desire the women of one State of this nation to vote any more than the women of another State.

I have no more interest as regards the women of New York than I have as regards the women of Indiana, Iowa, or any of the States represented by the women who have come up here. The reason why I do not wish to get this right by what you call the popular-vote method, the State vote, is because I believe there is a United States citizenship. I believe that this is a nation, and to be a citizen of this nation should be a guaranty to every citizen of a right to the voice in the Government, and should give me right to express my opinion. You deny to me my liberty, my freedom, if you say that I shall have no voice whatever in making, shaping, or controlling the conditions of society in which I live. I differ from Judge Hunt and I hope I am respectful when I say that I think he made a very funny mistake when he said that fundamental rights belong to the States and only surface rights to the National Government. I hope you will agree with me that the fundamental right of citizenship, the right to voice in the Government, is a national right.

The National Government may concede to the States the right to decide by a majority as to what banks they shall have, what laws they shall enact with regard to insurance, with regard to property, and any other question; but I insist upon it that the National Government should not leave it a question with the States that a majority in any State may disfranchise the minority under any circumstances whatsoever. The franchise to you men is not secure. You hold it to-day, to be sure, by the common consent of white men, but if at any time, on your principle of government, the majority of any of the States should choose to amend the State constitution so as to disfranchise this or that portion of the Supreme Court and by the legislation thus far there is nothing to hinder them.

Therefore the women demand a sixteenth amendment to bring to women the right to vote, or if you please to confer upon women that right to vote, to protect them in it, and to secure men in their right, because you are not secure.

I would let the States act upon almost every other question by majorities, except the power to say whether my opinion shall be counted. I insist upon it that no State shall decide that question.

Then the popular-vote method is an impracticable thing. We tried to get negro suffrage by the popular vote, as you will remember. Senator Thurman will remember that in Ohio the Republicans submitted the question in 1867, and with all the prestige of the national Republican party and of the State party, when every influence that could be brought by the power and the patronage of the party in power was brought to bear, yet negro suffrage ran behind the regular Republican ticket 40,000.

It was tried in Kansas, it was tried in New York, and everywhere that it was submitted the question was voted down overwhelmingly. Just so we tried to get women suffrage by the popular-vote method in Kansas in 1867, in Michigan in 1874, in Colorado in 1877, and in each case the result was precisely the same, the ratio of the vote standing one-third for women suffrage and two-thirds against women suffrage. If we were to canvas State after State we should get no better vote than that. Why? Because the question of the enfranchisement of women is a question of government, a question of philosophy, of understanding, of great fundamental principle, and the masses of the hard-working people of this nation, men and women, do not think upon principles. They can only think on the one eternal struggle wherewithal to be fed, to be clothed, and to be sheltered. Therefore I ask you not to compel us to have this question settled by what you term the popular-vote method.

Let me illustrate by Colorado, the most recent State, in the election of 1877. I am happy to say to you that I have canvassed three States for this question. If Senator Chandler were alive, or if Senator Ferry were in this room, they would remember that I followed in their train in Michigan, with larger audiences than either of those Senators throughout the whole canvas. I want to say, too, that although those Senators may have believed in woman suffrage, they did not say much about it. They did not help us much. The Greenback movement was quite popular in Michigan at that time. The Republicans and Greenbackers made a most humble bow to the grangers, but woman suffrage did not get much help. In Colorado, at the close of the canvas, 6,666 men voted "Yes." Now I am going to describe the men who voted "Yes." They were native-born white men, temperance men, cultivated, broad, generous, just men who think. On the other hand, 16,007 voted "No."

Now I am going to describe that class of voters. In the southern part of that State there are Mexicans, who speak the Spanish language. They put their wheat in circles on the ground with the heads out, and drive a mule around to thrash it. The vast population of Colorado is made up of that class of people. I was sent out to speak in a voting precinct having 200 voters; 150 of those voters were Mexican greasers, 40 of them foreign-born citizens, and just ten of them were born in this country; and I was supposed to be competent to convert those men to let me have as much right in this Government as they had, when, unfortunately, the great majority of them could not understand a word that I said. Fifty or sixty Mexican greasers stood against the wall with their hats down over their faces. The Germans put seats in a lager-beer saloon, and would not attend unless I made a speech there; so I had a small audience.

Mrs. ARCHIBALD. There is one circumstance that I should like to relate. In the county of Las Animas, a county where there is a large population of Mexicans, and where they always have a large majority over the native population, they do not know our language at all. Consequently a number of tickets must be printed for those people in Spanish. The gentleman in our little town of Trinidad who had the charge of the printing of those tickets, being adverse to us, had every ticket printed against woman suffrage. The samples that were sent to us from Denver were "for" or "against," but the tickets that were printed only had the word "against" on them, so that our friends had to scratch their tickets, and all those Mexican people who could not understand this trick and did not know the facts of the case, voted against woman suffrage; so that we lost a great many votes. This was man's generosity.

Miss ANTHONY. Special legislation for the benefit of woman! I will admit to you that on the floor of the constitutional convention was a representative Mexican, intelligent, cultivated, chairman on the committee on suffrage, who signed the petition, and was the first to speak in favor of woman suffrage. Then they have in Denver about four hundred negroes. Governor Routt said to me, "The four hundred Denver negroes are going to vote solid for woman suffrage." I said, "I do not know much about the Denver negroes, but I know certainly what all negroes were educated in and slavery never educated master or negro into a comprehension of the great principles of human freedom of our nation; is it not possible, and I do not believe they are going to vote for us." Just ten of those Denver negroes voted for woman suffrage. Then, in all the mines of Colorado the vast majority of the wage laborers, as you know, are foreigners.

There may be intelligent foreigners in this country, and I know there are, who are in favor of the enfranchisement of woman, but that one does not happen to be Carl Shurz, I am ashamed to say. And I want to say to you of Carl Shurz, that side by side with that man on the battlefield of Germany was Madame Anneke, as noble a woman as ever trod the American soil. She rode by the side of her husband, who was an officer, on the battlefield, she slept in battlefield tents, and she fled from Germany to this country, for her life and property, side by side with Carl Shurz. Now, what is it for Carl Shurz, stepping up to the very door of the Presidency and looking back to Madame Anneke, who fought for liberty as well as he, to say, "You be subject in this Republic; I will be sovereign." If it is an insult for Carl Shurz to say that to a foreign-born woman, what is it for him to say it to Mrs. ex-Governor Wallace, Elizabeth Cady Stanton, Lucretia Mott—to the native-born, educated tax-paying women of this Republic? I can forgive an ignorant foreigner; I can forgive an ignorant negro; but I can not forgive Carl Shurz.

Right in the file of the foreigners opposed to woman suffrage, educated under monarchical governments that do not comprehend our principles, whom I have seen traveling through the prairies of Iowa or the prairies of Minnesota, are the Bohemians, Swedes, Norwegians, Germans, Irishmen, Mennonites; I have seen them riding on those magnificent leads of wheat with those magnificent Saxon horses, shining like glass on a sunny morning, every one of them going to vote "no" against woman suffrage. You can not convert them; it is impossible. Now and then there is a whisky manufacturer, drunkard, inebriate, libertine, and what we call a fast man, and a colored man, broad and generous enough to be willing to let women vote, to let his mother have her opinion counted as to whether there shall be license or no license, but the rank and file of all classes who wish to enjoy the full license in what are termed the petty vices of men are pitted solid against the enfranchisement of women.

Then, in addition to all these, there are, as you know, a few religious bigots left in the world who really believe that somehow or other if women are allowed to vote St. Paul would feel badly about it. I do not know but that some of the gentlemen present belong to that class. So, when you put those best men of the nation, having religion about everything except on this one question, whose prejudices control them, with all this vast mass of ignorant, uneducated, degraded population in this country, you make an overwhelming and insurmountable majority against the enfranchisement of women.

It is because of this fact that I ask you not to remand us back to the States, but to submit to the States the proposition of a sixteenth amendment. The popular-vote method is not only of itself an impossibility, but it is too humiliating a process to compel the women of this nation to submit to any longer.

I am going to give you an illustration, not because I have any disrespect for the person, because on many other questions he was really a good deal better than a good many other men who had not so bad a name in this nation. When, under the old regime, John Morrisey, of my State, the king of gamblers, was a Representative on the floor of Congress, it was humiliating enough for Lucretia Mott, for Elizabeth Cady Stanton, for all of us to come down here to Washington and beg at the feet of John Morrisey that he would let intelligent, native-born women vote, and let us have as much right in this Government and in the government of the city of New York as he had. When John Morrisey was a member of the New York State Legislature it would have been humiliating enough for us to go to the New York State Legislature and pray of John Morrisey to vote to ratify the sixteenth amendment, giving to us a right to vote; but instead of a sixteenth amendment you tell us to go back to the popular-vote method, the old-time method, and go down into John Morrisey's seventh Congressional district in the city of New York, and there, in the sloughs and slums of that great Sodom, in the grog-shops, the gambling houses, and the brothels, beg at the feet of each individual fisticuff of his constituency to give the noble, educated, native-born, tax-paying women of the State of New York as much right as he has, that would be too bitter a pill for a native-born woman to swallow any longer.

I beg you, gentlemen, to save us from the mortification and the humiliation of appealing to the rabble. We already have on our side the vast majority of the better educated— the best classes of men. You will remember that Senator Christiancy, of Michigan, two years ago, said on the floor of the Senate that of the 40,000 men who voted for woman suffrage in Michigan it was said that there was not a drunkard, not a libertine, not a gambler, not a depraved, low man among them. Is not that something that tells for us, and for our right? It is the fact, in every State of the Union, that we have the intelligent lawyers and the most liberal ministers of all the sects, not excepting the Roman Catholics. A Roman Catholic priest preached a sermon the other day, in which he said, "God grant that there were a thousand Susan B. Anthonys in this city to vote and work for temperance." When a Catholic priest says that there is a great moral necessity pressing down upon this nation demanding the enfranchisement of women, I ask you that you shall not drive us back to beg our rights at the feet of the most ignorant and depraved men of the nation, but that you, the representative men of the nation, will hold the question in the hollow of your hands. We ask you to lift this question out of the hands of the rabble.

You who are here upon the floor of Congress in both Houses are the picked men of the nation. You may say what you please about John Morrisey, the gambler, &c.: he was head and shoulders above the rank and file of his constituency. The world may gabble over so much about members of Congress being corrupt and being bought and sold; they are as a rule head and shoulders above the great majority who compose their State governments. There is no doubt about it. Therefore I ask of you, as representative men, as men who think, as men who study, as men who philosophize, as men who know, that you will not drive us back to the States any more., but that you will carry out this method of procedure which has been practiced from the beginning of the Government; that is, that you will put a prohibitory amendment in the Constitution and submit the proposition to the several State legislatures. The amendment which has been presented before you reads:

ARTICLE XVI

SECTION 1. The right of suffrage in the United States shall be based on citizenship, and the right of citizens of the United Stated to vote shall not be denied or abridged by the United States, or by any State, on account of sex, or for any reason not equally applicable to all citizens of the United States.

SECTION 2. Congress shall have power to enforce this article by appropriate legislation.

In this way we would get the right of suffrage just as much by what you call the consent of the States, or the States' rights method, as by any other method. The only point is that it is a decision by the representative men of the States instead of by the rank and file of the ignorant men of the States. If you would submit this proposition for a sixteenth amendment, by a two-thirds vote of the two Houses to the several legislatures, and the several legislatures ratify it, that would be just as much by the consent of the States as if Tom, Dick, and Harry voted "yes" or "no." Is it not, Senator? I want to talk to Democrats as well as Republicans, to show that it is a States' rights method.

Senator EDMUNDS. Does anybody propose any other, in case it is done at all by the nation?

Miss ANTHONY. Not by the nation, but they are continually driving us back to get it from the States, State by State. That is the point I want to make. We do not want you to drive us back to the States. We want you men to take the question out of the hands of the rabble of the State.

The CHAIRMAN. May I interrupt you?

Miss ANTHONY. Yes, sir; I wish you would.

The CHAIRMAN. You have reflected on this subject a great deal. You think there is a majority, even in the State of New York, against women suffrage?

Miss ANTHONY. Yes, sir; overwhelmingly.

The CHAIRMAN. How, then, would you get Legislatures elected to ratify such a constitutional amendment?

Miss ANTHONY. That brings me exactly to the point.

The CHAIRMAN. That is the point I wish to hear you upon.

Miss ANTHONY. Because the members of the State Legislatures are intelligent men and can vote and enact laws embodying great principles of the government without in anywise endangering their positions with their constituencies. A constituency composed of ignorant men would vote solid against us because they have never thought on the question. Every man or woman who believes in the enfranchisement of women is educated out of every idea that he or she was born into. We were all born into the idea that the proper sphere of women is subjection, and it takes education and thought and culture to lift us out of it. Therefore when men go to the ballot-box they all vote "no," unless they have actual agreement on it. I will illustrate. We have six Legislatures in the nation, for instance, that have extended the right to vote on school questions to the women, and not a single member of the State Legislature have ever lost his office or forfeited the respect or confidence of his constituents as a representative because he voted to give women the right to vote on school questions. It is a question that the unthinking masses never have thought upon. They do not care about it one way or the other, only they have an instinctive feeling that because women never did vote therefore it is wrong that they ever should vote.

Mrs. SPENCER. Do make the point that the Congress of the United States leads the Legislatures of the States and educates them.

Miss ANTHONY. When you, representative men, carry this matter to Legislatures, State by State, they will ratify it. My point is that you can safely do this. Senator

Thurman, of Ohio, would not lose a single vote in Ohio in voting in favor of the enfranchisement of women. Senator EDMUNDS would not lose a single Republican vote in the State of Vermont if he puts himself on our side, which, I think, he will do. It is not a political question. We are no political power that can make or break either party to- day. onsequently each man is left independent to express his own moral and intellectual convictions on the matter without endangering himself politically.

Senator EDMUNDS. I think, Miss Anthony, you ought to put it on rather higher, I will not say stronger ground. If you can convince us that it is right we would not stop to see how it affected us politically.

Miss ANTHONY. I was coming to that. I was going to say to all of you men in office here to-day that if you can not go forward and carry out either your Democratic or your Republican or your Greenback theories, for instance, on the finance, there is no great political power that is going to take you away from these halls and prevent you from doing all those other things which you want to do, and you can act out your own moral and intellectual convictions on this without let or hindrance.

Senator EDMUNDS. Without any danger to the public interest, you mean.

Miss ANTHONY. Without any danger to the public interests. I did not mean to make a bad insinuation, Senator.

I want to give you another reason why we appeal to you. In these three States where the question has been submitted and voted down we can not get another Legislature to resubmit it, because they say the people have expressed their opinion and decided no, and therefore nobody with any political sense would resubmit the question. It is therefore impossible in any one of those States. We have tried hard in Kansas for ten years to get the question resubmitted; the vote of that State seems to be taken as a finality. We ask you to lift the sixteenth amendment out of the arena of the public mass into the arena of thinking legislative brains, the brains of the nation, under the law and the Constitution. Not only do we ask it for that purpose, but when you will have by a two-thirds vote submitted the proposition to the several Legislatures, you have put the pin down and it never can go back. No subsequent Congress can revoke that submission of the proposition; there will be so much gained, it can not slide back. Then we will go to New York or to Pennsylvania, and urge upon the Legislatures the ratification of that amendment. They may refuse; they may vote it down for the first time. Then we will go to the next Legislature, and the next Legislature, and plead and plead, from year to year, if it takes ten years. It is an open question to every Legislature until we can get one that will ratify it, and when that Legislature has once voted and ratified it no subsequent legislation can revoke their ratification.

Thus, you perceive, Senators, that every step that we would gain by this sixteenth amendment process is fast and not to be done over again. That is why I appeal to you especially. As I have shown you in the respective States, if we fail to educate the people of a whole State—and in Michigan it was only six months, and in Colorado less than six months—the State Legislatures say that is the end of it. I appeal to you, therefore, to adopt the cause that we suggest.

Sarah M. Grimke (1792-1873)

"An Epistle To The Clergy of the Southern States."

Antislavery crusader and advocate of woman's rights Sarah Grimke was born in Charleston, South Carolina on November 26, 1792. Her parents were wealthy, conservative, slaveholding aristocrats. Early Sarah showed dissatisfaction with her environment. Her sensitive nature caused her to resent the abusive treatment of black people. A trip to Philadelphia with some Quakers helped to clarify in her mind the discontent she had with her family as slaveholders. She and her sister Angelina persuaded their mother to allot them slaves and in response to that gift the sisters freed their charges. In time Sarah addressed small groups of women until she took the next step to the lecture platform. In the arena of the public platform she encountered much animosity. Sarah Grimke wrote the following discourse in 1836.

Printed with the kind permission of the Haverford College Library, (Quaker Collection) Haverford PA 19041-1392.

"And when he was come near, he beheld the city and wept over it, saying—If thou wouldst known, even then, at least in this thy day, the things which belong unto thy peace." Luke XIX, 11-12.

BRETHREN BELOVED IN THE LORD:

It is because I feel a portion of that love glowing in my heart towards you, which is infused into every bosom by the cordial reception of the gospel of Jesus Christ, that I am induced to address you as fellow professors of his holy religion. To my dear native land, to the beloved relatives who are still breathing her tainted air, to the ministers of Christ, from some of whom I have received the emblems of a Saviour's love; my heart turns with feelings of intense solicitude, even with such feelings, may I presume to say, as brought the gushing tears of compassion from the Redeemer of the world, when he wept over the city which he loved when with ineffable pathos he exclaimed, "O Jerusalem! Jerusalem! thou that killest the prophets, and stonest them which we sent unto thee, how often would I have gathered thy children together even as a hen gathereth her chickens under her wings, and ye would not." Nay, these are the feelings which fill the hearts of Northern Abolitionists toward Southern slaveholders. Yes, my brethren, notwithstadning the bon fire at Charleston—the outrages at Nashville on the person of Dresser—the banishment of Birney and Nelson—the arrest and imprisonment of our colored citizens—we can still weep over you with unfeigned tenderness and anxiety, and exclaim, O that ye would even now listen to the Christian remonstrances of those who feel that the principle they advocate "is not a vain thing for you, because it is YOUR LIFE. For you the midnight tear is shed, for you the daily and nightly prayer ascends, that God in his unbounded mercy may open your hearts to believe his awful denunciations against those who "rob the poor because he is poor." And will you still disregard the supplications of those, who are lifting up their voices like the prophets of old, and reiterating the soul-touching enquiry," Why will ye die, O house of Israel?" Oh that I could clothe my feelings in eloquence that would be irresistible, in tones of melting tenderness that would soften the hearts of all, who hold their fellow men in bondage.

A solemn sense of the duty which I owe as a Southerner to every class of the community of which I was once a part, likewise impels me to address *you*, especially, who are filling the important and responsible station of ministers of Jehovah, expounders of the lively oracles of God. It is because you sway the minds of a vast proportion of the Christian community, who regard you as the channel through which divine knowledge must flow. Nor does the fact that you are voluntarily invested by the people with this high prerogative, lessen the fearful weight of responsibility which attaches to you as watchmen on the walls of Zion. It adds rather a tenfold weight of guilt, because the very first duty which devolves upon you is to teach them not to trust in man.—O my brethren, is this duty faithfully performed? Is not the idea inculcated that to you they must look for the right understanding of the sacred volume, and has not your interpretation of the Word of God induced thousands and tens of thousands to receive as truth, sanctioned by the authority of Heaven, the oft repeated declaration that slavery, American slavery, stamped as it is with all its infinity of horrors, bears upon it the signet of that God whose name is Love?

Let us contemplate the magnificent scene of creation, when God looked upon chaos and said, "Let there be light, and there was light." The dark abyss was instantaneously illuminated, and a flood of splendor poured upon the face of the deep, and "God saw the light that it was good." Behold the work of creation carried on and perfected—the azure sky and verdant grass, the trees, the beasts, the fowls of the air, and whatsoever passeth through the paths of the sea, the greater light to rule the day, the lesser night to rule the night, and all the starry host of heaven, brought into existence by the simple command, Let them be.

But was man, the lord of this creation, thus ushered into being? No, the Almighty, clothed as he is with all power in heaven and in earth, paused when he had thus far completed his glorious work—"Omnipotence retired, if I may so speak, and held a counsel when he was about to place upon the earth the sceptered monarch of the universe." He did not say let man be, but "Let us make man in OUR IMAGE, after our likeness, and let them have dominion over the fish of the sea, and over the fowl of the air, and over the cattle, and over all the earth, and over every creeping thing, that creepeth upon the earth." Here is written in characters of fire continually blazing before the eyes of every man who holds his fellow man in bondage—In the image of God created he man. Here is marked a distinction which can never be effaced between a man and a *thing*, and we are fighting against God's unchangeable decree by depriving this rational and immortal being of those inalienable rights which have been conferred upon him. He was created a little lower than the angels, crowned with glory and honor, and designed to be God's viceregent upon earth—but slavery has wrested the sceptre of dominion from his hand, slavery has seized with an iron grasp this God-like being, and torn the crown from his head. Slavery has disrobed him of royalty, put on him the collar and the chain, and trampled the image of God in the dust.

"Eternal God! When from thy giant hand
Thou heaved the floods, and fixed the troubling
land:

When life sprung startling at the plastic call;
Endless her forms, and man the Lord of all—
Say, was that lordly form, inspired by thee,
To wear eternal chains and bow the knee?
Was man ordained the slave of man to toil,
Yoked with the brutes and fettered to the soil?"

This, my brethren, is slavery—this is what sublimates the atrocity of that act, which virtually says, I will as far as I am able destroy the image of God, blot him from creation as a man, and convert him into a thing—"a chattel personal." Can any crime, tremendous as is the history of human wickedness, compare in turpitude with this?— No, the immutable difference, the *heaven-wide distinction* which God has established between *that* being, whom he has made a little lower than the angels, and all the other works of this wonderful creation, cannot be annihilated without incurring a weight of guilt beyond expression terrible.

And after God had destroyed the world by a flood because of the wickedness of man, every imagination of whose heart was evil, and had preserved Noah because he was righteous before him. He renewed man's delegated authority over the whole animate and inanimate creation, and again delivered into his hand every beast of the earth and every fowl of the air, and added to his former grant of power, "Every moving thing that liveth shall be meat for you, even as the green herb have I given you all things." Then, as if to impress indelibly upon the mind of man the eternal distinction between his rational and immortal creatures and the lower orders of beings, he guards the life of this most precious jewel, with a decree which would have proved all-sufficient to protect it, had not Satan infused into man his own reckless spirit.

Permission ample was given to shed the blood of all inferior creatures, but of this, *being, bearing the impress of divinity,* God said, "And surely your blood of your lives will I equire, at the hand of every beast will I require it, and at the hand of man, at the hand of every man's brother will I require the life of man. Whoso sheddeth man's blood, by man shall his blood be shed, for in the IMAGE of God made he man." Let us pause and examine this passage.—Man may shed the blood of the inferior animals, he may use them as *mere means*—he may convert them into food to sustain existence—but if the top-stone of creation, the *image of God* had his blood shed by a beast, that blood was required even of this irrational brute: as if Deity had said, over *my l likeness* I will spread a panoply divine that all creation may instinctively feel that he is precious to his Maker—so precious, that if his life be taken by his fellow man— if man degrades himself to the level of a beast by destroying his brother—"by man shall his blood be shed."

This distinction between *men and things* is marked with equal care and solemnity under the Jewish dispensation. "If a man steal an ox, or a sheep, and kill it, or sell it, he shall restore five oxen for an ox, and four sheep for a sheep." But "he that stealeth a man and selleth him or if he found in his hand, he shall surely be put to death." If this law were carried into effect now, what must be the inevitable doom of all those who now hold man as property? If Jehovah were to exact the execution of this penalty upon the more enlightened and more spiritually minded men who live under the Christian dispensation, would he not instantly commission his most tremendous thunderbolts to strike from existence those who are thus trampling upon his laws, thus defacing his image?

I pass now to the eighth Psalm, which is a sublime anthem of praise to our Almighty Father for his unbounded goodness to the children of men. This Psalm alone affords irrefragable proof that God never gave to man dominion over his own image, that he never commissioned the Israelites to enslave their fellow men. This was

> "Authority usurped from God not given—
> Man over men
> *He* made not Lord, such title to *himself*
> Reserving, human left, from human free."

This beautiful song of glory to God was composed three thousand years after the creation, and David who says of himself, "The spirit of the Lord spake by me and his word was in my tongue," gives us the following exquisite description of the creation of man and of the power with which he was intrusted. "Thou hast made him a little lower than the angels, and crowned him with glory and honor. Thou madest him to have dominion over the works of thy hands: thou has put all things under his feet: all sheep and oxen, yea, and all the beasts of the field, the fowl of the air and the fish of the sea, and whatsoever passeth through the paths of the sea."

David was living under the dispensation to which slaveholders triumphantly point as the charter of their right to hold men as PROPERTY; but he does not even intimate that any extension of prerogative has been granted. He specifies precisely the same things which are specified at the creation and after the flood. He had been eminently instrumental in bringing into captivity the nations round about, but he does not so much as hint that Jehovah had transferred the sceptre of dominion over his immortal creatures to the hand of man. How could God create man in his own image and then invest his fellow worms with power to blot him from the world of spirits and place him on a level with the brutes who perish!

The same Psalm is quoted by the Apostle Paul, as if our heavenly Father designed to teach us through all dispensations of his mercy to a fallen world, that man was but a little lower than the angels, God's viceregent upon earth over the inferior creatures. St. Paul quotes it in connection with that stupendous event whereby we are saved from eternal death. "But we see Jesus who was made a little lower than the angels for the suffering of death, crowned with glory and honor; that he by the grace of God should taste death for every man." Here side by side the apostle places "God manifest in the flesh" and his accredited representative man. He calls us to view the master-piece of God's creation, and then the master-piece of his mercy—Christ Jesus, wearing our form and dying for our sins, thus conferring everlasting honor upon man by declaring "both he that sanctifieth and they who are sanctified are all of one: for which cause he is not ashamed to call them brethren." It is then, the Lord's brethren whom we have enslaved; the Lord's brethren of whom we say "slaves shall be deemed, taken, reputed, and adjudged, chattels personal in the hands of their owners and possessors to all intents and purposes whatever." Laws of South Carolina.

And here I cannot but advert to a most important distinction which God had made between immortal beings and the beasts that perish.—No one can doubt that by the fall of man the whole creation underwent a change. The apostle says, "We know that the whole creation groaneth and travaileth in pain together." But it was for man alone that the Lord Jesus "made himself of no reputation and took upon him the form of a servant." When he came before his incarnation to cheer his servants with his blessed presence, when he visited Abraham and Manoah, he took upon himself a human form. Manoah's wife says, "a man of God came unto me." And when he came and exhibited on the theatre of our world, that miracle of grace "God in Christ reconciling the world unto himself," what form did he wear? "Verily," says the apostle, "he took not on him the nature of angels; but he took on him the seed of Abraham:" Oh, my brethren, he has stamped with high and holy dignity the form we wear, he has forever exalted our nature by condescending to assume it, and by investing man with the high and holy privilege of being "the temple of the Holy Ghost." Where then is our title deed for enslaving our equal brother?

Mr. Chandler of Norfolk, in a speech in the House of Delegates of Virginia, on the subject of negro slavery in 1832, speaking of our right to hold our colored brethren in bondage, says:

> "As a Virginian, I do not question the master's
> title to his slave; but I put it to that gentleman,
> as a man, as a moral man, as a Christian man,
> whether he has not some doubts of his claim to his
> slaves, being as absolute and as unqualified as
> that to other property. Let us in the investigation
> of this title go back to its origin—Whence came
> slaves into this country?—From Africa. Were they
> free men there? At one time they were. How came
> they to be converted into slaves?—By the strategem
> of war and the strong arm of the conquerer; they
> were vanquished in battle, sold by the victorious
> party to the slave trader; who brought them to our
> shores, and disposed of them to the planters of
> Virginia.............The truth is, our ancestors
> had *no title* to this property, and we have acquired
> it only by legislative enactments."

But can "legislative enactments" annul the laws of Jehovah, or sanctify the crimes of theft and oppression? "Wo unto them that decree unrighteous decrees.....to take away the *right* from the poor of my people." Suppose the Saviour of the world were to visit our guilty country and behold the Christianity of our slave holding states, would not his language be, "Ye have heard that it hath been said by them of old time, enslave your fellow men, but I say unto you "Do unto others as ye would they should do unto you," and set your captives free!

> The sentiment—
> "Man over man
> He made not lord"—

is the sentiment of human nature. It is written, by the Almighty, on the soul, as a part of its very being. So that, urge on the work of death as we may, in the mad attempt to convert a free agent into a machine, a man into a thing, and *nature* will still cry out for freedom. Hear the testimony of James McDowell, in the House of Delegates, in Virginia in 1832.

"As to the idea that the slave in any considerable
number of cases can be so attracted to his master
and his servitude, as to be indifferent to freedom,
it is wholly unnatural, rejected by the *conscious*
testimony of every man's heart, and the *written*
testimony of the world's experience.............You
may place the slave where you please, you may
oppress him as you please, you may dry up to the
uttermost the fountain of his feelings, the springs
of his thought, you may close upon his mind every
avenue of knowledge, and cloud it over with artificial
night, you may yoke him to your labors as the ox which
liveth only to work, you may put him under any
process, which without destroying his value as a slave,
will debase and crush him as rational being, and the
idea that *he was born to be free* will survive it all. It
is allied to his hope of immortality—it is the ethereal
part of his being, which oppression cannot reach; it is a
torch lit up in his soul by the hand of Deity, and never
meant to be extinguished by the hand of man."

I need not enter into an elaborate proof that Jewish servitude, as permitted by God, was as different from American slavery, as Christianity is from heathenism. The limitation laws respecting strangers and servants, entirely prohibited cruelty and oppression, whereas in our slave states, "THE MASTER MAY, AT HIS DISCRETION, INFLICT ANY SPECIES OF PUNISHMENT UPON THE PERSON OF HIS SLAVE,"* and the law throws her protecting aegis over the master, by refusing to receive under any circumstances, the testimony of a colored man against a white, except to subserve the interests of the owner.—"It is manifest," says the author (a Christian Minister) of "A calm inquiry into the countenance afforded by the Scriptures to the system of British Colonial Slavery" that the Hebrews had no word in their language equivalent to slave in the West Indian use of that term. The word obed, is applied to both bond servants and hired, to kings and prophets, and even to the Saviour of the world. It was a general designation for any person who rendered service of any kind to God or man. But the term SLAVE, in the Colonial sense, could not be at all applied to freeman." The same word in the Septuagint which is translated servant, is also translated child, and as the Hebrew language is remarkably for its minute shades of distinction in things, had there been, as is asserted, slaves in Judea, there would undoubtedly have been some term to designate such a condition. Our language recognizes the difference between a slave and a servant, because those two classes actually exist in our country. The Burmese language has no word to express ETERNITY, hence a missionary remarked that it was almost impossible to convey to them any conception of it. So likewise among the ancient Greeks and Romans there was not word equivalent to humility, because they acknowledged no such virtue. The want of any term therefore in the Hebrew, to mark the distinction between a slave in the proper sense of the term and other servants, is proof presumptive to say the least, that no such condition as that of slave was known among the Jews of that day.

To assert that Abraham held slaves is a mere slander. The phrase, translated, "souls that they had gotten in Haran," Gen. 12: 5, has not possible reference to slaves, and was never supposed to have any allusion to slavery until the commencement of the slave trade in England, in 1563. From that time commentators endeavored to cast upon Abraham the obloquy of holding his fellow creatures in bondage, in order to excuse this nefarious traffic. The Targum of Onkelos thus paraphrases this passage "souls gotten, i.e. those whom they had caused to obey the law." The Targum of Jonathan calls them "Proselytes." Jarchi, "Those whom they had brought under the wings of Shekinah." Menochius, "Those whom they converted from idolatry." Luke Franke, a Latin commentator, "Those whom they subjected to the law." Jerome calls them "Proselytes." Here is a mass of evidence which is incontrovertible. Abraham's business as "the friend of God" was to get souls as the seal of his ministry. Would he have been called from a heathen land to be the father of the faithful in all generations, that he might enslave the converts he made from idolatry? As soon we might suspect our missionaries of riveting the chains of servitude on souls that they may have gotten, as seals of their ministry, from among those to whom they proclaim the unsearchable riches of Christ. Would heathen then, any more than now, be attracted to a standard which bore on it the inscription SLAVERY? No, my brethren; and if our downtrodden slaves did not distinguish between Christianity, and the Christians who hold them in bondage, they could never embrace a religion, which is exhibited to them from the pulpit, in the prayer-meeting, and at the domestic altar, embodied in the form of masters, utterly regardless of the divine command, "Render unto your servants that which is just." From the confidence which Abraham reposed in his servants we cannot avoid the inference that they clustered voluntarily around him as the benefactor of their souls, the patriarch of that little community which his ministry had gathered.

Again, it is often peremptorily asserted that "the Africans are a divinely condemned and proscribed race." If they are, has God constituted the slave holders the ministers of his vengeance? This question can only be answered in the negative, and until it can be otherwise answered, it is vain to appeal to the curse on Canaan, or to Hebrew servitude, in support of American slavery. As well might the bloodstained emperor of France appeal to the conquest of Canaan by the Israelites, and challenge the Almighty to reward him for the work of death which he wrought on the fields of Marengo and Lepsic, because God invested his peculiar people, with authority to destroy the nations which had filled up the measure of their iniquity. The express grant to the Jews to reduce to subjection some of the Canaanitish nations and to exterminate others, at once condemns American slavery, because those who derive their sanction to hold their fellow men in bondage from the Bible, admit that a specific grant was necessary to empower the Israelites to make bond-men of the heathen; and unless this permission had been given, they would not have been justified in doing it. It is therefore self-evident that as we have never been commanded to enslave the Africans, we can derive no sanction for our slave system from the history of the Jews.

Another plea by which we endeavor to silence the voice of conscience is, "that the child is invariably born to the condition of the parent." Hence the law of South Carolina says "ALL THEIR (THE SLAVES) ISSUE AND OFFSPRING, BORN, OR TO BE BORN, SHALL BE, AND THEY ARE HEREBY DECLARED TO BE, AND REMAIN FOREVER HEREAFTER ABSOLUTE SLAVES, AND SHALL FOREVER FOLLOW THE CONDITION OF THE MOTHER." To support this assumption, recourse is had to the page of inspiration. Our colored brethren are said to be the descendants of Ham who was cursed with all his posterity, and their condition only in accordance with the declaration of Jehovah, that he visits the iniquities of the fathers upon the children.—I need only remark that Canaan, not Ham, was the object of Noah's prophecy, and upon his descendants it has been amply fulfilled.

But we appeal to prophecy in order to excuse or palliate the sin of slavery, and we regard ourselves as guiltless because we are fulfilling the designs of Omnipotence. Let us read our sentence in the word of God: "And he said unto Abraham, Know that of a surety that they seed shall be a stranger in a land that is not theirs and shall serve them, and I will afflict them four hundred years, and also that nation whom they shall serve, I WILL JUDGE." That nation literally drank the blood of the wrath of Almighty God. The whole land of Egypt was a house of mourning, a scene of consternation and horror. What did it avail the Egyptians that they had been the instruments permitted to the inscrutable counsels of Jehovah to accomplish every iota of the prophecy concerning the seed of Abraham?

Appeal to prophecy! As well might the Jews who by wicked hands crucified the Messiah claim to themselves the sanction of prophecy. As well might *they* shield themselves from the scathing lightning of the Almighty under the plea that the tragedy they acted on Calvary's mount, had been foretold by the inspired penman a thousand years before. Read in the 22d Psalm an exact description of the crucifixion of Christ. Hear the words of the dying Redeemer from the lips of the Psalmist: "My God! My God! Why hast thou forsaken me?!" At that awful day when the dead, small and great, stand before God, and the books are opened, and another book is opened, which is the book of life, and the dead are judges out of those things which are written in the book ACCORDING TO THEIR WORKS—think you, my brethren, that the betrayer and the crucifiers of the Son of God will find their names inscribed in the book of life *"because they* fulfilled prophecy in killing the Prince of Peace? Think you that they will claim, or receive on this ground, exemption from the orments of the damned? Will it not add to their guilt and woe that "To Him bare all the prophets witness," and render more intense the anguish and horror with which they will call upon "the rocks and the mountains to fall upon them and from the wrath of the Lamb!"

Contemplate the history of the Jews since the crucifixion of Christ! Behold even in this world the awfully retributive justice which is so accurately portrayed by the pen of Moses. "And the Lord shall scatter thee among all people from the one end of the earth even unto the other, and among those nations shalt thou find no ease." And can we believe that those nations who with Satanic ingenuity have fulfilled to a tittle these prophecies against this guilty people, will stand acquitted at the bar of God for their own cruelty and injustice, in the matter? Prophecy is a mirror on whose surface is inscribed in characters of light, that sentence of deep, immitigable woe which the Almighty has pronounced and executed on transgressors. Let me beseech you then, my dear, though guilty brethren, to pause, and learn from the tremendous past what must be the inevitable destiny of those who are adding year after year, to the amount of crime which is treasuring up "wrath against the day of wrath." "A wonderful and horrible thing is committed in the land! The *prophets prophecy falsely*,   and the priests bear rule by their means, and my people love to have it so, and what will ye do in the end thereof?" "Thus saith the Lord of hosts concerning the prophets, Behold I will feed them with wormwood, and make them drink the water of gall."

The present position of my country and of the church is one of deep and solemn interest. The times of our ignorance on the subject of slavery which God may have winked at, *have passed away.* We are no longer standing unconsciously and care-lessly on the brink of a burning volcano. The strong arm of Almighty power has rolled back the dense cloud which hung over the terrific crater, and has exposed it to our view, and although no human eye can penetrate the abyss, yet enough is seen to warn us of the consequences of trifling with Omnipotence. Jehovah is call to us as he did to Job out of the whirlwind, and every blast bears on its wings the sound, Repent! Repent! God, if I may so speak, is waiting to see whether we will hearken unto his voice. He has sent out his light and his truth, and as regards us it may perhaps be said—there is now silence in heaven. The commissioned messengers of grace to this guilty nation are rapidly traversing our country, through the medium of the Anti-slavery Society, through the agents and its presses, whilst the "ministering spirits" are marking with breathless interest the influence produced by these means of knowledge thus mercifully furnished to our land. Oh! If there be joy in heaven over one sinner that repenteth, what hallelujahs of angelic praise will arise, when the slave-holder and the defender of slavery bow before the footstool of mercy, and with broken spirits and contrite hearts surrender unto God that dominion over his immortal creatures which he alone can rightly exercise.

What an appalling spectacle do we now present! With one hand we clasp the cross of Christ and with the other grasp the neck of the down-trodden slave! With one eye we are gazing imploringly on the bleeding sacrifice of Calvary, as if we expected redemption though the blood which was shed there, and with the other we cast the glance of indignation and contempt at the representative of Him who there made his soul and offering for sin! My Christian brethren, if there is any truth in the Bible, and in the God of the Bible, *our hearts bear us witness* that he can no more acknowledge us as his disciples, if we willfully persist in this sin, than he did the Pharisees formerly, who were strict and punctilious in the observance of the ceremonial law, and yet devoured widows' houses. *We have added a deeper shade to their guilt,* we make widows by tearing from the victims of a cruel bondage, the husbands of their bosoms, and then devour the widow herself by robbing her of her freedom, and reducing her to the level of a brute. I solemnly appeal to your own consciences. Does not the rebuke of Christ to the Pharisees apply to some of those who re exercising the office of Gospel ministers, "Wo unto you, Scribes and Pharisees, hypocrites! for ye devour widow's houses, and for a pretence make long prayers, therefore ye shall receive the greater damnation."

How long the space now granted for repentance may continue, is among the secret things which belong unto God, and my soul ardently desires that all those who are enlisted in the ranks of abolition may regard every day as possibly the last, and may pray without ceasing to God, to grant this nation repentance and forgivenes of the sin of slavery. The time is precious, unspeakably precious and every encouragement is offered to us to supplicate the God of the master and of the slave to make a "right way" "for us, and for our little ones, and for all our substance." Ezra says, "so we fasted and besought the Lord, and he was entreated for us." Look at the marvellous (sic) effect of prayer when Peter was imprisoned. What did the church in that crisis? She felt that her weapons were not carnal, but spiritual. And "prayer was made without ceasing." These petitions offered in humble faith were mighty through God to the emancipation of Peter. "Is the Lord's arm shortened that it cannot save, or his ear grown heavy that it cannot hear?" If he condescended to work a miracle in answer to prayer when one of his servants was imprisoned, will he not graciously hear our supplications when two millions of his immortal creatures are in bondage? We entreat the Christian ministry to co-operate with us to unite in our petitions to Almighty God to deliver our land from blood guiltiness; to enable us to see the abominations of American slavery by the light of the gospel. "This is the condemnation, that light is come into the world, but men loved darkness rather than light, because their deeds were evil." Then may we expect a glorious consummation to our united labors of love. Then may the Lord Jesus unto whom belongeth all power in heaven and in earth condescend to answer our prayers, and by the softening influence of his holy spirit induce our brethren and sisters of the South, "to undo the heavy burdens, to break every yoke and let the oppressed go free."

My mind has been deeply impressed while reading the account of the anniversaries held last spring in the city of New York, with the belief that there is in America a degree of light, knowledge and intelligence which leaves us without excuse before God for upholding the system of slavery. Nay, we not only sustain this temple of Moloch; but with impious lips consecrate it to the Most High God; and call upon Jehovah himself to sanctify our sins by the presence of his Shekinah. Now mark, the unholy combination that has been entered into between the North and the South to shut our the light on this all important subject. I copy from a speech before the "General Assembly's Board of Education." As an illustration of his position, Dr. Breckenridge referred to the influence of the Education Board in the Southern States. "Jealous as those States were, and not without reason, of all that came to them in the shape of benevolent enterprise from the North, and ready as they were to take fire in a moment at whatever threatened *their own peculiar institutions,* the plans of this Board had *conciliated* their fullest confidence: in proof of which they had placed nearly two hundred of their sons under its care, that they might be *trained and fitted to teach to their own population.*" The inference is unavoidable that the "peculiar institution" spoken of is domestic slavery in all its bearings and relations; and it is equally clear that the ministry educated for the South are to be thoroughly imbued with the slave-holding spirit, that they may be, *"fitted to preach to their own population,"* not the gospel of Jesus Christ, which proclaims LIBERTY TO THE CAPTIVE, but a religion which grants to man the privilege of sinning with impunity, and stamps with the signet of the King of heaven a system that embraces every possible enormity. Surely if ye are ambassadors for Christ, ye are bound to promulgate the *whole* counsel of God. But can ye preach from the language of James, "Behold the hire of your laborers which is of you kept back by fraud crieth, and the cries of them which have reaped, are entered into the ears of the Lord of Sabaoth." Multitudes of other texts must be virtually expunged from the bible of the slave holding minister; every denunciation against oppression strikes at the root of slavery. God is in a peculiar manner the God of the poor and the needy, the despised and the oppressed. "The Lord said I have surely seen the affliction of my people, and have heard their cry by reason of their task-masters, for I know their sorrows." And he knows the sorrows of the American slave, and he will come down in mercy, or in judgment to deliver them.

In a speech before the "American Seamen's Friend Society," by Rev. William S. Plumer of Virginia, it is said, "The resolution spoke of weighty considerations, why we should care for seamen, and one of those certainly was, *because as a class, they had been long and criminally neglected.* Another weighty consideration was that seamen were a suffering race."........."And who was the cause of this? Was it not the church who withheld from these her suffering brethren, those blessed truths of God, so well calculated to comfort those who suffer?" Oh my brother! while drawing to the life a picture of a class of our fellow beings, who have been "long and criminally neglected," of "a suffering race," was there no cord of sympathy in thy heart to vibrate to the groans of the slave? Did no seraph's voice whisper in thine ear Remember them which are in bonds?" Did memory present no scenes of cruelty and oppression? And did not conscience say, thou art one who withholds from thy suffering colored brethren those blessed truths of God so well calculated to comfort those who suffer? Can we believe that the God of Christianity will bless the people who are thus dispensing their gifts to all, save to those by whose *unrequited* toil, we and our ancestors for generations past have subsisted?

Let us examine the testimony of Charles C. Jones, Professor in the Theological Seminary. Columbia, S.C. relative to the condition of our slaves, and then judge whether they have not at least as great a claim as seamen to the sympathy and benevolent effort of Christian Ministers. In a sermon preached before two associations of planters in Georgia in 1831, he says: "Generally speaking, they (the slaves) appear to us to be without God and without hope in the world, a nation of HEATHEN in our very midst. We cannot cry out against the Papists for withholding the Scriptures from the common people, and keeping them in ignorance of the way of life, for we *withhold the Bible* from our servants, and *keep* them of ignorance of it, while we will not use the means to have it read and explained to them. The cry of our perishing servants comes up to us from the sultry plains as they bend at their toil; it comes up to us from their humble cottages when they return at evening, to rest their weary limbs; it comes up to us from the midst of their ignorance and superstition, and adultery and lewdness. We have manifested no *emotions* of horror at abandoning the souls of our servants to the adversary, the "roaring lion that walketh about, seeking whom he may devour."

On the 5th of December, 1833, a committee of the synod of South Carolina and Georgia, to whom was referred the subject of the religious instruction of the colored population, made a report in which this language was used. "Who would credit it that in these years of revival and benevolent effort, in this Christian republic, there are over TWO MILLIONS of human beings in the condition of HEATHEN, and in some respects in a *worse* condition. From long continued and close observation, we believe that their moral and religious condition is such that they may be justly considered the HEATHEN of this Christian country, and will bear comparison with heathens in *any country in the world.* The negroes are destitute of the gospel, and *ever will be* under the present state of things."

In a number of the Charleston Observer (in 1834,) a correspondent remarked: "Let us establish missionaries among our own negroes, who, in view of religious knowledge, are as debasingly ignorant as any one on the coast of Africa; for I hazard the assertion that throughout the bounds of our Synod, there are at least ONE HUNDRED THOUSAND SLAVES, speaking the same language as ourselves, who never heard of the plan of salvation by a Redeemer."

The Editor, Rev. Benjamin Gildersleeve, who has resided at least ten years at the South, so far from contradicting this broad assertion, adds, "We fully concur with what our correspondent has said, respecting the benighted heathen among ourselves."

As Southerners, can we deny these things? As Christians, can we ask the blessing of the Redeemer of men on the system of American slavery? Can we carry it to the footstool of a God whose "compassions fail not," and pray for holy help to rivet the chains of international bondage on TWO MILLIONS of our fellow men, the accredited representatives of Jesus Christ? If we cannot ask in faith that the blessing of God may rest on this work of cruelties to the bodies, and destruction of the souls of men, we may be assured that his controversy is against it. Try it, my brethren, when you are kneeling around the family altar with the wife of your bosom, with the children of your love, when you are supplicating Him who hath made of one blood all nations, to sanctify these precious souls and prepare them for an inheritance with Jesus—then pray, if you can that God will grant you power to degrade to the level of brutes your colored brethren. Try it, when your little ones are twining their arms around your necks, and lisping the first fond accents of affection in your ears; when the petition arises from the fullness of a parent's heart for a blessing on your children. At such a moment, look in upon your slave. He too is a father, and we know that he is susceptible of all the tender sensibilities of a father's love. He folds his cherished infant in his arms, he feels its life-pulse against his own, and he rejoices that he is a parent; but soon the withering thought rushes to his mind—I am a slave, and tomorrow my master may tear my darling from my arms. Contemplate this scene, while your cheeks are yet warm with the kisses of your children, and then try if you can mingle with a parent's prayer and a parent's blessing, the petition that God may enable you and your posterity to perpetuate a system which to the slave denies—

> "To live together, or together die.
> By felon hands at one relentless stroke
> See the fond links of feeling nature broke;
> The fibres twisting roused a parent's heart,
> Torn from their grasp and bleeding as they part."

A southern minister, Rev. Mr. Atkinson of Virginia, in a speech before the Bible society last spring, says: "The facts which have been told respecting the destitution of some portions of our country are but samples of thousands more. Could we but feel what we owed to him who gave the Bible, we would at the same time feel that we owed it to a fallen and perishing world not merely to pass *fine resolutions*, or listen to *eloquent speeches*, but to exhibit a life devoted to the conversion of the world."

Let us now turn to the heart-sickening picture of the "destitution" of our slaves drawn by those who had the living original continually before their eyes. I extract from the report of the Synod of South Carolina and Georgia before referred to.

> "We may now enquire if they (the slaves) enjoy the
> privileges of the gospel in their own houses, and
> on our plantations? Again we return a negative
> answer—They have no Bibles to read by their own
> fire-sides—they have no family altars; and when in
> affliction, sickness, or death, they have no
> minister to address to them the consolations of the
> gospel, nor to bury them with solemn and
> appropriate services."

This state of things, is the result of laws enacted in a free and enlightened republic. In North Carolina, to teach a slave to read or write, or to sell or give him any book, (the Bible not excepted) or pamphlet, is punished with thirty-nine lashes, or imprisonment, if the offender be a free negro, but if a white man then with a fine of two hundred dollars. The reason for this law assigned in the preamble is, that "teaching slaves to read and write tends to excite dissatisfaction in their minds, and to produce insurrection and rebellion."

In Georgia, if a white teach a free negro, or slave, to read or write, he is fined $500, and imprisoned at the discretion of the court. By this barbarous law, which was enacted in 1829, a white man may be fined and imprisoned for teaching his own child if he happens to be colored, and if colored, whether bond or free, he may be fined or whipped.

"We have says Mr. Berry, in a speech in the House of Delegates in Virginia in 1832, as far as possible closed every avenue by which light might enter their (the slaves) minds. If we could extinguish the capacity to see the light, our work would be completed; they would then be on a level with the beasts of the field, and we should be safe. I am not certain that we would not do it, if we could find out the necessary process, and that on the plea of necessity."

Oh, my brethren! When you are telling to an admiring audience that through your instrumentality nearly two millions of Bibles and Testaments have been disseminated throughout the world, does not the voice of the slave vibrate on your ear, as it floats over the sultry plains of the South, and utters forth his lamentation, "Hast thou but one blessing my father? *Bless me, even me also,* O my father!" Does no wail or torment interrupt the eloquent harangue?—And from the bottomless pit does no accusing voice arise to charge you with the perdition of those souls from whom you wrested, as far as you were able, the power of working out their own salvation?

Our country; I believe, has arrived at an awful crisis. God has in infinite mercy raised up those who have moral courage and religion enough to obey the divine command, "Cry aloud and spare not, lift up thy voice like a trumpet, and show my people their transgressions."—Our sins are set in order before us, and we are now hesitating whether we shall choose the curse pronounced by Jehovah, "Cursed be he that perverteth the judgment of the stranger, fatherless and widow," or the blessing recorded in the 41st Psl. "Blessed is the man that considereth the poor (or the weak,) the Lord will deliver him in the time of trouble."

And is there no help? Shall we be dismayed because our mistaken countrymen burned our messengers of Truth in Charleston, S.C.? No, my brethren, *I am not dismayed!* I do not intend to stamp the antislavery publications as inspired writings, but the principles they promulgate are the principles of the holy Scriptures, and I derive encouragement from the recollection that Tindal suffered martyrdom for translating and printing the New Testament— and that Tonstal, Archbishop of London, purchased every copy which he could obtain, and had them burnt by the common hangman. Now Great Britain is doing more than any other people to scatter the Bible to every nation under heaven. Shall we be alarmed as though some new thing had happened unto us because our printing press had been destroyed at Cincinnati, Ohio? The devoted Carey was compelled to place his establishment for the translation of the sacred volume beyond the boundary line of the British authorities. And now England would gladly have the bible translated into every tongue.

If then there be, as I humbly trust there are among my Christian brethren some who like the prophet of old are ready to exclaim! "Wo is me! for I am undone; because I am a man of unclean lips; for mine eyes have seen the King, the Lord of Hosts"— If to some of you Jehovah has unvailed the abominations of American Slavery, the guilt of yourselves and of your brethren! Oh remember the prophet of Israel and be encouraged. Your lips like his will be touched with a live coal from off the altar. The Lord will be your light and your salvation: He will go before you and the God of Israel will be your reward.

If ever there was a time when the Church of Christ was called upon to make an *aggressive* movement on the kingdom of darkness, *this is the time.* The subject of slavery is fairly before the American public.—The consciences of the slave-holders at the South and of their coadjutors at the North are aroused, notwithstanding all the opiates which are so abundantly administered under the plea of necessity, and expediency, and the duty of obedience to man, rather than to God. In regard to slavery, Satan has transformed himself into an angel of light, and under the false pretense of consulting the good of the slaves, pleads for retaining them in bondage, and they are prepared to enjoy the blessings of liberty. Full well be known that if he can but gain time, he gains every thing. When he stood beside Felix and saw that he trembled before his fettered captive, as Paul reasoned of righteousness, temperance, and judgment to come, he summoned to his aid this masterpiece of satanic ingenuity, and whispered, say to this Apostle, "Go thy way for this time, at a more convenient season, I will call for thee." The heart of Felix responded to this intimation, and his lips uttered the fatal words—fatal, because, for aught that appears, they sealed his death warrant for eternity. Let me appeal to every Christian minister, who has known what it is to repent and forsake his sins: Have you not all found that prospective repentance and future amendment are destruction to the soul? "The truth is, to postpone present duty, to get ready for the discharge of future, is just putting yourselves into the hands of Satan to prepare you for the service of God. Just so, gradualism puts the slave into the hands of his master; whose interest it is to keep him enslaved, to prepare him for freedom, because that master says at a convenient season I will liberate my captive. So says the adversary of all good, serve me to-day and to- morrow thou mayest serve God. Oh lay not this flattering unction to your souls, ye that are teachers in Israel. God is not mocked, and ye may as well expect indulgence in sin to purify the heart and prepare the souls for an inheritance with the saints in light, as to suppose slavery can fit men for freedom. That which debases and brutalizes can never fit for freedom. The chains of the slave must be sundered; he must be taught that he is "heaven-born and destined to the skies again;" he must be restored to his dignified station in the scale of creation, he must be crowned again with the diadem of glory, again ranked amongst the sons of God and invested with lordly prerogative over every living creature. If you would aid in this mighty, this glorious achievement—"Preach the word" of IMMEDIATE EMANCIPATION. "Be instant in season and out of season." "If they persecute in one city, flee ye into another," that your sound may go out through all our land; and you may not incur the awful charge,

"YE KNEW YOUR DUTY, BUT YE DID IT NOT."

It is now twenty years since a beloved friend with whom I often mingled my tears, related to me the following circumstance, when helpless and hopeless we deplored the horrors of slavery, and I believe many are now doing what we did then, weeping and praying and interceding, "but secretly for fear of the Jews." On the plantation adjoining her husband's, there was a slave of pre-eminent piety. His master was not a professor of religion, but the superior excellence of this disciple of Christ was not unmarked by him, and I believe he was so sensible of the good influence of his piety that he did not deprive him of the few religious privileges within his reach. A planter was one day dining with the owner of this slave, and in the course of conversation observed that all profession of religion among slaves was mere hypocrisy. The other asserted a contrary opinion, adding, I have a slave who I believe would rather die than deny his Saviour. This was ridiculed, and the master urged to prove his assertion. He accordingly sent for this man of God, and peremptorily ordered him to deny his belief in the Lord Jesus Christ. The slave pleaded to be excused, constantly affirming that he would rather die than deny the Redeemer, whose blood was shed for him. His master, after daily trying to induce obedience by threats, had him severely whipped. The fortitude of the sufferer was not to be shaken; he nobly rejected the offer of exemption from further chastisement at the expense of destroying his soul, and this blessed martyr died in consequence of this severe infliction. Oh, how bright a gem will this victim of irresponsible power be, in that crown which sparkles on the Redeemer's brow; and that many such will cluster there, I have not the shadow of a doubt.

Brethren, you are invested with immense power over those to whom you minister in holy things—commensurate with your power is your responsibility, and if you abuse, or neglect to use it aright, great will be your condemnation. Mr. Moore, in a speech in the House of Delegates in Virginia, in 1832, says:

> "It is utterly impossible to avoid he
> consideration of the subject of slavery. As well
> might the Apostle have attempted to close his eyes
> against the light which shone upon him from heaven,
> or to turn a deaf ear to the name which reached him
> from on high as for us to try to stifle the spirit
> of enquiry which is abroad in the land.....THE
> MONSTROUS CONSEQUENCES which arise from the
> existence of slavery have been exposed to open day;
> the DANGERS arising from it stare us in the face,
> and it becomes us as men to meet and overcome them,
> rather than attempt to escape by evading them.
> Slavery, as it exists among us, may be regarded as
> the heaviest calamity which has ever befallen any
> portion of the human race. (If we look back at the
> long course of time which has elapsed from the
> creation to the present moment, we shall scarcely
> be able to point out a people whose situation was
> not in many respects preferable to our own, and
> that of the other states in which slavery exists.
> True, we shall see nations which have groaned under
> the yoke of despotism for hundreds and thousands of
> years, but the individual composing those nations
> have enjoyed a degree of happiness, peace and
> freedom from apprehension which the holders of
> slaves in this country can never know."

The daughters of Virginia have borne their testimony to the evils of slavery, and have pleaded for its extinction. Will this nation continue deaf to the voice of reason, humanity, and religion? In the memorial of the female citizens of Fluvanna Co., Va. to the General Assembly of that Commonwealth in 1832, they say:

"We cannot conceal from ourselves that an evil
(slavery) is amongst us, which threatens to outgrow
the growth, and dim the brightness of our national
blessings. A shadow deepens over the land and casts
its thickest gloom upon the sacred shrine of domestic
bliss, darkening over us as time advances." "We can
only aid by ardent outpourings of the spirit of supplication
at a throne of grace.....We conjure you by the sacred
charities of kindred, by the solemn obligations of justice,
by every consideration of domestic affection and patriotic
duty, to serve every faculty of your minds to the investigation
of this important subject, and let not the united voices of your
mothers, wives, daughters and kindred have sounded in your
ears in vain."

We are cheered with the belief that many knees at the South are bent in prayer for the success of the Abolitionists. We believe, and we rejoice in the belief that the statement made by a Southern Minister of the Methodist Episcopal Church, at the session of the New York Annual Conference, in June of this year, is true: "Don't give up Abolitionism—don't bow down to slavery. You have thousands at the South who are secretly praying for you."— In a subsequent conversation with the same individual, he stated, That the South is not that unit of which the pro- slavery party boast—there is a diversity of opinion among them in reference to slavery, and the REIGN OF TERROR alone suppresses the free expression of sentiment. That there are thousands who believe slaveholding to be sinful, who secretly wish the abolitionists success, and believe God will bless their efforts. That the ministers of the gospel and ecclesiastical bodies who indiscriminately denounce the abolitionists, without doing anything themselves to remove slavery, have not the thanks of thousands at the South, but on the contrary are viewed as taking sides with slaveholders and recreant to the principles of their own profession. *Zion's Watchman,* November, 1836.

The system of slavery is necessarily cruel. The lust of dominion inevitably produces hardness of heart, because the state of mind which craves unlimited power, such as slavery confers, involves a desire to use that power, and although I know there are exceptions to the exercise of barbarity on the bodies of slaves, I maintain that there *can be no exceptions* to the exercise of the most soul-withering cruelty on the *minds of the enslaved.* All around is the mighty ruin of intellect, the appalling spectacle of the down-trodden image of God. What has caused this mighty wreck? A voice deep as hell and loud as the thunders of heaven replies, SLAVERY! Both worlds and spirits echo and re-echo SLAVERY! And yet American slavery is palliated, is defended by slaveholding ministers at the South and heir coadjutors at the North. Perhaps all of you would shrink with horror from a proposal to revive the Inquisition and give to Catholic superstition the power to enforce in this country its wicked system of bigotry and despotism. But I believe that if all the horrors of the Inquisition and all the cruelty and oppression exercised by the Church of Rome, could be fully and fairly brought to view and compared with the details of slavery in the United States, the abominations of Catholicism would not surpass those of slavery, while the victims of the latter are ten fold more numerous.

But it is urged again and again, that slavery has been entailed upon us by our ancestors. We speak of this with a degree of self-complacency, which seems to intimate that we would not do the deeds of our fathers. So to speak, argues an utter want of principle, as well as an utter ignorance of duty, because as soon as we perceive the iniquity of that act by which we inherit PROPERTY IN MAN, we should surrender to the rightful owner, viz. the slave *himself*, a right which although legally bested in us, by the "unrighteous decrees" of our country, is vested in the slave himself by the laws of God. We talk as if the guilt of slavery from its first introduction to the present time, rested on our progenitors, and as if we were innocent because we had not imported slaves originally from Africa. The prophet Ezekiel furnishes a clear and comprehensive answer to this sophistry. "What man ye, that ye use this proverb saying: The fathers have eaten sour grapes, and the children's teeth are set on edge..... Behold all souls are mine, as the soul of the father, so also the soul of the son is mine. THE SOUL THAT SINNETH IT SHALL DIE. If a man be just and doeth that which is lawful and right, he shall surely live. If he beget a son that hath opprest the poor and needy, he shall surely die; his blood shall be upon him. Now, lo! If he beget a son that seeth all his father's sins which he hath done, and doeth not such like, that hath not opprest any, neither hath spoiled by violence; that hath taken off his hand from the poor, he shall not die for the iniquity of his father, neither shall the father bear the iniquity of the son. The righteousness of the righteous shall be upon him—and the wickedness of the wicked shall be upon him."

Upon the present generation, rests, I believe, an accumulated weight of guilt. They have the experience of more than two centuries to profit by—they have witnessed the evils and the signs of slavery, and they know that sin and misery are its legitimate fruits. They behold every where, inscribed upon the face of nature, the withering curse of slavery, as if the land mourned over the iniquity and wretchedness of its inhabitants. They contemplate in their domestic circles the living examples of that description given by Jefferson, in his *"Notes on Virginia,"* of the influence of slavery, on the temper and morals of the master, and they know that there is not one redeeming quality, in the system of American slavery.

And now we have the most undeniable evidence of the safety of Immediate Emancipation, in the British West Indies. Every official account, from these colonies, especially such as have rejected the apprenticeship system, comes fraught with encouragement to this country to deliver the poor and needy out of the hand of the oppressor.

To my brethren of the Methodist connection, with some of whom I have taken sweet counsel, and whose influence is probably more extensive than that of any other class of ministers at the South, it may avail something to the cause of humanity, which I am pleading, to quote the sentiments of John Wesley and Adam Clarke. Speaking of slavery the former says, "The blood of thy brother crieth against thee from the earth: oh, whatever it costs, put a stop to its cry before it is too late—instantly, at any price, were it the half of they goods, deliver thyself from blood guiltiness. Thy hands, thy bed, thy furniture, thy house and thy lands, at present are stained with blood. Surely it is enough—accumulate no more guilt, spill no more blood of the innocent. Whether thou art a Christian or not, show thyself A MAN." Adam Clarke says, "In heathen countries, slavery was in some sort excusable. Among Christians it is an enormity and crime, for which perdition has scarcely an adequate punishment."

Yet this is the crime of which the Synod of Virginia, convened for the purpose of deliberating on the state of the Church in November last, speaks thus: "The Synod solemnly affirm, that the General Assembly of the Presbyterian Church have *no right* to declare that relation (viz. the relation between master and slave) sinful, which Christ and his apostles teach to be consistent with the most unquestionable piety. And that any act of the General Assembly which would impeach the *Christian* character of any man because he is a slave holder, would be a palpable violation of the just principles on which the union of our Church was founded—as well as a daring usurpation of authority granted by the Lord Jesus."

And this is the sin which the Church is fostering in her bosom—This is the leprosy over which she is casting the mantle of charity, to hide, if possible, the "putrefying sores"—This is the monster around which she is twining her maternal arms, and before which she is placing her anointed shield inscribed "holiness to the Lord"—Oh, ye ministers of Him who so loved the slave that he gave his precious blood to redeem him from sin, can ye any longer with your eyes fixed upon the Cross of Christ, plant your foot on his injured representative, and sanction and sanctify this heart-breaking, this soul destroying system?

> "Wo to those whose hire is with the price of blood
> Perverting, darkening, changing as they go
> The sacred truths of the Eternal God."

Brethren, farewell! I have written under a solemn sense of my responsibility to God for the truths I have uttered: I know that all who nobly dare to speak the truth will come up to the help of the Lord, and add testimony to testimony until time would fail to hear them. To Him who has promised that "the expectation of the needy shall not perish forever"—who "hath chosen the weak things of the world to confound the wise, and base things of the world, and things which are despised, hath God chosen, yea and things which are not, to bring to nought things that are; that no flesh should glory in his presence," I commend this offering of Christian affection, humbly beseeching him so to influence the ministers of his sanctuary, and the people committed to their charge by his Holy Spirit, that from every Christian temple may arise the glorious anthem.

> "Blow ye the trumpet blow,
> The gladly solemn sound!
> Let all the nations know
> To earth's remotest bound,
> The year of jubilee is come."

Yours in gospel love,
SARAH M. GRIMKE

Eleanor (Anna) Roosevelt (1884-1962)

"Restlessness of Youth: An Asset of Free Societies."

Author, lecturer, and diplomat, Eleanor Roosevelt was born on October 11, 1884 in New York City. After the death of her parents she was sent to attend school in England. She married Franklin Delano Roosevelt, a distant cousin, and her uncle President Theodore Roosevelt gave her away. Mrs. Roosevelt's social, political and educational interests led her to create a new role as first lady of the land. She advocated liberal causes and many times would be at the center of controversy. Appointed by President Harry S. Truman as a delegate to the United Nations she chaired a commission to draft the Universal Declaration of Human Rights. She lectured extensively in the United States and abroad, authored many articles and books, and was recipient of numerous awards and honorary degrees. She died at her home in New York City on November 7, 1962. In this speech to the *Les Jeunes Amis de la Liberte* in Paris in 1952 she encourages her youthful audience to "unite freedom-loving people" to resist oppression.

Department of State Bulletin, January 21, 1952.

Youth is never satisfied with things as they are. Young people in all countries wish to protest against the injustices they see about them. They are not easily fooled by facades of high-sounding words thrown up to conceal bad deeds. They tend to cut through words to the heart of an issue.

When they hear the phrase "free world" they want to know what is meant. They are not satisfied with the way things are going in any part of the world. They see great tasks and hard struggles ahead of them to make a better life. The "free world cannot be used as a pious phrase to suggest that the people in one part of the world have achieved the full freedom they seek. It is rather a phrase which points the direction toward which the peoples can move and are moving.

In the "free world" the dissatisfaction with things as they are, the striving for ideals and hopes, can find peaceful expression through free institutions. The restlessness of youth is a precious asset of free societies because it always promises regeneration of new vitality from decade to decade.

But where fundamental freedoms and human rights have been suppressed by ruling oligarchies, the youth has no outlet for its struggles against the status quo. Its dynamic urges are channeled through marching clubs, military machines, and propaganda organizations in support of a ruling class which is self-perpetuating.

While such a dictatorship is in the first bloom of its own youth, it can attract the youth by revolutionary words, by pageantry, and by vigorous activities. But tyrants grow old and become increasingly corrupted by arbitrary power.

Their high-sounding words soon stand in bleak contrast to their evil deeds. Their promises are in contrast to their performances. It is my deep conviction that any society which does not provide freedom for the upcoming generations to work openly and honestly for their aspirations contains within it the seeds of its own destruction.

A tyrant can never tell who is for him or against him because he cannot enter the secret heart of any man.

Youth's Obligations

Youth which is free to work for a better life in the open with the tools of human rights has first of all the obligations to strengthen this freedom and preserve it against all attacks. Young people who are still free to read, to discuss, to question and to seek the truth can find out for themselves how freedom has been bludgeoned in Eastern Europe and the Soviet Union. They can see for themselves the growing gaps between words and deeds behind the Iron Curtain. They can take direct testimony from those who are fleeing from these slave societies. They can read for themselves the new laws in the so- called peoples' democracies which state plainly that anything which is not published as a government hand-out is to be regarded as a state secret, and whoever inquires about such things is guilty f espionage or spying. They can see that these laws make it impossible for the people to find out from the public press or radio anything which the government doesn't want them to know.

Of course, these laws are in themselves proofs of the weakness and fear of the ruling minorities who try to impose them. You and I know that they cannot work for long, because people, and especially young people, have ways of satisfying their hunger for news and truth.

Yet, it is a sad thing to have to suffer long years of darkness, and to have to struggle for a new light of freedom.

You have precious freedoms which you do not have to lose if you will use them in your struggles for a better life and defend them against both the wiles of propagandists and the threats of aggressors.

You know from bitter experience what it is like to live under a dictatorship imposed by an aggressor. You know how precious freedom is by recalling your own experience of the Nazi occupation. And you know as we have learned in the United

States, that freedom can be preserved or rewon only by the collective effort of free men.

The United Nations is the greatest agency we have through which free men may cooperate to preserve their freedom by collective actions. In the United Nations they can work together for social and economic improvements, and thus strengthen their free societies. In the United Nations they can unite their moral, political, economic, and military strength for collective defense.

The forces against freedom understand that their only hope of imposing dictatorial regimes on new areas of the world lies in the disunity of the free world. Hence, they use every propaganda trick to sow confusion and dissention (sic) in the ranks of free peoples. They exploit every feeling of fear and antagonism to divide the free nations, and break the spirit for collective resistance to aggression.

If we are determined not to lose our freedoms, we must use our heads in an active campaign to expose the propaganda designed to divide us, and to promote the unity and cooperation of free people.

At this General Assembly, we are engaged in a great effort to keep the issues clear on the questions of peace and security, in the hope that the Soviet Union will recognize the determined will and clarity of thought of the people of the free world and abandon its policy of substituting propaganda for honest negotiation on real disarmament.

Truth vs. Slogans

We should realize that the truth about complex problems is harder to understand than slogans and emotional appeals that do not meet the issue. Therefore, those who wish to defend their freedoms have a difficult task of education to perform constantly in order to prevent the sloganized propaganda from misleading people.

One of the main issues on which we must all be clear is the question of peace and disarmament. As you know, France, the United Kingdom, and the United States joined in putting before the General Assembly a proposal for the limitations, control, and balanced reduction of all arms and armed forces. This proposal has been ridiculed by Mr. Vishinsky, who has put forward old Soviet proposals which are simple and beguiling. His main purpose is to confuse the issues of peace and to slow up or stop our actions to build collective security.

The people of this world want peace itself, not mere words in new pacts of peace. They get pacts of nonaggression from Hitler as his favorite prelude to his blitzkrieg. Now they want deeds, not words.

Let us remember that the making of war itself is an international crime. This was firmly established at the Nuremberg trials. This was accepted by every government which ratified the United Nations Charter. This means that the use of any weapon from a gun to an atomic bomb to attack or to threaten another state is prohibited. Regardless of what weapons may be used, aggression is a crime and is strictly prohibited. We have all signed the paper containing this promise. But this is not enough. the people want us to translate our promise into performance.

Knowing as they do the terrible destruction that armies, planes, and tanks and guns can cause, they will not accept a mere paper prohibition of one weapon. They want all weapons and all armies put under international control so that war itself if effectively prohibited.

When a nation only wants to prohibit the one weapon that happens to offset its mass armies, its hypocritical purpose is easy to expose. The real test for a nation is its willingness to submit to international control its whole military machine so that it becomes impossible for any nation to launch an aggression.

On the problem of the control and prohibition of the use of atomic energy for weapons, there is a perfect illustration of the need for clarity of thought on the part of free people in order not to be deluded by Soviet tricks of propaganda. Let me try to put the issue in the simplest way.

Suppose I held in my hand a small block of Uranium 235. It is often called "fissionable material." I am going to call it "the stuff that explodes." This stuff is what people the world over want to have put under international control so it cannot be used in weapons.

Suppose I held in my hand a piece of paper on which I had written these words: "Cross my heart, I promise never to use the explosive stuff in a bomb if you will agree to let me keep it and use it as I please."

This, in my right hand, is the stuff that threatens destruction. This, in my left hand, is the paper pledge to prohibit the use of it in a bomb.

Now I ask you: Do you want signatures of foreign ministers on this piece of paper, or do you want the United Nations to control this stuff? Which will be effective in prohibiting its use for destructive purposes?

Would you trust any signature on the paper if the signer refused to give up his possession of the stuff to an international authority?

Only Soviets say "No."

The United nations plan calls upon all nations to put this explosive stuff in the hands of an international guard. So far only the Soviets have said "no." They have insisted on having and controlling the explosive stuff to use for purposes they say are "peaceful."

They just want a new piece of paper which says none of us shall use this explosive stuff in bombs. After we sign such a piece of paper, they say we can probably work out some sort of inspection to find out whether anybody actually has any containers of this stuff labeled "bombs." However the inspectors will not be allowed for find out how much of this stuff anyone may have in containers labeled "peacetime use."

There is only one simple fact that people have to understand to see that this affords no protection at all. The simple fact is that the stuff that explodes is exactly the same for bombs as for peacetime use.

We say, "Let's have international control of the stuff that goes bang."

They say, "Let's just sign a paper promising not to let the stuff explode."

They ask the people of the world to take their word. We ask that the United Nations take control of the stuff itself so nobody can break his word.

Ah, but we are told that this would prevent countries from doing what they please with this explosive stuff. It certainly would.

The people aren't afraid of words and labels; they are afraid of the stuff that explodes. They aren't so simple as to feel safe if this explosive stuff is nicely labeled "peacetime use only," when they know it can become bombs by just putting it in special boxes marked "A-bombs."

The United Nations plan says each country can have as much of the stuff as it can use up in peaceful projects week by week, month by month. We must have an international authority to guarantee that atomic stuff is being used as each country claims it is being used.

But if each nation has a big warehouse of the atomic stuff, and it is even a secret how much they have, the labels can be changed overnight from "peacetime use" to "bombs." What kind of prohibition is that? Who would feel safe under that kind of control?

Why do the Soviet spokesmen reject the idea of getting what they need as they need it from the United Nations authority? Oh, they claim they couldn't trust the international authority to let them have what they need.

You see, we come back to the question of trust. They want us to trust them on their own word not to change the labels on this explosive stuff and use it in bombs. But they won't trust the authority composed of all nations to allot to them what they need for peacetime use.

In other words, they simply refuse to put this stuff under international control.

The United Nations plan is the best way advocated so far to control the explosive stuff and thus prohibit its use in weapons. We are ready to consider under any other plan that will control the explosive stuff as effectively. But we demand real control of the stuff that explodes.

This is only one illustration of why clear and realistic thinking is required if free men are not to lose their freedom in a fog of confusion and sophistry.

It goes without saying that no man would knowingly give up his freedom for mere promises of food or shelter or employment. Most people realize that these things have to be produced and cannot be promised or merely voted by politicians. The basic question is: Will they be produced by free men or by slaves?

Free men have never deliberately chosen the path of dictatorship. They have never in a free election voted for parties advocating totalitarian doctrines. In a clear contest between the principles of freedom and the doctrine of dictatorship, there is no doubt where the overwhelming majority will stand.

The danger comes from confusions and dissensions which the skilled propagandists of totalitarian parties disseminate—not primarily to win supporters but to divide and weaken their adversaries.

You have the good opportunity of helping this generation to face its problems with responsibility and realism. You can help unite freedom-loving people to prevent aggression and promote peace.

Geraldine A Ferraro (1935-   )

"Commencement Address at Virginia State University, May 21, 1989"

Author, lawyer, and past vice presidential candidate Geraldine Ferraro was born in Newburgh, New York on August 26, 1935. She attended Marymount College and took a Bachelor of Arts degree in 1956. She then taught in the New York public schools from 1956-1961. After receiving a degree from the Fordham University School of Law she went into private practice from 1961-1974. From 1974 to 1978 Geraldine Ferraro served as Assistant District Attorney in Queens Borough, New York. In 1975 she was a member of the U.S. Court of Appeals, 2d circuit. Moreover, as a Representative from New York she worked in the House from 1979 to 1985. During that time she held the position of Secretary to the Democratic Caucus (1980-1984). In 1984 she received the Democratic Candidacy for vice president. In 1985 Bantam Books published her volume *My Story*.

The text was provided by Allyn Singer of Geraldine Ferraro's office.

Thank you, Dr. McCLure, for that very kind introduction, and for that warm welcome. Let me start by offering my congratulations to each of today's graduates. It's always nice to stand up in front of a group of people who look so happy and so relieved. I can't tell who looks more relieved. Today's graduates or their parents. Or maybe those are professors.

But what makes me particularly happy as I look out from the podium is knowing that I'm not just looking at a graduating class, I'm looking at part of a return of my generation's investment in the future. For you, like thousands of other graduates throughout the country, are the most valuable resources our nation has. It is you who will inherit its past but it is also you who will determine its future in the decades ahead. Each of you is better equipped to face and solve the challenges that this country must meet in the years to come. I know that any school that can think up woo-woo's can teach our nation about teamwork.

A college education remains a privilege in this country, a privilege that many of us have sacrificed to achieve. That privilege is not yours alone. It also belongs to your parents. It belongs to me and millions more like me. For the education and training you have received here makes our investment in America sounder and more secure. Your education will help you realize not just your own dreams, but a nation's dreams as well.

Today I want to talk about a topic that, in one form or another, we see more and more often in the headlines. It is a subject to think about as you leave VSU today. The broadest term for it is ethics—but what it means in my book is defining an acceptable, shared moral vision for who we are as a people.

My goal, however, is not to define ethics — I make it a policy never to attempt in a half hour what has kept thinkers like Plato and Kant busy for centuries. Instead, I want to focus on how ethical issues face us as a society and what we are doing about them.

More than twenty years ago, Martin Luther King wrote: "Moral principles have lost their distinctiveness. For modern man"—and I'm sure he would agree that includes modern woman, too—"Absolute right and absolute wrong are a matter or what the majority is doing. Right or wrong are relative to the likes and dislikes and customs of a particular community."

If Dr. King were alive today, I think that he would see that our nation is in the midst of a great ethical revolution. Look around. Public discussions of ethics have become a major national growth industry. *Newsweek* has put ethics on its cover. Consider the headlines of the last months. The speaker of the house and the number two ranking republican in that body are both being investigated for questionable business deals, the Prime Minister of Japan resigned over a corporate scandal, and Michael Milken is being tried for insider trading that has given him an annual salary of half a billion dollars. The players and issues may vary, but the theme is the same: what we, as a society, define as acceptable ethical behavior.

America has embarked on our ethical *Glastnost*. We are examining everything from our hospitals to our schools. From our corporate boardrooms to our factory floors and our government offices. It affects the career and life choices every one of you graduating today will be making. It doesn't matter whether you majored in business administration or biology, agriculture or education. You can expect ethical decisions to affect not only how you work but how you live your lives as well.

We have begun a great, freewheeling national conversation to decide what is, and is not, acceptable. We, as a society, are taking ethical decisions out of the closet, onto the front page. Topics once considered private are now public, subject to open discussion and decision. Television shows explore the ethics of allowing euthanasia of the terminally ill. Commentators ask if it is ethical to allow polluters to just walk away from environmental damage. A half million people march on Washington to protest the ethics of forcing pregnant women to bear children. We debate surrogate parenthood and giving needles to intravenous drug users to stop the spread of aids, we ponder limiting the sale of deadly assault weapons in the name of human life and safety.

With these and a hundred other issues, one thing is clear. As the number of decisions have multiplied, so has the number of people making them. Once upon a time, the rules of what was acceptable tended to be made by a narrow class of relatively similar, relatively homogenous people. And most of us in this room weren't in that class.

But that is no longer the case. Today, different *types* of people are getting in on the act. Codes of appropriate behavior and values are being set by much larger, more diverse, constituencies. Women. Seniors. Blacks. Medical patients. Consumers. The disabled. Not so long ago, we were neither expected or allowed to debate such issues. Now, for a change, the human beings who are most affected by the outcome of our nation's ethical decisions are standing up and demanding a voice in making them.

In this very state, 170 years ago, Thomas Jefferson wrote: "I know of no safe depository of the ultimate powers of society but the people themselves. And if we think they are not enlightened enough to exercise their control with a wholesome discretion, the remedy is not to take it from them, but to inform their discretion."

Of course, Thomas Jefferson neglected to mention that this process can get messy at times, as cultures and different values clash. Things were much neater in Virginia in 1816, when the nation's decisions were agreed upon over drinks in a restricted club. Of course, to get into that club, you had to be powerful, wealthy, white, and male— and like Thomas Jefferson, a landowner. But today, America has begun to change that. We have said that real life is not a republican convention. We have stood up for that radical idea— first voiced by the founding fathers of this country— that our nation is healthier for this pluralism. In my view, bringing the discussion of ethics into public view does not require apologies, but applause. Such debate is not a sign of decadence, but of democracy.

There is no more important area for these ethical discussions than politics. That is because breaches of ethics betray the very foundations of a free republic. An administration has just left Washington setting a record of 560 appointees at various level indicted for ethical violations, 470 of whom were convicted. Today, the speaker of our House of Representatives, Jim Wright, and Newt Gingrich, the Republican whip, are under investigation for blurring the line between public service and private gain. This month we learned that former President Reagan will earn $2 million dollars [sic] from a major Japanese corporation for a one week visit to Japan, the negotiations for which may have begun while he was still in office.

More than ever before, we are right to ask for higher standards from the people who make and enforce our laws. More than ever before, we must stand up to that kind of behavior, and say: "Sorry, Not Acceptable." We must borrow a phrase from Dr. McClure, and restate what VSU has said in another context: "The party's over."

Such ethical lapses trickle down into the private sector as well. What do we say to the pharmaceutical companies who ship third world countries medicines that have been shown to be toxic by our more stringent standards? Who says "Not acceptable?" What do we tell the tobacco companies who send their cigarettes to Japan removing the warning on their packages advising pregnant women that smoking can be dangerous to the fetus? Sorry, the party's over.

What do we say to the news network who toned down its criticism of the white house because the President was personally popular and the criticism might affect their ratings and therefore their profits? Not acceptable.

What do we say to liquor and tobacco companies who concentrate advertising in poor neighborhoods. When studies show people in those areas have a higher rate of disease and death from smoking and drinking? Not acceptable.

What do we say to an Exon, whose corporate disregard has killed countless fish and animals, destroyed the livelihood of whole towns, and ruined some of America's most pristine wilderness, for decades to come? Who says not acceptable?

Just as ethical challenges are surfacing in politics and in business, they touch all of us in our private lives as well. As a nation, we are talking openly, and making a collective judgment about all kinds of choices that were previously private. Many are choices that our parents could not have thought of a generation ago.

We can create a test tube baby, but we have not resolved the issues it raises. We cannot say what happens when a couple dies before their fertilized ovum is implanted, as happened a few years ago. Nor do we know what to do when, as was recently reported in The New York Times, a couple divorces in the middle of test tube fertilization. Is their mutual fertile product property or is it progeny? Do we respect its rights, or her right, or his rights—or just throw it away if it is not needed? A decade ago, this was pure science fiction. Today, it joins a long list of medical-ethical dilemmas that suggests no easy answer.

That list is growing. Because we now have reliable blood tests for exposure to the Aids virus, that does not mean it is ethical to compel people to take them. Just because medical science had advanced enough to offer prenatal tests for a wide variety of genetic disorders, it does not mean that our ethical understanding has also advanced enough to cope with the answers those tests provide.

Just because health care experts project that we lack the money to care for all Americans who will get sick in the next decade, that does not mean we are justified in rationing care to the old, the very ill, or those too poor to pay. Just because most hospitals now have the technology to keep a body alive, its heart beating indefinitely, that does not make it a fitting way to care for a human being. In every area, the fact that we can does not mean that we should.

Every day presents ethical challenges we have never before imagined, and we are scrambling to find new answers. The kinds of discussions that VSU encourages on campus— something like your commonwealth lecture series or the recent symposium you held on the black church— are a part of this national discussion. Each of us— in our private, professional, and political lives— must make peace with the question: Is what is possible also desirable? We know that our era has given us the wherewithal, but where do we find wisdom to use it? Our ethical challenges aren't just scientific.

It is a fair bet that many of you will eventually find yourself in a place where someone is asking you to do something you are not comfortable with. In New York City, there was a recent case of a young woman in her twenties, who worked for a Wall Street wheeler-dealer. Well, it appears her boss was being investigated by the government, and in the course of that investigation, this young woman testified on his behalf. But, trying to protect him, she lied under oath.

Before she knew it, she was convicted for perjury. Now she says she was just taking his orders, that she didn't know it was wrong...But the fact is, she has a criminal record, her career is ruined, she has made herself an ethical victim— who did what was wrong because someone told her to. That defense did not work after World War two at Nuremburg, it did not work for President Nixon's men in Watergate, and this month, we saw that it didn't work for Oliver North.

Your work life will almost certainly bring you such ethical questions, times you will be asked to do things you think are wrong, times when you have to make your own personal judgment about what is right and what isn't. In those cases, speaking as a former prosecutor, I can promise you that nobody will care if you didn't know it was wrong. I can also promise you that you will do yourself a favor to have thought about these issues before you face them.

I expect that this has been a good place for you to do some of that thinking. That is what your education is all about. Yes, you may learn the details and specifics of business administration, agriculture, or aquaculture. But the harder part will be to put that knowledge to work ethically. You alone can make sure that the businesses you work in will be honest ones that provide jobs and help lives, that the food you create will help feed the world's hungry. Whether you are graduating in agriculture or science, business, education, humanities or social science, you must create your own personal moral, and ethical framework to make decisions. It may be shaped in philosophy, economics, or history class, in a public forum series as VSU, or in late night talks down at Mitchell's but is ultimately up to you to think through some of these issues, to clarify and refine, not just your intellectual tools, but the ethical and moral tools you will call on throughout your life.

You will face a lot of murky, difficult questions, and believe me, there are no quick fixes. But I would at least like to suggest a few possible directions that might help us sort things out.

Let us start with the most obvious: that we are right to be grappling with such issues, and right to try to forge new solutions. In any period of ethical reassessment like today, some people will tell you that the solution is to turn back the clock. All we need, they say, is to return to the good old days, the way things used to be. To those people, I say: "You are living in a dream world.'

Let's face it: the reason we are having this great national conversation right now is that the status quo is frayed at the seams. The 1989 graduating class of VSU faces problems that many of us in your parents generation never even heard of. Never forget that new problems demand new answers.

Looking to yesterday for solutions to today's ethical challenges is giving up on what America has always done best. It is the attitude of those who lack either the courage to envision better rules, or who are too lazy to try.

It is no accident that the loudest voices for "Traditional Ethical Values" are those same rich, powerful, white, and male interests who have always been in control.

To them, let's offer a simple answer: What was "Just fine" for them is no longer food enough for us. Our nation expects, and deserves, better. America has not grown great by pining for yesterday, but by looking to tomorrow.

That is why I think this great national conversation about ethics strengthens and empowers America. That is why what you are doing at VSU is so important. I have confidence that Americans can come up with better answers. We always have and I, for one, think we always will.

But a caveat. . .When I say better answers, I do not necessarily mean more rules and regulations. We will not solve our problems by passing more laws. Ethics does not boil down to a matter of black and white, legal and illegal. The hard questions come in the gray area. Too often, our current debate centers on spelling out the limits on conduct— what are the exact rules and how far can you push them, what you can do and still get away with it. When you think that way, dotting all the I's and crossing all the T's, it is easy to fall into the same way of thought that creates abuses in the first place. This preoccupation with what's allowed, that is, the bare minimum you can do in a job and still squeak by, misses the point, what we need are not just a set of limits on behavior, but a different attitude.

Let us strive instead for what I call positive ethics. That means living up to certain standards not because we have to, but because we want to. Positive ethics means concentrating a little less on what we must prevent— and a little more on what we want to accomplish. By openly discussing a full range of opinions among people of good will, then in the long run we will all get a whole lot further. Positive ethics is not about scratching our heads and just saying no— it is about opening our hearts and just saying yes. Saying yes to the kind of companies, and country, and lives, we want to create together.

We must not waiver from our demands for the highest ethical standard for those in office. In a democracy, ethics concerns the separation of truth and lies. When those in high places lie to us— whether, like Ollie North, in the belief that they are above the law, or like corrupt officials who lie to personal gain— we must hit back, and hit back hard. This democracy is a fragile thing, and rests on the principle of the consent of the governed. But we cannot consent to what is hidden from us. Lying or concealing facts from the public, is the most unpatriotic of acts. Unless we treat it as such, we will weaken our nation and our future.

As to the more personal ethical challenges, let me take a stab at answering the hardest question of all: How can we know when we ourselves act in an unethical way? I think, when all the lectures and learned words are done, the real test of ethical behavior comes not in your head, but in your heart. It may seem naive, but I think that you can feel when you do something that is morally wrong. It is something that you don't want others to know about you. It is something you wouldn't tell your mom.

As we debate these questions in private and in public, remember that this ethical soul-searching can only strengthen and empower America. Each day that we do not put our nation's ethical house in order is a day we weaken ourselves— economically, politically, and morally.

You have spent your years here learning theories, tools and practices to be personally and professionally successful. But you also need a coherent ethical framework to let that success blossom. That is what will let you take the education that you have gotten here at VSU and put it to work for the good of yourself, your generation, and our society.

And that is my message to you today. You are free to rise as far as your dreams will take you. Your task is to build the future of this country and of our world. Whatever you do, I remind each of you that your potential and possibilities at this juncture of your lives are limitless.

Virginia State university has given you the skills to make this world a better place. It has offered you the vision to make it more humane and compassionate. For my part, I wish you the courage to stand up for what you believe is right. If that is the challenge you set for yourselves, you cannot help but triumph. Again, my congratulations to you and your parents.

Thank you.

Julie R. Kidd (1974-   )

"To Love and Serve Humanity."

A high school student and a prolific public speaker from Frewsburg, New York Julie Kidd has competed in several oratorical contests. Up to this time she has "spoken fourteen times about a variety of different topics." Her subjects have included: the U.S. Constitution, volunteerism, the homeless, the Statue of Liberty, and outer space. Her interests are in teaching and in the area of communication. The following speech appeared in *Together* magazine, Spring, 1991 issue. She presented this award winning address to an enthralled audience at the 6th Annual Arts and Science Award luncheon in Albany, New York.

Reprinted with the kind permissions of the author and the Editor of *Together* magazine.

Where will you go tonight? Will you return home for a warm dinner and a good night's sleep in your own comfortable bed? Yes, perhaps you will, for you have a place to call home. But where will the homeless families of our nation go tonight? Many will try to sleep in abandoned buildings, or airports, or bus terminals, for, unlike you and I, they have no place to call home. Many of us picture the homeless as the Oakies in Steinbeck's *Grapes of Wrath,* or a bag lady lying on the floor of Grand Central Station, or an unshaven bum panhandling on the street for his next bottle of cheap wine.

The National Coalition for the Homeless reports that today of the estimated 3,000,000 homeless, 28% are families with children. Yes, families. Families are the fastest growing segment of the homeless population. Congress recently issued a report stating that within the next fifteen years more than 20 million Americans will be homeless. "Most of these will be families with young children."

I would like to tell you of a homeless family I know of. Close your eyes and picture, if you will, a family of six, huddled close together for warmth in the cold of early evening in a deserted city park. Only the youngest has a coat. You can see the mother and father are pale and tired, but most of all notice the look of defeat on their faces. What pride could they possibly possess? Their children wear no designer jeans or named brand sneakers, but instead wear tattered second-hand clothing and unmatched shoes. The oldest boy leaves his family to search for an abandoned car for the family to sleep in, while the mother scrounges through a nearby trash barrel in search of scraps for the evening meal. Who are these people? And where are they from? They are homeless and they are from my hometown, or maybe yours.

Dr. Martin Luther King, Jr. believed that all people, black or white, male or female, were entitled to a home, a job, an education, pride, dignity and being a part of the beloved community, but unfortunately in 1990, we have this astounding number of homeless families in our bountiful nation who are denied these rights.

In his quest for the creation of the beloved community, Dr. King created a dynamic heritage which can be applied to the national crisis of the homeless families of today. King said, "Yes, if you want to, say I was a drum major. Say I was a drum major for justice. Say I was a drum major for righteousness." I believe that if King were alive today he would indeed be a drum major for the homeless families.

What can we do. . .to be drum majors of the homeless? We can devote our time and efforts and we can give monetary contributions to shelters and soup kitchens, but these serve only as band-aid or temporary solutions. The best approach in dealing with the crisis is to offer assistance that will have a long term, beneficial impact on the families. The solution is to provide affordable permanent housing, for this will provide not only shelter, but it will restore a sense of pride and dignity. Two major nationwide programs of which we can become part are The Better Homes Foundation and Habitat for Humanity.

The Better Homes Foundation is a national non-profit organization created in 1988 by the editors of *Better Homes & Gardens* magazine. Its goal is to provide the counseling, medical aid, training and housing search assistance needed to help these homeless families become self-sufficient members of the community. Already the foundation has made direct grants to 50 programs in 23 states. Funding comes from individual readers, businesses and other groups.

A second approach to the problem is Habitat For Humanity. Founded by Millard Fuller. It is an organization of volunteers building homes for the needy. Currently, Habitat is in 277 cities across the United States and plans to build 2,000 houses this year, 6 per day. As Fuller says, "We can be a conscience about the plight of the poor. We can show that something can be done about people not having a decent place to live."

The success and accomplishments of the Better Home Foundation and Habitat For Humanity illustrate Dr. King's principle of love and prove that giving of ourselves in an unselfish way, we can provide permanent homes for these homeless families.

History shows the progress of the human race has depended on the dreamer. Like Dr. King, I, too, have a dream. I have a dream that by the year 2000 there will not be one homeless family in the United States. It is a dream firmly rooted in reality and practicality and it is a dream that can be achieved by Dr. King's ideals of love, brotherhood and the creation of a community.

I'd like to leave you now with one thought. The true genius of Dr. Martin Luther King, Jr. was his ability to perceive there is something noble in humanity, that once tapped is powerful enough to transform the world. I truly believe that if we follow Dr. King's examples of love and service to humanity, that once tapped is powerful enough to transform their world. I truly believe that if we follow Dr. King's examples of love and service to humanity, and if we give of ourselves, we cam make it work today. Then every homeless family in America will have a place to call home.

This bibliography is divided into five sections. The first section is a selected list of the standard volumes in American Public Address. These books are then subdivided into two areas: 1) anthologies of American Public Address, and 2) books and articles about speech criticism. The second section includes books and articles pertaining to African Americans. Much has been written about the African American but little attention has been given to compiling anthologies of their speeches. There are a few collections of black orations on the market but there are many extant speeches that need to be published. The third section includes books and articles pertaining to Mexican Americans. There are a limited number of scholars studying in the area of Chicano rhetoric and presumably they will publish more collections. The fourth section includes books and articles pertaining to Native Americans. Again, there are a few anthologies of native American oratory available but more of the available orations need to be compiled. And, the fifth section includes books and articles pertaining to White American females. Anthologies of white American females have been appearing on the market and it is assumed more will be forthcoming

ANTHOLOGIES OF AMERICAN PUBLIC ADDRESS

Auer, J. Jeffrey, ed. *Antislavery and Disunion, 1858 -1861: Studies in the Rhetoric of Compromise and Conflict.* New York and Evanston: Harper & Row, 1963.

Baird, A.C. and L. Thonnsen. *American Public Addresses, 1740-1952.* New York: McGraw-Hill, 1956.

Brandt, Carl G. and Edward M. Shafter. *Selected American Speeches on Basic Issues: 1850-1950.* Boston: Houghton Mifflin, 1960.

Brigance, William N. *A History of American Public Address.* 2 vols. New York: McGraw Hill, 1943.

Graham, John, ed. *Great American Speakers of the Twentieth Century,* New York: Appleton-Century-Crofts, 1970.

Hochmuth, (Nichols) Marie. *A History and Criticism of American Public Address.* New York: McGraw Hill, 1955.

Holland, DeWitte, ed. *America in Controversy: A History of American Public Address.* Dubuque, Iowa: William C. Brown, 1973.

Oliver. Robert T. and Eugene E. White. *Selected Speeches from American History.* Boston: Allyn & Bacon, 1966.

316   SELECTED BIBLIOGRAPHY

Platz, Mabel, ed. *Anthology of Public Speeches*. New York: H.W. Wilson, 1940.

Reid, Ronald F. ed. *Three Centuries of American Rhetorical Discourse: An Anthology and a Review*. Prospect Heights, Illinois: Waveland Press, 1988.

Ryan, Halford Ross, ed. *American Rhetoric from Roosevelt to Reagan*. Prospect Heights, Illinois: Waveland Press, 1987.

_____, ed. *Oratorical Encounters: Selected Studies and Sources of Twentieth Century Political Accusations and Apologies*. Westport, Connecticut: Greenwood Press, 1988.

Ryan, Halford Ross and Bernard K. Duffy. *American Orators Before 1900: Critical Studies and Sources*. Westport, Connecticut: Greenwood Press, 1987.

Wrage, J. and B. Baskerville, eds. *American Forum: Speeches on Historic Issues, 1788-1900*. New York: Harper & Row, 1960.

BOOKS AND ARTICLES ON SPEECH CRITICISM

Andrews, James R. *A Choice of Worlds: The Practice and Criticism of Public Discourse*. New York: Harper & Row, 1973.

_____."Reflections of the National Character in American Rhetoric." *The Quarterly Journal of Speech* 57 (1971): 316-324.

Baird, A.C. and L. Thonnsen. *Speech Criticism.*. New York: The Ronald Press, 1948.

Baskerville, Barnet. "Principal Themes Of Nineteenth Century Criticism of Oratory." *Speech Monographs* 19 (1952): 11-26. .

_____."The Critical Method in Speech." *Central States Speech Journal* 4 (1953): 1-5

Bitzer, Lloyd. "The Rhetorical Situation." *Philosophy and Rhetoric*. 1 (1968): 1-14.

Black, Edwin. *Rhetorical Criticism: A Study in Method*. New York: Macmillan, 1965.

Hauser, Gerard A. *Introduction to Rhetorical Theory*. New York: Harper & Row, 1986.

Hunt, Everett Lee. "Thoughts on a History and Criticism of American Public Address." *The Quarterly Journal of Speech* 42 (1956): 187-190.

Scott, Robert L. and Bernard L. Brock. *Methods of Rhetorical Criticism*. Detroit: Wayne State University Press, 1980.

Smith, Ralph R. "The Historical Criticism of Social Movements." *Central States Speech Journal*. 31 (1980): 290 -297.

Starosta, William J. "Roots for an Older Rhetoric: On Rhetorical Effectiveness in the Third World." *Western Speech* 43 (1979): 278-287.

Wrage, Ernest J. "Public Address: A Study in Social and Intellectual History." *The Quarterly Journal of Speech*. 33. (1947): 451-457.

BOOKS AND ARTICLES CONCERNED WITH AFRICAN AMERICAN MALE AND FEMALE RHETORIC

Allen, James E. "Samuel Ringgold Ward." *Negro History Bulletin*. 8 (1941): 41.

Asante, Molefi K. "A Metatheory for Black Communications." *The Journal of Black Psychology* 1 1975): 30-41.

Benson, Thomas W. "Rhetoric and Autobiography: "The Case of Malcolm X." *The Quarterly Journal of Speech*. 60 (1974): 1-13.

Blassingame, John W. ed. *The Frederick Douglass Papers*. Ser. I, vols. 1, 2, and 3. New Haven: Yale University Press, 1979, 1982, 1985.

Bradford, Sara H. *Scenes in the Life of Harriet Tubman*. Auburn, N.Y.: 1869.

Burke, Ronald K. "Eight Alabama Clergy vs. Martin Luther King, Jr." in *Oratorical Encounters: Selected Studies and Sources of Twentieth-Century Political Accusations and Apologies*. Halford Ross Ryan, ed. Westport, Connecticut: Greenwood Press, 1988.

_____."The IMPARTIAL CITIZEN of Samuel Ringgold Ward." *The Journalism Quarterly*. 49 (1972): 759-760.

_____."Samuel Ringgold Ward: Christian Abolitionist." Ph.D. diss. (Syracuse University, 1975).

Campbell, Karlyn Kohrs. "The Rhetoric of Radical Black Nationalism: A Case Study in Self-Conscious Criticism." *Central States Speech Journal.* 22 (1971): 151-160.

Cooke, J.W. "Freedom in the Thought of Frederick Douglass: 1845-1860." *Negro History Bulletin.* 32 (1967): 6-10.

Duster, Alfred M. ed. *Crusade for Justice: The Autobiography of Ida B. Wells.* Chicago: University of Chicago Press, 1970.

Edwards, Michael L. "A Resource Unit on Black Rhetoric." *Speech Teacher.* 22 (1973): 183-188.

Douglass, Frederick. *Life and Times of Frederick Douglass: Written by Himself.* 1892. Reprint. London: Collier-Macmillan, 1962.

_____. *My Bondage and My Freedom.* New York: Miller, Orton, and Mulligan, 1855.

Erickson, Keith V. "Black Messiah: The Father Divine Peace Mission Movement." *The Quarterly Journal of Speech.* 63 (1977): 428-438.

Foner, Philip S. ed. *The Life and Writings of Frederick Douglass.* 4 vols. New York: International Publishers, 1950, 1952, 1955.

Fulkerson, Gerald. "Exile As Emergence: Frederick Douglass in Great Britain, 1845-1847." *The Quarterly Journal of Speech.* 60 (1974): 69-82.

Fulkerson, Richard P. "The Public Letter As A Rhetorical Form: Structure, Logic, And Style in King's 'Letter From Birmingham Jail.'" *The Quarterly Journal of Speech.* 65 (1979): 121-136.

Golden, James L. and Richard D. Rieke. *The Rhetoric of Black Americans.* Columbus, Ohio: Charles E. Merrill Publishing Co., 1971.

Gregory, James M. *Frederick Douglass: The Orator.* Springfield, Massachusetts, 1893.

Hale, Frank W. "A Critical Analysis of the Speaking of Frederick Douglass." M.A. Thesis. University of Nebraska, 1951.

Hawkins, Hugh, ed. *Booker T. Washington and His Critics: Black Leadership in Crisis.* Lexington, Massachusetts: D.C. Heath & Co., 1974.

Heath, Robert L. "A Time for Silence: Booker T. Washington in Atlanta." *The Quarterly Journal of Speech*. 64 (1978): 388-399.

Hertha, Pauli. *Her Name Was Sojourner Truth*. New York: Avon Books, 1962.

Hill, Roy L. *The Rhetoric of Racial Revolt*. Denver, Colo.: Golden Bell Press, 1964.

Holland, Frederick May. *Frederick Douglass: The Colored Orator*. New York: Funk & Wagnalls, 1895.

Hooks, Bell. *Ain't I A Woman: Black Women and Feminism*. Boston: South End Press, 1981.

Johnson, James Weldon. *Along This Way: The Autobiography of James Weldon Johnson*. Reprint. New York: De Capo Press, 1973.

_____ "Our Democracy and the Ballot" in Carter G. Woodson, *Negro Orators and Their Orations*. Reprint. New York: Russell & Russell, 1969. pp. 663-671.

Kennicott, Patrick C. "Black Persuaders in the Antislavery Movement." *Speech Monographs*. 27 (1970): 15.

King, Andrew A. "Booker T. Washington and the Myth of Heroic Materialism." *The Quarterly Journal of Speech*. 60 (1974): 323-327.

King, Martin Luther, Jr. "I Have A Dream," in *American Rhetoric from Roosevelt to Reagan* by Halford Ross Ryan. Prospect Heights, Ill.: Waveland Press, Inc., 1987.

Ladner, Cornelius A. "A Critical Analysis of Four Antislavery Speeches of Frederick Douglass." M.A. thesis, State University of Iowa, 1947.

Lerner, Gerda. *Black Women in White America: A Documentary History*. New York: Random House, 1972.

Loewenberg, Bert James and Ruth Bogin. *Black Women in Nineteenth Century Life: Their Words, Their Thoughts, Their Feelings*. University Park: Penn. State University Press, 1976.

Loggins, Vernon. *The Negro Author: His Development in America*. New York: Columbia University Press, 1931.

Lomas, Charles W. *The Agitator in American Society*. Englewood Cliffs, N.J.: Prentice-Hall, 1968.

McFarlin, A.S. "Hallie Quinn Brown: Black Woman Elocutionist." *Southern Speech Communication Journal*. 44 (1981): 72-82.

Miller, Gerrit Smith (Papers). Syracuse University, Bird Library (Arents Room) Syracuse, New York. For speeches and writings of African American and White abolitionists.

Penn, I. Garland. *The Afro-American Press and Its Editors*. Reprint. New York: Arno Press and the New York Times, 1969.

Price, Melva L. "The Negro in New York." *Negro History Bulletin*. November, 1941. Entire issue devoted to New York's social activists.

Quarles, Benjamin. *Black Abolitionists*. Oxford University Press, 1969.

_____. *Frederick Douglass*. New York: Atheneum Press, 1968.

Richardson, Marilyn. *Maria W. Stewart, America's First Black Political Writer*. Bloomington and Indianapolis: Indiana University Press, 1987.

Ripley, Peter, ed. *The Black Abolitionist Papers*. 2 vols. Chapel Hill: University of North Carolina Press, 1985.

Scott, Robert L. and Donald K. Smith. "The Rhetoric of Confrontation." *The Quarterly Journal of Speech*. 55 (1969): 1-8.

Smith, Arthur L. *Rhetoric of Black Revolution*. Boston: Allyn & Bacon, Inc., 1969.

Sorin, Gerald. *The New York Abolitionists: A Case Study of Political Radicalism*. Westport, Connecticut: Greenwood Publishing Corp., 1971.

Sterling, Dorothy. *We Are Your Sisters: Black Women in the Nineteenth Century*. New York: W.W. Norton, 1984.

Terborg-Penn, Rosalyn. "Afro-Americans in the Struggle for Woman Suffrage." Unpublished diss. Howard University, 1977.

Turner, Leslie. *The Voice of Black Females in White America*. New York: New American Library, 1970.

Wagner, Gerard A. "Sojourner Truth: God's Appointed Apostle of Reform." *Southern Speech Communication Journal*. 28 (1962): 123-130.

Ward, Samuel Ringgold. *Autobiography of a Fugitive Negro*. Chicago: Johnson Publishing Co., Inc. Reprint. 1970.

Williams, Jayme Coleman and McDonald Williams, eds. *The Negro Speaks: The Rhetoric of Contemporary Black Leaders*. New York: Noble and Noble Publishers, Inc., 1970.

Woodson, Carter G. *Negro Orators and Their Orations*. New York: Russell & Russell, 1969.

BOOKS AND ARTICLES CONCERNED WITH MEXICAN AMERICAN MALE AND FEMALE RHETORIC

Acuna, Rodolfo. "An Interview With Bert Corona." *Western Journal of Speech Communication*. 44 (1980): 214 -218.

_____. *Occupied America: The Chicano Struggle for Liberation*. San Francisco: Canfield Press, 1980.

Baez, Joan. *And A Voice to Sing With: A Memoir*. New York: Summit Books, 1986.
_____. *Daybreak*. Garden City, New York: The Dial Press, 1968.

Castro, Tony. *Chicano Power: The Emergence of Mexican America*. New York: Saturday Review Press, 1974.

Cisneros, Henry G. "A Survival Strategy for America's Cities," in *Contemporary American Speeches* by Johannesen, Allen, and Linkugel. Dubuque, Iowa: Kendall/Hunt Publ. Co., 1987.

El Malcriado. United Farm Workers (UFW) newspaper, Keene, California.

Galarza, Ernesto. *Spiders in the House and Workers in the Field*. Notre Dame, Indiana: University of Notre Dame Press, 1970.

Gonzalez, Alberto. "'Participation' at WMEX-FM: Interventional Rhetoric of Ohio Mexican Americans. *Western Journal of Speech Communication*. 53 (1989): 398-410.

Gonzales, Rodolfo "Corky". "Why A Chicano Party?" *La Raza*. New York: Pathfinder Press, 1970.

_____. *I Am Joaquin*. New York: Bantam Books, 1972.

Gutierrez, Jose Angel. *A Gringo Manual*. Crystal City, Texas: Wintergarden Publishing House, n.d.

_____. "A Youth Manifesto," in *Manifesto Addressed to the President of the United States from Youth of America* ed. by Alan Rinzler. London: Collier Books, 1970

Hammerback, John C. and Richard J. Jensen and Jose Angel Gutierrez. *A War of Words: Chicano Protest in the 1960's and 1970's*. Westport, Connecticut: Greenwood Press, 1985.

Hammerback, John C. and Richard J. Jensen. "The Rhetorical World of Cesar Chavez and Reies Tijerina." *Western Journal of Speech Communication*. 44 (1980).

Jensen, Richard J. "An Interview with Jose Angel Gutierrez." *Western Journal of Speech Communication*. 44 (1980): 204.

Jensen, Richard J. and John C. Hammerback. "An Establishment View of the Chicano Movement: Henry B. Gonzalez." *Texas Speech Communication Journal*. 7 (1982): 27-36.

Larralde, Carlos. *Mexican American Movements and Leaders*. Los Alamitos, California: Hwong Publishing, 1976.

Levy, Jacques. *Cesar Chavez: Autobiography of La Causa*. New York: W.W. Norton & Co., 1975.

Marin, Christine. *A Spokesman of the Mexican American Movement: Rodolfo "Corky" Gonzales and the Fight for Chicano Liberation, 1966-1972*. San Francisco: R and E Research Associates, 1977.

Martinez, Elizabeth Sutherland and Enriqueta Longeaux Y Vasquez. *Viva La Raza!* Garden City, New York: Doubleday and Co., 1974.

Meier, Matt S. and Feliciano Rivera. *The Chicanos*. New York: Hill and Wang, 1972.

Moore, Joan W. *Mexican-Americans*. Englewood Cliffs, New Jersey: Prentice-Hall, 1970.

Nabokov, Peter. *Tijerina and the Courthouse Raid*. Albuquerque: University of New Mexico Press, 1969.

Powers, Lloyd G. "Chicano Rhetoric: Some Basic Concepts." *Southern Speech Communication Journal*. 38 (1973): 340-346.

Rodriguez, Eugene, Jr. *Henry B. Gonzalez: A Political Profile*. New York: Arno Press, 1976.

Sedano, Michael Victor. "Chicanismo: A Rhetorical Analysis of Themes and Images of Selected Poetry from the Chicano Movement." *Western Journal of Speech Communication*. 44 (1980): 177-190.

Steiner, Stan. *La Raza*. New York: Harper & Row, 1970.

Tice, Robert. "Rhetoric of La Raza." Unpublished manuscript. Chicano Student Collection. Arizona State University. Tempe. 1971.

Yinger, Winthrop. *Cesar Chavez: The Rhetoric of Nonviolence*. New York: Exposition Press, 1975.

BOOKS AND ARTICLES CONCERNED WITH NATIVE AMERICAN MALE AND FEMALE RHETORIC

Armstrong, V. I. *I Have Spoken*. Chicago: Swallow Press, 1971.

Astrov, Margot, ed. *American Indian Prose and Poetry: An Anthology*. New York: Capricorn Press, 1962.

Balgooyen, Theodore. "A Study of Conflicting Values: American Plains Indian Orators vs. the United States Commissioners of Indian Affairs." *Western Speech* 26 (1962): 76-83.

Bellecourt, Clyde. *Akwesasne Notes*. 10 (1978): 8.

Berger, Thomas. "Native Rights Movements." *Indian Law Support Center Reporter*. 11, #1. Boulder, Colorado. (1987).

324   SELECTED BIBLIOGRAPHY

Boas, Franz. *Race, Language, & Culture.* New York: The Macmillan Co., 1940.

Bosmajian, Haig A. "Defining the 'American Indian': A Case Study in the Language of Suppression." *Speech Teacher.* 22 (1973): 89-99.

Boudinot, Elias Cornelius. *"The Indian Orator and Lecturer." The American Indian Quarterly.* XIII #3. (1989).

Brown, Dee. *Bury My Heart At Wounded Knee.* New York: Bantam Books, 1970.

Buswell, Lois E. "The Oratory of the Dakota Indians." *The Quarterly Journal of Speech.* 21. (1935): 323-327.

Cohen, Felix S. *Felix S. Cohen Handbook of Federal Indian Law.* Charlottesville, Virginia: The Michie Co., 1982.

Calden, Cadwallader. *The History of the Five Indian Nations.* Ithaca, New York: Cornell University Press, 1964, 1969.

Deloria, Vine and E. Lytle. *American Indians, American Justice.* Austin, Texas: University of Texas Press, 1983.

Deloria, Vine. *Behind the Trail of Broken Tears: An Indian Declaration of Independence.* New York: Dell Publ. Inc., 1974.

_____. *Custer Died for Your Sins: An Indian Manifesto.* New York: Hearst Corporation, 1970.

_____. *God Is Red.* New York: Delta Books, 1973.

Ek, Richard A. "Red Cloud's Cooper Union Address." *Central States Speech Journal.* 17 (1966): 257-262.

Green, Rayna. *Native American Women: A Contextual Bibliography*: Bloomington: Indiana University Press, 1983.

_____. *That's What She Said: Contemporary Poetry and Fiction by Native American Women.* Bloomington: Indiana University Press, 1984.

Hertzberg, H.W. *The Search for an American Indian Identity:* Modern Pan-Indian Movements. New York: Syracuse University Press, 1971.

Jones, L.T. *Aboriginal American Oratory: The Tradition of Eloquence Among the Indians of the United States.* Los Angeles: Southwestern Museum, 1965.

Lake, Randall A. "Enacting Red Power: The Consummatory Function in Native American Protest Rhetoric." *The Quarterly Journal of Speech.* 69 (1983): 127-142.

Means, Russell. "For the World to Live, 'Europe' Must Die," in *Contemporary American Speeches* by Johannesen, Allen, & Linkugel. Dubuque, Iowa: Kendall/Hunt Publ. Co., 1987. pp. 115-123.

Merritt, Frank W. "Teedyuscung—Speaker for the Delaware." *Today's Speech.* 3 (1955): 14-18.

Morris, Mabel. "Indian Eloquence." *Western Speech.* 8 (1944).

_____. "Indian Oratory." *Southern Speech Communication Journal.* 10 (1944).29-36.

Morris, Richard and Philip Wander. "Native American Rhetoric: Dancing in the Shadows of the Ghost Dance." *The Quarterly Journal of Speech.* 76 (1990): 164-191.

Neihardt, J.C. *Black Elk Speaks.* New York: Pocket Books, 1975.

O'Donnell, John H. "Logan's Oration: A Case Study in Ethnographic Authentication." *The Quarterly Journal of Speech.* 65 (1979): 150-156.

Parker, Arthur C. *Red Jacket, Last of the Senecas.* New York: McGraw-Hill, 1952.

Philipsen, Gerry. "Navajo World View and Culture Patterns of Speech: A Case Study in Ethnorhetoric." *Speech Monographs.* 39 (1972): 132-139.

Sandefur, Ray H. "Logan's Oration—How Authentic?" *The Quarterly Journal of Speech.* 46 (1960): 289-296.

Vanderwerth, W.C. ed. *Indian Oratory.* New York: Ballantine Books, Inc., 1971.

326 SELECTED BIBLIOGRAPHY

Verble, Sedelta, ed. *Words of Today's American Indian Women: Ohoyo Makachi.* Wichita Falls, Texas: Ohoyo Resource Center, n.d.

BOOKS AND ARTICLES CONCERNED WITH WHITE AMERICAN FEMALE RHETORIC

Anderson, Judith. "Sexual Politics: Chauvanism and Backlash?" *Today's Speech.* 21 (1973): 11-16.

_____. *Outspoken Women: Speeches by American Women Reformers,* 1635-1935. Dubuque, Iowa: Kendall/Hunt, 1984.

Bosmajian, Haig A. "The Abrogation of the Suffragist: First Amendment Rights." *Western Speech.* 38 (1974): 218-232.

Brake, Robert J. "Women Orators: More Research?" *Today's Speech* 15 (1967): 20-22.

Campbell, Karlyn Kohrs. "Femininity and Feminism: To Be or Not to Be a Women." *Communication Quarterly* 31 (1983): 105-107.

_____. "Stanton's 'The Solitude of Self': A Rationale for Feminism." *The Quarterly Journal of Speech.* 66 (1980): 304-312.

_____. "Style and Content in the Rhetoric of Early Afro-American Feminists." *The Quarterly Journal of Speech.* 72 (1986): 434-445.

_____. "The Rhetoric of Women's Liberation: An Oxymoron." *The Quarterly Journal of Speech.* 59 (1973): 74-86.

Coughlin, Elizabeth Myrtle and Charles Edward Coughlin. "Convention in Petticoats: the Seneca Falls Declaration of Women's Rights." *Today's Speech.* 21 (1973): 17-23.

Donaldson, Alice. "Women Emerge As Public Speakers." *Speech Monographs.* 18 (1951): 54-61.

Flexner, Eleanor. *Century of Struggle: The Woman's Rights Movement in the United States.* Cambridge, Massachusetts: The Belknap Press of Harvard University Press, 1959.

Foss, S.K. "Equal Rights Amendment Controversy: Two Worlds in Conflict." *The Quarterly Journal of Speech.* 64 (1979): 275-288.

Gold, Ellen Reid. "The Grimke Sisters and the Emergence of the Women's Rights Movement." *The Southern Speech Communication Journal.* 46 (1981): 341-360.

Hancock, Brenda Robinson. "Affirmation by Negation in the Women's Liberation Movement." *The Quarterly Journal of Speech.* 58 (1972): 264-271.

Harper, Ida H. *Life and Work of Susan B. Anthony.* New York: Bowen-Merrill, 1898.

Hillbruner, Anthony. "Frances Wright: Egalitarian Reformer." *Southern States Communication Journal.* 23 (1957): 193-203.

Japp, Phyllis M. "Esther or Isaiah?: The Abolitionist--Feminist Rhetoric of Angelina Grimke." *The Quarterly Journal of Speech.* 74 (1985): 335-348.

Kendall, Kathleen Edgerton and Jeanne Y. Fisher. "Frances Wright on Women's Rights: Eloquence Versus Ethos." *The Quarterly Journal of Speech.* 60 (1974): 58 -68.

Kramer, Cheris. "Women's Speech: Separate but Unequal." *The Quarterly Journal of Speech.* 60 (1974): 14 -24.

Linkugel, Wil A. "The Rhetoric of American Feminism: A Social Movement Course." *Speech Teacher.* 23 (1974): 121 -130.

Lutz, Alma. *Susan B. Anthony: Rebel, Crusader, Humanitarian.* Boston: Beacon Press, 1959.

Mansfield, Dorothy M. "Abigail L. Duniway: Suffragette with Not-so-Common Sense." *Western Speech.* 35 (1971): 24 -29.

McDavitt, Elaine E. "Susan B. Anthony: Reformer and Speaker." *The Quarterly Journal of Speech.* 30 (1944): 173-180.

McPherson, Louise. "Communication Techniques of the Women's Liberation Front." *Today's Speech.* 21 (1973): 33 -38.

O'Connor, Lillian M. F. *Pioneer Women Orators: Rhetoric in the Ante-Bellum Reform Movement.* New York: Columbia University Press, 1954.

O'Neill, William L. *The Woman Movement, Feminism in the United States and England.* London: George Allen, 1969.

Riegel, Robert E. *American Feminists.* Lawrence: University Press of Kansas, 1963.

Rosenwasser, Marie J. "Rhetoric and the Progress of the Women's Liberation Movement." *Today's Speech.* 20 (1972): 45-56.

Stanton, Elizabeth C., Susan B. Anthony, and Ida W. Harper. *History Of Woman's Suffrage,* 1881-1922. 6 vols. Reprint. New York: Collector's Edition, 1971.

Yoakum, Doris G. "Pioneer Women Orations of America." *The Quarterly Journal of Speech.* 23 (1937): 251-259.